Three Plays

THE
SEAGULL
LIBRARY OF
GERMAN
LITERATURE

Three Plays

RECHNITZ
THE MERCHANT'S CONTRACTS
CHARGES

Elfriede Jelinek

TRANSLATED BY GITTA HONEGGER

Seagull
BOOKS

LONDON NEW YORK CALCUTTA

This publication has been supported by a grant from
the Goethe-Institut India

Seagull Books, 2019

Rechnitz (*The Exterminating Angel*) and *The Merchant's Contracts*
originally published as *Rechnitz* (*Der Würgeengel*) and *Die Kontrakte des
Kaufmanns* © Rowohlt Verlag GmbH, Reinbek bei Hamburg, 2009

Charges originally published as *Die Schutzbefohlenen* © Elfriede Jelinek, 2013
Published by permission of Rowohlt Verlag GmbH, Reinbek.

First published in English translation by Seagull Books, 2015, 2016

Translation, Introduction, Preface © Gitta Honegger, 2015, 2016

ISBN 978 0 8574 2 712 0

British Library Cataloguing-in-Publication Data
A catalogue record for this book is available from the British Library

Typeset by Seagull Books, Calcutta, India
Printed and bound by WordsWorth India, New Delhi, India

CONTENTS

INTRODUCTION TO *RECHNITZ* AND *THE MERCHANT'S CONTRACTS*

GITTA HONEGGER

I am very sorry that I can't be with you. I am sure Gitta explained why. But instead, you can accept Gitta as the author. She is my stand-in and she stands up for me. I translate myself, so I know what it means: one follows someone's text which one actually wrote oneself before. Or maybe one writes in the wake of a text by jumping in—catching it is always a close call, but one always catches it, if one is a translator like Gitta (yes, you must translate this, I am merciless!). And the other half of the text is by all of you. I think that a text for the theater is only one half of the whole. The rest is written (not just put on stage!) by a team of actors, director, designers to make it a play (which is no longer a play by me). I am only there for the kick-off. I kick the ball and it flies off. You have to get it into the goal.

> —Elfriede Jelinek, in her opening-night greetings to the New York cast of *Jackie*, March 5, 2013.

More radically than most other authors of performance texts, Elfriede Jelinek challenges her directors (and translators) to become her co-authors and she fully acknowledges them as such. She does not consider those texts "plays," but rather "texts for speaking" as distinguished from her "texts for reading." "I want to put language itself on cothurns," she says.[1] Jelinek's lines "for speaking" are literally "figures of speech," it is up to the production team to orchestrate and embody them, that is, to "play" them or rather to play *with* them. Her texts become "play" only in performance.

It is not surprising, then, that innovative directors have a special affinity to Jelinek's texts. Some first gained or significantly expanded their international recognition as "Jelinek directors" for their brilliantly "co-authored" stage versions.

Since the drama in her texts does not unfold in the action but is buried in the language itself—quotes from literary and philosophical canons, from historical sources, popular culture, political speak, and the Web—it is up to the directors of Jelinek's plays to cull the narrative they will stage from the 150-odd pages of texts (in the German published version). "*Textflächen*," Jelinek has called them (literally, "planes of text"), a term that has become a cliché in Jelinek scholarship and journalism. Planes of texts have only a few, if any, designated characters and hardly any paragraph breaks. They are triggered by current events and their mythologization by the media, with motifs from Greek tragedy and with the relics and waste from the history of Western culture to the contemporary consumption embedded in it. Mostly homebound because of her acute anxiety

---

1 Elfriede Jelinek, conversation with Gitta Honegger, January 26, 2011. Unless otherwise noted, all translations are by Honegger.

illness, Jelinek has become more or less exclusively dependent on mediated information, which she deconstructs in her
writing. If Plato's definition of reality is a play of shadows,
then Jelinek's texts stage the shadows of shadows.

Jelinek's strategy of quoting is a form of ready-made
speech acts taken from trashcans and the canon. They are
not sorted out to restore an "original" masterpiece or give it
"new life." Unlike the archeologist, who carefully culls the
fragments of the "real thing" from the rubble, Jelinek does
not discard anything from the garbage heap of words, which
she spreads on her flat surfaces. As a trained musician, she
is attuned to—not to say obsessed by—the algorithmic pat-
terns in the cacophony of sounds. The past and the present
merge and expand in the unstoppable process of her writing.
The truth—or untruth as the ultimate ugly, devastating
truth—reveals itself not in a well-reasoned or emotionally
charged linear argument or dialogue. Rather, it lurks in the
most harmless-sounding words, their reverberations in
homonyms and the cultural histories contained in each of
them, in their (mis)pronunciation, their function in neolo-
gisms or in the platitudes derived from them. This of course
is also the stuff of comedy. Jelinek's strategies are akin to
Stephen Colbert's method of turning the logic of politicized
media spin against itself by taking the sentences literally "by
their word(s)" and pushing them way over the top until they
say the complete opposite of what has been said to begin
with, which, more often than not, was utter, if not highly
toxic, nonsense. The truth is in the pudding; it vanished in
the—in every sense—tasteless, sticky corn(starch). In the age
of instant global communication, the "original" source of
information can no longer be identified. Both Jelinek and
Colbert (as well as Jon Stewart) demonstrate this through
choruses who pass on and drill into us, in endless repetitions,

the latest "facts." For the TV comedian, it is the chorus of TV pundits. Jelinek, writing for the stage, goes back to the classic device of the chorus. Standing in for contemporary society, the speakers root the tragic facts in ancient mythologies and, in the process, construct the new myths that generate faith in the invisible Gods of current ideologies. In *The Merchant's Contracts*, a "Comedy of Economics," it is the commandments of the Market, the invisible creator of fatefully invisible wealth.

In *Rechnitz (The Exterminating Angel)*, a chorus of messengers reports what they have been told about the circumstances that led to the massacre of 180 Jews, which took place towards the end of World War II during a wild party for provincial Nazi administrators at a castle in the Austrian–Hungarian border town of Rechnitz. The bracketed subtitle is an allusion to Luis Buñuel's 1962 film *El ángel exterminador*. The mystifying title (Who has heard of Rechnitz, even in Austria, which ultimately is the point of Jelinek's cultural critique? And who could instantly think of Buñuel's movie?) suggests some kind of demonic ritual. This sets up the uncanny ambiguity of the messengers and the sources of their information, as I will discuss in this introduction. Both in *Rechnitz* and in *The Merchant's Contracts*, the horrifying facts of the massacre are linked to classic myths, most prominently of Dionysus and Zarathustra in the former, and of Hercules, his twelve tasks, and his children in the latter. The most revealing thematic connection between Jelinek's texts is hidden in a word game that no longer resonates in modern English: the German term *Schuld* for guilt is the root of the plural *Schulden*, meaning debts. "And forgive us our debts, as we forgive our debtors," says the King James translation of the Lord's Prayer, which might have hastened the birth of modern capitalism in England.

As mentioned before, Jelinek leaves it up to her directors to find the connecting threads in the overabundant material. Jossi Wieler and Nicolas Stemann are experienced "Jelinek directors" who staged defining versions of her work. Their approaches could not be more different. Wieler, born in 1951, honed his elegant minimalist aesthetic in the wake of the late modernist tradition. Stemann, born in 1968, dismantles the techniques of the great masters of *Regietheater* with the playful exuberance of their brilliant student. His appropriations of performance styles correspond to (and sometimes parody) Jelinek's use of quotes. The calm beauty and surreal humor of Wieler's approach make the underlying horror even more unbearable. While Wieler fills the rigorously pared-down lines with resonant silences, Stemann attempts to thrust every single word on stage in all possible methods: read, sung, declaimed, taped, projected, spoken, and overlapping at top speed. Some words and phrases are repeated. They are the markers across the powerful cascades of words and their possible meanings.

In addition to these two "model productions," I will also discuss site- and culture-specifics stagings that further reflect the pliability of the texts. Finally, or rather to begin with, in the context of this translation, there are the translator's considerable challenges, which I will discuss in the final section of this introduction.

I

LANGUAGE OF GUILT

Rechnitz (*The Exterminating Angel*)

The Jews have their wailing wall, we have our wall
of silence.[2]

On February 12 and 13, 2011, the distinguished Munich
Kammerspiele presented its outstanding production of
Elfriede Jelinek's *Rechnitz* at the Cameri Theatre of Tel Aviv.
It was an historic event on many levels. As Jelinek's transla-
tor, I had the good fortune to meet the company in Israel.

The revolutionary momentum sweeping the Middle
East at the time highlighted the precariousness of Israel's
position. The evening of their arrival, as actors and staff
gathered in the hotel lobby for their first foray into the city,
Hildegard Schmahl, the luminous grande dame of cutting-
edge German theater, burst in with the news she had just
watched in her room: "(President) Mubarak has just
resigned!" The next evening, the German company would
perform a play that deconstructs rituals of remembering
past atrocities—the ongoing attempts of "speaking the
unspeakable," as Jelinek called it in a conversation.[3]

Rather than a "docu-drama," her text focuses on the
transmission of historic memory. The actual events leading
up to the party, the gathering of the victims and their murder took place during the night of March 24–25, 1945,
shortly before the arrival of the Russian army. Ironically
enough, it was the night before Palm Sunday, the Christian

---

2 From Margareta Heinrich and Eduard Herne, *Totschweigen*, documentary film, 2006; DVD, docushop, 2009).

3 Jelinek, conversation with Honegger, December 26, 2011.

holiday in commemoration of Christ's triumphal entry into Jerusalem. The predominantly Catholic inhabitants of Rechnitz and their descendants have never come forward with detailed information about the massacre.

Rechnitz Castle was owned by Count Bátthyany, the descendant of a historic aristocratic line, and his wife Margit, the heiress of the Thyssen dynasty of industrialists and art collectors. During the war, the castle served as the residence of local Nazi leaders. The victims were brought to Rechnitz from a nearby forced-labor camp of approximately 8,000 inmates in the small town of Köszeg. As the Russian army approached Hitler's Reich, the Nazis began to build fortifications along the eastern border, the so-called East Wall. The more than 180 inmates who were transferred by train to Rechnitz were too sick or weak to work. During the night of the party, the Gestapo chief of Rechnitz, Franz Podezin, one of the prominent guests and, according to gossip, Margit Bátthyany's lover, received the call with the order to pick up the victims from the train. They were put up at the estate's stables, and shot. Though the site of the massacre is known, the mass grave with the remains of the victims could not be found to this day. Jelinek's messengers recount the events from different perspectives. Though the Thyssen heiress was at the party, it is not known whether she actually participated in the shooting.

With the exception of Hildegard Schmahl, who was born in 1940 in Pomerania (now Poland), the Munich ensemble members belong to the post–World War II generation, ranging in age from thirty-three to fifty-eight. Jossi Wieler, then fifty-nine years old, is the son of German Jewish parents with many family ties to Israel. After completing his studies in theater at the University of Tel Aviv, he moved to Germany, where he quickly established himself as a leading director of his generation with a special affinity to Jelinek's texts. Wieler was concerned that *Rechnitz* might be perceived (and misunderstood) as yet another play "about" the Holocaust. As he and his dramaturg Julia Lochte point out in numerous interviews and introductory events preceding the performances, Jelinek did not write a documentary about the incident. In fact, a 1994 documentary film *Totschweigen* (Wall of Silence) by Margarete Heinrich and Eduard Erne is just that. Following the most recent failed attempts by members of the Jewish community to locate the mass grave, the film features interviews with villagers remembering the shooting, as well as with relatives of the victims and with the initiators of such searches since the 1960s. Their accounts inspired Jelinek's chorus of messengers, who report bits and pieces of information, remembered, passed on, and modified in the process. Though her outrage over the massacre is Jelinek's starting point, she does not attempt to reconstruct history. Rather, she examines the construction of memory. Her focus is on the accountability of the present, not for past crimes (at a time most contemporaries have not yet been born) but rather for current strategies of silence about mass killings anywhere in the world, which more often than not impel incessant talk around the core of silence. As one of Jelinek' messengers describes their mission: "[A]voiding all talk by giving a speech, the same one, over and over again."[4]

"The Jews have their Wailing Wall, we have our Wall of Silence" comments a resident of Rechnitz in the documentary. In contrast to the heavy, static image of a "wall of silence" suggested by the film's English title, the German title *Totschweigen* (literally, "killing through silence") is a verb

---

4 Elfriede Jelinek, *Rechnitz (The Exterminating Angel)*, p. 106.

turned into a noun, indicating an action in process. Jelinek orchestrates this unfinished process: a verbal massacre still in the making.

For the Munich company, sharing the ambivalent legacy of their culture, and the uncompleted struggle to come to terms with it, with an Israeli audience was a profoundly moving challenge, a once-in-a-lifetime "dream come true," as Hans Kremer, one of the actors, put it. Nonetheless, it was anticipated by all (including the local German diplomatic community and also myself) with heightened nervousness. As actor André Jung, an experienced, inspired Jelinek performer, put it during the post-performance discussion: "We speak the language of the perpetrators in this terrible tragedy. And here we are in Israel."[5] Not only does the text unearth yet another gruesome incident of the Holocaust, but, as conceived for a German audience, through the chorus of messengers, it also addresses the spectators as like-minded accomplices, if not directly in the crime, then in the continued circumventions of the truth, which add up to yet another pernicious process of extinction. How could German performers involve an Israeli audience as participants in such a conceit without being perceived as outrageously insensitive? Steven Scharf explains: "Well, we couldn't play it with the sort of coy attitude: that's not really how we think, we are different, we are just playing these awful people. We had to fully commit. And we were pretty tense."[6] The result was an electrifying performance in a packed house. In the uncanny presentness of the theatrical encounter between performers and

---

5 Conversation with Gitta Honegger, Cameri Theatre, Tel Aviv, February 20, 2011.

6 Ibid.

spectators, the actors themselves were the messengers. Rather than performing the roles of the messengers, they executed the task of the messenger. Their relentless, remorseless delivery straight in the face of the audience made them perpetrators in the present. Or so it seemed to this visitor whose native language is also German. As a spectator, but also insider "to the game," she was linked to the perpetrators as well. But that was only one part of the production's uncanny impact.

Characteristically, Jelinek cuts back and forth across centuries and cultures. All sites everywhere are haunted by the undead of the past. Borders blur and get reinforced. A member of the chorus alludes to the conflict between Israel and Palestine:

> The sign of the cross has led to many mistakes, the crusaders already wanted to get to Palestine and ended up in the Gaza Strip instead, where, of course they were thrown out, because it was already full, the boat there was full, something like that, but one thing is correct: everyone gets thrown out of there except those who either must stay or tear down the fence, and if mistakes are made, they can't always be ironed out the way it is done with the graves here . . . [7]

The perpetrators' language seeps into their victims. "Language is a virus," according to William S. Burroughs, as quoted by the performance artist/musician Laurie Anderson, a contemporary of Jelinek. The latter's couriers are its carriers. No one is safe from contagion.

The undead dominate most of Jelinek's work. They are no longer individually recognizable as they mingle with the

---

7 Jelinek, *Rechnitz*, p. 133.

present. Perpetrators escape and settle with changed identities in all parts of the world, spreading the virus like any other contagious disease. Communicating electronically, today's messengers are anonymous. Facts can't be verified, untruths have almost instantaneous performative impact with the speed they hit their targets. As a trained musician, Jelinek is acutely aware of time. "Music is time that is heard," states one of her messengers like a voice on the radio announcing the daily program "The Banality of Evil." The passage the brief quote is taken from is worth citing at length, as it is a good example of Jelinek's method and the dramaturg's and translator's task to tease out the cross connections of meanings behind the banality of the message.

> You just heard our daily program about the banality of evil, but you know all about it anyway; it's yesterday's news, and now more music. Those tunes are from the day before yesterday; don't you know anything newsier, anything new, or even the newest? Then put it on. Put it all on the line. We also have one of last year's tunes, which is newer than this one, but the tunes of tomorrow and even the day after tomorrow have just come out and we will put them all online already today. They are like all things past: music comes and it passes the moment it is put on; music is time that is heard; generally, what's past must first have come to pass, but there are things in the past, which should not and could no longer come to pass. What's been committed here should disappear; it should be admitted, I mean, omitted, but never permitted to be committed again; whatever has been committed should be thoroughly cleaned up, so that no one will ever have to submit to it again. Not again,

please! But tomorrow you can tune in to see and listen to another banal program; it won't even deal with the banality of evil, but it will certainly be banal.[8]

Acknowledging the influence of the great Austrian satirist Karl Kraus, Jelinek highlights the banality of the so-called *Bildungsbürgertum*, the educated middle class (the majority of theater audiences and art "connoisseurs") and those trying to work their way into and possibly beyond it. (The Thyssen dynasty fits both.) Insertions of quotes from Euripides's *Bacchae*, Nietzsche's *Thus Spoke Zarathustra*, and T. S. Eliot's poem "The Hollow Men" not only locate the unspeakable drama of Rechnitz at the crossroads between myth, history, and revisionist spin; they also serve the characters as linguistic stirrups onto the societal–cultural high horse even as the speakers keep getting entangled in them. They are the pratfalls of Freudian slips, malapropisms, and absurd gaffes, while the horse turns out to be the Trojan kind, filled with the scenarios of Greek tragedy, Thyssen arms and money and Nietzsche's darkly mocking laughter.

In her contribution to a book about the work of Wieler, Jelinek explains her approach to *Rechnitz* and her dramaturgy in general:

How can one put on a stage that which could not be, but nevertheless could do so quite well? I tried to write a play around a blind spot, because one cannot speak about the event itself. It is like enclosing a pencil sketch with the messengers' reports (the empty spot is in the middle just as it is in our midst, that spot, just as others could not be in our midst. That, which was not found: the mass grave,

8 Ibid., p. 104.

is nonetheless in our midst); their accounts also speak of our way of handling it, because they speak of everything, my stage figures never leave out anything, they always say everything, they come to be out of this "everything" they say and they have to be extracted out of this everything, not liberated, but first of all, they must be created.[9]

In the same essay, Jelinek describes Wieler's production of Paul Claudel's *Partage de Midi* (The Break of Noon). It indicates her special appreciation of Wieler as a director

who steers a boat with stranded people before the shipwreck and what they think is their truth and what they enunciate as the truth. But to get one to see it as anything but the truth is the director's job. He has to produce/construct it in such a way that one realizes this truth has been produced/constructed. It has not been withheld. In Claudel, the silence speaks; in my work, the speaking never keeps quiet.[10]

Jelinek challenges the director with an apparent paradox: How can the truth be "constructed" or "produced" in the sense of being manufactured and, at the same time, not be withheld—particularly in view of the endless strings of words that keep wrapping themselves around the truth to the point of choking it, at the very least making it invisible, even to themselves, which ultimately is the conscious or unconscious intent of the speakers? The director's and actors' task then is to find a physical language which, rather

---

9 Elfriede Jelinek, "Die Leere öffnen" (Opening the Void) in *Jossi Wieler* (Hajo Kurzenberger ed.) (Berlin and Köln: Alexander, 2011), pp. 117–18.

10 Ibid., p. 105.

than "expressing" some psychological truth "deep inside" the speaker, makes the paradox visible. In other words, Jelinek asks for an embodiment rather than an illustration of her linguistic strategies. Because her figures are doubles, their "double speak" disrupts the surface of the language in her "planes of text."

As Jelinek further elaborates: "It has often been said that people at best see only their own shadows without recognizing them as such. Why then should I not borrow their shadows, their shadowlike speaking, which had always been said before them by someone else, nothing but shadow-boxing, their speech acts! So why not borrow them without returning them?"[11]

Shadows are doubles, so are actors, according to Plato. He goes even further, denouncing the latter as the shadows of the shadows of all perceived reality. They are doubled doubles as it were. The actors in Wieler's production of *Rechnitz* perform messengers, who are also doubles as they literally "incorporate" the speech of another and, in the process, embody it. They talk of the banality of evil in an equally banal language, in contemporary vernacular, which is both instantly familiar and strange—uncanny, *unheimlich*, in Sigmund Freud's paradoxical meaning of the word due to the many resonances of its antonym *heimlich* (homey, cozy or secret).[12] I briefly retrack Freud's etymological excursion as it leads directly into the uncanny space of Jelinek–Wieler's production:

The word root *heim*, the English "home", contains multiple connotations, that make the home itself *heimelig*, cozy

11 Ibid., p. 104.

12 Sigmund Freud, *The Uncanny* (David McClintock trans.) (London: Penguin, 2003), p. 125.

(or *heimlich* in its earlier usage). *Heimelig/heimlich* as it may be, it is what makes the *heim* also *unheimlich*—uncanny, because what's done *daheim*, at home, is often done *heimlich*, that is, secretly. After painstakingly tracking down every possible connotation of the term, Freud arrives at the conclusion "*Heimlich* [homey, cozy, secret] thus becomes increasingly ambivalent, until it finally merges with its antonym *unheimlich* [uncanny]." The uncanny, in Freud's definition is "a species of the frightening that goes back to what once was well known and has long been familiar."[13] This is precisely what makes the banalities of Jelinek's messenger-speak (and arguably, all political speech) so frighteningly uncanny, a comfy and homey (*heimelig/heimlich*) quilt of familiar platitudes, truisms and jokes, "*Sprachfetzen*" (patches of speech), as she refers to them, cut up and rearranged over and over again in different, unfamiliar combinations. In the process, the familiar, comfortably worn-in native speech turns into an uncannily "foreign" language. This foreignness is all the more resonant in Wieler's staging of the silences Jelinek speaks of in the preceding quote: they fill the spaces left by the passages that Wieler omitted. Taking his cue from Buñuel's surrealist imagination in staging a society locked into its own repressive politics, Wieler stages Jelinek's hunting party in a stripped-down interior. As designed by Anja Rabe, the minimalist set suggests a combination of hunting lodge and shooting gallery. As familiar, popular sites in rural areas, their merging has an uncanny effect. The wood-paneled walls are lined with adjacent doors and folding seats equipped with earphones. The only decoration on the greenish plaster walls above the paneling is a stag's trophy antlers in the center of the back wall.

---

13 Ibid., p. 124.

The actors enter to the well-known motif from the overture of Karl Maria von Weber's popular opera *Der Freischütz*. Dressed in elegant evening clothes, they are waving, smiling, winking conspiratorially at individual spectators like seasoned entertainers to their fans, their body language and gestures promising "a gay ole time" (as the Devil sings in *Black Rider*, Robert Wilson's adaptation of *Der Freischütz*; music by Tom Waits, lyrics by William Burroughs). Their opening conversation seems to continue an argument about the birth of Dionysus, which segues into an exchange of well-known war stories. They have been told over and over again: about the Russians, their looting sprees, their brutal rapes of German women, ironically counterbalanced by the fact that it was the Germans who first raped Russian women. Bits and pieces of information are strung into puns that lead to contemporary biases against Russians as "uncivilized" yet well-paying tourists.

In the course of their "reports" and conversations about them, they begin their sexual foreplay, surreptitiously at first, then with increasing boldness, always also coolly aware of the audience as they strip themselves of their clothes and intertwine in various erotic configurations. Towards the end they change (back?) into more or less timeless servants' costumes and contemporary street clothes that they wear as they leave the stage. Retrospectively, they might have been the servants at the tragic event slipping into the clothes and roles of their fleeing masters before the dreaded arrival of the Russians. Wieler leaves us thinking that the characters might have performed their narratives as witnesses and messengers since the end of World War II or passed on their messages along with their mimetic skills to the next generation. From their accomplished performances it is clear that these characters have performed the story many times.

Mimicking the speech acts of the perpetrators, the undead continue to live on through them. It is what makes their presence so *unheimlich*. The ambiguity of the set captures the uncanny *Heimlichkeit* (secrecy) of the enclosed space, with its doors opening into even smaller enclosed spaces, or leading to an indeterminate number of rooms and closets. Beyond the doors could be another interior, that even if it led outside, is bounded by the threatening barking of unseen guard dogs. The messengers' repeated exits and returns with popular take-out food, from pizza to fried chicken to frosted cakes (resulting in the familiar but eerily slow-motion pie-in-the-face routines) mirror our own fast-food culture as reminder of an incessant cycle of leftover food, garbage, and human remains disposed of in a dump. In Wieler's final Marxian tableau, the circle closes at the point where past and present merge around Rechnitz, the "empty spot in the middle," as Jelinek calls it. The truth is a pie in the face. Marx's famous adage of history repeating itself turns tragedy into farce also applies to Jelinik's "shadows." In her essentially tragic scenarios, the messengers as history's doubles are not only uncanny in the sense of "weird," but also "weird" in the sense of "funny."

Unlike Wieler's production, Jelinek's complete text does not end with the messengers' story but with a grotesque satyr play: a conversation between a cannibal and his consenting victim about the process of preparation and consumption, based on an interview with the "real-life cannibal" Armin Meiwes, a German man, known as "the monster from Rotenburg," and his willing victim, Bernd Brandes, whom he met on the Internet.[14] Embedded in Jelinek's

---

14 Gunter Stampf, *Interview with a Cannibal: The Secret Life of the Monster of Rotenburg* (Pat Brown ed.) (Beverly Hills: Phoenix Books, 2008).

ritualized comedy-of-manners dialogue are references to the Bible (John 14) and to the hunter's deal with the devil in *Der Freischütz*. As a macabre coda to the monstrous orgy at Rechnitz Castle, it would have completely derailed Wieler's disciplined, sensitive exploration of historic memory.

Another production of *Rechnitz* by the Schauspielhaus Zürich, which opened on December 19, 2009, directed by Leonhard Koppelmann, is a telling example of what happens when Jelinek's choral dramaturgy is altogether ignored and the narrative retooled into a portrayal of the countess. Conceived as a one-woman show that suggests the countess's escape and arrival in Switzerland, the production completely missed the larger critical implications of Jelinek's staging of society's multiple strands of inherited manipulated speech. The text was cut to thirty-seven pages and radically rearranged to fit the quasi-site-specific staging by Leonhard Koppelman. Each performance was presented at an unannounced "secret" location in and around Zürich. I saw the production's guest performance in Berlin, hosted by the legendary Deutsches Theater. The audience first assembled in the theater's lobby. An actress (Isabella Menke), dressed in a drab uniform suggesting a tour guide, addressed us with the opening paragraphs from the text before we were put on a bus and taken the longest way around the new and historic sights of Mitte, the city's rebuilt center, past the Brandenburg Gate to the Swiss Embassy (as in Zürich, without prior announcement of the site) to the soundtrack of Richard Strauss's tone poem "Thus Spoke Zarathustra." A drive through the landscape around Rechnitz was simulated on video screens, along burning fields past the remains of the castle grounds, punctuated by the reading of Eliot's "The Hollow Men." It felt a bit like a theme-park ride, to give the passengers the sense of people fleeing or, maybe even more awkwardly, of being transported to an unknown destination like the victims of Rechnitz. At the embassy, we were put through an elaborate security check, handed a chair and shown to the embassy's recital hall, where the actress joined us again, wrapped in a coat, apparently arriving at an elegant location after a strenuous journey. Was she a messenger bringing the news across the border to the safe haven of Switzerland? (Fittingly enough, the embassy is located across from Hauptbahnhof, the main train station, which, in times of the Berlin Wall, was the last stop before crossing into the Eastern section. A rather small building, the embassy stands like a last defiant fortification in a wide, open area right between the modern structures of the new chancellery and other government buildings, a relic of the city's past. Much to the annoyance of the city planners, who intended a harmonious, progressively modern aesthetic for the new government, the Swiss refused to move their embassy, like other countries, to another location.) Once inside, the actress appeared to morph into the countess, recounting the events during the night of the massacre from her perspective. If willing to "play along," so to speak, given the specific space of the Swiss Embassy, audiences could imagine themselves as like-minded fellow travelers, if not perpetrators in exile, perhaps even victims of the Nazi regime, who managed to escape. Though cleverly concep-tualized (in Zurich, each performance took place in a differ-ent undisclosed location) and very well performed, the production is a good example of how the characters in Jelinek's late texts resist individualization. The attempt to compress the multiple voices into a single, "full-fledged" character with a linear, psychological subtext missed the complex political underpinning of Jelinek's linguistic strate-gies. The linearity of Koppelman's production made the text seem "mono-logical," resulting in a tediously indulgent, oddly disconnected confessional. Quite ironically, the chilling uncanniness of the messengers as doubles amid or inside ourselves is diffused by the virtuosity of an actor's solo performance.

The Merchant's Contracts: "Doing God's Work"

If, arguably, *Rechnitz* is Jelinek's best performance text, then her "comedy of economics," *The Merchant's Contracts*, is her most "accessible" and most obviously "funny" text, at least on the surface. With capitalism having gone global and Wall Street as its neo-mythical Walhalla, English has taken over as the market's universal language. Even in their respective native languages, speculators' lingo and media spin is babble to the ears of most small investors, who, after all, were and continue to be the biggest losers worldwide in the economic crisis.

Jelinek finished the script of her "comedy of economics" in the summer of 2008, just a few weeks before Lehman Brothers filed for bankruptcy on September 15, 2008, which set off the avalanche of the global disaster. Initially, *The Merchant's Contracts* was written in response to two Austrian investment-banking scandals, both involving the near collapse of the respected institutions and the catastrophic loss of the life savings of small investors who naively and greedily put their trust in the good name of both. That Jelinek's text is based on very specific Austrian corruption scandals does not limit it to local audiences as the banks in question and their collapse and resurrection were intimately tied to their US trading partners. From a dramaturgical perspective, the specifically Viennese strategies of intrigue and deception, honed during centuries of imperial statesmanship and manners, give the specific details of the banks' collapse the patina of an absurd operetta. Laced with the comedic strategies of a Jon Stewart or Stephen Colbert and situated in a local circumstance, *The Merchant's Contracts* nevertheless has the alienating effect and universality of a Brechtian fable. In the age of global economy, Jelinek turned the merchant of Vienna into a universal comedy of errors.

The text's prologue alludes to the BAWAG bank, acronym for Bank für Arbeit und Wirtschaft (Bank for Labor and Business) that belonged to the Austrian Labor Union. After its near collapse due to the bank's shady deals made possible by hidden accounts with offshore companies and the now defunct US financial service company REFCO, it was purchased by the powerful US company, Cerberus Capital Management. Widely known for its purchase of Chrysler and General Motors' financial arm during the economic crisis, Cerberus made news when it put up for sale US's largest gun company, the Freedom Group, after it came under pressure in the wake of a gunman opening fire and killing 20 children and 6 adults at the Sandy Hook Elementary School in Newtown, Connecticut, on December 14, 2012. Cerberus owner Stephen A. Feinberg stepped up as a prospective buyer of the company.[15]

BAWAG's deals (with Morgan Stanley, Goldman Sachs, Credit Suisse and others as trading partners) were masterminded by Wolfgang Flöttl, the Austrian-born, Harvard-trained son of BAWAG's former long-time director Walter

---

15 Peter Lattman, "Cerberus Owner Might Buy Its Gun-Making Group," *New York Times*, April 17, 2013. Available at: http://dealbook.-nytimes.com/2013/04/17/feinberg-of-cerberus-considers-bid-for-its-gun-maker/?_r=0 (last accessed on October 29, 2014).

Flöttl. The younger Flöttl is well known in New York's banking world, where he advanced his career to vice president at Kidder, Peabody & Co., before he founded the Bermuda-based investment firm Ross Capital Markets, where he financed his high-risk speculations with BAWAG money. He further deepened his ties to the US with his first marriage to, divorce from and remarriage to former president Dwight D. Eisenhower's granddaughter Anne. After seven years of criminal investigations and trials, he was acquitted of all charges in May 2013.

Jelinek's primary focus in the main part of the text entitled "The Real Thing" is Austria's historic gourmet coffee and grocery dynasty started by and named after Julius Meinl, its phenomenal expansion through a complex web of offshore accounts and investment companies, and their collapse following the US subprime crisis, leading to criminal investigations against the current head of the family business, Julius Meinl V. His great- great-grandfather Julius I (all male descendants destined to lead the company were named Julius) started out selling roasted coffee beans in Vienna in 1862, eventually building a coffee empire which served the entire Habsburg Empire. The company's logo, generally known as the "Meinl Moor"––a dark-skinned boy wearing a fez, the traditional Turkish headwear, a cone-shaped red hat with a flat top and black tassel—assured instant brand recognition since 1924 despite occasional criticism from Austria's diversity-conscious circles.

Julius V happens to be a British citizen on account of his Jewish grandmother, who fled with her family from the Nazis to London, where "V" (as he is often referred to) was born. He studied at the famous School of Management, at the University of St. Gallen, Switzerland, and perfected his investment skills in London and New York, which served him well when he took over the family-owned Meinl Bank, a small savings bank he turned into an investment bank and fund-management firm.[16]

The quasi-leitmotif of Jelinek's text—"the firm which has our name but isn't us"—is drawn from Julius V's scheme of setting up offshore firms and shadow companies under the respected Meinl name and managed by the Meinl Bank without formal connection between himself and the firms. Best known among them was Meinl European Land (MEL), a real estate investment firm he developed from the family properties in Eastern Europe. Share certificates were sold mostly to small investors, who in turn were charged substantial service fees. According to the *Economist*, 60 percent of Meinl Bank's profit came from its investment-banking services to MEL. In 2007, MEL issued seventy-five million new share certificates, most of which went to an Antilles-based subsidiary of a Meinl trust in Liechtenstein. When Eastern European real estate values began to drop as a result of the US banking crisis, MEL bought back over two-thirds of the certificates without informing the investors. The strategy misfired. The crash could not be avoided. The scandal broke with catastrophic consequences, as everywhere else, for ordinary folks, represented in the text as the Small Investors' Chorus.

Jelinek's appropriation of the myth of Hercules slaughtering his children in a fit of madness is based on an actual case of a thirty-nine-year-old Austrian public relations manager who lost all the family's money in toxic stocks. With an

16 *Economist*, "A Viennese Grind: The Troubles of Julius Meinl V Illustrate the Complicated Consequences of the Property Crash," July 30, 2009. Available at: http://www.economist.com/node/14120267 (last accessed on October 29, 2014).

ax he purchased for his purpose, he first killed his wife and seven-year-old daughter (whom he wanted to save from a bad start in life, as he claimed) in their Vienna villa, then drove 150 km to kill his parents in Arnsfelden, a small town in Upper Austria, from there to nearby Linz to murder his father-in-law, then back to Vienna to finish the night in a bordello. His family, he said, would not have been able to cope with the financial losses. He did not kill himself, he explained, after seeing how long it took his victims to die (at least 18 blows with the ax each).[17]

That the current owner of BAWAG, Cerberus, took its ominous name from the three-headed dog that guarded the Greek underworld fit perfectly into Jelinek's associative approach. Interweaving both the BAWAG and Meinl scandals, she renamed her stand-in for the Meinl Bank's newly created investment management firm "Hercules," after the Greek hero, whose defeat of Cerberus was the final of his twelve labors. Thus the name Hercules (or Herakles) pulls multiple current events (not to forget the disastrous economic collapse of Greece itself) into a mythological underworld, which resurfaces in the actual present as the corrupt dog-eat-dog underworld of global capitalism. An avid reader of crime mysteries, Jelinek challenges dramaturgs to do detectives' work, following the leads inside and connections

---

17 *Spiegel Online*, "Lebenslange Haft für fünffachen Axtmörder" (Life Sentence for Five-Time Axe Murderer), November 7, 2008. Available at: http://www.spiegel.de/panorama/justiz/wien-lebenslange-haft-fuer-fuenffachen-axtmoerder-a-589185.html (last accessed on October 29, 2014). *News At*, "Volle Schuldfähigkeit: 5-facher Axt-Mörder aus Wien hat Familie bewusst erschlagen" (Full Accountability: Five-Times Axe Murderer from Vienna Slayed Family Intentionally). Available at: http://www.news.at/a/volle-schuldfaehigkeit-5-facher-axt-moerder-wien-familie-216237 (last accessed on October 29, 2014).

between words, like needles in a haystack, rather than expecting and looking for a straightforward unraveling of events. As it turned out, the actual cases followed a similar pattern. Even at the time of writing this, Jelinek's plot is not finished, as it still unravels in real life in different parts of the world.

In 2009, Julius V was arrested and released after two nights in jail with an unheard-of bail of 100 million euros deposited at BAWAG (at US$130 million, it is six times the amount of Bernard Maddoff's bail), which he managed to raise in that brief length of time. At the time of writing this, he was refunded 90 percent of the bail after four years of legal battles and still-ongoing investigations. That doesn't keep him or the Viennese, for that matter, from partying together. In April 2012, he celebrated the 150-year anniversary of the family business, sponsoring an evening of songs from famous operettas at Vienna's historic Volksoper (The People's Opera) titled *Wiener Musik and Melange* (Viennese Music and Coffee).[18]

As the Austrian news magazine *Profil* reported, over the years, the tactics of Meinl's star lawyers managed to make "the alleged perpetrators appear as the victims."[19] Three years before the publication of the article in April 2012, Jelinek had already highlighted this strategy in her text.

A crucial connection between BAWAG and Meinl was (and continues to be) the friendship and business collaborations of their respective directors with none other than

18 Michael Nikbakhsh, "Julius Meinl: Geld im Getriebe," *Profil Online*, April 14, 2012. Available at: http://www.profil.at/articles/1215/560/-324823/meinl-julius-meinl-geld-getriebe (last accessed on October 29, 2014).
19 Ibid.

Austria's former finance minister Karl Heinz Grasser, whose political career began with Austria's far-right freedom party before he turned Independent and joined the Conservative Party's coalition with the Freedom Party as finance minister from 2000 to 2007. His shady business transactions led to long-drawn criminal investigations, which are still in process, while his financial future is well protected by his second wife Fiona, the heiress of the Tyrol-based international firm Swarowski crystal.

Jelinek uses such details to provide a sense of the bizarre mix of slapstick, farce, tragedy, and melodrama which is the ordinary citizen's experience of banking and politics everywhere. In the spirit of Jelinek, directors and their dramaturgs are free to mine her massive texts for material to construct their performance narratives within their specific cultural contexts. The consequences of such contracts as Jelinek depicts have become evermore urgent and global over time. By necessity, she has kept the text open since its by-now legendary "ur-reading," the first over-five-hour-long reading at Vienna's Akademietheater (which is part of the Vienna Burgtheater) in March 2009, staged by Nicolas Stemann. Accordingly, Stemann, an experienced Jelinek director, developed an open-ended dramaturgy that would allow the interweaving of new topical and site-specific material with a group of superbly trained Jelinek-savvy actors. They call themselves STE (which stands for *schnelle theatrale Einsatztruppe*, "instant theatrical task force," for their quick intervention in current events). For the Cologne world premiere in April 2009, Jelinek provided a fourteen-page epilogue, titled "Schlechte Nachrede," freely translated as "Bad Rap." (*Nachrede* means gossip; in a theatrical context, it suggests an epilogue, a bad one at that, according to the title, which also suggests the idiom for bad behavior or criminal deeds having a *böses Nachspiel*, literally, a bad "after-play," which translates into "bad" or, in the case of the text, "bloody" consequences. Given the topic of the play, it also evokes a post mortem *Nachruf*—a "bad eulogy.") In an instance of life imitating art, Meinl's lawyer accused the prosecutor of acting in a "blood rage" when he ordered the arrest of his client and set the record-breaking bail, whereupon the prosecutor's office, at the instigation of the Ministry of Justice, initiated investigations on the grounds of *übler Nachrede*, slander, which in German is also implied in the epilogue's title.[20]

As none of the above alternatives has equally suggestive resonances , I followed Jelinek's advice: "Find something completely different, as long as it captures the spirit." This led me to the tongue-in-cheek "Bad Rap" of all the rumors and anxious speculations surrounding the post-crash banking world with a wink to Jelinek's own often ironic self-references in regard to criticism of her writing style.

The epilogue is a response to the immediate aftermath of the crash. Now the revolt of the small investors and its reversal are staged as a mad Dionysian spectacle that culminates in their offering themselves to the speculators as ritualistic sacrifices to be burnt, now literally, by the bankers. The strategies of Meinl's legal team are turned into a satyr play concluding the inherent tragedies. (See appendix for the translation of this text.)

A co-production of the Schauspiel Cologne and Hamburg's Thalia Theater, *The Merchant's Contracts* was transferred to Hamburg in January 2010. In the meantime, the avalanching economic disaster necessitated another adjustment, which turned into over forty additional pages

20 Ibid.

from which Stemann interpolated about a quarter into the production, titled "Aber sicher—Eine Fortsetzung" (idiomatically, in the context of the text, "You bet—A Sequel"). Again, the enigmatic German title makes it a treasure chest for wordplay and for frustrating, but ultimately liberating, challenges for translators, so typical for Jelinek. Out of context, the banal phrase *aber sicher* translates into "but of course." The multiple meanings of *sicher* include "sure," "certain," "safe," and, most importantly, "secure," both in the sense of personal security and risk-free, the latter happily leading into investment vocabulary. In the context of the banking world, the banal idiom—delivered either as a calmingly reassuring "for sure," a persuasive "trust me," a casual "sure thing," or a cocky assertion "you bet"—encapsulates the cynical vacuity of market spin. While "sure thing" might be the closest in expressing the "events" of the piece, I chose the active "you bet" for the title as it ironically wraps up the "action" of the entire text. The additional text maps the devastation wrought by the global speculation frenzy. Stemann had Jelinek reading on screen the new text's opening passage (which comes up later in his staging), of a stranger walking through a deserted, foreign landscape of abandoned, deteriorating homes, copper pipes ripped out, sinks, toilet bowls, appliances stolen, their former owners living in tents, SUVs, in parks, under bridges or at relatives'. Walter Benjamin's angel of history comes to mind, moving forward but turned backward, looking at the havoc wrought in our times by economics, which continues on its destructive path. In the author's soft, melodious voice, it becomes a dirge, a sad eulogy turning into a "bad rap" when the focus shifts to the small investors' lament segueing into outbursts of anger alternating with despair and self-accusations. Caught in a loop, the nearly unbearably obsessive iterations are driven by two key words (to continue in Jelinek's punning mode, they also provide the alternating tonal key for the performance): the earlier mentioned German *Schuld/Schulden*, for guilt/debts, and *Versicherung*, for both "assurance, to assure" and "insurance, to insure." The chains of wordplay reemphasize (in every sense) the "pathetic" connection between religion and capitalism in their reliance on faith, the immateriality of both further reinforced in a world gone viral.

In yet another instance of reality imitating art, half a year after the Cologne premiere of *The Merchant's Contracts*, Goldman Sachs CEO and chairman Lloyd Blankfein seemed to be a player in Jelinek's script with his much-quoted statement in an interview with the London *Times* that "banks are doing God's work."[21]

Still later, Jelinek added a brief second part to "Aber sicher." In her stage directions, she concedes that it "can be left out, like everything, so that nothing remains." She wrote it after the discovery, in May 2009, in the Institute of Forensic Medicine at Berlin's Charité hospital, of a ninety-year-old headless corpse of a woman, believed to be the "real" Rosa Luxemburg (hitherto assumed to have been buried in 1919). The inspiring, controversial Marxist theorist and communist activist was shot dead on January 15, 1919 by rightists and found in Berlin's Landwehrkanal. Though Stemann never included that part, in retrospect, the surfacing of Luxemburg (whose murder continues to be commemorated in a controversial annual public march in the former Eastern sector of Berlin) adds another dimension

21 Reuters, "Goldman Sachs Boss Says Banks Do 'God's Work,'" November 8, 2009. Available at: http://www.reuters.com/article/2009/11/08/us-goldmansachs-blankfein-idUSTRE5A719520091108 (last accessed on October 30, 2014).

to the original text's character of an angel quoting from Marx and Engels (note the latter's name's similarity to the German *Engel*, for "angel"). As Jelinek told me, she first introduced the angel as an homage to Tony Kushner's *Angels in America*, which she frequently watches in Mike Nichols's DVD version for HBO. In conjunction with the corpse found in Landwehrkanal, the German *Kanal* (canal) provides another chain of associations as it means both "channel" and "sewer." In the sense of "channel," the *Kanal* is a reminder that the Meinl Bank's offshore companies are located in the channel islands of Jersey and Guernsey; in the sense of "sewer" or "canal," it alludes to the cross-border leasing of sewage systems Jelinek satirizes in the main text for taking away even the shit from the local population. The issue of the name of Rosa Luxemburg floating between two drowned bodies parallels one of the main themes in the primary text's main themes: of "the name that belongs to us but isn't us."

When Stemann's production was chosen for the prestigious Berlin Theatertreffen in spring 2010, Jelinek, at her director's request, provided the site- and occasion-specific six-page piece "Im Wettbewerb" ("In Competition"), read by the actors lined up downstage as a sort of interlude. Self-referentially, the author (who, in addition to the 2004 Nobel Prize in Literature, has won many prestigious prizes throughout her career) contemplates the contradictory consequences of any competition.

Finally, when the production traveled to Vienna's international Festival Weeks in June 2010, Stemann restored passages he had cut from the original version, as they alluded to persons and events only an Austrian audience would understand. By then, *The Merchant's Contracts* had turned into a cult event.

Many repertory companies presented their own versions the following seasons when it became one of the most-produced plays in the German-speaking theater. In the summer of 2012, Stemann's production was invited to the Avignon Festival. As of this writing, it continues in the repertory of Hamburg's Thalia Theater with the original cast as an ongoing "work in progress," ready to respond to new stages in the global economic drama.

Such flexibility continues to be possible as Stemann, in his many productions of Jelinek's performance texts, had already developed a distinct, partly improvisational performance vocabulary with some of the actors and two musicians with whom he had formed a rock band long before his directing career. In contrast to other directors, Stemann wanted to present the complete text with only the standard minimal cuts. After the ur-reading, it was clear that this could be done only with text in hand and Stemann on stage, both as performer and director/conductor, as new additions required rearrangements, which necessitated the eliminations of other passages. Segments of the text are delivered at top speed, sometimes in overlapping choruses, at times as pop songs or cantatas, occasionally as stand-up comedy acts or Grand Guignol and horror-movie style. The latest political and economic developments are projected on the side walls of the stage and the auditorium. If it is impossible to grasp the entire text this way, its frantic performance reflects the degree society is able (or unable) to absorb the onslaught of stock market lingo (an unintelligible language for most).

If the practical dramaturgy of *Rechnitz* is comparable to an archeological dig, *The Merchant's Contracts* brings to mind a fashion designer and cutter's work, cutting different models from a huge bale of fabric. Jelinek's love of fashion has been much discussed and well documented in numerous photographs. She frequently stated that if she hadn't become a writer, she would have become a fashion designer like her aunt. Fashion is a theme in several of her texts, most notably *Jackie* and her most recent *Schatten. Eurydike sagt* (Shadows. Eurydice Says) and *The Street. The City. The Attack* (Vienna Burgtheater, January 2013, and Munich Kammerspiele, December 2012, respectively). In another context, she speaks, tongue-in-cheek, of her performance texts as an *Angebot*, an offer, a "special" in the commercial sense of offering a surplus of material to the consumer.[22] There were plenty of unused remnants of text for state and municipal repertory companies in Austria, Germany, and Switzerland to tailor-fit the verbal fabric to local conditions.

Two productions by smaller companies, both pared down to eighty minutes, stand out as opposite poles of site-specific versions in the wide range of settings and focal points of other stagings. One, presented in June 2010 at the Hans Otto Theater in Potsdam, the capital of the (formerly East German) state of Brandenburg on the outskirts of Berlin, staged the evolution of capitalism on a planet of gorillas evolving into investment bankers without shedding their apish features, with allusions to Stanley Kubrick's *2001: A Space Odyssey*. German theaters are haunted by the ghosts of their long history. The director Lukas Langhoff is a third-generation member of the famous East German dynasty of stage directors; his grandfather Wolfgang Langhoff, as artistic director of Berlin's Deutsches Theater, hosted Brecht's legendary production of *Mother Courage*; his father and

---

22 Elfriede Jelinek, "Notes on Secondary Plays" (Gitta Honegger trans.), unpublished manuscript. German version: "Anmerkung zum Sekundärdrama". Available at: http://www.elfriedejelinek.com (last accessed on October 30, 2014).

uncle, Thomas and Matthias respectively, directed at the Berliner Ensemble under Helene Weigel's leadership. A state-sponsored institution, the Hans Otto Theater, founded under the reign of King Frederick II of Prussia in 1795, went through several dramatic political changes, destroyed buildings and new homes. In 1952, it was named after Hans Otto, a communist actor and union leader who was murdered by the Nazis in 1933. Not surprising perhaps, in view of both the theater's location and history, and the director's background, was the production's unrelentingly ugly depiction of capitalism. Though sociopolitically quite interesting, it made for a rather leaden evening.

The other production, the 2011 Swiss premiere at the Theater St. Gallen, was also notable for its location. The University of St. Gallen is well known for its management school and its noted and notorious alumni. Apart from Julius Meinl V, the university is also alma mater of Prince Adam II, head of state of Liechtenstein, and two prime ministers of this tiny neighboring state of Switzerland, both famous tax havens. Austria's former finance minister Karl-Heinz Grasser's Liechtenstein Foundation protects a formidable international network of subsidiaries and turned out to be a major player behind the scenes of the ongoing Meinl and BAWAG epics.

Another link to the actual economic crisis was the St. Gallen theater production's young Icelandic director Thorleifur Örn Arnarsson, whose country's economy was one of the first among the European states to crash. To further foreground the ironic site-specific subtext, Arnarsson cast thirty local citizens from all walks of life for the chorus of small investors to read short passages from the text. Production dramaturg Karoline Exner describes:

In the production, one person at a time came to the microphone (in front of the still closed curtain). During the reading, a photograph with a "business card" of every person was projected: name, age, profession, motto for life. All remained on stage after they read so that the space got pretty crowded. This is how we gave identity to the people who lost their money anonymously.[23]

During early rehearsals,

> people were somewhat hesitant, because it was clear that the topic would be finances and Switzerland is a very wealthy country with a banking secret that also seems to be important to ordinary citizens. One doesn't talk about money here [. . .]. Many were shocked that the director asked them about their income (a breach of taboo) and what effect the financial crisis had on them. We were truly amazed how many of them had actually lost money and, even more surprising, how much. But of course, with that much money around, a lot can be gambled away [. . .].[24]

Chance played another University of St. Gallen alumnus—a classmate and later "hunter" of Julius Meinl—into the company's hands, which eventually led even to his brief appearance on stage: St. Gallen resident Wolfgang Vilsmeier, who had lost a substantial amount of his money in Meinl investments. After seeing another production at the theater, he asked two actors about other shows he should see. When they told him about *The Merchant's Contracts*, in which they were also cast, he indicated his relationship to Meinl and

---

23 Karoline Exner, email interview with Gitta Honegger, June 14, 2013.
24 Ibid.

was willing to meet with them. Briefly, the head of two Meinl investment firms (Meinl Investment Company and Meinl International Power), Vilsmeier discovered during an annual analysis that the majority of deposits originated from a single IP address abroad. As a graduate of the St. Gallen Business School he instantly understood his fellow student's strategies and took legal action which recouped some of the investors' money.[25]

In response to Vilsmeyer's story, the cast created their own fundraising project named HENRI, in German the acronym for University Ethics Emergency Pennies Initiative, that would help the university hire an ethics professor for their business school. During the intermission, actors announced the project and distributed piggy banks around the theater for contributions. The university was not amused. It requested a panel discussion in the theater between company members and university faculty to emphasize the university's commitment to ethics and its openness to artistic experiments.[26]

---

25 Karoline Exner, email to Gitta Honegger, June 19, 2013; Michael Nikbakhsh, "Ein Strategiepapier der Meinl Bank enthüllt Pläne zur Diffamierung von Gegnern" (A Strategy Paper of Meinl Bank Reveals Plans for the Defamation of Opponents), *Profil Online*, September 29, 2009. Available at: http://www.profil.at/articles/0939/560/251995/exk-lusiv-ein-strategiepapier-meinl-bank-plaene-diffamierung-gegnern (last accessed on October 30, 2014).

26 Exner, June 14, 2013.

II

TITANIA'S ASS

> Bless thee, Bottom, bless thee! Thou art translated!
> —William Shakespeare,
> *A Midsummer Night's Dream*, 3.1.123

As is evident Jelinek has a unique relationship to her directors. The linguistic strategies of her later "texts for speaking" add an entirely new dimension to the old adage that plays are completed only in performance. Her earlier plays are provocative from a feminist/Marxist perspective under the influence of Brechtian politicized dramaturgy. (As is well known, Jelinek was a member of the Austrian Communist Party from 1974 to 1991. As she once told me, she originally joined the party because it was the only one that was outspoken about Austria's involvement in the Holocaust.) After the collapse of communism in 1989, the formation of the European Union, and the expansion of global capitalism, her concerns with Austrian issues necessarily expanded to examine them in their interrelatedness with the new challenges for the emerging global connectivities. Interestingly, after the publication in 1995 of her opus magnum, the 666-page novel *The Children of the Dead*, she turned more and more to the theater. Her only novel after the Nobel Prize in 2004 was *Neid* (Envy), which she posted on her website in serialized form, as soon as she finished each chapter. As she stated, she also meant it for reading on the Web, rather than in print. Intended as a gesture against the globalized commercialization of the publishing world, the novel remains on her website only and will not be published in print. As she led an increasingly secluded life due to her anxiety illness, she followed and responded to world events all the more intensely on the Internet. Unlike the established publishing route, the serialized novel offered her an immediate extended contact with the world. So does the theater. As we have seen, *The Merchant's Contracts*, necessitated by current events, took on the form of an instantly serialized performance project. Theaters in the German-speaking countries responded with more and more commissions for texts on current events or existing literature they thought might fit Jelinek's concerns and strategies, as was the case with *Rechnitz*. Buñuel's film *The Avenging Angel* was suggested by the Munich Kammerspiele. An outspoken political activist unafraid to participate in public events and demonstrations in her earlier years (such as the weekly marches against the extreme rightist Freedom Party's participation as coalition partner in the federal government), Jelinek transferred her interventionist agenda to the theater. The dramaturgical methods could only be developed in the already mentioned intense symbiotic relationship with directors. This does not mean that she interfered in the rehearsal process. Rather, Jelinek's dramaturgy was as much influenced by some of the outstanding directors' work on her texts, as her work influenced their approach to the plays of other writers, especially the classics.

Fully aware of the (albeit brilliant) excesses of Regietheater, she challenged her directors, many of them the masters of Antonin Artaud's battle cry "No More Masterpieces" (although appropriated for their political–aesthetic purposes), who were attracted to the freedom her texts offered, with the invitation: "Ihr könnt mich verarschen," "You can make an ass of me." It wouldn't be Jelinek if the encouragement did not resonate with a popular quote from Goethe's play *Goetz von Berlichingen*: "Lick my ass," sometimes enhanced with an invitational overtone—"You can kiss my ass."

To further understand the genesis of Jelinek's planes of text and their staging methods, it is useful to look at some defining productions of her other plays.

The controversial German director Frank Castorf was the first to literally respond to Jelinek's provocation in his (in)famous 1995 production of her still conventionally structured play *Raststätte* (Service Station), a raunchy adaptation of Mozart's *Cosi fan tutte*. At the end, a giant naked sex doll with Jelinek's features and signature hairdo entered the stage, with blinking nipples and an opening and closing vagina. Jelinek, a great admirer of the visual artist Paul McCarthy, accepted the figure as a shocking but dramaturgically justified provocation, while her husband Gottfried Hüngsberg, usually a calm and gentle presence, was ready to storm the stage. Nevertheless, Castorf, in his characteristic manner, broke not only the taboos of more traditional audiences (though even those were used to taboo-breaking Central European directors); more importantly, he broke with previous directors' already standardized stereotypical approaches to Jelinek's outrageously subversive travesties of pornography and other clichés of the "feminine mystique." Since then, it was clear that the right to "making an ass" of the author had to be earned by a thorough understanding of her sociocultural critiques and new ways had to be found to get to the core of her strategies. In regard to the former, Shakespeare might provide a clue.

"Bless thee, Bottom, bless thee! Thou art translated!" shouts Quince at the sight and sounds of his fellow player transformed into an ass. For Peter Quince, the carpenter, "translation" is embodiment profoundly different from the role-playing the artisans are rehearsing at the moment.

Shakespeare, of course, plays with the uncanniness of translation and the transformative power of performance on all levels of the theatrical process. Bottom, the loud-mouthed player is translated into a braying ass; a weaver by profession, Bottom's acting like an ass gets interwoven into the dream-and-fairy world. Titania's gaze, blinded by her jealous husband's magic potion finds her "ear is much enamored of thy note," her eye "enthrallèd" *to* his shape.[27] In seventeenth-century parlance, she is thrilled to find herself held in bondage of the ass, aroused by his foreign "speech." Thus she is "making an ass" of herself. The same could be said by Jelinek's use of the male canon, except that unlike Titania, she is fully conscious of her infatuation with the uncanny familiarity-as-foreignness of her native (literally "man"-made) language, not the mother but the father's tongue, to play in her spirit on Jacques Lacan's variations on ("translations" of) Freud. Thus she invites her trusted (mostly male) directors, who "enthralled" her with the shapes into which they "translate" her texts, to "make an ass" of her; more than that, she coyly provokes them to do so in her stage directions and by occasionally inserting herself as the author's voice into the text.

Arguably, Stemann, the youngest among Jelinek's defining directors, has won his place (and her heart) as her most congenial director in a sort of flirtatious, quasi-mother–son working relationship. It is reflected in his staging himself in her texts and in her protective defense against criticism of his irreverent, though loving and dramaturgically astute aesthetics.

In his first Jelinek production, the 2003 world premiere *Das Werk* (The Plant) at the Vienna Burgtheater, Stemann

---

27 William Shakespeare, *A Midsummer Night's Dream*, 3.1.65–66.

introduced a wig with Jelinek's signature role and braids, which was tossed about and trampled on by the men in the play. What could be perceived as shockingly brutal and offensive was in fact an accurately graphic "translation" of the ways her real life detractors verbally attacked her, and continue to do so. The fetishized wig became a trademark of Stemann's subsequent productions of Jelinek's new works. In his 2006 Hamburg production of *Ulrike Maria Stuart*, Stemann wore it himself as he read lines from the text rendered in a melancholy voice in Jelinek's Viennese lilt (as perceived by a Northern German), while a photograph of the author was projected on a screen. Speech, image, and doubling emphasized the author's vulnerability. In the meantime, the wig has become a standard prop in the increasing number of Jelinek productions by the disciples of the master directors.

Before Stemann, the late Einar Schleef took on the part of Jelinek's self-representation (sans wig or drag) as "Elfi-Elektra" in his seminal 1998 eight-hour production of *Sportstück* at the Vienna Burgtheater. Rather than "making an ass" of himself or Jelinek, his performance of the author's lines was an inspired insertion of the classic fool, thus highlighting the affinity between Jelinek's linguistic strategies and the subversions of meanings in the language of Shakespeare's fools. Schleef was also the first to highlight the importance of the chorus to Jelinek's sociopolitical critique.

Among Jelinek's internationally renowned directors, the late Christoph Schlingensief's approach as her co-author was the most radical. Responding to her texts as litanies or mantras that have a therapeutic effect on him, her repetitions and variations set him off on his own non-linear visual narrative: chains of images spun off one or more of the multiple connotations of her lines or individual words that wove into his provocative performative universe.

Schlingensief, who died in 2010 at the age of fifty, corresponded with Jelinek during his long battle with a rare cancer. The result was her text "Tod-krank.doc" (Death(ly)-ill.doc), which he included in his "readymade opera" titled *Mea Culpa*, among texts, compositions, and images from Bach to Wagner to Schönberg, from Nietzsche to Jean-Luc Nancy to Slavoj Žižek, staged as a drawn-out celebratory dance with death (-in-progress, so to speak) at the Vienna Burgtheater in 2008.

Previously, Schlingensief had staged his response to Jelinek's reaction to the First Gulf War, *Bambiland*, also at the Vienna Burgtheater, with excerpts from the text only as a soundtrack. He explains his collaboration as "co-author":

In *Bambiland,* for example, there's the line: "Finally, he's coming." In (my) take on it, it was shown in the form (of a film clip) of a US citizen, a porn actor, getting jerked off by a porn actress and ejaculating on the American flag. It's a ridiculous image, but it is charged by the two actors, both icons of many Fassbinder movies, Udo Kier and Margit Carstensen standing (on stage) in the background. So it is not a 1:1 illustration, but it opens up a world that connects Udo Kier with Andy Warhol, Paul Morissey, the Frankenstein movie and Dracula. It is this blood, this having-to-bleed in order to live again . . . my images don't illustrate, rather they are pictures that let another organism breathe. One picture develops out of the other, they are shapes coming into being.[28]

---

28 Christoph Schlingensief, "Christoph Schlingensief im Gespräch mit Teresa Kovacs" in Pia Janke (ed.), *Jelinek Jahrbuch* (Wien: Praesens 2010), pp. 15–29; here, p. 18.

Jelinek remembers their collaboration in a tribute after his death:

> Getting back to my question, why we had so much and at the same time so little to do with each other: because I as a consumer could stare at, admire all that kept appearing and disappearing, humans and human material, literally, the stuff that dreams are made on, weaving across the stage like overloaded trucks; while he didn't know what to do with my texts, and even when he used them occasionally in small doses, I think it had to do with this kind of compulsive bringing out and putting away again. (Which often is a pushing away! A pushing away in bringing it out, this is how I perceived our collaboration, which never was one. I can still see him in my home, how he turned out sketch after sketch to show me those appearances in his *animatograph* plus additional appearances, plus only projected appearances, which also were alive once, etc.; how he imagined it all, how he had to bring it all together, force it together, irrespective of whether it wanted to come together, he knew exactly how, and there was no room for other things.) Thus he proved, perhaps not to himself but to me, that what he wanted to accomplish was not possible with my texts.[29]

---

29 Elfriede Jelinek, "The Terror of Fusion" (Gitta Honegger trans.) in Klaus Biesenbach, Anna-Catharina Gerbers and Aino Laberenz Susanne Pfeffer (eds), *Christoph Schlingensief*. (Köln; Walther König 2014) pp. 109–11; here, p. 110.

Nonetheless, it was Schlingensief who best summed up her importance to literature:

> This is another form of literature, it's rather meant for the future. I find it awful when [Jelinek's] texts are approached in small-minded ways. They don't do justice to them. It would make no sense, for example, to reduce her texts to a feminist aspect. That's only what society would like. In reality her texts are texts of the future. When some day extra-terrestrials will arrive, they will find this weird speak trash of hers, which is a thousand times more important than all the information about Michael Jackson, which was in the news today.[30]

Thanks to Jelinek's uniquely "open" dramaturgy and special interest in contemporary visual and performance art, innovative directors have advanced their careers with provocative confrontations with her texts. As a notable exception, Jossi Wieler's rigorous minimalist aesthetic and psychological as well as philosophical discipline highlight Jelinek's deep roots in the classical tradition. His understanding of the writer's larger cultural context is related to Austrian filmmaker Michael Haneke's award-winning film based on of her novel *The Piano Teacher*.

Though women have also successfully staged her works, only one, Karin Beier (born in 1965), has achieved the wide recognition and power of her male colleagues. As head of the Schauspiel Cologne and, as of 2013–14, the first woman to head Germany's biggest theater, the legendary Hamburg Schauspielhaus, she commissioned several of Jelinek's recent works, most notably a response to the collapse of the Cologne City Archive in 2009 caused by flooding during the

---

30 Schlingensief, *Jelinek Jahrbuch*, p. 18.

construction of a subway line. The text, ambiguously titled *Ein Sturz*, is another instance of Jelinek's untranslatable titles: as written, it means "a fall." If read aloud in one breath as *Einsturz*, it is the German word for collapse. The piece opened the 2010 season, which focused on themes of "visionary constructions and real catastrophes." *Ein Sturz* was introduced as the final piece in a triptych of Jelinek texts: *Das Werk / Im Bus / Ein Sturz*, which included Beier's new staging of *Das Werk* and a brief text *Im Bus*, originally written for Schlingensief but never performed. *Das Werk* (The Plant, as in a power plant, but also connoting a work as text or any work of art) deals with the construction of the Austrian mega–power plant in the Alps near Kaprun. Planned in the 1920s, it was built during the Nazi regime with forced laborers and prisoners of war, many of whom perished under the dangerous working conditions, and completed in 1955. The first production at the Vienna Burgtheater in 2003 was directed by Stemann, then, at age 35, one of the most promising upcoming directors, who firmly established his fame with this (his first of many) staging of a new "work" by the author. In contrast to Stemann, who created a culture-specific and critical performance space suggesting Austria's obsession with the Alps, their mythologization by blood and soil visionaries, high-risk athletes and *Sound of Music* cultists, Beier's performance space suggested an oversized, unadorned workspace of a contemporary architectural firm. The bare stage was filled with rows of white-topped tables, each supplied with bottled water, which the chorus, all dressed in black and white, eventually created elegant little fountains and waterfalls in elaborate spitting games. They were an ironic counterpoint to that specific text and a prelude to the evening's third piece, *Collapse*, which climaxed in the break of a massive pipe causing the stunning eruption of a powerful waterfall that flooded the entire stage. *Im Bus* (In the Bus), about an accident during the construction of a subway line in Munich, serves as a brief clownish interlude between the two major pieces. Beier stands out for her razor-sharp articulation of Jelinek's texts (though they also are radically pared down) and her postmodern operatic imagination. Jelinek/Titania's ass turned out to be what he always was: The victim of an imperial power game uncontrollable by ordinary humans. It might have taken another woman to expose the bottom of it all.

For her 2011 season, Beier commissioned a brief text for an evening of short pieces to the theme "Demokratie in den Abendstunden" (freely translated, Democracy in the Twilight Hours) from Jelinek among other contributors such as Thomas Bernhard, Joseph Beuys, Rainer Maria Rilke, André Breton, Richard Wagner and Al-Qaeda, with music from Franz Schubert to John Cage. As happens so often with Jelinek, requests for short pieces result in nearly full-length performance texts, while commissioned full-length texts expand into over-eight-hour-long performance material. Whenever a theme is suggested to her, she interweaves it with most recent contemporary concerns. In this case, it was the 2011 tsunami and nuclear catastrophe of Fukushima. Titled *Kein Licht* (No Light), it featured an orchestra's first and second violinist, two undead after the disaster. Their text, in Jelinek's linguistic technique, orchestrates the resonances between music and physics, light and radiation, through the concepts of time, "splitting", a play on the German *Spaltung* as in *Kernspaltung* (nuclear fission), and "split tones" as in half and quarter notes, which indicate the *Tonwerte*, the tonal values. The German *Wert* also comes up in *Halbwert* for the English term "half-life" in the terminology of nuclear physics. *Wert* as value—personal, artistic, and commercial value of a composition—connects the text to the issues raised by *The Merchant's Contracts*. A major concern in all of Jelinek's recent texts, the term has, of course, also great personal meaning for Jelinek herself, whose "market value" rose considerably after the Nobel Prize.

Needless to say, *No Light* was of specific interest to Japan. A production of the text, in the award-winning translation by Tatsuki Hayashi and directed by Masahiro Wiwa at the Tokyo Metropolitan Playhouse, was the centerpiece of the Festival Tokyo 12, which was dedicated to Jelinek's work. Besides performances of Jossi Wieler's production of *Rechnitz*, the festival presented her older text *wolken.heim* (literally, clouds.home, suggesting "cloud-cookoo-home"), featuring the widows of Nazi officers taking on the language of their fallen "heroes," also translated by Hayashi and directed by Nobusuke Kakashima. Most significant, perhaps, for its site-specific approach was Akira Takayama's "tour performance" of *Light II*, a sequel titled "epilogue?" [sic] Jelinek had written in the meantime, featuring a "Mourning Woman" with the stage direction "she can do what she wants." The text mourns what happened in the wake of the tragedy. The radioactive contamination is again followed by commercial pollution: "The same people who built those silos of the dead are building new houses, which—and that's also all new—are all clean. And that's how we should keep them. No shit." (Here is one of those harmless German words—*sauber*, for clean. With a slight undertone, it becomes an [Austrian] slang I replaced here with "no shit" to retain the ambiguity, albeit at the expense of the faux polite tone.)

In the Japanese version by the same translator, the director let schoolchildren from the vicinity of Fukushima choose and read those parts of the text that had special significance for them. No one advised or coached them. Audiences were given earphones with the recording of the children's readings and sent on individual tours through the Shimbashi district of Tokyo with a tour book and postcards that turned out to show pictures of the disaster and its aftermath. The tour was invited to the 2013 Vienna Festival Weeks with spectators guided through Vienna with pictures of Fukushima while listening to the children's readings in German and Japanese.

As the Tokyo transcultural event has shown, Jelinek's performance texts are not limited to the collaboration with German-language directors. Most importantly, their interventionist reach and relevance also include non-Western artists and cultures. (Her novels have already been translated into more than 35 languages.) The worldwide interest in Jelinek's performance texts introduces another challenge for translators, dramaturgs and directors: the translation and staging of surtitles. The issue goes beyond Jelinek's works. In our time of global theater/performance festivals, which include more and more experimental forms of interweaving performance cultures, it is surprising how little attention is being paid to the creative inclusion of surtitles. Jelinek's linguistic strategies make it all the more important, if not imperative, to confront the challenge of staging the drama of translation: the tensions, both intra- and inter-linguistic, and the drama of the politics of translations. But more often than not, translations are commissioned as an afterthought, when a production has been selected for the festival circuit (as happened to me twice, when I was asked by the Berlin Theatertreffen four weeks before the presentation of Jelinek productions). Among others, Robert Lepage and Ariane Mnouchkine have already shown how to imaginatively stage titles, not just in the standard abbreviated fashion of surtitles, but also as an integral part of the world they are showing and all of us are living in.

TRANSLATION IN PERFORMANCE

Translation is another word for the impossible.
—Jacques Derrida[31]

I take it as more than a fortuitous coincidence that this volume is published by a British company, although based out of Calcutta, India, and distributed by an US American University Press: for the Austrian American translator into English of an Austrian German–language writer, whose "texts for speaking" stage the historic debt of language as a language of guilt, it is a challenging reminder of the complex colonial and revolutionary histories resonating in what has become the language of global communication. The question "Whose English is it?"—what, whose histories does it carry; what politics are embedded in its use—has become a crucial issue for translators. As the translator of a poststructuralist writer such as Jelinek––a woman, in a culture with the legacy of an empire of diverse cultures, albeit within Europe, who takes on the male canon, who ruptures language to expose the cultural performances inscribed in it, I am indebted to Indian literary scholars Gayatri Chakravorty Spivak and Homi K. Bhabha for their analyses of the multiple performances of translations from a postcolonial/ feminist perspective.

---

31 Jacques Derrida, *The Monolingualism of the Other* (Patrick Mensah trans.) (Stanford, CA: Stanford University Press, 1998), p. 57.

As we have seen in *Rechnitz*, Jelinek's messengers, not unlike the colonized subject, adopt and mimic the language of the master. As Bhabha has shown, the minoritized, the "minoritarian majority" do not become like the other but, rather, like his uncannily distorted double. A freak. Like Jelinek: a woman, appropriating the male canon of *Dichter and Denker*, of poets and thinkers, and subverting it. And getting the Nobel Prize for such blasphemy!

The politics of translation are always embedded in Jelinek's dramaturgy and most poignantly so in *Rechnitz*. The messengers are also translators—of memory, of history. Ultimately, Jelinek stages herself as a messenger in her dramaturgy of appropriating found texts from different epochs and disciplines. Not unlike her messengers, she communicates in a language that is not her own but that of the patriarchal literary canon. (It is a problem her generation of Western feminist thinkers such as Julia Kristeva or Luce Iragaray have struggled to come to terms with.) As a feminist writer, Jelinek draws the radical consequences by enacting "culture's double" in the sense of Bhabha's explanation of the "colonial paradox": "[T]he repetition of the 'same' can in fact be its own displacement, [it] can turn the authority of culture into its own *non-sense* precisely in its moment of enunciation."[32]

For example: one of Jelinek's favorite play on words is based on a shift of intonation: "Nicht wahr?, *nicht* wahr!"—"True, no? NO! that's true." Idiomatically, it would be "Right? no? NO! that's right." In English, the twist is not quite as clean as in the German. It needs some help with an

---

32 Homi K. Bhabha, "Articulating the Archaic: Cultural Difference and Colonial Nonsense" in *The Location of Culture* (New York: Routledge, 1994), pp. 175–98; here, p. 195.

extra "no." But in both languages, the double meaning of the phrase only becomes clear when it is enunciated. It is not surprising then that Spivak challenges the translator to *stage* the text "as one directs a play, as an actor interprets a script."[33]

Rechnitz is ultimately a play not *about*, but *on* translating, on translation in performance, and the multiple roles of translators in action. The location of Rechnitz on the Austrian–Hungarian border is also a linguistic border—not only between the local Austrians and the Hungarian or Roma-speaking slave laborers, but also between the dialect of the local peasants and the strained High German of the out-of-town Nazi elite. (Quite revealingly, the above-mentioned German documentary about Rechnitz features select German subtitles for the local rural accents as well as for the Hungarian-accented German of some interviewees of the Jewish community.) Jelinek's source for quotations from Elliot's "The Hollow Men" is a German translation she found on the Internet. Sometimes she uses lines from the English original. A translator herself (of Thomas Pynchon's *Gravity's Rainbow*, Christopher Marlowe's *The Jew of Malta* and, most recently, of plays by Oscar Wilde and Georges Feydeau), she draws attention to the process of translation.

Spivak, the translator into English, not only of Jacques Derrida's *Of Grammatology* but also of late-eighteenth-century Bengali poetry as well as of short stories by Bengali writer Mahasweta Devi, speaks of translation as the most "intimate" act of reading. For her, this is the experience that goes beyond knowledge; it goes back to a culture's songs

---

33 Gayatri Chakravorty Spivak, "The Politics of Translation" in Lawrence Venuti (ed.), *The Translation Studies Reader*, 3rd edn (New York: Routledge 2002), pp. 312–30; here, p. 314.

"sung day after day in in family chorus before memory began."[34] It is a child's intimate experience of her first language. It takes a native speaker's deep experience of the language and its cultural codes to translate. Jelinek could not agree more. Some of her wordplays and local idioms need translations from *Austrian* German into *German* German, all the more so because, as we have seen, each is just a small, easily overlooked link in a large net of sociopolitical maneuvering. The blandest "line" (in its theatrical sense) might contain a nearly invisible/inaudible clue that links it across long distances to other apparently bland or nonsensical lines and clues. Together they map the jigsaw puzzle of doublespeak and doubles speaking.

Bhabha's essay "Articulating the Archaic" takes him via Freud from "colonial nonsense to metropolitan bourgeois truth," [35] which he finds in the uncannily lifelike doll Olympia in E. T. A. Hofmann's story of "The Sandman" (more widely known from Jacques Offenbach's opera *The Tales of Hofmann*). The doll's stunning mechanical imitations of a "real woman" have a similar effect on patriarchal society as Jelinek's performances as a writer: her obsessive repetitions of cultural gestures suggest the automaton's uncanny mechanism. (Jelinek herself talks of her obsessive automatism in the act of writing.) Moreover, her performance as a writer exposes the mechanism of language. In Hoffman's story, the automaton's maker Coppelius destroys the doll and flees with the parts of his creation for fear its inhabitants will kill him for his fraud. In Walter Felsenstein's legendary 1958 Brechtian production of the opera at (then East) Berlin's Komische Oper, Olympia gets savagely torn

34 Ibid., p. 313.
35 Bhabha, "Articulating the Archaic," p. 195.

apart by her upper-bourgeois audience. The doll's truth, which is the artifice of her behavior, exposes, like Jelinek's writing, the artifice of "civilized" society. The truth is patriarchy's fraud. No wonder one of the oldest (male) members of the Nobel-awarding Swedish Academy resigned in protest over Jelinek's selection.

By an ironic twist of fate, Jelinek won the 2004 Nobel Prize for literature a few weeks before Jacques Derrida's death. For a long time, Derrida had hoped to receive the award. Though Jelinek and Derrida did not know each other, the kinship between their explorations of language brings to mind Freud's assessment of Arthur Schnitzler. What the psychoanalyst wrote to the playwright also applies to the difference between the postmodern philosopher/writer and the postmodern artist/writer: "I have often asked myself in astonishment how you came by this or that piece of secret knowledge which I had acquired by a painstaking investigation of the subject, and finally came to the point of envying the author, whom hitherto I have admired."[36]

Jelinek deconstructs the patriarchic language as she uses it. For Derrida, deconstruction is the tracking of *différance*, which is a "game of the trace . . . which has no sense and is not [present as matter] . . . ." It is "'a game in process,' in which the *differing-from* charts a trace, which will again be erased." [37] In that sense, Jelinek's performance texts score the appearance and disappearance of traces. As we have seen in both *Rechnitz* and *The Merchant's Contracts,* performances of her texts embody the playing of traces. In Bhabha's analysis, both the colonized "other" and the automaton have

36 Sigmund Freud, "Entry for 8 May 1906" in Letters of Sigmund Freud (E. L. Freud ed.) (New York: Basic Books, 1961), p. 251.

37 Heinz Kimmerle, *Jack Derrida* (Hamburg: Junius, 2000), p. 87.

picked up the traces of the "master." In the cracks between their appearances and disappearances, the "archaic" shows up in the other: the "native" and the absent "real" woman, that is, Elfriede Jelinek. As some of the media's visceral, aggressively personalized attacks on Jelinek's work show, the encounter with a (woman) writer's Derridaesque "absence as presence" in her writing as well as in her "real" life as a (involuntary) recluse, can be deeply traumatizing.

Coincidentally, Shakespeare's *Merchant of Venice* provides the stage for both Derrida's and Jelinek's playing with traces. While Shakespeare's merchant resonates in Jelinek's title, Derrida, in his text "What Is a 'Relevant' Translation" examines how *The Merchant of Venice* itself stages translation in action on every level, from the economic (money in exchange for a pound of flesh) to the law (in its relationship to the divine), as interpreted by a woman disguised as a male lawyer, which forces the conversion of Shylock, the Jew, to Christianity.[38] Derrida finds all those meanings contained in a single word: "mercy," going back to the Latin *merces* (pay, wage, reward, compensation, monetary recompense)[39] to "market, merchandise mercenary, reward, literal and sublime."[40] In Derrida's deconstruction of Portia's famous trial speech, as in Jelinek's orchestration of the chorus of messengers, translation itself is put on trial. And it is also a single word, *Schuld*—for debt and guilt—that links Derrida's

38 Jacques Derrida, "What Is a 'Relevant' Translation" (Lawrence Venuti trans.) in Lawrence Venuti (ed.), *The Translation Studies Reader*, 3rd edn (New York: Routledge 2002), pp. 365–88.

39 See Dictionarium latino-anglicum (Latin-to-English Dictionary). Available at: http://browse.dict.cc/latin-english/merces.html (last accessed on November 5, 2014).

40 Derrida, "What Is a 'Relevant' Translation," p. 375.

analysis of Shakespeare's play to both *Rechnitz* and *The Merchant's Contracts*. Antonio's debt, which he acknowledges, becomes Shylock's irresolvable guilt vis-à-vis Portia's command "Then must the Jew be merciful."[41] He either must break his oath and thus Jewish divine law or—thanks to a loophole Portia finds in his contract with Antonio, the bond, the IOU—become guilty of murder according to Christian law if he is not merciful. Both Western law and the market deal with the forgiveness of debt as a divinely inspired act. As Jelinek's and the world's "real" merchants' contracts show, it is now the banks that in the name of the law under the God of one nation must be forgiven.

Jelinek, by her own account, had not read Derrida. She did not have to. The link between them (as well as with Spivak and Bhabha) is Martin Heidegger. All of these thinkers critically pick up on the controversial philosopher's investigation of origin, his interrogation of history and culture, and his critical search for their traces in linguistic roots and the performance of language. Not quite surprisingly, all five are known for the length and density of their writing style. More than anything, their texts exemplify that, in Derrida's words, "translation is another word for the impossible."[42] The translator takes hope from the enigmatic statement: If indeed translation stands for the impossible, the word suggests that translation actually performs the impossible; thus translation shows itself possible in the act. Both Jelinek and Derrida share Heidegger's (obsessive) use of

---

41 Ibid.

42 Jacques Derrida, *The Monolingualism of the Other; or, the Prosthesis of Origin* (Patrick Mensah trans.) (Stanford, CA: Stanford University Press, 1998), p. 57.

punning, his etymological rooting in roots, so to speak, and apply them to their respective deconstructive projects.

While Derrida was deeply influenced by Heidegger's philosophy since the late 1940s, Jelinek, an early member of the first post–World War II generation, came of age when the relationship between Heidegger's path-breaking philosophy and early support of the ideas of Hitler's National Socialist project were the subject of impassioned public debate. The controversy is the catalyst for her 1991 play *Totenauberg* (*Death/Valley/Mountain* in the English published version). It explores the impact of Heidegger's philosophy and its ambiguous legacy from his time to the present through the lens of Hannah Arendt, his Jewish student and lover in 1924. *Totenauberg* marks an important turning point in Jelinek's dramaturgy from the radically feminist approach of her earlier plays to the wide scope of political and cultural issues woven into her later "(planes of) texts for speaking." Her submersion into Arendt and Heidegger's changing political–ethical discourse in the context of the Holocaust, their diverging careers yet renewed contact after World War II gave Jelinek the foundation for the complex themes and innovative dramaturgy of her later work. In retrospect, *Totenauberg* can be read as the first part of a trilogy that directly connects to the world of *Rechnitz* and leads to the global scenario of *The Merchant's Contracts*, all haunted by recycled Heideggerian sound bytes. Therefore, I am taking a short detour through this text. This does not mean that an audience needs to be familiar with Heidegger's thinking and language. The play is not "about" Heidegger but about the performative force of his language to this day. The speakers of "Heideggerese" are as unfamiliar with Heidegger's writing or flummoxed by what he is actually (*eigentlich*) saying (which needs intra-linguistic translation for nearly everyone) as the uninitiated audience. That's Jelinek's point.

Totenauberg alludes to Heidegger's secluded cottage outside the village of Todtnauberg in the Black Forest. Essentially, the play is a meditation on the relationship between Heidegger and Hannah Arendt, in the context of Arendt's first visit of Heidegger in 1950, seventeen years after their two-semester affair. In the meantime, Arendt herself had become an acclaimed political theorist and philosopher living and working in New York. The dirge-like mood of their meeting frames a series of grotesquely comical episodes that demonstrate how Heidegger's concepts were appropriated in the post–World War II culture of forgetting. Heidegger's legacy continues to metabolize in trendy popular culture, as cultivated in fashionable academic discourse, marketed by the tourist industry and practiced by sports, nature, and perfect-health enthusiasts, young mothers grooming their babies for competitive superiority, and local peasant entrepreneurs of deadly alpine athletics. In a scenario that foreshadows the themes of the texts included in this volume, the undead among the mangled limbs and corpses of fellow tourists (commercially exploited, though welcome foreigners as opposed to refugees) evoke both the ghosts of fascism and the precarious situation of native and migrant foreigners in our global world.

While Derrida develops and challenges Heidegger's philosophical discourse on the stages of academia, Jelinek pursues and subverts Heidegger's traces on the screens of mediatized everyday life. Inevitably, she would have had to come across Derrida's ideas, intertwined as they are with Heidegger's philosophy. Not surprisingly, then, the two masters echo each other in Jelinek's linguistic scenarios. As processed in media speak (and dramatized by Jelinek), the fashionable philosophers' discourse deteriorates into speechifying, its "truth" into what Stephen Colbert would term truthiness, recycled into the various jargons of current fashions.

Heidegger's terms for "discourse" and "speak" are *Rede* and *Gerede*. Unfortunately, the standard academic translation of "discourse" and "idle talk" does not show the active relationship between the terms. *Ge-rede* also suggests the scattering of something that's whole, composed (both in the sense of put together and calm), such as a *Rede*, speech, a lecture. In the context of Jelinek's dramaturgy, "speech" versus the vernacular noun "speak" or "speechifying" comes closer to their interactive dynamic. Heidegger's authorial speeches in search of the truth "fall" (in Heidegger's sense of *verfallen* for "deteriorate, dissemble") into various "speaks" in Jelinek's choruses. Furthermore, as a chorus, its individual members also reflect another important Heideggerian concept: Their *Mit-Sein*, their "Being-With" a group, that is, their adapting to society's norms and expectations, as opposed to "Being-There," fully open to the moment. The obscene activities and criminal actions reported by the chorus of messengers in *Rechnitz* are a devastating travesty of Heidegger's pontifications. The German pronoun for man ("one" as in "one doesn't do that") expresses Heidegger's Being-With.

Jelinek's messengers almost exclusively use "man," which, unlike "you" or "they," is general enough to unwittingly imply them as well, as they try to distance themselves from their reports, while or "you" or "they" unequivocally sets up the distance. The use of "one" in English immediately elicits outcries of "sounding translated." A translation for performance must keep a delicate balance between the natural flow of Jelinek's language and the undercurrents of meanings. Ultimately, the choices between "one" or "they" or "you" will have to be made in performance.[43]

To ease US theater folks' fears of theater waxing philosophically, Jelinek, if anything, satirizes such waxings (both in philosophical and cosmetic practice). The truth comes out in performance or, as Plato fretted and Bhabha asks: "What is the truth of the lie?"[44]

That said, I will conclude with Jelinek's take on what is a key word to Heidegger's pursuit of "Being" (*Sein*): *Das Eigentliche*, commonly translated as "the authentic." It is the enigmatic title for the main part of *The Merchant's Contract*. Tellingly, the term does not come up in the actual performance text and, in the sense of "authentic," it has nothing to do with it. But the German term in its multiple meanings can be read as a tongue-in-cheek reference to the philosopher as well as a coded stage direction. *Das Eigentliche* is the noun of the adjective *eigentlich*, meaning factual, real, true, in its straightforward dictionary translation. As mentioned, in English translations of Heidegger, *eigentlich* stands for "authentic" as opposed to "inauthentic." The term is fundamental to Heidegger's investigations of the relationship of pure Being (*Sein*) and Being-There (*Dasein*), for truly being in the world (as opposed to being stuck). But Jelinek's title suggests yet another idiomatic use of "*eigentlich*" as a modal

---

43 In dramaturgical discussions for the 2013 American premiere at the Women's Project Theatre of my translation of Jelinek's solo performance text *Jackie*, the issue of the character's frequent use of "one" came up. In Jelinek's spirit, I suggested they use "you" or "they" instead, as they saw fit. During the rehearsal process, the team discovered that "one" in most instances actually worked best for their staging of Jackie (Onassis)'s self-performance.

44 Bhabha, "Articulating the Archaic," p. 197.

particle, one of those uninflected words so dear to German-language speakers as a qualifier or indicator of mood or attitude. In that sense, it is difficult to define even in German. I found the best German definition of *eigentlich* buried on a blog: "It should be this way, because it would be right this way, but it isn't."[45]

This definition captures Jelinek's take on Heidegger's linguistic acrobatics, and her subversion of them in *The Merchant's Contracts*—the transformation of *das Wahre*, the truth, into *Ware*, commodity, ware, things. The connection between *Wahre* and *Ware* goes beyond the homophonic. It goes back to the root word "*eigen*" in Jelinek's title *Das Eigentliche*. *Eigen* also comes up in the noun *Eigentum* (property), and in the verb *aneignen* (acquire), where it clues us into the plot of the play, the plotting for property (plots)–the real truth, searched for in philosophy and revealed in religious ecstasy. The ticket to it all is a certificate, a contract, which actually is worth nothing and leads into (existential) nothingness. Heidegger's truth, *das Eigentliche*, like the real thing in the real world, turns out to be nothing. Heidegger's "Nothing" permeates *Rechnitz*, where the Jewish laborers are perceived as "nothings." The narratives of the massacre of those "nothings" open up the chasm of nothingness, where Heidegger meets Nietzsche in Jelinek's uncanny scenario. The roots of greed branch out into the language of both plays.

---

45 Maeve Dragon, in "Wer kann die Bedeutung des Wortes 'Eigentlich' erklären?" (Who Can Explain the Meaning of the word "Eigentlich"?), Yahoo Answers. Available at: http://de.answers.yahoo.com/question/-index?qid=20080727104345AAjWA4W (last accessed on November 5, 2014).

In the multivalent Austrian vernacular, the adjective *eigen* is also a synonym of "uncanny" in the sense of weird, strange, different. In Jossi Wieler's staging of *Rechnitz*, the messengers' behavior is "funny," both strange and familiar—*eigen*, uncanny. The site of the massacre is the property/ *Eigentum* of the hostess, a member of the Thyssen dynasty, whose financial power straddles two world wars and the present of global economics. The aristocratic legacy of the countess's husband is the value of historic aristocratic status added to the big investors' money. The victims are strangers, uncanny, because of their emaciated state. Initially valuable for their slave labor in the service of the economics of Hitler's war of extermination, they have become valueless, as they had already been worked to death by the master race.

The currency of a name connects the past with the present and the economy of both plays. A case in point is the self-description on the current website of the ThyssenKrupp AG, titled "Developing the Future," which states: "Innovations and technical progress are key factors in managing global growth and using finite resources in a sustainable way. With our engineering expertise in the areas of 'Material,' 'Mechanical' and 'Plant', we enable our customers to gain an edge in the global market and manufacture innovative products in a cost- and resource-efficient way."

The title and terms in quotation marks could be straight out of a Heidegger glossary—the present leads to the future, its quality arising from the past that is inscribed in two resonant names. The wording offers an example of Jelinek's ongoing preoccupation—to stage the use, manipulation, and

---

46 ThyssenKrupp, 'Group', official website of ThyssenKrupp AG. Available at: http://www.thyssenkrupp.com/en/konzern/index.html (last accessed on November 5, 2014).

impact (intended or not) of Heidegger's terminological tools in the fashion and marketable jargons of business, politics, and the bourgeoisie.

POSTSCRIPT: MERCY ME . . . *MERCI* . . .

In her characteristic laconic fashion, Jelinek acknowledges her sources at the end of her texts. For the heading of that section in *The Merchant's Contracts*, she even trumps herself with the ultimate untranslatable word game: *Dank-und Bitt-und Versagungen.*

Starting from the commonly used Dank*sagung* (nominalized plural of "saying thanks"; "Acknowledgments" in English publishing terminology), she shifts to the neologism Bitt*sagung* (her nounification of "saying please"; in this context, an appeal for mercy), and tops it all with *Versagungen*, the plural of her distortion of *Versagen*, or "failures." But that's not all. Sleeping in the last word is the verb *versagen*, which can mean "to fail," but also to deny something to somebody. Jelinek's final word might be a hidden warning to anyone attempting to translate her work. In the spirit of Jelinek's literary mode and one of her theatrical ancestors' opening line, the word game could be completed with *merde*. But this would not be in the humbly ironic spirit of her acknowledgements. Thus I conclude my translation with:

My thanks to Elfriede Jelinek and our audiences: Merci me—Mercy . . .

November 2014

RECHNITZ
(The Exterminating Angel)

A castle in Austria. Hunting trophies on the walls. Messengers, male and female, are arriving from everywhere, partly in shabby evening clothes, partly dressed as bicycle messengers; they are running in ever-shorter intervals until at some point the room is crowded. No one leaves the room. All are dressed in contemporary outfits. Please no suggestion of the past, except for small quotes, such as hairstyles, etc.! A man in underpants (by Calvin Klein or Hugo Boss) is checked by two messengers, while his chauffeur watches. Every now and then someone enters in a somewhat sloppy but very elegant evening get up, carrying a gun. This person pushes his/her way between the messengers, shoving them to the side to get to a window, from where he/she shoots out every now and then.

Every now and then, especially when the subject of the conversation is Germany or Germans, one or the other messenger performs a make-belief suicide attempt, which is instantly recognized as fake. Maybe he/she pulls a plastic bag over his/her head and tries to tighten it around the neck— something like that—as an ironic suicide attempt.

Only the messengers are talking (it could however also be just one person, that's up to the director). Everyone tries to hold back the armed person or push him to the window, so that the shot goes outside. Of course, it can also be done completely differently, as always with my plays.

You want to tell us you saw a man, who was extracted from his mother's womb by a flash of lightning like a bone from a chicken? Don't even try, I wouldn't believe it! Did you see the smoking ruins of a burning castle—despite the ban on smoking that weighs so heavily on our souls? No? So this then is still to come! Set on fire, like everything that has ever been set on fire since Hephaestus or Prometheus or the Russians, for that matter; the Russians were the last ones who brought us some fire, who put a bomb under us. Well, I am telling you: If they haven't been here yet, they will come. And they will come soon, a messenger just like yourself is telling you, and you know how much to believe us. The Russians have the conqueror's pride now, but they always ruin everything they conquer and steal the rest and ruin that too. The Russians are the gods of fire, but where does this persistent reputation come from? Their jubilations in the distance sound like shouting to us, where does it come from, when will they be here? When? What if I say I will not wait? Who will pull out all the stops on Stalin's Organ, that multi-barrel rocket launcher? Which raging swarm, wrapped in skins made of uniforms and watches of strangers and the lives of strangers and their own blood and their own torn flesh, and the skins of torn horses and in their own torn shoes, running across their own torn earth, over the bodies of raped foreign women, well, yes, back home they let the Germans rape their own women. One hand washes the other. Except for this one incident, the Russians always did and had to do everything themselves. They marched right through themselves, because a Russian only knows himself, he thanks us by raping our women and marching on while constantly checking the watch he stole from us: Is there time for another one?, there always is; and did the raging empire on the run wear down its soles already? All those Huns with their top guns? Those rich Huns from the Reich, they stick to their guns. At least they still wear halfway decent shoes. Something you have never seen, a good pair of shoes! You have never seen how it is when the Russians are coming and coming all at once, all at the same time. A gigantic stream that makes a racket like a buffalo herd pounding on tin. All at once. A gigantic human avalanche. You might get to experience something like that in a few decades hence, in the Alps perhaps, in Kitzbühel or Wengen or Mürren, or, altogether different, in St. Moritz, where horses play ball and people are gliding instead of racing down the tracks. I don't just mean they all got scared, all at once, and packed up and took off, but rather: a one-shot occurrence, that's what I mean by only once, all of a sudden, one time only. One of a kind. We won't live to see something like that again! So we might as well forget it again. Besides, there's no need for me even to mention it: No one could imagine anyone staying when the Russians are coming. Hello! Everyone here? No, but quite a few! In the end the Russians will also bring down prices. The Russians are coming to Kitzbühel, St. Anton, St. Moritz, St. Neverland—holy, holy, holy shit! We are leaving! We are running! We are so winning, we could have stayed, but we've got the runs, yes, no, we gotta run, we are running from the enemy with a discrete smile about the enema's purging effect on us.

The end will be our burial plot, I was told to pass on to you, there's no way you can bypass it. Meanwhile the distinguished professor has been cutting and pasting his purged spin on his ass—because people on the run can be seen only from behind—and he wants you to know that people rushing to save themselves from the infernal fires of their own homes have no time for orgies and other bullshit all across the Christian Occident, the land of dusk, the *Abendland*, all the way to the Orient—land of dawn—my ass!, fucking all night until the morning's twilight of men, which in the end gets you nothing but the shit hand drawn from a blood-soaked jacket. You want to stay in a house that is home to every lust and vice, you don't just run because the stranger gets here early. As for us, everyone's always coming too soon, before we are finished. At least let's stay till the very last moment. There is nothing left to loose and we want to get all we can as long as it lasts, one last one-and-only experience, which, alas, has been repeated a thousand times since. Let someone whisper to you: Haven't we been here before? Isn't this why we want to stay so long now, to the very last moment, savoring it, licking it out of one or several dripping people? It was a feast for followers, most definitely, a feast for followers, one followed the other and then, at 11 p.m., the phone rang, in the middle of the feast and fifteen people left. Thus speaks the messenger. So, slip in the tongue as long as you can! Keep licking, get the wrong message and spit it out again. Bon appétit! A professor of history unwrapping his daily vegan lunch and then burrowing for something tasty, would not be able to imagine such a feast. He is busy wondering if bits of meat might still be hiding there and how he could get them out of his Stayfresh lunchbox with lime detergent. Caustic lime, on the other hand, must be poured over everything, so nothing will ever show again. They won't show up again. Twenty-seven times; the truck went back and forth twenty-seven times, then the delivery was complete. All flesh must go. No time for moans and howls of lust. No time for senseless firing through the window. Just time for packing and splitting. This is how the history professor in his airtight eco-friendly box, which voluntarily transformed into a Mercedes Benz after he had read a lot and written even more about it, imagines the scene. But I too once was a box, I too can be recycled. Who wants me? I could become a wristwatch! Even before the professor is out for lunch for good and might as well be ready for recycling. Though should one try, there would be nothing left. If *Der Russe*, "*The Russian*"—here we always use the singular—if "*The Russian*" is really coming, and that seems unavoidable, everybody will run, that much is certain, that's clear to everyone, it's a constant in world history: "*Der Russe*," "*The Russian*" is hell for anyone thinking in terms of a solitary figure, because he always comes in high quantities and wastes no thoughts on anything, though he got plenty. This one has a photo of Gogol, no, Gorky in his wallet. He isn't just one, one of the Russians, rather: there are many of him, they are always many, because they don't have enough machines to take over their work. It wouldn't be worth mentioning that they are so many, let me be no nearer in death's dream kingdom!, yes, he is the site of mass escapes but at the other end, the Western end, the West's end: where all things come from except the gas. The gas will come later, after it will have been stuffed into a pipeline called Nabucco or something, which does not yet exist. And later still, even those pipes will line up against each other, because there can only be one Pied Piper, as there can only be one conductor. As for the semiconductor Iran, let this be my one and only, but all the more emphatic, warning. But now the war is over, practically over, it gave us kiss-asses a real good licking; the winners are always the same, so are the losers, so then I don't understand why wars are waged at all, reason becomes a play on words, capital a free gift of weapons for the less well off, its owners are in another country, that's why the other country remained neutral all this time. As long as they let it stay that way, it stayed laid back: and it paid off. Everything still on wheels is on its way there, they can stay there, because back home everything gets slaughtered, not only the first-born, but all born, except the born barons. The masses are ready to go, they are chasing one another and don't know whereto. Here comes the masters' automobile. It stashed away gas like a shake and fake fucking bakery before the arrival of the hordes of soldiers, who will find nothing but empty shelves. Anything still able to move, moves out, but not far, because we stick to our roots, and to our story, but also to each other. The aristocracy, seedbed of great emotions and great risks, take the limo; I, as a messenger, am constantly overtaken and must inhale the exhaust fumes.

Stretch limo at the very least; the duchess has to give a ride to her lover and also to another gentleman, who is also a lover—a lover of expensive wines, he carries responsibility, and there is another gentleman, who also carries responsibility, and there is all the luggage to take along too. No, it will be just the opposite: they must shirk responsibility; nowadays responsibility means charge, gotta charge up your battery, get in charge, before you get charged, it doesn't come free of charge, responsibility, but here we have a case of liability, an insurance case with no-fault benefits; responsibility, however, constantly defaults on us, it charges at us when, if we don't immediately accept it and sign the messenger's return receipt, and then it lets go of us again; we are and will always be in default. We can always pay the next time.

With direct eyes, they cross to death's kingdom, those Holy Thursday warshippers, I mean, they cruise, or do they actually cross right through it? Remember us, if at all, not as lost, violent souls, but only as the hollow men, the stuffed men, they stuffed themselves, we stuffed ourselves, why are they hollow and we are not? Hollow men? Holed up men?, what do I know what kind we are. Kind we are not. And we also have to take along Messrs. P. and O., thus killing two birds with one bloody stone, because these are the really hollow men, everything fits into them. Or are those others the hollow men, because they're nearly starved to death? Hollow versus hollow. Their path led to a potter's field. If the Russians can't behave themselves, we'll deduct all the people they might need from their paychecks in advance so they won't kill them afterwards for nothing. The stuffed men. The mended ones. There, their tree is swinging over there, but they aren't hanging from it. Their money rests safe and sound in another sort of nursery, where its worried mother won't have to pick it up every day. You can just get it when you need it and when you have the time. Money doesn't stink, money doesn't scream, money doesn't yell. Business hours can be ignored. The bank belongs to us, the times don't get away from us, we have nothing to worry about. Our bank is our castle, armed and secure, no, not like this one lighting up the sky with blood-red flames, as the countess and the accomplices to her wild rites and rides are on their way out as well.

But first let's get a good fire going to turn up the heat for the Russians' arrival. The poor locals will keep quiet about it, they always do. They are too busy saving themselves. That's how they are wasting their time, no wonder they stayed poor and always will stay poor, forever and ever. The rich don't have to save themselves, they are already safe from every possible danger; they take refuge in their own blood supply banks, which are left unscathed in times of crises together with all their bloody money, so the owners won't be left high and dry, and something could still happen to them. How they jump about in the water, their gills wide open with greed!, they miss their capital, their cash and assets, their real estate, their natural habitat, they can't wait to reclaim it all again! They'll get it back soon, a little patience, please; we process one claim after the other. Their souls are waiting, albeit impatiently, no, not the banks', they have no soul, of course, they only have a board, but no control, they are out of control, but they always bounce back all on their own, luckily they belong to someone who has the patience to wait, who is humane and Hungarian, and Dutch or Swedish for a while, which means he won't have to go Siberia, while in the meantime Siberia has gone to great lengths to come to us. As if they didn't have enough snow there too. Well, this chairman of the board goes the opposite way, good thinking, he must go there anyway, he must get to Siberia, while most are getting out of there, I mean most Siberians, but there are many more who are sent in the opposite direction. So the chairman stays for a few years in Siberia, where it freezes your peepeeria, he goes wherever they send him. No, the money stays here of course. And the souls of the dead? And the dead souls of the living? Who'll deport them on the school of life bus?, well, what about them? They are hanging from their mouths like dirty rags, while they let their chauffeur clean out their spark plugs. So, now they noticed our tongues, so they tear out those rags as well. We are not here to listen to some biblical bull, we are here to get out of here. Therefore this story can't be true, says the historian, who did a colonoscopy on history, at least that's what he planned to do, he looked into history from the other end as it were, but it stayed dark in Munich, in Münster, in Germany, no, in Austria, in Burgenland, way down East, that's the way, makes no difference anyway, he would have seen only darkness from any direction. He wouldn't see a thing, even if it were shown to him in a picture, because he is used to finding out everything from pictures. Would he finally see nothingness there, having seen the end already? No. His story, history, hasn't even happened yet! At least it hasn't come to an end, if it ever started. Come back tomorrow. Then you might hear: This is the way the world ends This is the way the world ends This is the way the world ends. Not with a bang but a whimper. And if you missed the beginning, it's okay, the beginning is a poem, but that's okay, just for you his story starts any time, history starts anew every moment, but this time it rages in other people and—due to a shortage of people it could make short thrift of—, also in other cities. In every proper history the wealthy, the stuffed man, the stuffed-up man has his representative, who handles all his stuff and takes care of his shit, I mean he has to take care of all the shit in place of his master. History only tunes its instruments, but it rarely gets to play. Life is very long. But today is one of those days history is playing with us as if life would never end. We are its instruments. We are in tune. We bring history in tune with us. Our testimonies must hit the right tone and we should all sing to the same tune. No, we never get it right and no one listens to us anyway. So the story should be looked at in peace and quiet once it's over; but while it is happening, it should be also left in peace; better not look at it, its Gorgon's gaze might turn us into stone. Or better yet, history should be dragged into a heated room to let it thaw, cheered on by all. We should all thaw, finally, it won't hurt, it's warm and comfy there. And it's nice to see people finally show up and warm up to us again. We missed them. But as soon as they got here, they messed up our lives again. Here history, for once, has the chance never to happen again, the chance that is, history will or maybe not, have the chance to be listened to in peace and quiet. It is giving a lecture, who else would know better. Between the conception and the creation between the emotion and the response falls the shadow. It isn't necessary to see it talking, because whatever can be seen is real and therefore could be lost. Soon the fire will shine bright and red, it will shine on our bed and then the bed will also be gone and so will we. The red-hot revelers want to get just one last high, they kick up their legs for the big leap and then run, baby, run! Fifteen persons leave the castle after the weapons have been distributed and arrangements made for the dead. No, the dead can only be properly arranged afterwards. It must not be that courage, the best slayer, an instant slayer of outrage, would suddenly show itself with such raw and even jubilant brutality. After all, they already had plenty opportunities to do so at least a thousand years ago.

Who would have thought they'd drag in those dregs at the very last moment!, not a stitch of clothing on their bodies, so many dropped stitches, all in the ditches, and they didn't even have to clean up the mess, no, not in the ditches, they had already been stripped before, stripped of their Hungarian citizenship and then they stripped themselves, they were specifically told to "please take off your clothes!"; "Bitte legen Sie ab," "Take it all off" was the softly forceful order; that was all that was needed; it was all they needed; they could not fight them anyway and their bodies wanted to take off for a long time; they refused to stay at home with them. Couldn't take it anymore. Just dropped to the ground! There was no need for an extra push, they could have saved themselves all the trouble with the guns—, shooting down those last helpless creatures just for the heck of it, instead of saving their own skin first, which is worth much more in death's twilight kingdom, and time is also very valuable, so it's high time to cash in on time before there is a crash. Get rid of foul deeds! Quick, quick, get out of the bull market! Bolt! No, we still must settle a couple of things before we set this castle on fire and send the sun on vacation—we don't need it just now, we've been doing for a long time what the sun can do: more shine than substance, so much so that one cannot see the substance for the shine; so, while others laid in the deep sleep of exhaustion, their bones all picked and resting in peace, we have to settle a few more things. The party is over, the fire bursts from the hollow barrel, the Gods are cheering that the right guys won for once, but one can't hear them, one only hears the people how they cheer no more, and haven't for a long, long time. They collapse silently, like houses of cards. They don't have much weight anymore and never had. Who needs them? They are bound for eternity, but before they get there, they have to be put to good use. Lust for power?, yes, we got plenty, in good condition, in stock. But who could call it addiction, when those high on top want to get down for power. There really is nothing sick about that. They better get it all done now, the powerful, tomorrow it's probably all gone, their power. They'll have to get used to being lonely up there without friends to invite and wine to flow and red-hot barrels shooting into thin air until the mountain comes to the valley and the storms in the highlands down to the beckoning Glenns, where they read *Der Stürmer* for news on the Fox hunt to prepare for it. In this upcoming, unbecoming situation one can only count on oneself and you better know how to count without the count. We also suffered. We got our share. We are the shareholders of the Raging Reich, the emptied empire! We lost everything, in the end the Reich itself. We had to write off Division *The Reich*, but didn't know on and to whose account. That something like that had to happen! It was the first time it happened and it certainly won't happen again. We swear. We foreswear. We lost everything, except for what we still have, fortunately. Only smart people deserve such a fortune. Or can you think of anything better than holding on to what hasn't even been lost? Losing more than everything is not possible. So all one can do is hold on to it. One has a choice. It's their own fault, those dumb dead—why didn't they have a voice to give orders or the strength to obey? Oh well, we would have killed them anyway, no matter how much life was left in them, all of it had to go; the last blush blown from every cheek, sleep must be scared away, even before it comes and if it comes, then the right way: forever. Not so different from falling asleep every day. We don't mind sleeping every day, so why not die when sleeping is so pleasant?, well, thanks a lot. They were so weak we could have blown them out like a candle. Why even bother to cock a gun? No problem, the hunters and their cocks do it for their mistress, the countess, but even more so for their own kicks, they'll do anything for any master, especially if it's themselves. Those lords and masters must be carefully studied. You just have to tell them who's the master of the moment and they'll be happy to do it, our masters' game wardens; they'll cock any gun before the cock's third crow, and then they'll deny everything, they'll even deny they were also masters, masters at their game and everyone else's game, they'll deny having ever been or had or known personally or seen from afar a master, you are welcome, don't mention it. *Nieder zur Erde*. Down to the ground with those shivering limbs, hurry up! *The* Russian is coming, the great, but not the only son of Stalin who has millions of them, and they will level the castle down to the ground and then they will burn it or they'll do it all at once.

What did you do with your *Fang*, your kill? Did you sink your fang into the flesh? Did it get stuck there, your tooth? The tooth of crime? Did the Hungarian crown, I mean the dental-crown hold up, was there no metal inside to cause an allergic reaction, a cause for legal action? The Hungarians have specialized in this kind of dental procedure at bargain prices, and why not, the borders are finally gone, it's only to our advantage, history has also been changed several times, the third time we adjusted the angle somewhat, so the front teeth don't stick out so unbecomingly. Since your second change of history—and that's been quite a while now, you can no longer tell the difference to your own, very individual tooth with its individual history of face-changing procedures! We offer a package deal that includes hotel and spa, no, not the one for spastics, the one for the healthy, of course, with sauna and Jacuzzi. On request, the Hungarians will make you a new face or straighten out the old one, naturally it'll cost you more not to look so natural anymore, but it's worth it. For now! I hope you will see the difference to your own face, your own nature! Let's see if they still want the old gold crowns or if they let us charge it on plastic, yes, they let us charge, any time, let's see whether someone else will have to take charge of our return trip! Oh no, we got used to the guy in charge now. For an additional charge, they offer: breast implants, historical implants, dental implants and human plants, which deliver spare parts. They have to come from somewhere, don't they? We guarantee that those plantations are continuously reforested and replenished, yes, just like your upper jaw, which was carved out of your hipbone, if it wasn't grown artificially from a few cells. They'll rebuild your jaw completely. Or did you make another kill? Did you do it with your own teeth? Or was it you who shot this man who saw everything and would have talked too? And the dog, did you shoot him too? Well now, that really wasn't necessary, a dog can't talk, right, no?, that's right. So, that witness is taken care of. Is there another one? Another candidate for your game? Yes, that one there, in the car, the only one who survived. Now you can shoot him at your leisure, now you have all the time in the world. Back then you didn't take the time, it was a mad hunt, a great rush, but one guy got away and now we pop him in his car, so he won't talk anymore. We pop them all, some sooner, some later and now we got them all. Now there are only tooth- and face-shopping and saving tourists. Lots of them. No wonder, since our teeth got stuck in the flesh of foreigners and we need replacements. No wonder this one didn't last, the dental cement was already loose, I can't think of another explanation. But it's your own fault too. Why did you have to bite with so much force? Didn't we explain to you that you have to go easy for a while, until the bone is bone dry and no longer to distinguish from the rest of your body? But you left a clear imprint and you better get out while you can. No wonder you already need new teeth again! No wonder you have to get rid of the last witness of your killer bite to make room for more to kill, we make sure the bite is right and we do it for much less money than those stupid Austrians. But this can't go on forever, sooner or later everything will be ruined by your toxic spit and then your jaws won't hold up at all anymore, not one of them, not even the movie, that super-killer, then it's only ground meat with mashed fries and not even that, because the ground is full. The grounds are filled with them if they haven't been dug up again and buried some other place. Everything is possible. The former *Gauleiter*, the governor of Styria and Strudelgau still knows all the construction foremen, he even knew the Führer himself, but no one lasts for long with him. No one lasts long around that man. He drove away whole herds of people, but new ones kept coming all the time. A phenom, that man. One would think this land would be empty at some point. But no, no emptiness anywhere. It won't be empty, because now they are buried in another place. No emptiness for Herr Gauleiter and Mr. Governor, and Commander of the legion of horror and Knight of the Burning Pestle, all in one person, all one person, they can't take it, they can take everything only all at once, a phenom that man, who came as if he were more than one, as if he were many, I am telling you, he can't stand it in his *Gau*, his state, his grounds anymore, he won't stand his ground much longer, his ground zero, though his state was Styria, strictly speaking, it was hysteria, so what, who cares, he also lorded it over Burgenland, our land of castles, though strictly speaking he wasn't our Lord, and now, in his fancy burial ground he can't grind his teeth anymore, although he took such good care of them. Or not. Will he also have to go to Hungary? It would stand to reason, somehow. He has lost his bite. His skill or his kill didn't last. Or was it taken some other place—by the bulldozers of the Mengele and Co. perhaps? Did they dig somewhere else? Did they bury something some other place? I can see that, easily; It's a good guess; technically, it's possible, no doubt; with good construction machinery, it's a cinch. We got plenty of gravel pits, and the *Herr* Governor is a friend of construction as well as restrictions, for farmers, among others, whose friend he is not. Construction companies are his big buddies. It's just that he misses his kill, our Mr. Ex-Governor, his bite is what's missing. He can dig up everything, he can dig in everything, but not with his teeth, he misses them badly, how could he not? Even though we use only the best ceramic and the best gold in Austria, from the Ögussa company, whose name used to be Degussa, which delivered gas for humans, or am I mixing things up here?, yes, I must be, I am always mixing up everything, and not always with something else. I get put in my place. I was out of place. I was misplaced. I am displaced. But you are never sure with the Hungarians, whatever they use, they mix up the hard currencies, which they put in our mouths; it often won't stick, whatever they stuff in there. Not even if they use a hammer to get it in. Every male knows the problem, he can put himself in that position, he can even put it in himself, women also know this huge problem they often had to put up with and put out, and we, and by that I mean all humans, are supposed to put things back in their place, while not even a tooth can stay in place anymore! We are to wipe up the mess there, before the victors get to wipe us all out; those victors, who turned losers a while ago, though they still keep their hold on us, but: they could not hold up our trains. They clearly were too late for that. What's your problem, it's the most efficient way of heating! Gas, of course! Why do you think we built all those pipelines, partly through former enemy territory, partly through future enemy territory, all in an effort to clear the air for good?, it's all good, those ovens simply can't be improved upon, and they can't hold any more either, simple as that, they throw it in as a tablet at the top, the gas, and it comes out pure below, couldn't be easier, no, that's all you can run through the pipelines, the pipeline pigs run on their own, they run through several countries we recently befriended or at least want to befriend, because it's cheaper there; besides, we also offer a guarantee—*we are from*

Austria!—for your crown. The Hungarians can't compete
with that! Okay, I admit, they are cheaper, but there is nothing else I'll admit, or remit, at least not too much, no, not
the least bit, and that's it. Hungarians don't guarantee anything, that's how they are, every now and then they will
guarantee citizenship to a German war profiteer, what's there
to profit, they didn't win the war, as you know very well; I
feel for you, but first not wanting to be a winner and then
not wanting to be a loser, as some do, is not how they play
it. Although it wouldn't be a bad idea! Only skiing is better,
and winning in skiing is the best, therefore it's best to live in
Switzerland or Austria and win in Adelboden or Grindel-
wald or Arlberg if you like skiing, but it's pleasant there anytime, even in the summer. Yes, also in the summer. Anytime,
really. Don't worry if you don't find your way around here
anymore, you'll learn quickly, ashes are ashes, ruins are
ruins, dirt is dirt, there are others who know the ways here
and an aristocratic predicate comes with your predicated
wine for no extra charge, but that's only a tiny predicate for
this magnate, whose art collection is a magnet for the hungry masses, no, I am sorry, I am totally wrong, I meant the
art collection is a magnet for the well-fed masses, because
art doesn't like to be collected, it wants to be diverted, like
us, it wants to get out and divert others as well, and it's a lot
of trouble to catch it again, for the masses, whose eyes are
not here. The eyes are not here, they wander, but they don't
look at the works of art, no, there are no eyes here, we deny
everything, the eyes didn't keep up with all the beauty they
saw, the eyes couldn't keep in anything, because they were
drunk, because they were drinking, drink, O eyes, as much
as your lashes hold, no one can keep up with that, no, we
don't have eyes here at all. If you question us, we'll deny
everything before you finished your question. Art is for the

masses, but it can't be explained to them. Art is basically inexplicable. Only two or three people get it. It's a phenomenon; it is sightless, senseless, useless. The eyes come by every now and then, but in vain, because art has refused to collect itself, sightless, unless the eyes reappear as the perpetual star multifoliate rose of death's twilight kingdom the hope only of empty men. The empty men. Yes, the empty men have been buried somewhere, okay, but there really was no need for it. What's empty is empty and does not have to be buried. What's hollow is hollow and cannot be art. It doesn't take an artist to be hollow. And it doesn't take much to be empty.

Now, they do allow you to become a citizen through marriage, death or transfiguration, but otherwise they don't guarantee anything, you can yell and scream all you want, but you won't get it, even though Hungary has become a rapidly expanding fat land, land of the fat and the free, fat land and flat land all in one, of plains and plans and inexpensive management of pain by experts who are free to settle in the plains and will settle for plain deals among free, wheeling-and-dealing plain folks with plenty of plain old healthy selfishness, in a land of plenty under the flat but full moon with plenty of moonshine. Why should it be any different there from here, where there is either darkness or light, where it's either a lite or a dark. Why should it be better there? It isn't better anywhere. Only here it's never good. Go someplace else! It's not good here and it will never be good again. That's what I say!

If it weren't differently different here with us than different elsewhere, huh, different than if we were different elsewhere, somewhere else, where we would be someone else, huh, why then did this man, a real German become Hungarian of all things, go figure, what figures did he play with to figure out how this will pay off for him, how he can get away with it? One can be Hungarian or Dutch or Belgian or whatever, but better not in Hungary or the Netherlands or Belgium, at least not when the time isn't ripe yet, because once the time is ripe, those countries will spit us out, those countries will no longer like the taste of us, but they'll still have to swallow us. We are hard to take, but easy to get and we take what we can. This is well documented, I brought all the files. History just handed me another pile. History doesn't do us much honor, we'd do better as Hungarians or Dutch, and that is what we now are. It was later than we thought, later than we intended it to happen. We are in South Africa now. We are in Argentina. It makes no difference, for wherever the German, *DER Deutsche*, gets to, you should be anywhere but where *Der Deutsche*, THE German is, and that means every German, for that is who we are, or at least have been, even though we are not now, not anymore, and of course we should not be in Germany either, not in Germany of all places, first to go, last to get there. The whispers, not the bang. But if Germany just whispers, there are big bangs everywhere. But if two Germanies collapse into one another with a soft whisper, a whimper of millions of voices, it's without a bang, it's just this whisper, and afterwards, no one dares even to whisper. Let alone speak out loud. No, that's wrong. I can hear the Germans talk loudly everywhere; they out-scream one another on top of their lungs. Then they notice other people just a short distance away and they shout them down like razor heads cutting through grass. Not one blade will ever bounce back there. No one will. That's not talked about. Why are the Germans coming here if they like it so much at home back home? Why do they come here and voice their opinions about everything, especially about facts and circumstances which are not so simple, why can't they just whisper? Germans are the busiest travelers and talkers I know, and they do it just so that afterwards they can come back to Germany again. *Jawohl.* They live to talk and love to travel. They are dying to travel. But when they are coming we better be elsewhere. Otherwise they come up with a war again. They've already been here with everything else. Once the Germans are here, we should be where that *Here* is not, but this applies only to times of danger, thus it is willed by the German mind, a heavy mind. When you see it, don't lift it, it will break your back, and if you drop it, the rest of him will break too! And if the rest is also kaput, then its ruins are scattered all over the world and it will be a lot of work to clean them all up, he is a piece of work, our hardworking German, he comes in many small pieces, every piece a heavily armored think tank, though prone to sink from time to time; but the work gets done; anyway, I am talking nonsense, thank you, as always, for the much appreciated applause, at least by one!, so then this German, recreated by all his travels, then wrecked and reconstructed again, in record time, for the umpteenth time, well then, there he is, sunglasses, swimming trunks and bikini, lying around everywhere, wherever it's nicer than back home, clad in tiny bits of cloth, he is the pits, I mean, the last bit of humankind, this German, because a bit of humanity is left in him. We couldn't take that away from him. The German *Sturmbann*speaker, the storming S-S-Super-man-of-his-word, The Man, *Mann* for short because everything German is manning the storm and never questions itself, ever. Kindness to other people makes him tremble. Fear of what could happen also makes him tremble. He has learned that much in the meantime, in these mean times. That he is to be feared. All that can happen because of him and what it takes to make him happy. He has learned his lesson. Therefore don't worry, be happy, in Germany, in peace and quiet, not in the storm, all is calm, because even with the German there, he finally got his peace, his piece of cake, which he now also eats, but he also gives some peace, so there is no danger at all. Then they all sit on their high horse and they are easy to find, all way on top, and from up there they see things smaller than how they are seen from down below. An unpleasant situation for the rest of us, whom they didn't finish, but not for them. We are the ones down on the ground, not they. Even if Germany is down on the ground, it still stands tall, and that's stupid, of course, because it's an easy target that way. All Germans are a target and they stay on target. Their voice, their mastermind's voice, always speaks their mind before THE German, *der Deutsche*, who equates his power with violence and stirs in some morality before he pushes millions into the oven, ever starts thinking.

A SPECIAL MESSENGER

Halt halt halt! Now that we finally gained a cognitive distance to these times of extremes, you shouldn't just wager that distance in the casino of thinking! Now that you finally learned how to think and act for yourself. So hold on to your marbles. Don't lose them now. At least stop betting on just one color and don't bet the whole distance or your view on what was. Better be happy you finally won! Hold on to it now, your view! But what am I talking about? Much as I try, I can't be completely unbiased, it's already hard enough to remember everything I have to report. A totally self-absorbed woman hammered it into me. How lucky you find her so unappealing! I didn't remember everything anyway. Anywho, if no one is in charge, and it's everyone for himself, we have chaos, and no messenger can be expected to deal with that. My main concern here is not ideology, as you constantly accuse me and the woman, who again prompted me my lines, but people and how they conduct themselves, because most people's actions are contradictory and their views change over the years due to circumstances. Well then, let people change their views, I don't care, but as a reporter my view has been set, even if somewhat late, because I can't report something before it happens, right, so then, I already calibrated this view for you, as it was willed by a woman, which, luckily, doesn't count, and you can take it, my view, just the way I hand it to you, fine with me, you can also have my character, because my character is more durable than my opinion, which I cannot insert in my report anyway as was laid out to me by that lady, who knows the lay of this land, or is it lie?, anyway, who plays it as it lays. You keep insinuating that I shoot off my mouth mostly stuff I memorized as you accuse this lady of shooting off nothing but memorized bullets. And what's the upshot of this? She asked me to return her guns! So what am I supposed to do without those great equalizers which balanced my views, because originally I had to borrow a few and had to give them back even before I had a good view of my own origins. The countess and a few others, who don't count anymore, gave me these bullets and who benefits from them now? You do, armed with my bullets, which I had to borrow myself! I never had any protection, not even for my limpest limb. You insinuate I hate Germans? Seriously? Hating Germans? But now I can finally say to you, regardless of what I said before: I am proud to be German. Wir Deutschen unter unseren Duschen. We Germans, in our germ-free showers, the real showers, of course, should once again dare to show our nationalist spirit, which would send everyone else to the showers, although we (Austrians) are not really Germans, I am saying this here and now, because this kind of courage will have been lost for a while and *die Opfer*, the—victims, the dead, and their survivors, yes, they too, the victims, I say, well then, *die Opfer*, the victims more than anyone else will work with all sorts of foul tricks to get what they want. Victims always want something, even if they are no longer and haven't been for a long time and have never wanted to be victims, the victims—*Die Opfer*. However, we know that especially in extreme situations certain people can play a big role, and each and every one and his role is important, it counts, and here they are, playing grand opera, no, *Opfer*, they play enormous roles, they play those big parts until they get too big for them and they just drop them. Until they are sick of their power over others. Until they are sick of their shtick. And then they get back to doing what everyone else is doing. And that is what they are doing now, before the future will have begun. The Germans aren't driven by fear of themselves and that is their greatness. They have an inner compass they always follow, even at great risk. They always followed their inner compass needle. Who am I to judge them, I can't change the position of the north. They approach the others, the Germans do, but they don't torture them anymore. They learned from history, they were happy to learn, because they wanted to be happy, who doesn't? Everything I will have said about torture will be correct but no longer topical. Had we known, what we know today! We wouldn't have believed it. We had to learn the hard way. We wouldn't have believed we would be asked the typical questions of those who came after. But we are preparing for our turn to do something about the arrogance of posterity. We are turning now, this is the *Wende*, the turning point, now we are turning to you and then we will address you, though without any redress; you can't expect redress from us too, oh yes, we are turning, but without returns for you. You ask for returns as soon as we turn our backs for a moment, I can't believe it! How can you prevent what has already been done? So you want redress from us! You expect us to say this is how it was, but if what was were to be today, we could say about ourselves that we certainly would have hidden persecuted individuals or other criminals. And this is exactly what we are doing. We definitely would do it. We will have known how parents and grandparents should have acted, and today we finally are able to judge for ourselves, and at long last, as messengers we no longer have to parrot what we are told, what we are told to do and say. We don't have to hide anymore. I am not about to spare you the effort of thinking for yourself! As long as I as a messenger don't have to think for myself. Now you are taking care of it. All right. Where were we? We are not entitled to take on the roles of judges, neither are you. We always were—just a minute, let me just put away my heavy historical luggage some place where it's not in the way, would you have a little room for it, just a small one would be fine? Thanks, just a moment, thanks, wait, just a moment, don't push me, don't pull me, I have to first put away my luggage, can't you see that! I know you are mesmerized by stories of those horrible times, you are not interested in anything else, I can see that, and by staring at the horrible crimes this country committed, you once again make Germany the navel of the universe! Don't you understand? As a messenger, I don't care, it just makes me more important, but it's not good to make Germany a navel again, you better make it an ass, then you can sit on it, I am sorry, okay, navel, but navel in a negative sense. That's no good. Ass would be better, and also more practical. When do we messengers have a chance to sit down in peace and quiet?, so I can sympathize with Germany. But navel is not so good. Oh well, why not, everyone has a navel, and quite a few take themselves for the navel of the universe, with everything circling around them, all waltzing, what nonsense, but why should I care. However, to avoid this kind of fixation on the past, in the future you might want to go someplace else, if you're still alive, South Africa perhaps, Argentina, yes, Argentina is best, that's the easiest to get to, no matter where you stand on Germany, no matter who stands by Germany at the moment, and then continue your reports! You always can go to Argentina. Once there, wait and see and then report. Yes, I know, I should first put my own house in order, but there's always such a mess at the door, all those messages in the mail, mostly advertisements, although I strictly prohibited the delivery of such junk. So, while I am still busy throwing all that stuff into the trash can, I can hear a voice from above, it probably doesn't belong to a licensed messenger, and the voice calls out: You should never act the lawmaker for others either! No, you shouldn't. The voice is right. A man's voice and a woman's voice. They both are right. I know someone else, who does it all the time, he makes laws as he is talking, every word a law, but now he regrets it very much. He has been regretting for decades that everything he says becomes law. He regretted a lot, also being a woman, he regrets that too, it's very embarrassing for him, but he regrets most that for the longest time he has made himself the law for what others should think. He has no right to do that. Since he is a woman, he has no right to anything anyway, but most of all he does not have the right to make the law. Germany is teeming with such moral fanatics and moral watchdogs, it is teeming like an anthill, slips of paper are found and thrown out again, I too have already thrown out tons of paper around here, I don't even look at them anymore, I can tell it's advertisement stuff, you can't throw it out fast enough, you can't throw out human stuff fast enough either, there is always more on the way. We just add our own scraps of information about all that, garbage doesn't care, it can't feel a thing, it has no feelings, not enough for us at least, whose feelings are still valuable; once it's in the garbage you can't tell if the mail was free or a stamp had been glued to it, under great pain, glued together what had been broken, oh, excuse me, I slipped into the wrong line, yes, I know, you excuse nothing. More paper still. And even you, many of you, don't want to acknowledge it: there are already signs of fatigue. After the thirtieth prospectus, which I throw out because the future turned out different than described, I take a break. If, in a few decades, you will ask a high-school graduate about his biggest pain, he will tell you it was this time, the time he didn't even live through and only knows from messenger reports. Those terrible years the messenger describes, if he ever gets to it—with all that paper piling up he can no longer see our door and the slit, through which he should slip his little message. Then the messenger would have to admit that those few years have assumed a position that is disproportionate to the over-all distribution of his messages. Now, if one takes this posi-tion to be somewhat elevated, because it's there to see on three hundred tons of paper scrap, papal crap?, all for pulp, holy shit,! no, scrap, scrap for pulp, an alp of pulp, not yet disposed of, then one knows for sure, what everyone else would have done, and what one's own actions would have been, namely: the exception. Every man for himself. This is not resistance, it is exempted from resistance, and this is surely what you would have done at that time. That is, had you done anything at all, it would have been the exception. There are so many shades of gray when it comes to moral issues, as we all know. But in those brochures, everything is colorful, so that one can't even tell the executioner from the victim. But there is no need to tell, it's all just a matter of placement, which can be changed any time, just take your ballpoint or felt pen and change it! You don't have to accept my calibration either, it makes no difference, no difference at all nowadays, everyone knows who the executioners were and who the victims; but those brochures also show the grayish tones in special colors and those must go right away. They have an appointment. At a place for the healthy men, the wholesome men, where they have an appointment they must observe, those grayish tones; they have to go; no, they don't have to observe anything; there is nothing to see, because there is no more difference between true and false, there is only an in-between; no more grayish tones; no more upper tones; the Reich, uhm, the rich are already gone, so are the poor; I forgot, what else is gone, and whatever remained must go now too. That's it.

The voice you are hearing now is the voice of a blower fan, no, it's a real fan, a real fanatic no one warned us about, whose overblown voice and vision fill the elevators and restaurants and malls, yes, they come from everywhere through the air, there is no getting away from this voice, and its hour, the voice of the hour, uhm, the hour of the voice is always. And it always just arrived, perhaps to talk about good and evil, to make it a topic for the new generations, who are already busily roaming about, bringing love of neighbor to their neighbors, untiringly, like branches from the burning bush, no need to beat around the bush with them, they don't have any use for it at home: the love of neighbor behind the chain link fence, well, what did I want to say, what message can I relay to you from the Germans, the main criminals of old? But in our new times we have different, better criminals. The Germans want you to know they won't be able to come today, because right now they are way on top, and they don't want to come down again too soon. They first want to savor the view down to the valley, where all the others are. Only afterwards will they be ready to get down from their old self-importance, for they all purport to know what's good and bad for mankind, and therefore it is always their hour, the Germans' hour, the Germans' programs are running all the time, they are carried everywhere, the Germans are on and in the air all the time, while Austrians are always up in the air, Germans will be happy to reclaim them, it just takes a while to reclaim anything from Austria, be sure to include a self-addressed envelope; destination is destiny, the messenger is the messiah, who gladly accepts his mission as his final destiny until he is more finessed in finishing his mission than the one who sent him flying and of course also more finessed than the ones who were fit for the pits; okay, now let's fit all the pieces together, until they can't be seen anymore, until they are no longer perceived as especially chosen, let's get the surface nice and smooth, without showing how it got that way, and how we made the news, not necessarily willingly, on account of the work of so many, far too many, which are not really fit for print. You don't want to know now about the workings of destiny—when did you ever want to know anything?, before or after, it's best to know nothing, with all the important stuff, which you don't want to know, buried right in it. They are buried all right, they are right here among us, but we don't know it, right, no?, that's right!, no, it's not true,

NO!, that's the truth; true or not true, it makes no difference, what's the point, when it comes to smoothing things out, the Austrian in the meantime has become smoother than the German, who remembers everything and keeps reeling it off and spelling it out for the world to come under his spell again. Germans notice everything and they make mental notes of everything, all the beautiful vacation spots in foreign countries for example, which were so beautiful, they would love to set up camp there forever. But Germans remember nothing forever, only that they would love to vacation forever. But then they also notice faster than others everything that's wrong in those countries, anything that is distributed unfairly. They want to redistribute everything. They want to dispute everything. Whereas *Aussis*, no, *Ösis* for *Österreicher*, Austrians, forget everything. But they don't forget that on principle they are against forgetting anything. That is division of labor. *Wer vergißt glücklich ist . . .* or: forget and you'll be happy, just remember that you did forget something. If you forget without remembering, everything will just stay the same. Today, they asked me to tell you, but unfortunately I forgot who forgot what: you will, of course, get some kind of warranty for the hot springs, valid beyond the next hour, yes, when it comes to business, the German grows way above and beyond himself, he reaches out, grabs onto things, gasps for air and takes it wherever he can get it, our world export champion. In this last of meeting places, we grope together and avoid speech, no, Germans would never do that, they talk and take action, they can do both at once, and more often than not, they can speak English. Incidentally, they won't be export world champions for much longer, those Germans, we will soon catch up with them, no, this time we won't follow them, we Austrians, we stay here, winning as we are, we don't have to become

Germans anymore to be winners, who take all, we are winning already and always were, firstly because of our language, which was created for us to speak English in other
places; but now it is China's turn, now China is coming, the
Middle Kingdom, it comes after our kingdom of mediocrity;
China doesn't talk, but it takes all the more actions and it
undertakes all kinds of transactions. Now it is pushing trade.
I am sure you want to know more about the so-called
Europa Warranty, which we added to your package, so you
won't be scared: it guarantees that Europe's hot springs function free of harmful germs of foreigners, but only if no foreigners are let in, we'll also guarantee the spa, although I
hear that the heat is supposed to be quite good for the ger-
mination of germs in the warm, moist zones of Regina Coli,
or is it *Coeli*?, it seems to be working well for our heavenly
queens and also the kings, they spread beyond control, for
theirs is the kingdom, let them for all I care, we are up shit
creek anyway, why not let them germinate if we want to
propagate another master race?, in principle, everyone can
become a master and castigate his slaves and, in principle,
anyone can also become one of them: slaves, until they drop.
But that's shooting ourselves in the foot! Shoot! We can't
come to an agreement, we can only agree on who is master
and who is slave, but it's never too soon to kill those germs
right in the bud. Then why did we buy them in the first
place, why did we bring them here? We didn't! All right?!
Now you know. We lost the warranty; we have no proof
where we got them, no proof we bought those slaves. They
covered their tracks. That's logical. The victims were thrown
into zigzag ditches or they fell in, some were still alive for
sure, because killing is a lot of work, you can't imagine how
much work that is, so we throw the victims, dead or alive,
into the ditches, on top of one another, a mass of men, quite

a mess; the question is: how to shove the biggest number of people into the smallest possible space; tourism is not alone in asking this question. The fact is that these zigzagging ditches can be cleared of all remains at any time, though preferably during the night; but heavy construction machinery makes it an easy job. Those graves will never be found, because we turned gravel pits into graves, every healthy construction company knows the *Kiesgrube*, the pit filled with crushed rock, every contractor personally owns or personally knows one, where else would they get this crucial building material of the future? Rocks and pebbles. The bedrock of all construction. The peanuts and the dough. Every healthy economy must make as much of it as possible and then of course it must be spent again. Small change and dead presidents. *Handel und Wandel*; Trade and Transformation. It's possible they are in there, but I don't know for sure. I can't guarantee it. Well, okay, there is a warranty for the products of the Degussa company, where did I put it now?, no, not the bank, I mean the Degesch company, short for Die Deutsche Gesellschaft für Schädlingsbekämpfung, the chemical firm and pest-control company, we saw how effective they were, we tested them on millions, we wanted to be absolutely sure they couldn't leave alive, but otherwise there's no guarantee for anything. No guarantee for a product that isn't ours, that isn't German, a product from *Deutsch Österreich*, from German Austria, but from other nations, like Hungary or another one of those *Rumpfländer*, those leftover parts from the former imperial body; those countries didn't even exist before, or, as the name *Rumpfland* implies, something incomplete or in the form of laborers and maids, it's time to give these people their own forum!, they were totally dependent on us, those countries, if it wasn't one thing, it was another: export quotas, then immigrant quotas, both for one single purpose: to revoke or grant people citizenship to make sure they won't be the same people they were when they were born and they'll be different than they have been once they were born. Now I ask you: What German would voluntarily become Hungarian? People don't go there, they are either taken out of Hungary or they leave voluntarily. They have every reason for it. But they are also taken out for no reason, some of them anyway, lots of them, taken to the train station, they are processed under close control, when they are finished, they are finished, they've had it, so they end up in the pits. Only someone all the more proud to be German because of such patriots' acts would visit Hungary in such a precarious situation. Much better to bring Hungarians here, then we don't have to go there. Anyone who could stay there anyway moves to another country, or he might as well stay, it would make no sense for him to leave. He would become an illegal. He would become ill; he would be worked to death and thrown into a pit and that would be it. A German abroad: that's best of all. That way he gets away from himself and to another place, who would he want to be? Who wants to be German? His money stays in Germany, it can call the shots by itself, so it's quite convenient that it's already in a beautiful bank and won't have to shoot for a safer haven. All of it belonged to us once, yes, *alles*, and now it does again, all of it, *alles*, *über*, no, over and over again, and Austria too, it was and always will be German and now we know why, yes, the teeth too, they once belonged to us too. When we were younger and still had them. Back then everything was centrally regulated. A central office is an absolute must as one finds oneself playing briefly in a different league in a land not meant for us. Suddenly you are a Hungarian and you don't know why. You have nothing to do with Germany, you might have something to do in Germany, war always needs something, it always loses something, now a gym bag, then a toothbrush, a tennis racket, ski poles, then life, something is always missing, people miss deadlines, thus they put themselves on the line, they will soon be missing themselves. We are missing some. We'll find them! We'll find them all. The headquarters are in Berlin, another one in Düsseldorf, the head will soon be in Siberia, on the next train, but it'll take a while till he gets there. The owner of it all, or at least half of it, is in Switzerland and will stay there for the time being, he wouldn't run away, as traveling was still dangerous at that time. We transfer good and evil to where we are not. That's how it's done, it's called outsourcing, I think; the good ones in your pot, the bad ones wherever, but I am just the messenger. I forget that sometimes. I think I have to throw up. Then falls the shadow and I remember where I am, on the ground I see what came out of my mouth.

Even I got myself central heating when I was half frozen to death, though unfortunately, the messenger is not where his heat is. He always has to run or ride his bike, but at least it keeps him warm. Now go, and do likewise! What, you don't have a car? They have cars even in Hungary, even during the war, if not too many. By the way, or rather: most importantly, you should have taken better care of this tooth, Madam Countess, you might need a new crown, and you might even have to walk a few streets to get it, the same way you acquired the count's crown through marriage. It was a very small count, but a count nonetheless. The Hungarians are and have always been cheaper, why pay more, when you can get a Hungarian crown, a crown is a crown and Hungarian crowns have always been cheaper and they still are!, but not much longer, and they don't just give them away either. They came as a gift to us once again, courtesy of the EU; we are delighted. But we aren't there yet; it's still pretty foggy. Petty biases, puny bonuses and phony penalties are still the order of the day, all waiting to be put to use. And we use them, even if they don't want us to.

I am charged to report the guns have been delivered to your chambers; they can be picked up any time. The chambers are charged. They will discharge. They will overcharge until the barrels glow red hot. I must thus inform you that they were ready to lend their willing hands, and their rosy cheeks—mentioned earlier by the charming black-booted colleague—did not change color, truth to tell, we did not see any blush, except on the countess, though countess only by marriage, which puts an end to being the one and one and only one and all alone, and all of this in Hungary, where one wouldn't want to live if it still existed, I mean, Hungary exists in multiple shapes and in many places, yes, also in Austria, but you don't want to be there, Switzerland is better. A Hungarian in Switzerland is best, though, as I said, we can put on a very small count's crown only, but it was cheap, it was reduced, it was not taken down all the way, it must never be taken down, but it was reduced, it's not the main line but a side line, which will be sidelined once we have the right— um—uhm—empire. Still, it is a big task, no idea what sort of task the people will be burdened with. We don't want to shell out too much though, we'd rather save the shells for the guns and pistols we'll be handing out, no, not the pistols, those we carry strapped to ourselves, we hand out only the guns, the long guns, no, we don't let them have them, we let them have it, and maybe the red on the countess's red hot cheeks was as artificial as her lipstick, those cheeks were aglow from an inner blaze, what else?, yes, I believe it was her, at least that's how she was addressed, as Countess. I couldn't positively identify her among all those tall, armed men in black. That's no joke. And yourself? Armed too? Good. Black, as everyone will tell you, makes people look bigger and more terrifying, like clean slates. Anything that could be written on it would seem smaller, I mean, the slate, the blackboard immediately seems smaller the moment something gets scribbled on it. Black, however, is indescribable, still, it gets described constantly, it seems to ask for it. Something's scratching the surface. All Germans here, everything German, all in elegant black, down to the boots, but luckily they are not in Germany, where the first slates are beginning to break and can be inscribed only in part, like shards of clay. The relicts of cave men. Holed up men. Of hollow men. No longer readable. No more time. The New Time is coming to an end, now what?, we used up the old one a bit prematurely, before we even got the new one, as soon it was announced. But it turned out differently. Only when the countess picked up a gun did I know for sure it was her. It is her right. It comes with her title. The weapon comes with her title and goes with her temper. And of course she wanted to shoot too. There is a hierarchy in shooting, the highest in rank shoots first, at the highest ranked game, which isn't man, not just any old stag, it is the royal stag; the big buck that must be stopped and shot right here. Men are small fry and after the first one is taken out, the others can take out the rest of them. There is plenty for everyone. Who is counting? Not the countess. I only realized much later, when I saw her again after many years, that she must have been a shy, reserved woman. Was that finally the banality of evil I had heard so much about, although much too late, otherwise I would have recognized that woman by her banality, wouldn't I? Actually, I wasn't around long enough to see how evil got to be banal. Lying down, flat on her back, pretending humble submission, yielding to the desires of groping hands, but despising wisdom in all her humility and servility and piety and complacency and complicity—that's all we need, but it's all we got. That's how it looks when the powerful make themselves small. And they always know when they have to make themselves small, without really being small, of course, or they wouldn't have to pretend. And if they disappeared altogether, as if they had died, that's okay too, that's what they wanted and they always only disappear as long as they want to. Unlike the dead, they emerge again, they emerge in the gap between the idea and the reality, between the motion and the act, yes, that's exactly where they emerge, that is where the shadow falls, which we may have. At least we may see a photo of it. Many of us believe it is they, the mighty, for theirs is the kingdom, life is very long, but for the most part, we can't see it. Humility can also be very wise! They disappear only to return again, the high and mighty. Their money disappears before they do. They saw to it that it could show up later when they needed it. Luckily it can be thawed any time, their frozen money. For the high and the mighty life is theirs, is their way, which is the world the way it ends, this way to the end, the way of the world ends not with a bang but with a you-know-what.

Luckily, we are not humble is what the messenger has been charged to pass on to you; I tell it how it is, I tell you what I was told, literally: we hate anyone who does not resist, those are the kind of people we have lined up. And we, the messengers, have this message for you: it is the humble ones we, the brave, love to order for take out. And we let them eat their hearts out. They are game, already delivered, ready to serve and they are served right away. And quickly taken out again. Naturally, they repulse us. We cannot touch a single bite, because they did not resist at all as we rounded them up. Those naked men just swallowed everything we threw at them: the venomous spit, the mean looks—that was their slave mentality, totally wrecked by work; my taste goes for different kinds of victims, but it never gets them, it only gets those who are already half dead and rotting, and this is exactly how we want them. All that was boiling over before is cooked now. Still, we wouldn't want to eat their flesh. Not even touch them! Beat them, why not, shoot them, sure, no problem, but touch them? Never! And it is quantity that counts; it makes up for the lack of human quality. Between my concept of quantity and the creation of quantity (do I mean The Creation here?), between the emotion and the response falls the shadow, which I mentioned earlier, but it is dark already. We step aside, so the shadow won't fall on us. And suddenly our smoking top guns with their bazookas set heaven and earth and all those people on fire, what a blast!,—a word that's often used for this kind of thing, I can't think of another one right now. As a messenger I should always have several words on-hand ready to use, but as I said before, the words have been forged and hammered and solidly soldered, they bonded quickly in the high heat, I can't pry them apart anymore; the heat was on us back then, everything had to go very quickly, quick, quick! Killing two or three people is peanuts, but two hundred! Hold on, I am told it was one hundred and eighty, nearly two hundred defenseless, I should say: perfectly defenseless men, just to point out one more time the perfection of it all, of both counts and accounts. Nothing, no one is left, they fall like bowling pins, those hollow men; no, not holy men, those are the hollow men, while we are the stuffed men, *die Ausgestopften, Stroh im Kopf*, straw in the head, *ach, diese hohlen Männer*, straw men?, *nein*, just their headpiece filled with straw. Unfortunately, the stupid computer didn't do a great job translating the poem, I could have done better, but, basically, the message comes across, it's like a messenger of the poem, what a mess though, the hole thing. Actually, those holed-up men look like real people, just hollow because they never ate, their dried voices hollow when they whisper together, they whisper, they don't holler; and as wind in dry grass or rats' feet over broken glass in our dry cellar, they are meaningless. Okay, now the computer blew a fuse. There is nothing we can do with those men. That's why we locked them up in the cellar. But it was a beautiful cellar, whitewashed even, it used to be the rec room for the horses, yes, that's right: nice and white, not filthy, we kept them in a clean cellar, in a huge former barn, scrubbed, whitewashed, that's where we put up the hollow men and, though hollow, they were perfectly human, all there, but without form, shaded shape without color, paralyzed force, gesture without motion, that's what we turned them into, and still: perfect men, absolutely perfect, like us—perfect— it's just a word, just like love, which is also only a word, but this time the word landed perfectly, better than usual, it works with a lot of things, as a side dish, thank you very much, that much perfection is more than enough for me, that much perfection is an absolute must, that much time is an absolute must, we must not take too much time! Still, it doesn't pay to shoot them all, but here they are, so we must do it, they never wanted to live here, but they had to, born to work, no, not born, made to, not born to be a woman but made to, everyone spits at the other, if given the opportunity.

We, however, we shoot and we kill, unfortunately it's nothing to write home about, since these men were simply handed to us for this purpose; there was a telephone call, and then, around 1:30, 2 a.m.: screaming. It didn't help to shut all windows and doors and cover one's ears: screams, screams, screams, horrific screams, can't they be more considerate, we want to sleep at that time, everyone wants to sleep at that time, except those who don't want to or aren't allowed to; there was this phone call and the weapons were distributed; it will be decades before the petty political cash can be collected, but without interest, because the kill was made without a plan, and it was up to us to get rid of them, they are here, they must go, simple as that, not much left of them anyway, but left right here, so here they stand, ordered and also delivered; those who have crossed us with direct eyes, to death's other kingdom remember us, but they won't have the opportunity to do so; they were sent to us, assigned to us to be shot and shooting is our privilege. The privilege of people who are not hollow, who are stuffed, stuffed with straw, in contrast to the others, who are not stuffed, at least not with straw. Those are not Steiff stuffed-animal toys propped up by their pelts. Just a moment, please; I can see them; I see them, those men, the hollow men! The ones who have crossed with direct eyes to death's other kingdom still remember us now, but not for long; if they remember everyone, they will also remember us. Take them out! Out, out, out. Although it's no fun. It's only fun if you can get completely smashed before, that much time is needed and we got it, the time is now. Then everything gets to be fun, even fucking, it is like daylight on a gaping hole, right there, which is closing again; it is a tree growing, no, swinging, and voices blowing in the wind, more distant and more solemn than a fading star, now I don't know, does he mean a rock star, or whom or what?

You just heard our daily program about the banality of evil, but you know all about it anyway; it's yesterday's news; and now more music. Those tunes are from the day before yesterday; don't you know anything newsier, anything new, or even the newest? Then put it on. Put it all on the line. We also have one of last year's tunes, which is newer than this one, but the tunes of tomorrow and even the day after tomorrow have just come out and we will put them all online already today. They are like all things past: music comes and it passes the moment it is put on; music is time that is heard; generally, what's past must first have come to pass, but there are things in the past, which should not and could no longer come to pass. What's been committed here should disappear; it should be admitted, I mean, omitted, but never permitted to be committed again; whatever has been committed should be thoroughly cleaned up, so that no one will ever have to submit to it again. Not again, please! But tomorrow you can tune in to see and listen to another banal program; it won't even deal with the banality of evil, but it will certainly be banal. It's unbelievable! If you want to believe it, go ahead, but it *is* beyond belief. Take your eyes off! Eyes off everyone! Why? Eyes off! In this sink, there are no eyes here in this sink, this hollow sink. Nonetheless, eyes off everyone. Still, don't miss it! It will get interesting any moment now. No, it doesn't. Nothing again. So piss off already, will you!

This is the feast that features the killing of the true lamb, whose blood guards the doors of the faithful. Well, nothing is right about that line. Not only should I not have delivered it, it also makes no sense. Who smeared all that red paint on all the windows and even on the door? A messenger has to always look where he puts his hand. I'd get myself all dirty knocking on doors, knock, knock! How many doors and windows do you think I have to pound on every day? How could I function with everyone smearing their crap all over them? What killing is to be prevented here? None. Just the opposite, the killing is to be arranged and done at close range. For it is not man who sacrifices God, no, not even God sacrifices God, and God doesn't sacrifice himself for his father either, no, no, no, I have seen many killings, not this one, but so many messengers told me about it that I better believe it. But it is wrong. God does not sacrifice himself. God is no victim. He gifts himself to the world. I don't see the difference, but I can understand God. Before I let myself be beaten up and crucified, I'd also be happy to gift myself to the world! I can't second-guess God, let alone outguess him, but before I have myself beaten up, you can have me even for nothing. You could have me as a free gift that comes with God for no extra charge. The countess also sacrifices herself, but I don't know for whom. I believe, she does it for her horses, that's what I was told. She'll soon leave in her car, with her two mates, no, aids, no, adjutants, no, celebrants, no, not that for sure, what would that woman have to celebrate? Almost two hundred, all done, 180 you say? It happened just once. It just happened. A celebration might be possible in ten years at the earliest, and at that time they will have other concerns and other reasons to celebrate. Celebrations as commemoration will come much later, not exactly a reason to celebrate; the eyes will not be there, the eyes will never be there, among those celebrants, now perpetual commemorators, those commemorating perpetrators, in this hollow pit of broken jaws, of broken bones. Now we also have to bury it all, in this pit, this cesspit, in this last of meeting places we will search sixty years later or so, maybe seventy, eighty, 180?, I'd say around sixty, but it could be more, we will search for this last of meeting places, together, groping together, avoiding all talk by giving a speech, the same one, over and over again, which at some point will be swept away by this river of memory, on this beach of the tumid river, sightless today, sightless tomorrow, unless the eyes would reappear again, but they don't, not even in our dreams, those eyes. No sacrifice—no sacrificial feast! Feasts come later and then, paradoxically, the victims will be celebrated, not us, not us. We will celebrate with the victims; we will celebrate their sacrifice, because the victim is the gift is the sacrifice is the son. The father will be delivered from sacrifice, he will be delivering the victim; thank God, for once it's the father who delivers, so he'll know how difficult that is. There will be blood, lots of blood, well, yes, but not on windows and doors, please. Someone might get his hands in it without looking, always without looking, then what! So then, God does not sacrifice God, not himself, he gifts himself, he gives himself, it is self-abandon, out of love, not a sacrifice. Christianity on principle does not sacrifice anything alive; remember that once and for all! It never did, it never sacrificed living life. Where would that get us? It would get us exactly to where we are now! Now we are stuck with our crock of crap. It just came in. One victim more or less—better one more in death's twilight kingdom. The hope only of empty men was rising, of empty men, so what's the difference? They were empty and still are.

Well, to me, whatever the countess is doing is not a sacrifice, no, and clearly not for her, as she does it willingly! And what you do willingly, is well done, uhm, not done, uhm, no, it's just better than what one does unwillingly. Don't mention it. My pleasure. It was a pleasure. And later it won't be mentioned and it won't be a pleasure. Strange. The hope of the empty men doesn't get them to rise, though they are light and crinkly, like kites.

Oh yes, the countess! Had nothing to say but plenty to do all the time. Instead, her family talked all the more and all the more loudly, they still had decades ahead of them, to be filled with plenty of cheers and checks but certainly no balances after the pits were full; the countess is talking now, quiet everyone!, the deader that woman was—don't worry, that was much later—the more her relatives talked, they easily drowned out the countess. But today she wants to say something, and she wants to have a say in everything, though she doesn't have to know anything about it and today, and also on the day we have been told to tell you about, and then on the day we must under no circumstances tell you about, she is very appealing to Messrs. P. and O., the Men in Black, stuffed with straw, I distinguish here between the hollow men and the straw men, who cannot be held responsible, since this is what they are: straw men, meaning they are not stuffed with flesh inside their skin; and we don't know their names. Not flesh. But straw. Stuffed with straw. The hollow ones with nothing. The others with straw. The countess with nothing, nada, nix, zero, zilch, okay, that'll do for now. She is one of those *Nichten*, those nixes, or is it nieces?, who are *Nichts*, nothing, nix, nada, anyway, her own niece will be something, though much later, decades later, she'll be somebody, it's not her doing, but she'll be more and somewhere else than we, by chance she will be where we are, she'll be everything, she'll be everything to herself, she'll be everything to everyone else as well, a perpetual star, a star, the star multifoliate of the twilight kingdom, this time not death's. Yes, her niece, ten years later, the countess's niece, not every niece a *Nichte* of the countess, the empty men's hope—though only theirs—instantly rises six inches, no, theirs doesn't either, here no one gets up again, back then a star of the unborn, the niece, the *Nichte*, the *genichtete Nichte*, the *noch nicht gesichtete Nichte*, in plain English: the nixed niece, the not-yet-in-the-pix niece, a star among other unborn, she even is the opposite of nix, she is not a *Nichts*, no nix, no, definitely not a Nixon, a nothing, no, she is the opposite of nothing, she is the highest of all, well, maybe not that high, but the highest we can imagine; but she is not the kind of branch, not a high branch she could saw off, she only married the family tree, though she herself is also a branch, but one she can sit on, why would she sit on a branch she could saw off, she sits on a foreign family tree, there, it's all in the papers, there she goes and here we go, we look at her picture in the paper, her naked ass in this rag, prickly pear all around, perky pricks?, pesky balls?, wreckers' balls? so we go 'round this prickly pear at five o'clock in the morning and at six it's all done. Here, in this magazine. Here she is, that woman, there she stands, firm and fast, when its time to move the firm, not the mother, the aunt, I am not quite sure who she is, in any case a sister, aunt, mother? No, not mother, yes, the mother is also in the paper!, oh, now I see she also is a mother, and surely also a daughter, right?, wouldn't work any other way, so here she is, right in this paper, and she is looking, between the desire and the spasm between the potency and the existence between the essence and the descent, where the shadow is falling, she looks here and there, she looks everywhere, but she can't see a place for her to sit, because she has no family tree which she could climb even higher if things get too hot on the ground, but no one should notice that she still has to get there first. There now, she got one, now she is on top. All the way on top. She got it, a tree, prickly pear, prickly pear. Now she sits on the highest branch, an *Erzherzogin*, if something like that existed. Archduchess? No, it doesn't. We don't have it, whatever it is. Or is it *Erz* for ore?, gold or iron ore?, gold ore for the Iron Lady? No, that's another country. That's okay. No, that's not the UK, it was k.k., for *kaiserlich königlich*, for the Habsburg Empire, the Austro-Hungarian monarchy, the Kaiser and the King, k.k. okay, no, really? That clan? Even in Hungary? No, that was another clan, but she is now in Switzerland. So could it be that our lady, our arch lady, with the heart of gold and gold for art and art for gold, that *the* lady is a tramp? Whose heart has been trampled on? No, that's impossible! Not even a Trump? Oh no, it's impossible that it's impossible. She is probably just one that is trumped up, tripped up and torn down to us in the media jungle, it's not really a jungle, not even a forest, on the contrary, it's the low lands where one can see very far, many want to come here, some to lay low here. Many want to be dukes and move here, getting things moving, but only a few get elected, I mean selected. To settle here, to set up business here. What would she be without it, this pretty woman? Well, it's what she would like to be, pretty, and she is. It'll do. It would do for me. That does it. Since we no longer have a foundation for golden arches, there are no more archdukes wrapped in their golden fleeces, and what will keep them warm now?, animals need their fleece to stay warm, otherwise they freeze to death or dry up like cactus in a cactus land. You couldn't find a decent fleece today, with the environment poisoned and animals feeding on polluted grass; and if you find a fleece, after a long journey, it no longer fits the animal that wore it before it was torn off its body, the animal perished, the fleece too, and anyway: Once upon a time they hunted animals only, once upon a time a man took another wife, then he took two pieces of children, then three, then all of it got taken away again, so he took another wife and still another, but on principle everything always gets taken away, one way or another, and we are working against that principle. The animal, whose fleece was stolen, used to jump across creeks and rocks and hollows, inspired by a spirit, no, not a spirit, whatever, inspired by something, maybe just an idea, yes, the idea of Germany, but it might as well be any other idea, almost any idea will do, almost any other idea will fly, it's there and it flies, well, my ideas keep flying away, I can't hold them back, maybe they aren't even ideas, I am pretty sure of that. Even if one isn't there, one thinks of Germany, the dead land here, the cactus land, where stone images are raised, that's how strong they are here. Just a moment now, I see this isn't an animal, let the messenger first take a look what it is before he sets the tone with a fork. Forking out the right notes takes quite a fortune, no, hitting the right note can bring a big fortune, well maybe just a small one, since no one would want to hear the same tune several decades from now. But Germany would do better if she were in Hungary or Switzerland or rather: if she stood there, Germania, so she would remain upright and no one could hurt her, though everyone keeps trying, but they can't hack her, they can't get her on her knees, they can't kill it, this kingdom of death, they can't hack it, only death himself can hack it, he who hacks last, hacks best, but still, just the idea of Germany keeps you going, if not running, even if Germany must go down. But then let's not have all of Germany come down to us to go for broke, let them go broke in their own country, then let them break their news to themselves, break a leg, guys, but no closing session in the twilight kingdom, please! We can see for ourselves that the twilight of the gods has arrived and then someone switched on the light again, and if one dares the big leap, no, not the long march, that would be too slow and we are too few and in the wrong country at that, but the big leap would work, one giant leap, or is it a small step, no, a grand leap, whatever, if one dares the grand leap, one lands in the present, from the past into the present in one single leap, and we also need the Germans right now, someone has to do the work, right, and someone has to get it done for them, the work, so someone will always have to produce a lot of work, be labor intensive, and it's not the Germans, they are growing, it'll be others who haven't been axed yet, not yet erased from the face of the earth, but who will be axed as soon as there is the threat of a crisis, no matter what kind, they'll explain everything to us, the Germans will; explaining everything better is what Germans do better than anything else, they can explain even wars, no, that leap won't cut it, it might go down and cut a zigzagging crack into the ground; and that kind of pit can easily be cleared during the night with heavy construction machinery, no, it doesn't go, jump is what it does, as its name tells us, jump and cut the crap, I mean the crack, and that's the pits, but it won't jump to conclusions, and the jump from man to animal is so inconclusive; it happened so long ago, and the jump from animal to man has not yet been concluded; so why not keep jumping around, and as we leap we see a man sitting on a fir tree, a local, of course, anything foreign wouldn't grow here, and something is holding us back, though nothing can hold us back here in our stronghold; we saw the blood on the door, ordering us like a red light: Angels, please keep moving! There is nothing to see here, shoot and move on, and now we'll repeat this about two hundred times, no, but the blood says yes, no, the blood doesn't say yes, the blood says no, please, don't kill, don't ask for more blood, please, we have enough already, please, we have already felled fir trees at Christmas and birch trees for Maypoles, all bloody ancient tasks, but what can we do with them? And what should we do with the blood? We can't use every drop for a transfusion. All the towels are already soaked, so we'll just smear it on windows and doors. Yuck! It's disgusting! If you don't look and get your hand right into it! As messengers we'll be the first to whom it will happen, no doubt about that. Unfortunately, we'll once again be the first who must get their hands dirty. But we hope no one will be looking and no one else will put his hand in the dirt, which is still wet.

We can take it. We can take care of it. We throw the gravel in an arch; the moment someone sits on the tree, they throw dirt at him, then they just tear the branches off this beautiful tree, which took so much effort to grow, and they throw about their arms like batons, their arms with the branches, they rise, the arms rise, the arms with the branches, why else should they rise?, to regulate the traffic?, traffic in what? Why twist arms, why twirl weapons like a majorette, like a major, if they have nothing in hand on those people, those 180 naked people, and nothing on us, who will have to report it?, just a moment now, there is no charge against us. First they raise their hands, they all do, just for the heck of it, whether or not they have something in their hands, they don't care, they raise their hands; but the man for whom they yank up their arms has taken too strong a stand for us to understand, we couldn't move him from his position under any circumstances, we can see that right away, but the countess understands where he stands, women always understand everything, that's their job, and if they don't get it, they at least want to, they want it all. So then the snoop sits way up there, I am afraid he can't tell me more, I am afraid I am in the wrong play now, I beg your pardon, but I get carried away, I can't help it, the game fled into our forest, it is in our camp now, Austria is also in our camp, but there still is room for these animals here, where they can't be seen, that's where the game is, it doesn't want to be seen, so it can't be shot, but it must be shot, so it must be chased up the tree or into the clearing, so it can be caught, so then, many arms take up their arms, and those are not weapons of the spirit, those are the weapons which are to produce the spirits! They'll take care of that all right and then they'll finish off whatever is left of the spirit, Now we shoot, the offshoot gets pulled out, the womb is fertile still, but it can't be pulled out, on the contrary, the uterus decomposes last, the very last, that's been proven, those men will decompose before our uterus, each of us has only one, one piece of uterus, which, however, will last much longer, but not forever and not for whatever it was originally intended, one more tactlessness of the hearts of women, who are capable of anything, they'll go to extremes, even with their organs, which everyone wants to play, so they really must go to extremes, because people have no heart anymore, so what's left to beat? The beat comes out of their ears, whence music spurts like a viper's venomous foam, no, not like whipped cream, especially, if the ear doesn't fit tightly, I mean the earplug, which, however, must first be plugged into the unit, one end into the unit, the other in the ear, which better not come loose, or all that beautiful music just fizzles out for no reason. Then nothing will come out. It will come to nothing. Nothing like it anymore. There is no more. They have everything anyway. However, the woman who comes with all that, who calls to the heavens, but no more flames light up the sky, she has some sort of foam around her mouth, I just noticed, and it ain't whipped cream either, my, my, her twisted gaze is vacant, I am afraid she is no longer conscious, still, better than dead. With her arm she grabs his—the countess, I mean, *Frau*, countess, Ms. Margit, that doesn't sound right—anyway, she grabs his left arm at the wrist, the left arm of that man over there, that's the truth, no? No, that's the truth. She could have seized him from the right, but he hasn't had any rights for a long time, so she grabs him from the left and plants her foot upon his chest, she can do that, it was she who shot him after all, now wrenching away the arm at the shoulder, his shoulder joint that is, now that wasn't necessary, really! It was not the force of her arm that finished him, nor the force of her charm, but the force of fire, her fiery arms, the arms not of a God—no God was present—I would have loved to report to you about a present or an absent God, but I didn't see any in that mess, everyone totally drunk, of course, why should we hold on to all that stuff for the Russians, who won't get a hold of us in the castle, which we won't hold for them either?, well then, what did I want to say, hands on the trigger, go, tear up the flesh, that's it, finished. The bullets are a big help but we must also give a hand or the bullets will be powerless. Screams and whimpers, cries of pain emanate from the shredded, lacerated bodies, ouch, that must hurt, it's supposed to hurt, but with a gun it's over relatively quickly, the hollow men were lucky that way. If they hadn't already been wrecked by work, the bullets would have taken care of what was left of them, but what we got were already the left-overs, they were hollow when they were delivered to us, before we delivered the goods. And now, of course, they are fed up. Hungry, but fed up with us. The same old story. Always fed up with us. As if all Germans should be held responsible. But nothing ever happens to us. It goes right by us, like nothing. The shouts resounded all around, I heard them myself, how else would I know about them?, this one here is still breathing, no, if you ask me, he stopped breathing long ago, it makes no difference; one woman carried off his arm, another his foot, there were no clothes, they had to take them off before, they might still be good for something. It turns us on when people are stripping and we are tripping. The windows are smeared with blood, the doors too, we too; now we could also throw their limbs around like balls, their balls too, if they got any, yuk, that's dumb!, or we could do something altogether different with them, for our arms were given their grace by the God we created for that purpose. *Sieg Heal—No—Heil*!, it's okay, it'll heal! You know what else I could tell you? I could tell you where in the dense underbrush or in the ground, next to the stables—we have two stables, not one, but two, less wouldn't do—where they are buried, where they could be buried, where they would have to have been buried, if not in, than next to one of the stables, but which one is the one where they would have to be?, well, they don't have to be anywhere to do anything anymore; they had to before, but not after; well then, which stable is it? Tell us, will you now, or shut up for good! What do you think of my gravel-pit theory, for which I don't have the faintest lead, but I still can lead anyone on and around, all on my own, though maybe not much longer. They wouldn't have been eaten, would they now, those 180 men, roasted in the fire in the castle? Dig up, cover up, dig up, cover up, even the corpses are beginning to get bored of it! I could also tell you where it will not be easy to find those bodies, no, nothing will be easy to find, but I say nothing, otherwise it would be too easy a find and much too easy a finale.

Well then, in the end, those 180 men also lost their lives in the war. This then is the end of it. I didn't know at the time how to report it. I don't know now either, but I go on reporting, although nothing is going to happen. They would tear the bands from their heads, but we wouldn't have blindfolded them. That's only for deserters, or an adversarial attorney or an adversary in the general trial of all those adverse to trials. Or Lady Justice herself, she'll get one too. Fuck them all. Those men don't get anything from us, period. They do not have a claim on life; they did not register in time. They cannot claim a thing. They cannot even claim they lived, but they cannot leave either. All they can have is our sticks and stones, our spears of fir and even the big Speer, they can have him! Hush, the naked man there is still speaking: Mother, it is I, your own son, the child you bore! I am also every man, whom you also bore, no, you did not bear them all, I made a mistake, I mistook you; if you had given birth to all of them, it would have been quite a few. And what hasn't been born, at least not by you, mother, would even be more. Why are you acting so hysterically? What's with the weapon? Put it down! Now! No, there is nothing to discuss. Here a son does not get murdered for his misdeeds, he is a son, but not the countess's. He is every son. He is a son. But not yours. So, what's your problem?

May I also say something, please? She doesn't need it, that title; she already has one, even if it got a bit small for her. She acquired a reputation but she can still stand on her own, held up by her title, brought down by the communists, no longer brought down by the Austrian lords of hammer and sickle, her homeland's brave, so proudly hailed at the twilight's last gleaming. She has bite, the archduchess, like a shepherd who bites off a sheep's umbilical cord. I think I am a sheep, because I always have to run and eat and then thirst is eating me, at least it gnaws on me. Oh, what a life! A messenger's life! Oh, poor us! And yes, so much hunger, hunger for life, which others satisfy, but not mine. Around me, nothing but sheep. Just sheep, all of us. Still, better than people, because animals are much better than any people. But not all people are still around, some are missing, some will always be missing, or can you see anyone? Yes? Still? But are you missing anyone? There you go! The very fact that we miss them is what makes them people. Because we are always missing some. It shouldn't be too many though. Are you missing something, somewhere?, up there?, so you see things, which aren't there? I must have done something wrong then. So they still exist after all, I knew it; I was lied to! There would be no need for me as a messenger if I had no message for no one. I'd have only puzzles and bitterness in my heart, if I went somewhere to deliver my messages. Now I am confused, the victors, those with their feet firmly on the ground are not the ones I had something to report to. No, maybe they don't exist, what do I see?, no, it's nothing and no one, I am alone again , and want to stay that way, naturally, with clear skies and open seas, and another afternoon will surround me, and I will not have reported anything to anyone, and I will try again tomorrow, when I will have found my friends, but there is nothing I can tell my friends, they always know everything in advance. So now, the light is still, that's good for the un-alive, there is the un-alive and there is art, the unloved: unloved, because it doesn't live, we only love what is alive, we, who are able to bring to life anything by simply looking at it, must still kill people to get them to stand still, according to our standstill agreement, just a moment, a moment doesn't count if one stands still, I've seen this kind of art a few times, if only from afar, you can buy it, I hear, if you can, you can, and of course people are still around, and you can buy them too. There'll always be people, one just has to look for them long enough, there'll always be miracles, yes, those too, at least now and then, while art must be found, you cannot look for it, well, naturally, there'll also always be art and you'll always be able to buy it, but there will be more people, and those who are no more cannot be bought either, of course. It won't increase their value, however, rather decrease it, would be my rule of thumb as my index finger pulls the trigger. The living will always be in the majority, but they will be overpowered by art till they drop; oh, no, the dead won't bother them in any way, they are gone for good, they are powerless, they have made room for good. You can't squeeze blood out of a turnip. There are also the living dead, I saw them myself and I should have reported about them; all you had to do was touch them with your pinkie and they dropped, those people, yes, especially them, a 180 pieces, there they lie, their work put them through the wringer for hours on end, like rags, but that didn't get them any cleaner. Those who can't get their hands dirty aren't fit to rule; they can't give orders either. A house that can't be smeared with blood can no longer hold up, it lacks the inner cohesion that only a blood-bath can provide. But here we make an exception. This house falls, this hand falls, no more hands raised in suppli-cation; hands that would shiver like leaves in the forest hang still; no cry even of beasts. Those men no longer listen with pricked ears, evidently they don't care anymore, their eyes no longer roll with frenzy, they don't lift up their arms anymore, those men no longer give a shit, they are done, done in, they are nothing special, it's everyone's lot, all of us are done in by our work, why not those men? They just were done in differently for a change. The countess is committed to getting it right, whatever is committed comes out right and just, uhm—whatever—I don't commit, I'm just an ordinary kind of guy, I don't commit, I don't commit to the right, I don't commit to commies, I don't commit so I won't be committed, I commit to memory what others have committed, I am too clumsy to commit what they committed, I'm just a messenger, just a minute ago I still was a messenger, that's about all I could manage, I massage the message, others just want the massage; if they can't get their message right, which would be the messenger's real job, they go to a parlor, their job was to manage the mess, that was our message, which they missed and then they went to mass and that's all they wrote; but the others are no better either, if only I knew who they were, I would certainly tell you: They won't hold up, they won't last much longer, that's why they'll be cheap like the Hungarian prostheses, no point collecting them. There are a lot more of them where they come from, but there's nothing in it for us if they stay there. Well, yes, of course, now we easily go there ourselves; nothing to stop us anymore. No borders, no guards. Now you can get yourselves something new there anytime, messengers, prostheses, teeth, the supply is inexhaustible except of art, otherwise they have replacements for everything and everything is still cheaper there; then we get them to Austria, those living dead, we get them going in Austria, the dead, who were alive once, those dead, who are so dear to us; they are cheaper if they are still alive, let them come, on sidetracks, or main tracks, we can let them come, in compartments with boarded up windows, on tracks with signals always set on

GO, green light for the unfit!, their shit and piss can go into a food pail in a pinch, we'll pull out some floorboards to empty it, we can allow for things to come, it won't harm us to make room for what's coming and dispose of those who came. Whatever we do, will not have been seen; it will seem to not have been done; and those dead, who one day will not have ever been, will end in literal Nothingness, I am afraid, coming from Hungary going Nowhere. They are already collecting themselves all by themselves just to get somewhere, anywhere, they don't need to be pushed, all one has to do is give an order and instantly the light goes still with happiness that we caught so many beautiful people again, well, not all are beautiful, but human beings are essentially beautiful, don't you think so?, yes, even the others, and I bet it is safer, it is better and safer, better still, it is better altogether, generally and specifically better, even safer, no, not safer, one can go wrong, but basically it is better to collect art. You won't get blamed for that. Unless it is stolen, then the lawsuits start, a bit late, but better than never. Then there'll be a thousand "oh's" and "dear's" that this art was stolen. That's not easy either, not easy at all, collecting art and catching people, snatching art and collecting oneself for the act, at least once a day, not so easy, but it can be managed. Everything can be managed. Where I look for people, I only find art, where I look for art, I only find people, they are moving about, they are hard to catch, you can't get them, there's no way to get them for all the money in the world, and still they are worth nothing. A puzzle. No wonder we couldn't solve the puzzle of human existence, this sudoku for the prosperous and progressives?, no, the pros; and also the cons then?, no, not the proles, not the poor, they need no puzzles, no wonder we found ourselves turning to art in the end, no, not our end, and: just so you know, the archduchess also finds it okay, to this day, she told me yesterday, when she found it in New York, and the day before, when she found it in Croatia and Slavonia, where no one found anything before, while no one found anything profound about it before, I am to tell you that she finds art, where it is and where it's not, I mean, where she and art happen to be at the same time, both of them, by accident, and when she isn't there or it isn't, can't remember which, she keeps looking until she finds it. She looks for what she finds beautiful. She finds something. What does she find? How does she find out? That's what I'd also like to know. People are drifting about, I am driven by fear, but I stay here, though I long for people's laughter, a laugh that won't be driven away, so I could rest awhile, the archduchess must be driven too, driven away, by her driver, who drives her crazy; she even has her own, special laugh, designed exclusively for her, which I saw just yesterday in a magazine again, flashing between her lips, like something Zeus had thrown, a shot, a light installation, there, another one, over there, projected onto the mountain, all that gorgeous light, oh my God, how much effort you put into letting it be light!, well, it must come from somewhere, doesn't it? And you say it comes from you. I see. And you want us to believe that? This lady has paid for it! And you, God, haven't even sent us a bill for the light yet. Yes, those are firebrand folk; I never saw a fierier bunch. And the most disgusting animal, the parasite always among them, somehow. The elite of our kind, out of their mind because they still have to wait, had only one choice: being mean animals or mean animal tamers, and of course they chose the latter, though I wouldn't want to build me a cabin, where people want to tame and subdue, those black uniforms with their skulls and bones and boots and their boot jacks and boot lickers, those guys will have to wait but not for long, for the game they themselves should be but naturally don't want to be. The game is here already and corralled in the pen. They are above all that, those skull-and-bones guys, who smoked the men, whose skulls those were, in their pipes; they walk and run and climb and dance and finally they fire. Fire, finally. Someone must have unloaded the guns, then load the guns, someone would have to lead the guests; they like to have their *lieder* to sing, as they get loaded. You may sing along, I am to tell you, this is an invitation; yes, of course, the guns will also be loaded. Those who taught people to fly, to New York, London, Mumbai, Tokyo, wherever, moved all existing border stones, now they will have to turn to art, because only art knows no boundaries and never did, art throws all those rocks high up in the air, art rocks, let's get it, let's shoot for art, we must aim at it, we must overcome our inner boundaries to reach the arts, which are boundless, but we'll just need a rifle or a pistol, so that their projectiles land where they can shoot the crap and seal the deal. Borders must be established, but where?, no idea, some day they'll be torn down again anyway. Why bother with any today? Now look, I am to tell you that rifles have many advantages; first of all, they have long pipes, like the messenger, who needs strong pipes not to run out of breath on his long runs; nonetheless, he also does shorter runs, when he is tired or got the runs or is sick and tired for many other reasons, but that comes later; so then, the projectile in this long metal pipe is exposed for a longer time to the—how shall I put it?—the force that triggers the explosion, the explosive force, which is to accelerate the projectile; when the explosion is triggered, this explosive mixture, this gas or whatever it is, propels the projectile through the barrel, faster and faster, longer rifles allow the gas more time to work, like in a car, which can accelerate faster and slower, and after the acceleration is complete, the projectile shoots out of the barrel as fast as it can, as much as it could be accelerated and it strikes like lightening, you see, the muzzle velocity—I am telling you now, once the projectile leaves the muzzle, it's too late, it's all very fast, I am telling you ahead of time, because the projectile will always catch up with me, the poor messenger—anyway, the muzzle velocity as well as the muzzle energy depend on many factors, such as length of the barrel, kind and weight of projectile, amount and kind of powder charge and the respective cartridge. And I am not even talking about a specific type of cartridge; I am talking of all types, would you like a short list? No, you don't. This will do for our purposes. No, you don't see a flash, what a dumb question, it would be a waste of energy, a pistol flashes, not a rifle, I think, but whatever comes out of the raging barrel, though raging, the messenger stays cool in the meantime, he waits until the flesh of the defenseless targets is broken, torn to pieces the flesh of the helpless, the tired, the empty men they hit, the effect is almost beside the point, who would believe that they are in the Father and the Father is in them? There is nothing in those hollow men, the jacketed hollow point bullet is where it belongs, the hollow guys could use a jacket, right, but they stand naked in front of the firing line, they all fired, I saw it, only we, the messengers didn't, we just have to sit and wait for what we'll be told, what they order us to do, and then we run, counting the prisoners, giving our account, but the helpless can't be referred to as "killed in the war," right?—It would dishonor all the war dead who were not helpless, and Germans need honor, really now, leave them alone, the Germans, right now!, I am waiting! And he who is hit knows his hour has come. For whom the bell tolls. Someone will be left an orphan, while they are coming home, to their Father. Finis—finished.

Schluß, aus, Ende. But he knows very quickly, almost before he was born, that there is nothing he will be able to do about any of it. No matter how many times, how happily you came here and came in a woman, you might have even come together, for all I care, though, personally, I wouldn't want to be a woman, anyway, now it is time to go, what else is there to do. Others will come and they will also have to go again.

The hunters are already waiting with their rapt crew of holy women led by the countess, naturally; she was graced with a natural nobility, even before she could marry into it, but she ain't no crew, this lady, no cruiser either, she just looks like one, no, the crowd divides all by itself in front of her, like reeds in a lake, not the Red Sea, that was a mistake in translation, the sea of reeds dividing, it's not a big deal, unlike art, which can be a fantastic deal; this lady makes big waves wherever she goes, so, now she has called to arms, the short and the long ones, and the *Schutzstaffel SS*, her personal security detail, is with her, at least two of them, but others too, a certain Mr. P. and a certain Mr. O., so there must have been about thirty people but only fifteen received arms and the permission to shoot at the hollow ones, yes, also the countess, why not, it's all good as far as I'm concerned, what good would it do if it weren't? So, I'm good. As a messenger I will have become worthless and wordless. They won't bail me out. So this man wants to lead the *Sturm*, the storm, the troops, so he nails a skull on his jacket, maybe he just tacked it on, now he needs a cap, a cap makes a man seem taller, so they won't suspect him to be soft: And now, we'll shoot them all, he screeches, his voice cracked a while ago, so now this man is done paying his dues to mankind, nature is laden with dew, the caresses have stopped, a stop-gap is needed, so let's shoot them now, let's finish them now, no, not the caresses, only those who want to exchange caresses, but have nothing left to exchange. No woman has carried those men in her womb the way they look now. And if it was a woman who carried them, they no longer show it, skeletons, even in life. Not pretty in death. I see them right in front of me, not even a professional messenger could describe them any other way. That's not what life turns men into; it's labor that does it. Only work turns men into animals, in this regard Marx wasn't right, if you ask me. Thank you for not asking, I would have had to explain this in greater detail, and I don't dare to look at the details. I really don't want to know all the details. That's enough for me. Now it's time to clean up. We don't need lawless rage, we don't need mad intent, we don't have to sneak up to the Great Mountain Mother, the countess has already taken care of the weapons, take one, please, don't be shy, would you like another one? My pleasure!, mink slung around her shoulder, or was it her lover?, tossed over the shoulder, or she over his? No? How else then operate the gun?, perhaps the other shoulder?, no, that one's already in use; smashed out of his mind, this man, if you ask me, but he's still able to shoot, maybe not hit the mark; no—I wouldn't want him to hit on me either, not even when the moon shines brightly as tonight would I want to meet him in the dark, he can meet me in the moonshine, but he won't, since there is no darkness once the moon is bright like that; so, the moon is doing its job, but how should this man in his condition still be able to aim?, well, of the 180 targets he should at least hit one, but he shoots several, if not with precision, not a chest hit, not through the heart, some of them are still alive as they go down into the pits, to take a look at the family's pits, the

Thyssen pits of the Thyssen company, oh, the Thyssen pits of the Thyssen family, very interesting what's going on in such a pit, thank you for not asking, it's cold outside, we better shoot outside, we can't have the bloody, stinking mess inside, we'll trample the hills down flat and tear open the green valley, we'll dig a grave no one can find, that's overlooked by all, I can see it already, I can foresee it, it won't be somewhere in the clouds, nor in the air, the grave stays here, right here with us, it's here to stay, the grave. The messenger on a perch, that would work, from that towering fir I could see much better, I could have a much better view of their shameless but jolly activities. Well, all right then, I'll work a miracle. I bend the highest branch of a great fir, okay, now what?, what should I do with it?, I bend it down, forcing the mighty fir down to the ground by hand and I sit on it, let no one else sit with me, they don't sit well with me, and let the trunk rise straight up, slowly and gently so it won't hurl me off too soon, like the gun its bullet, aimed at the target, because not having a target would be counterproductive; I am supposed to watch, and with my head spinning I am towering way up high, and later I will always be spinning my report, that's only natural, of course I will spin the report or, better still, I won't talk about it at all, they won't let me anyway, so why bother? Can't shoot more bullets than you got and there is no need for it. Now rage, vengeance, rage in radiant glory. Gore his throat!, kill without mercy earth's monstrous spawn! Done! All right, but now calm down again, okay!

Now the messenger lets us hear his laugh, it is not a human laugh, he can't hear it himself; he would go into shock and choke if he heard himself laugh. The hounds drive in a stag with a man tied to it. We fixed him good up there, he doesn't hold up so well, but he's still whole. He must not look at a naked goddess, this fast-moving Actaeon, who wants to get everything he can out of this action, he must not look when they shoot, there are so many, someone will be hit, although they aimed at the stag, they hit the man, not a big hit, if you ask me, but as a consolation he will not be torn apart by his own dogs as if he were the stag, those dumb and goofy, but unsurpassed scent hounds. Such extravagances were still allowed at the time, and I am not talking about Greek antiquity, today it's done swiftly, without the crap of crystal-clear springs and stags, goddesses, nymphos and a hot hunter, today humans get tied into bundles and set on fire all at once, or they get shot, several by one bullet, if possible, they are pretty soft, and afterwards, if some are still alive, so what, well, maybe not completely, but the important parts should be dead, it would be better for them than dropping into the pits alive, but they have to get in there, why else did they have to dig them? We take these men as they come, dead or alive, and whatever they will plead in their own name will not be complied with, the job will be completed, we'll take whatever comes our way; so there is a stag, and there's a man on top of it, right, a flash-pan hunter out of magic bullets, he won't give us any more of his bull, up there, tied to the stag, caught at his own game, now stuck on top of it, that was to be his punishment, but at that time the dukes and the counts could still be moved to pity, don't worry, later they didn't give a damn, the archdukes didn't either in their ancestral hunting castles or their titled spouses' ancestral hunting castles, or their titled ancestral in-laws' hunting castles or outlawed in-laws' tilted hunting castles, whatever, lawless entitlements in any case, titles to hunting, grounds and lodging, in the woods, the happy hunting grounds, I'd say, someone has to cultivate these woods. And what does the prince have to say to all this? Whoever can kill the stag and get us out of the woods, I mean, that man, that hood in our woods, who just violated all laws of our civilization, which has gone bonkers in its bunkers, I mean it is half as bonkers as one would assume, no, it is not half as bonkers, only one half are bonkers in their bunkers, the other half are bankers, they have not gone as bonkers, they have gone to their banks, they love our game, what's there to do?, the game was not to come to the banks before the bankers came to the game, I am confused now, okay, so the shooter shoos, no, shits, no, he shoots, the stag stumbles, and the game thief, except for some scratches from thorns, was unhurt. Where am I? I bet not even you can tell, even though you can see me quite clearly, or don't you? From then on the aristocrats paid all their bills on time, except for limo charges, because those are certainly not gaming debts, those are fixed fares discretely rounded up, I know from experience. They don't pay, they rather collect. They collect one painting after another. Why don't they just collect the money? You betcha, they also collect the money. Let me tell you what I learned. They collect money but they don't brag about it like the average Joe, who thinks he got some leverage for once. One collection of money has taken place already, there are more to come and now, whatever hasn't been shot has been collected. There will be no collection for the families of the victims. Or will there? I am afraid I am wrong again. I think it's easier to collect money than to collect oneself. If one collects oneself, one gets to a dump like Purkersdorf or Mauthausen, where no one camps anymore today, although it is free of charge, or is it? No, it is or it isn't? A place, in any case, where celebrities sing and act and camp it up in local pubs for a good cause; they try to make a vulgar impression, without having ever been impressive. Their wishes are facing a wall that's soft; a wall of people who don't have what they want, but get what they deserve. Those people are exactly what we want but do not deserve. They come at the right time. That's also the reason, why they went off the rail the moment they saw us. They drove into this wall, luckily it was on their way home, I hear; at least that's how they look. They gathered but they didn't collect themselves. Collecting comes later. Collecting at the collecting point is, after all, the point of it all, but not the end, not by a long stretch. It goes on until long after midnight, into the early morning hours. Okay, the money has been collected, preferably in the form of paintings. What form money takes is up to the collector. Money is more beautiful as a picture, more beautiful than the picture that's on the money. No discussion. Period.

As for the rest . . . what's a staff good for? She looked through the window across her valleys and asked her neighbor, who also had dropped all his clothes together with all responsibilities, and more than once at that, anyway, he also had a gun but nothing else to wear: Can you guess how high my peaks are? You are welcome to take a look, and I can also ring the bells, like Heidi K. over there, who just now peaks into the future through the mirror that shows our futures, now she is looking right at us, with such a sweet and saucy grin, all happy and content. We too are doing okay. So he replies: What peaks are you talking about? Heidi has given them names, she calls them bells! Just tell me please, which is which so I won't confuse them when the Lord calls me to mass, the Lord, who is the way, the truth and the life, a bit much all at once, wouldn't you say? On the other hand, though, one has to admit, they didn't laugh when they were arrested and handcuffed, those men, who came as foreigners and didn't really want to pass for friends, but certainly not pass away, and in the end were shot as game. That they were shot as game must have been a mix up, no, no one was game, here the countess calls the shots and she called for a hunt and later a game, you go play your games some other place! Earlier they had to dig their own grave, those naked men, no, those are no stags, take another look, will you!, before the blood starts running out of them and they lose their shape, slowly, but surely, I mean, it would be more practical, if they would somehow be—how shall I put it?—well—smaller, but either way, there's not much left of them. They don't have to be shrunk, they are zeroes, with nothing in front and nothing above them, they are so cold, those zeroes, because they got nothing in front. They must confront it head on, they must front for themselves. The earth was pretty hard, large or small, everything had to go in or must everything eventually go again, at the everything-must-go sale? Of course, everything must be gone again, or they would be found, the dead, one 180 in all, it won't be easy to transfer them. We can think about that later, now let's get them in first. All that blood should have softened the hard earth; there is a hand still sticking out and there a foot or whatever it is. The earth maybe, but not us, we won't be soft-ened, not even by blood. Well, the ditch will be done sooner or later, they don't have to be too careful digging in a zigzag line—a good design if nothing is to be found and a lot has to go into the smallest space, because afterwards no one is supposed to know where it is, the ditch. Well, a few will, but they won't tell, and if they do, we kill them too, no problem; It's much simpler to kill just one rather than a 180; if we can manage 180, we can easily handle one or two more. Since they shouldn't be found again it shouldn't take too much energy—digging those graves, those zigzag traps, they promptly fell into, every single one, though in groups, but nevertheless, one big hole they dug themselves into! Slow AND clumsy!, can you believe it, and those guys were to build a wall of defense against the East! Sure, it makes no sense, but the digging must go on. Not all graves are sense-less, on the contrary, we need them, but underground defense tunnels are senseless, they don't stop the enemy, while some graves can't even stop decomposition, others do, it depends on the ground. Nothing would have become of them anyway, those men would have never made it to the big city, those foaming fools, Zarathustra's apes who couldn't pick a better ancestry, they only have themselves to blame. I could have told you that they would never get away from here, why would the countess and her escorts P. and O., whom history had to keep mum about until their death and it's still hush hush, but maybe one of them is still alive, maybe both, no, I think they died long ago, because their life was a lot of work, and in the end they worked for noth-ing, they might as well have let those 180 live, maybe they are dead, only history hadn't been informed, we messengers, after all, must not get overworked under any circumstances, but, whatever the circumstances, this is not unjust, as history keeps silent anyway, no matter how much one keeps dig-ging, deep or shallow, or it keeps talking incessantly, fraught with sins of pride, no one sinned as much as he and he and he, and those are the ones we are talking about and we'll be happy to take responsibility for part of the guilt, no, we don't, we weren't even born then, why should we?, still, we are proud of our sins and we talk about them, because what sense would sinning make if we couldn't talk about it after-wards, and no matter how long the digging continues, his-tory keeps mum, or it talks to us, it tells us we should be ashamed of ourselves, no matter who we are, I say: They did it and I am proud of it, as if I myself had been shot by them, that's very important—pride of penance and regret, why else would the castle's occupants let those people dig if they couldn't be proud afterwards and regret and repent? Which they didn't, do you know how this could work at the same time, proud to sin and proud to regret? What's going on? I don't hear anything!, just pound the ground with a hollow staff, and if no certified local wine pours out, we have come to the right place and we will regret to have made the trip. But if wine indeed is pouring out, we have nothing to regret anymore, we would actually prefer it that way, but no chance. So we are digging here, we could as well dig over there, no one will find the grave, let alone the naked men, we are *die hohlen Männer*, the stuffed, *ja, die Ausgestopften* leaning together, straw in the *Kopf*. Alas! Anyway, even the naked must have gotten wind of the game while they were digging and that it made no sense to dig and that the game was elsewhere and they were the game that still had to be shot; they only knew that they couldn't get out, which was not a good enough reason to proudly sin and proudly regret, that's exactly what we have to do now, we commemorate them proudly and ruefully, piece by piece, if not always peacefully, though not for long, the church clock just struck, but it wasn't a hit, it struck the time but it wasn't the right time, where will all this lead to, I'd like to know and as a messenger I should. This can't be happening, and it could not have happened that way, but they are still digging, I can't believe it! What if they dig up something after all that digging! But as long as they keep digging in the wrong place I couldn't care less. Everything happened to us, no, it always only happened to others, otherwise we would actually be missing something; we would miss the penance and regret, and our pride would be all that's left to us. I know they are off track everywhere they dig, as long as they haven't found the right place, maybe a second stable? The sign of the cross has led to many mistakes, the crusaders already wanted to get to Palestine and ended up in the Gaza Strip instead, where, of course they were thrown out, because it was already full, the boat there was full, something like that, but one thing is correct: everyone gets thrown out of there except those who either must stay or tear down the fence, and if mistakes are made, they can't always be ironed out the way it is done with the graves here, in our beautiful state, yes, sir, they got depth there, those dirt diggers get all the way to the bottom, then they can bury themselves in there for all I care. And then start ironing, while the young shep-herd squirms with shame that he can't find the grave he knew at that time. No one can find it; no need for him to be ashamed. This grave does not want to be found and it won't be found. Because, well, anybody can see that: the way they are digging, they won't dig up anything, nothing could be dug up their way and if, then only for a very short time, and then it all gets buried again, way to go!, again and again and all over again; and most importantly, they are digging, their golden locks blowing in the wind, but sadly in the wrong place. Too bad. I already said that. As a messenger I say what they tell me to say, and I did see it myself, after all: a man lying there and there and over there. Those people saw me coming from afar, that's the way it usually is with messen-gers, you can always see them from afar, and then they start screaming, they might even drop dead on the spot, even before they could hear the bad news let alone pass them on, a bit prematurely, if you ask me; then we howl, then we scream, then we start scribbling again, well, at least I am, will this never end?, and then, finally, we tell what we have to tell, what was told to us by someone, who no longer exists, but even if he'd still be around, he'd also be crying for help like a dog, so here we are all screaming at each other, though we are more used to people screaming rather than dogs. But this dog really screamed. They all kept screaming all at once, how is a messenger supposed to remember anything in such a noise? How could he concentrate? Should he first say how much help this dog needs or should he first say how much help this person needs? He doesn't know. He hesitates. He shouldn't do that, a snake might come and bite him in the throat and he won't be able to say anything. Strange. But I would never tell them the right place later, just so they can dig those men out again!, I guess, they have nothing better to do, those born after, in their dreary solitude that makes them stand out in their sinful pride, I mean their pride of sin, those outstanding people; if I were them, I wouldn't want to drag up anything anymore but rather regret in peace and pride, but there they are, digging again, digging in the right places and the wrong ones—it's always only in hind-sight that we realize what's right and what's wrong—they want to get something out of there, if it's the graves, they are down there already, they don't have to be dug. Men had to swallow their pride there, but we are not going to do that, we will be proud of course, of our sins, our nature. So they have something to talk about, those who came after, those born after, born to come after us, who are coming after us. So they have something to shut up about. Or so they can bad-mouth us once again, they don't need messengers for that, everyone bad-mouths us, even radio and television, and we ourselves worst-mouth us, no one can stop us, no one can top us. It is just so unjust that the others even want to try, that they are after us with a vengeance; they want to undermine our repentance! While those men remain unavenged, unbelievable!, absolutely unavenged, to this day. And now, of all people, those bands of fast-talking pavement pounders!, I mean, as soon as they start running, they stick pounds of Band-Aid around their heels and toes, because they are so sensitive, those born after, some put on the Band-Aid even sooner, before they join the race, so they won't get sore during the historic run, which serves the memory of what has passed—and no one knows what that's supposed to be—that's why it has passed, simple as that, without anyone stopping it; well, it wasn't all that simple, what did I want to say, we were told there'll be a party, people will be shot, but then off we go!, the castle also has to go, luckily the bank is somewhere else. Those are not cattle, those are men who took off everything, like animals, who, nevertheless, took off to serve us as nourishment, now they just have to be skinned, I mean skimmed off the present, off the premises, no, we don't eat human flesh, not yet in any case, we bury them, maybe that will make them more tender and easier to chew, and then they fall, like grazing cattle into our arms, no, into our unarmed hands, yes, we do this with our bare hands, no, we got our fire arms, what did I want to say, no one escapes our tearing apart and blowing up and hollowing out and digging out or—how shall I put it?—as a messenger I should know, I should be able to instantly distinguish, in principle, the different ways of death, I should have learned that in math class, I mean, in messenger class, what's a hidden variable and what's in plain sight, or how to ascertain the root and how it looks above ground, well, here we see an undernourished man (that's the difference to a calf, the difference between a man and a calf, the calf gets fed; those 180 men, however, did not get fed), a man in his fleshly wrap, yes, made of flesh and blood, as ordered, a victim should be alive before it is sacrificed and killed, not much flesh, more blood, we see us tearing apart the chosen one, I mean, the one we picked, we picked up and tore apart with our strong arms, with our powerful fire arms, whatever; we see limbs mangled, ribs ripped out, feet unprotected by split hoofs, unfortunately, and then thrown into the ditch they dug for themselves, and they dug and dug and dug. Those old bones won't tell your story,! I must give the lie to the old song, I wouldn't be a good messenger if I didn't, things would forever stay the same, one wouldn't have to listen to new old songs, wounds would be produced as usual. Okay. We are ready. This bullet drives into the flesh, let it drive, for all I care, it doesn't have to walk like some poor messengers, and that one over there, that bullet has a driver's license, its energy is measured in joule, the mass of the projectile in kilograms and the muzzle velocity in m/s. However, the calculated energy value is nothing to cheer about, I mean, it doesn't tell us anything about a projectile's impact (something is written here, which I can't copy on my computer, it is a v with a lowered zero next to it, are they talking about me, a zero at a lowered price? But my prize has gone up, though no one seems to notice. Strange . . .), anyway, we are talking about a projectile's impact over a certain distance, since the bullet loses speed as it is flying, right?, or about its stopping power or about its impact on us as targets ironclad as we are against everything, in other words, we are not targets to get something out of, targets usually have it coming, and without those data we have no information, all I know is the number one 180, that can be a lot or a little, it all depends . . ., it's not up to the messenger to provide information, although: no one will have seen it except myself as one of several messengers who came a long way, from very far away, one who won't make it much further. So I'll stop here. I certainly will not cast the first stone, it might come back at me; I can run pretty fast, but I might not make it all the way out when push comes to shove. I might get lost and they kill anyone who knows anything; the rest they killed already. That's what everyone thinks around here. Ask anyone. First die, then talk. I think the servants also keep their mouths shut, they know, and they have to keep mum. We keep even mummer, well, okay, they keep painters, because their products are worth something, they'd also keep mummers if they knew any, but they just don't keep company with mummers, those SS gentlemen, and they are not a steamship crew, those guys are a special sort of mummers, assigned to guard their troupes and also their mom, who's quite a trouper, because their honor is loyalty. Therefore mum was also the word for their surprise party and the fire they lit for special effects and for a special purpose: so that the Russians won't find a thing, not even the house. That sparked off some excitement. I'd love to have that much fire in me. The Russians will find the graves and they will immediately cover them up again. A little later no more graves will be found. Soon the castle itself will give off sparks of fire. We find nothing special about that and whatever we find in the castle, we take, so the Russians won't find it. Nor will they find the countess and her loyal entourage. All they'll find is the ruin of the castle. If you can make millions disappear, a few saps here and there won't make a difference. They aren't from here anyway, as we always were told by our *Gauleiter*, our governor, that peaceful, friendly man, who was not so stupid to drop dead too soon, he'd rather die much later and in his own bed. And what does his wife have to say? She says they shouldn't dig forever for the goners, but for the gold, which those men had buried earlier, so of course they had to follow it, as they did not want to part with it. They cling to their gold, everyone knows that. The Jew and his money, that's an indivisible unit. Where there are Jews, there is gold, any gold, all the gold. Even though it is unsanitary to decompose next to one's gold. Well, it won't hurt the gold. And they kept digging and digging and digging. But that's none of my business, I am only the messenger of what has happened in the past and though I can see what will happen, I am not telling, and you'll want to hear something completely different about the past, let me tell you, talk to you later. They will spin it in such a way that they are repenting and atoning, but that they will also have been allowed to take pride in being able to be proud and guilty. We are proving herewith that the past is the present, until the present is once again the past, and then—yes, you guessed it—once again the same as the future, which will then again be the present. What else can I say? An advance messenger of the future will call you shortly, please turn on your voicemail in case you don't want to have been here when this messenger will foretell you the future, which, strictly speaking, he doesn't have to do, as it will be both the present and the past. If, however, you have time to wait at least three hours to get to listen to this kind of thing, press the pound key, followed by a "1," now. Then wait those three hours, then press, upon request, the respective number. Feel free to choose one you like.

Here now the voice of another messenger, who came from even farther away and might not ever get away from here again. You already turned off the buzzer, thank you, I am ready. Ladies and gentlemen, please stop the shooting for just one moment, I know you are having so much fun, but men—the most courageous among animals—must first prepare the ground for other, less courageous animals, who don't dare to go all the way to the abyss. That's no abyss, that's just a grave!, that's ridiculous, not even six feet under, umpteen millions are already in there, well, maybe not exactly in this one but in another, in several others, in many others, but all the same, they are there, even if not in this one, not to worry, they all fit in, do not push, please! Kindly wait until we are ready, then press One for Yes, for No please press Two. Wait you must, no getting around that. First those ditches must be dug, since they can't do abysses, so that our great guys, our blue bloods, no, those are elsewhere, I mean our native blue party boys, the real freedom fighters, with their seeing eyes and blind weapons, no, the other way around, their blind eyes and seeing weapons, whatever, anyway, so our guys can party with God and Fatherland, whoever may be their God of the day, well, everyone knows who that is, except those men, who might not know until they finally start firing, those gorgeous hunks plus one dame, who is a real lady and loaded, with her husband, all of them creatures who can't be recreated, there is nothing to match their greatness, their creator would have to be greater than they and they venture into the thickest, most tangled woods, where only poets dare to go, but then they still don't know why, they know nothing; and with such bitterness in their hearts, these special people who carry their pain—which, however, they did not feel back then, because they were too young back then, yes, in those days, it was a pain they had to experience, unknowingly, unconsciously, like happy islands in a dump of rags—and with such bitter memories they would become, no, they will have been allowed to become, in the afternoon of their lives, bookkeepers or mail carriers or teachers or physicians. Those are also nice professions after all. Those people are also needed; yes, they are still needed. The dead, of course, are no longer needed but the others are, they are still alive, so we can be kneaded to rise with remorse and take pride in ourselves again, at least as much as we once did. Doctors, for example, may practice for a very long time; forty years later they are still searching for them, for 50K or so, that's not even worth it, we used to clean up a lot more, and still it vanished again in thin air, like Atlantis in the sea! Such an old doctor could never practice the kind of murder he was trained for! He is totally harmless now! He retired a long time ago! Government, keep your money! Murderer and doctor, doctor and murderer, Dr. Jekyll and Mr. Hyde: tried both—no comparison! In the evening we often got together for a couple of beers, in unmixed company, definitely not mixed, we made sure of that; it was not mixed with Watusis but with what? Doozies?, what Doozies?, peoples, with what other peoples?, the messenger observes: Here is one and there are more over there, ducking in the public square, giving themselves to men to satisfy their lust, yes, this is how wealthy these people are, they can just spread their lust, such wealth of gorgeous—whatever, so they can stuff their pits real good, even if not with their best stuff. It sticks. So do we. We stick to our plan. Otherwise the work would go on piecemeal forever. While we still have to take care of roughly two hundred pieces, but not before we take them out first, before they can resist their pretty cramped accommodations. I don't know what's more work, surely the digging of the graves, I mean, of course, the gravel pits, we let them take care of them, naturally, since their doomed heads got into our hands. Why shouldn't we get something out of it too? There is no more room in the house, but those filthy men just tore up the grounds outside and now they are dying for a shower. Digging holes like crazy, digging and digging. What sense does it make to dig if the hole cannot be found again? Whatever. The holes are done now, we are not done yet, we let those who need the holes do the digging. That's what they came for. That's how we all can come clean. That's where they should go, don't you think so? But this isn't how it goes. They could also skin them and tie their pelts around their bodies while they are at it, before those animals are buried, for they are no longer humans. They are not human anymore. They won't become human again. We would bury humans too, but only if we don't need them anymore. Or if they leave us voluntarily. Really? Already? What else do you want? It all works out! We don't need them anymore and they can't go on anymore, so we play into each other's hands. It works out perfectly! Of course, the messenger is only reporting, he must not interfere when the wise old goat songs fill the air and the old wisecrackers crumble all over the beds, so one can't sleep in them anymore. I overheard my colleague say to the man who would be the first to fall into the ditch he dug: Stranger, not on my own account I take you, but at the behest of another. Those were the days when people could still count on one another, and were held accountable, for who would protect us if we meet misfortune. There you go! Someone has to take responsibility. Freedom in a blasphemer's hand is unpleasant but necessary; otherwise one gets over-whelmed by fear and thrown into a dungeon's desolate dark-ness. But no matter where one gets thrown, the main thing is to be in, at long last. No, it's always better to push the oth-ers in while we stay out forever. We must get all hands used to weapons; we must get all water used to showers for even water wants to shoot out once in a while for our own good. My colleague had the full understanding of his victims. It was an order, after all! But others who were rounded up have disappeared I hear, footloose and fancy-free, they simply swarmed off, whatever, in any case they are gone. First I saw them, then once again and then never again. Probably following their God, whoever that may be, makes no difference, he is that he is, no matter what. Speaks but one word and breaks. But he isn't saying anything. Please stop for a moment saying nothing! It's also too early to shoot! You may do it later! Yes, I'm telling you! I'll give you the signal, don't worry; as for you, just give me a small sign of your impatience, please. I am the one to give the signal! The messenger thinks: Must not what *can* happen of all things, have happened, been done, run by before?

Now the following: You can see for yourself that they have gone mad. Nothing can be done about it now. Just as nothing can be done about the sun rising and setting. It is a force of nature, you better believe it! All we need now are choruses of women at the foot of the mountains. But the countess alone makes no chorus. Still, she is welcome to sing along, until a hot fire bursts from her, brighter than a thousand suns, no, sorry, wrong play, brighter than a forty-watt light bulb is what I mean. The countess will not be sleeping tonight. No way will she let slumber dissolve her; resting her head on boughs of fir, she cocks the trigger shouting for joy; she shouts some more and aims and shoots. And shoots. I warn her not to hurt herself. When it's all over, it won't have happened that way—that she herself was also shooting, don't worry! When it's all over, we messengers will make sure it didn't happen that way! We will contradict one another, some will say nothing, but without us you would know nothing, without the others you would know more, so be glad you don't know, at least not from us, but from others: that the countess was here at all, because soon she'll be gone again. And then all threads of life will have been neatly cut.

Rubbing the bloom of soft sleep from her eyes, without a moment's hesitation she forsook sleep, ignored constraint, statute, necessity and consequence and purpose and will and good and evil and drank 'til everyone dropped, danced right over dead bodies, because for the sake of this lightest being of all, the hard part had to be done and faced too, yes, the hard and the grave are part of it, so she started to shoot, the countess, the reports contradict each other already, what's going to happen next, and, most importantly, to whom? And she kept shooting, the countess, bang, bang, she shot them down, and she shot and shot, or did she not shoot at all? Did she just shoot off from the castle? And we confused it with her usual freewheeling antics and our far-fetching semantics (remember now, we weren't there). Letting her gorgeous hair fall over her shoulder, she shot out the window, or from wherever, the men kept falling; they fall as if from far away, that's where they came from, after all. But Hungary isn't as far as it could be; it hasn't come far at all. Before she gets going, this woman straightens out her deerskin, she gets her race horses to safety, she gets her lover to safety, but only after the horses, the other lover too, of course—no, that's later, he'll come later, for now he shouldn't be so sure, the lover, of her love, and she starts shooting only after she made sure he got her drift; she only starts shooting once the horses are safe and secure, and her lovers out in the cold, in cold blood, for lack of conscience, which will also keep them in the dark, unless they are brought back so they can shoot again. *Laßt lustig die Hörner erschallen*, let your horns sound merrily, no, we do it without horns, the count got the horns, we do it without the horns and the goo, I mean ado, come now! *Jetzt auf! In Bergen und Klüften tobt morgen der freudige Krieg!* In mountains and ravines the gay ole war will rage in the morning, but today we'll have a gay ole time, we

don't want to keep these decomposing men, these compost-
ing men, *die hohlen Männer,* the hollow men in the dark any
longer, because they won't see the light one way or another;
they will never see it, the light of day, that's for sure; they'll
never find it, their shed, in the light of day; nothing to shed
light on what happened that night; though we looked everywhere, we found nothing; not a shred of evidence, least of
all in our conscience, because it wasn't us. How often do I
have to say it: We only report. The countess frowned.
Everything she could behold was a prize for her sure barrel.
Evenings she brought home a rich bag and, as if about her
good luck, surely threatening to the killer, her loving gaze
lit up—something like that. Like out of an opera. When dusk
falls gray again, and horror once again breaks through the
dawn of day, now for the second time, shall echo, cliffs and
gorge resound, just a moment, we start in the morning, keep
going through the day and throughout the night and then
we stop, so we better say: in the morning gray, no one but
us will see the dawn of day. And then it dawns on the countess she needs a break from the horror; she'd be much better
off some other place, Switzerland would be much better.
There she would not be chastened by humility; she would
not be chastised by mediocrity, no one would intimidate her
there; she could show her hot-blooded self, that's even
required there. She must have the master's proudly domi-
neering mind, as we must have the messenger's sinfully
proud mind, but they won't let us have it, they only let us
have it. All they let us mind is our report, which must be
mindless. All in all, it makes no sense, but we don't mind.

It doesn't have to make sense. She has to have some sense,
the countess. But who cares! The sense of it must be her

being there. That must do. That must be it. That much time is a must. Once everyone is gone, there is no reason for her to have been there. She girds her evening gown with snakes or whatever it is, looks like snakes, doesn't fuck around for the dappled fleece of some wild beast, she'll shoot humans right away, just a moment, yes, ready, now! She jumps for joy, waves only to the leaves, a lover's salute to the leaves. No dark powers ensnare her, no despair takes hold of her, no taunts torture her, and not one single ray of light pierces the night, only the spray of gunshots, does fate rule blindly here? No, we look through the finder, we look through field glasses, but there is nothing left to find, the victims were pushed directly in front of our rifles and pistols, is there no living God? This question I can answer with an unequivocal no. She is quick-tempered, this countess, she wants to do nothing, nothing big, nothing small, just nothing at all, but here she goes; nothing going on so far, but soon, soon you will see how it goes; the going is good; it seems like it's going all on its own, white legs kicking, getting down and dirty and bingo, for her it's a cinch, she is used to it from hunting, long walks in the dusk, no, the urge hasn't come yet, not one of us had it, the urge to report any of it. The messenger keeps silent. Other messengers will tell, but no one will believe them. No one will report that. No messenger around when one is needed. Period. Valid in perpetuity, as of today. But where is pride of sin to come from, if no one knows about it? It comes from deep down inside us, I think. It is something very deep. Those ditches are nothing by comparison. I am to report there are places where there is nothing to risk and everything to win. So they made it from Switzerland to this place and back again, as a colleague already told you earlier, no, I'd say they made out good, I've heard one can escape taxation as well as annexation, no *Anschluss* for

Switzerland. Switzerland is not a joiner. It doesn't shoot, it rather shuts out, anything under 100K, but it does not sell out. It rather sits it out, all by itself. Business needs calm so it can grow, so, hush, little baby bunting, Daddy's gonna hunting. In Switzerland, money sleeps, that slow spider: it only moves when new prey approaches, in which case it moves very quickly. Money also sleeps in Frankfurt, Berlin, New York, and so on, no matter in what bed, it can sleep anywhere, undisturbed, while everyone else is gone or dead, or wounded so badly, that the money no longer belongs to anyone, there is no one left to protect it. Now the banking laws must protect the money. Sleep in heavenly peace, my dear money, which goes through thick and thin with me, if necessary. But you can't call that sleeping, for in order to multiply, all concerned must be alert, that's been proven, for the prudent passion of the propertied bursts out of them, it bursts into laughter, it laughs and laughs, such passion does not climb every mountain, it mounts its own mounts of climbing amounts in vaults where it vaults higher and higher without hitting the ceiling. Such passion isn't resting, it is arresting. And then, before you know it, the bank's wide wings are closed again; that sounds harsh. You'd never have guessed they were open for everything coming their way. Up to anything. Pleasure and innocence are the most shamefaced things, they like to hide: you shouldn't be looking for either, for when they are found, they only get in the way. One should have both, but not look for them. One should look for guilt and pain, but not for pleasure and innocence. Those about to perish should be loved, but they no longer notice. A train arrives, a ship is coming and then the door closes again. And the moon arches behind the apple orchard in full bloom, in dead silence, above the house, it stood still just a moment ago, now it is gone, the whole castle burnt down, it burnt for a long time, now it is gone, it is some place else, in the Ticino, no, that's the villa, of course, the favorite, fortune's darling, still standing strong today, beaming in the boom, well, anyway, here's our message: The castle is big, and now it's no longer, can we agree to that? You save me a lot of messaging if we can, so there it stood, the castle, which many wanted to enter, but weren't allowed to, while others did not want to, but were forced to, hurry on, into the cellar, into the shed, the stable, where they live, the hollow men, there it stood, the castle, standing around the men, idly, well, now it doesn't stand anymore, it stood still, as if it were property, which it was, in principle, because principal is property, the countess's. Her family bought it for her, so now it is her property. This family buys a lot and loves it. The only limit would be weight, art, however, isn't bought by weight, but rather by its weightiness. Though if they can get it, they also buy the lighter stuff. That's history's lesson: carry no weight at the right time! The dog stands frozen in horror, where he had been standing before, quiet as the castle; reduced to a pile of embers, it no longer appears to be property; the dog responds to the name Nero and waits for the command Nero, he obeys no other commands; and the sky is bright as day from the fire, but, if you ask me, I didn't see it myself, and as a proper messenger, who always has the proper answer and refuses to correct himself—let others do that—, I cannot attest to it, so if you ask me, if you keep asking me that way, I will say: nothing. If you ask me another way, I will say: They set the fire themselves, according to that Nero command, a decree thought up by dogs for dogs, which I first understood as an order meant just for dogs, yes, that's how I understood it, I am sorry, animals only listen to such short, clipped orders. Commands tailored to them, as it were. We messengers understand more complicated assignments as well. Poor Nero gets abused so badly, all he ever did was play the guitar and sing. If he could walk on water, he would have jumped into the river and kept singing. Animals—they only understand this sort of command. Go get'em. I sort of understand it, though I can't quite get it. But I want to be guilty and proud of it.

Okay, I heard there are so-called close seasons, there's no shooting then. *Laßt irre Hunde heulen um ihres Herren Haus*—Let mad dogs howl outside their master's house—, because it's gone, but don't leave the house to anyone else. The house knows no close season, no matter how big it is, it just goes, whenever it wants to, it goes up in flames, for example, or it goes someplace else; how nice when a man gets fired up by his work, the same goes for castles, of course. Here there are no laws against shooting, and if there were, they would apply to animals only. Someone lost his mind here, another one over there, and there yet another; luckily, they could tie up the rest of them, before they also start looking for meaning. No; to answer your question: There is of course no close season for those animals. For other animals there is, they will be protected from close calls. So you will soon reside in the Alps—in Switzerland; very interesting, and you'll be much better off there than here? That's what I thought! The count wants me to tell you, other alps don't really interest him, as they are partly in enemy land, in the enemy's hand, and you never can tell what will become of that enemy, maybe a friend and a friend's land, let's wait and see, we have time, the money is getting bored, but still, let's wait, who knows, yes, who knows how long it will be until it is a friend's land again. I don't think it will happen in record time. It will take quite a while. But they already live here, those friends, in the castle, out of their minds, blowing their minds to the sound of flutes, smelling of incense and flowing like milk out of the earth or isn't it milk? What then is pouring out of the ground; did you discover a spring of champagne?, bet you can market it in fifty years at the latest? But for now leave us alone. After they are tapped, the champagne supplies will last for at least one year. Or rather, they would last. They wouldn't do for us, but they'd do for the well-to-do, who are restless and don't stay anywhere for long. When they go away, the champagne simply starts flowing somewhere else. I understand. The last supplies must be used up, before this house, this castle with its holy wines and holed-up men, the cavemen, who are the hollow men, caving in, heads in pieces stuffed with straw, goes up in flames. Straw burns so fast, so festive. What a shame! Their dried voices when they whisper together are quiet and as wind in dry grass or broken glass or rats feet paralyzed in our dry cellar they are meaningless. We already contemplated, translated and communicated all of that! We delivered the message of the hollow men; there is nothing more to deliver. In the cellar. Yes, those cave men, the hollow men, right there, in the cellar, at least until the fire was lit, but by then they were already gone; where there's no cellar, there's no way, where there's no will, just get away, away, away! Up, up and away! Attaway!

One is often lonelier in twos than by oneself, so let's stuff a few more people into the car, is that a Daimler? Already taken, sir, take the boxcar we were kind enough to assign to you! No, no one's left in the cellar. None of the lost violent souls is still present in the cellar. The car is present, but not for long. We must go. I have to look in the back to see what I got myself into up front.

At some point there will be nothing but such hollow men, but right now they are all gone. You can't get them anymore. And we won't get a new supply. Shape without form, shape without color, paralyzed force, gesture without motion; let's go, guys, now! Wow! I am surprised, I say let's go and they are really gone. Well, from now on I won't say a word, or I run the risk—as a messenger I do enough running already— I run the risk of finding a lot of that musty straw in my own mug again, though I never lost it, my sweaty old mug. I just went off the wagon for a bit, when the train went off the tracks. The straw could have rubbed off on me with its licking flames, I could have been burnt by its red hot zeal. Therefore I better hold my tongue, my licking tongue. Yes, and we will also unload the train. We must take the time it takes to make it pass quicker for those people. To make them pass quicker. Whether one knows guys like me will certainly depend on one's own value system and sensibility with regard to such things. I can think of a lot of people, who would never think about things like that. Therefore I won't either. Every messenger knows when to keep silent. That's what he learned. That's what he learned in this country. In this country we are leak proof, everything is leak proof, even the cesspits, at least that's the regulation, so that agriculture can hold its water a bit longer, we have no sewage system here, we once had a cellar, but no sewer, never a sewage system. So, to protect the environment from our exhaust gases, those cesspits, where we dump everything, have such perfectly sealed foundations. No outside grants for our artists, we got them all in there. Haven't you already heard my stories from another messenger? Well, I would never believe this story if someone else had told me, and no one ever tells the truth anyway. Who then will tell what can't be true. The messenger! The last resort for the momentous power of truth. Exactly! The one you depend on in this regard. Please wait; your messenger will be dispatched to you shortly. He is the one surrounded by jugs filled to the brim, but none for him; he is the one they say "was abroad," if he returns and talks; he is the one, who takes precautions, returns them and turns out more and more nonsense, the messenger I mean, before I even know what he means, is the one who saw with his own eyes how they prepared, on the eve of Palm Sunday, with blood sausage and shots of schnapps for the slaughter to come, at a party thrown by the countess to which she invited between thirty and forty intrepid guests. No, not us, we are only the messengers who had been ordered, but not picked up, ordered but returned again; the local secret police, the registered party youth and the youth-club youth with or without clubs have already arrived. They are already smeared with blood, the clubs. The messenger is the one who reports, that among them are the organizations heavy hitlers, uhm hitters, the stars of the storming squads, the SS, the aces of the race with nothing to relay, whose honor would be loyalty (*jawohl: Meine Ehre bleibt die Treue*), if they knew what that is and when they all became disloyal they still remained loyal to the club, swinging their fists, roaring like animals, riding the subway to the suburb in the west, where I live, unfortunately. Accosting foreign passengers, they keep rolling along, the train rolls out of the station, that's part of the deal, the messenger shouldn't leave before it arrives, he is supposed to be objective, but he is a bit high strung and sometimes twists the arm of fate not to wrap strings around his neck before he can wrap it all up tight himself, Ur-Mother Eartha put her coils of string around his wrists to wind into balls and spin a fate; the balls of the future dangling on Ur mom's strings; the future stranglers tangled up in—what shall I call it—fatal spin—wrapped up so tightly that no one can disentangle it and at that point our entanglement becomes simply impossible but not simple—he knocks them down now, the messenger, he cuts them up, the strings, fate's yarn, the ropes of fate, he struggles, he kicks his legs in his fashionably loose trousers held up by fate's belt which had been much tighter before. The messenger testifies that the party lasted from 9 p.m. until early morning, so what I just told you was wrong again, like so many times before, because I thought that the party had started in the morning and ended only at the end of the following night, no wonder I never get invited. It doesn't matter. And so they kept going and going and going, until the 29th or rather the 30th of March of the same year, in which they had encountered surprisingly little resistance, which did not counter their kicks and punches, the messenger could not see it so well, while I saw and even heard it quite clearly, just before the last stop Vienna-Hütteldorf was called, my station, but not only mine, called by an invisible voice, who was calling me here?, I am following you!, by a recorded voice, not my voice or was it the conductor's voice? The messenger confirms that the party lasted from nine pm until the early morning hours, so what I just told you was wrong again, like so many times before; I thought the party started in the morning and ended only after the following night, no wonder I never get invited, so here I am, with the wrong ticket, which I had to pay for myself!, and nothing is about to happen; they say I should come again the next morning; meanwhile, downtown the brittle bones are trembling—oh yes, *Es zittern die morschen*

Knochen—and also the glassy eyes of those duds, such inno-
cents, who looked at us so dearly and were so dear to us, but
they could no longer see. There was nothing to loose, now
they know it, because they had lost everything long ago, and
the rest better get lost, for the only thing they were allowed
to do was lose. And so it happened that there were only losers. Everyone a loser except us. You get our message, but you
have no faith? So you lost your faith? If you lost face, you
don't want to face us. So you can't hear us. So what.

No, that doesn't sound right. Obsessed with the God of
Destiny, no, possessed by the God of ecstasy, people don't listen to us messengers anymore, we talk and we talk, foaming
at the mouth, no one listens to us, though we got it right,
they gave us the right instruments, everything sounds right,
pure and true, so then, obsessed with the God of Destiny
they won't hear a thing. Those obsessed with their possessions, I mean possessed by the God of Destiny, no one takes
anything away from them. One reports about them. If anything were taken away from them, there would be nothing
to report. They would be nothing. They would look for
cover, though they would have nothing to cover up, we
would have our hands full recovering them, uncovering
them, we would have nothing to cover. They have no coverage, but they have deeds and things that happened and now
they happen to go to Switzerland. And that is indeed the
destiny this God had planned for them: they should become
the objects of our explanatory and interpretative investigations, but the messenger interprets nothing. That's your
problem. You have to get on top of that problem. You have
to stay on top.

Listen, everyone stay together now, don't anyone run away. Don't anyone carry off an arm, a leg, shoes, don't anyone tear out any ribs and run off with them! All of it belongs together and stays together! The hollow men still look quite alive, as if they still held on to our forceful breath, but that can't be, they have long lost hold of themselves, and they have nothing to hold out for, and now, everyone of us, yes, everyone will throw their limbs about like balls, and those too, yes, that's what we are going to do right now. It's really quite superfluous, they are already almost fluid, we shot through them so many times, but that's what we will do now. And if we had to put them in a container so they won't come apart completely. And it's just a rumor that the countess impaled the head of one of those holed up men she shot on a stick and brought it back like a wild beast's head. I should know! She wouldn't be so stupid to bring such a grisly prize triumphantly—to Switzerland of all places, where only money walks on foot, because there is too much of it, because it is too much for it just lying around, it wants to get some exercise, it wants to fuck, maybe it will multiply without having to work. Well, at the border at the latest, nothing unexpected will happen to them; they'll happily cross the border, unsuspected, uninspected, the countess and her two men, those big children, who want to have fun and always had their cake and ate it too; as long as they won't get inspected, nothing will happen; how long and where they expect to stay as long as everything is still up in the air;—what?, everything gone up in thin air?—,whether and where they will prospect without inspection, I don't know. That little bit of booty, a man's head, my ass; with direct eyes, to death's other *Reich*, no, kingdom, what do you want, they are already there, remember us—if at all—not as lost violent souls, but only as *hohle Männer, Ausgestopfte, ja?*, no, wrong translation, so what, no one remembers. At the Swiss border, at the latest, she would have had to give up the head for sure, they would have confiscated it. They would have confiscated her trophy, even if she told them it was a golf trophy. The import of hollow men and stuffed heads is prohibited. Only the import of money is permitted, but that's already there anyway. And her hunting buddies, the leaders of the *Sturm*, those two gentlemen in the car with her, whom she took along, whom she treated with a trip to Switzerland, so they can't say anything in Germany, so they can't talk in Germany, only abroad, those horny, I mean stormy men blowing their horns after they blew the heads off those holed-up men, all those hollow men, just what a storm does to thunderheads, that's its job, so it will clear up again, so we'll be clearheaded again, so we can be heady and horny as before, and headhunt as before, what did I want to say? So then, her hunting buddies who made her catch such a success, the victors, no, the losers now, no, later the victors, winners in the long run, even if it should take some time, they avoid all sights of awful sorrow and take an apartment in Switzerland. One of them lives in an apartment above a bar in Lugano, Switzerland. The other: don't know, but there surely must still be some who know where he lived, when he was still a loser. As a winner he looked for another place, but winners don't look like him, so no one recognized him. Because all this time we were looking for a winner. But I am getting ahead of myself, since I can't see anything from where I stand. I am not allowed to say anything. Tough for a messenger. He runs and runs, he is running out of time, time will tell, but now he is not allowed to tell what he has been trained for. He is trained to tell our dear old tales, which tell of our trespasses. We can be proud, regardless of what. So there is the countess and where she is, is Switzerland or a stud farm near Bad Homburg or some other spa to purify the blood, but that comes later. It'll come, but we are not coming anymore. Straw makes a better bed than good old Mother Earth, but we don't need the straw, not for stuffing and not for comfort rest. The hollow men are gone. They don't need anything anymore, thank you very much. Pudency and pious awe of the sacred, no matter how loudly the sacred screams, was not their thing, those being the hollow men, who are *die Ausgestopften*, though without a doubt those qualities, I repeat, pudency and piety mark the most beautiful and also the wisest of mortals.

Okay, so let her keep silent, the countess. Silent night, all is calm, and she is bright. She is silent in Switzerland, she is silent in Germany, she is silent in England, she is silent in Hungary, and she is silly rich, which keeps everyone silent. Or whatever.

Soon the dark firs' shadows will fall on the burnt out castle's roofless cave. Soon nothing will fall anymore, for the castle itself will have completely fallen apart. Not a bad idea, come to think of it. There—those naked men—we can handle them, they're only two hundred or so, we don't need dark rooms for them, no one talks about them, there are no photographs of them, there are no names; no faces, no names. You think, at least there must be names?, even though there is no light; no light, no photograph; what they also do is die, they do it in the dark, in the darkest dark, silently, no point to get into it now, there is nothing to get out of it either, no car has to carry them into the woods, the way one of us will be carried off, and some others as well, those men can still walk on their own, but not for long. Just a bit further. That's all. They are lucky, they don't have to line up for hours in front of the dark room, you can still see the dark frame here in this photo, it was shot exactly through this opening here, but there was shooting all the time, line up here please; no, please!, here they line up to hand in their clothes and their lives, one after the other. You know what I mean. Later, they'll move into the light once more, but they won't be seen then. They won't see the light anymore either. And they are not allowed to sit among the reveling women, but neither will they have to see all those bodies, writhing, gagging, like young shepherds, twitching, their faces distorted, so many of them, their tongues hanging black and heavy from their mouths. We don't have to see the pale dread in their faces and we may believe, that technically speaking, such things can't be possible. Such belief comes easier than believing in God. So, every one of them has his tongue hanging out of his mouth, naked as they all are, with black tongues, like snakes, hanging from their mouths, they tear at the snakes, they tear each other's tongues out of their mouths, the snakes, they must be sleeping not to notice!, so the hands are tearing at the tongues, there is writhing and gagging all around, they tear and they tear, but the tongues won't tear, it doesn't work. Then it cries out of the earth: Bite! Bite! But the tongue-snake is no longer alive, the head sticks stiff inside the throat, no, the slit, no, the throat, now I can see it, the throat's been slit; bite, bite off the head! a scream slips out from the depths of the messenger's heart, you better believe me! anyone who saw such things could never put the boot in anyone again, he could boot no one ever off a boat that was too full; but no one saw it. No one. No one. No one. And those who saw it are some place else today and proud of it to boot, though they are sinners and guilty somehow, I don't know how. Please consider this incident unseen. What you actually saw is not the truth. The people were told they will take a shower, but then it happened the other way around: the people are waiting in front of a shower room, which isn't one, which is too small for so many, the people are waiting in front of a dressing room—a chamber, all the clothes go in there, not out, the people also go in, but not out, what did I want to say, you saw it the other way around in the movie: the people wait for the chamber, those poor people, as even their guard himself called them, I heard it myself, with my own ears, that's the only ones I got, but there was nothing personal or embarrassing, even though all the women were naked as they were waiting in front of the chamber, the women already undressed—the men will go in later—waiting for the chamber, which really is a shower. Since that's not possible, it didn't happen, therefore I didn't put much effort into my report. It's all about nothing anyway, this report.

I saw it with my own eyes, at least I think they were my own, there were so many!, and later there were none, I saw it myself and I also heard how those men were moved to the castle, while none of the guests and none of the servants from the village and none of the rangers in the forest and none of the lilies in the field were moved at all, only those assigned to it were moved inside the pelt of their humility, what else should they have done? What else could they have done? Those with black tongues in their mouths, with snakes in their mouth; who is the shepherd who is yet to come one day? Well, I do know the lord who is my shepherd. But who is the shepherd with the tongue snake, no, the snake tongue, no, the fire and then the heaviest, blackest stuff hanging from his mouth? As a messenger I must inquire and have them spell the name because of their unmelodious pronunciation. There are many names I don't even know yet, they are unspeakable, but not unspeakably valuable, still, we are happy to learn. So then, in those chambers the black shepherds dig in and bite and bite, with a good bite, what the Black Cook has cooked and the snake spews their heads far away, not the other way around, the thinker saw that wrong, most thinkers see things wrong, because they look at only them, so they see things reversed or not at all, the guilty become innocent, the innocent guilty, because in reality the thinkers do not want to see anything, they just want to think about it, the messenger, however, revises the mess and makes sure not to mess up his message. But he didn't see, the messenger didn't see how the shepherds spit out the snakes' heads, the messenger saw nothing as usual, but he doesn't miss a beat and he goes overboard, no, not he, that's the others, he goes to mass, where he gets the message, all he does is report it, he only reports he knows nothing, but he dismisses the thinkers and he reports; that's all he does: report he is not guilty, we are not guilty, even if there are hundreds more of us, they wouldn't be guilty, because no one sees anything, there is no one there to see anything, as all of us are here, and from where we are, there is nothing to see; no, no one returns from where he could have seen anything, no one is changed by death into someone with something he can at long last laugh about, he will get the last laugh, the best laugh, I mean, he will be the best at laughing, and then he will become an adviser, somewhere, and then he will—whoever he will be, he will have been one of us—he will stretch a provisional heaven above the provisionally produced people, and then he will take a look-see if it was good, and then he will try to turn his fiction, because that's all it was, into all the facts fit to print, he did a good job piecing the facts together, yes, and he can determine, what about man is fragment, a riddle, a dreadful accident.

We can save those who wreak havoc every day by making up something about them, that's not a problem, everyone probably knows such hollow men (or women) in their own community, don't you think so? I for one know one, no, two men, that's all the men I know. And this is why it was not the way it was; it sounds hollow nowadays, it is all about the hollow men at this last of our meeting places, where we were searching together, searching for the men, fumbling, avoiding all speech; we shouldn't have done that, we should have reported, we, the messengers; because we messengers can just as well, no, even better!, save the past and reinvent, no, circumvent, no, all that was, until it is our will alone that speaks. It was, because I willed it. It happened that way, because we, the messengers wanted it that way. The messenger can also have something going for himself, something beautiful, it just shouldn't be too heavy. He who laughs last, laughs best, and that will be us, we, the messengers long for a laugh that is to come after the people will have swallowed their tongues in all their blackness. But then no laughter will come at all. They can't spit them out again, those tongues. They don't laugh, they don't even scream, or do they? It gnaws us messengers how they are unable to laugh; they don't even laugh last in a place they could win something and be winning on account of their laugh, but we are not to blame. We couldn't bear to die, but we see it every day, we see every day how that goes. We have nothing more to report. It is too dark. We could not see anything. No one could see anything. This time we have nothing to report.

Some day it will be the last time I'll be going to these people. But I've had it with them right now. They have had it long ago!

Well, I've never seen anything like it, except perhaps with different eyes, the same. The one I saw spoke: You are arrested. You are not yet humble enough. I must get you off the street; and your brake linings are worn through to the steel, you'll see what happens when you brake the next time, yes, and you definitely will hear it too, the frame is rusted through, the headlights don't work, how are you planning to drive at night, and night always falls? And the ropes that hold together the full load have two inches play and you are playing with it now, while the load flies all over the street; it could kill several people, who want to also get there, albeit after you. I must order you off the street this minute, a warning apparently won't do for you, I don't like it, but the license plates must come off right away, the vehicle is confiscated, its walls, its underside are too thin in any case, for any chase. But your humility has the toughest hide, which is not even a hide, I can see that already, you are telling me this pickup is your only source of income and if I take it away from you, you might as well shoot yourself. Well, I don't know, maybe it's like a car, your humility, waiting for an upgrade? On the other hand, if it is a car, it can't be humility. They simply don't work together. Except if you need a car for a living, then it gets tricky. As soon as anyone has a car, he gets arrogant. When his car gets inspected for damages, he becomes humble again. Humility, however, wants an undisturbed, wholesome world, while a car wants to wreck the world. Yours will do it swimmingly, if I don't confiscate it right now and get it off the road. Anyone owning a car is no longer humble, because he immediately wants a bigger one with more power. You'd be happy if you could just keep yours, I understand, and you can keep it all right, but you can't drive it anymore. A guy with a hummer like yours likes to put down others, but you can't do that anymore, though your baby put out the most, took them right out. It'll be the downfall of us all some day, the car, besides many other things right beside us, but down we go in any case, and we are not so fortunate as to have our own special chamber for it, except in the hospital if they push us into the bathroom there, because you were in a deadly crash and all other rooms are occupied. But the dying is done by others, who have more room for it. But why so soon?

The countess and her bright, manly rippers would know, in step with their *lieder* they beat all the odds and painful endings, but nothing hurts them anyway. Can something other than this car steer our next steps, please?, the car can't accomplish such a feat, instead it pulls the steps from under people's feet. The car is our ruin. It also takes away the air we breathe. Before, something else was our ruin, now, luckily, it's only the car. As a messenger I must walk and bike a lot, so I am almost always out of breath and talk too much, when the days are long and the breath is short, my word hasn't yet moved any mountains or Autobahn—we're happy we got one, finally, what would we do without it?, we'd all stand still, though we, the messengers aren't even allowed to use the Autobahn. But still we try. For the hell of it. To get the hell out. No chance. Not a single wheel would turn. And what would we do without *Kinder*? We'd all run away, because we'd be without responsibility. The present would come to an end with us. One way or the other, nothing works without, everything works without, dying works much better without clothes, because there is no extra weight.

Nonetheless, I'd still work my way to those men, completely naked, to tell them the kinds of things naked people have to tell them, a naked man has no pockets for someone to reach inside, he, on the other hand, must not hold back anything either, he has to report what he remembers, it all depends on how it all connects. If everything stood still, we would run, the clock would run, the second hand would run, everything would run by itself, but I am still not getting through to you, I am not getting anything on you, time itself doesn't get anywhere either, though the hand keeps turning and turning, as long as the battery still got juice. I am here only to report. Let me in! The boss wants me to tell you that he accepted your money. All he said was: What do you know? The dew falls on the grass, when the night is most silent.

I saw with my own eyes, how those naked men—the others, not the messengers, they wore their cycling tights, that's even better than naked, that's at least as good as naked, naked like those naked men—how those were mocked and flogged, I saw no reason for it, they had no trouble finding their way also at night, the hunter and the countess; and herded ahead of them some unemployed or unemployable or welfare cases, entitlement hunters, entitled victims, all of them are always victims, everyone dying to be one, we too, but that's not possible; not everyone can be a victim!, someone has to want to be the perpetrator, please, step forward, we need every perpetrator we can get, so we can count ourselves among them and no one would notice, we urgently need perpetrators we could join if we just tried a little harder especially once the ultimate sacrificing is over, that's their cue, the catch, time to catch on, their turn to say that the next time they definitely want to be part of it, but as perpetrators among the sacrificial victims, so they have something to regret; well, I am not quite sure whose victim they want to be this time, but when I last saw them, some other time, they were busy digging, completely off the books, of course and their employer did not register them, of course, so they can't claim any benefits; then the contractor gets sued, but not before he dissolves the company, so nothing is left. So what's left for them to do, if they can't even get the minimal wage? They just thought they finally found their own way, those illegal workers of the pits and the defense wall, quite opposite constructions, I know, but they haven't found a way, not yet, to dig their own grave, until they finally had to dig, as I said, those strange ditches. Those hollow men I saw there were no longer good for anything anyway, certainly not for work. Their legs were probably shaking, I can imagine, they shivered with fear, if they weren't too tired even for that, but I can't swear to it. So then a few shots were fired and some disappeared in the ditches, but now there weren't enough ditches, and too many people were still around, now what?, after the shots came the screams, but there's always screaming, I think it's the next group's turn to dig, please step forward, there are almost two hundred of them, 180 or so, the digging will take some time, especially with this hard ground, which produced an equally hard breed of men over the centuries, hard at work, go, go, go!, no wonder, stubborn as they are, I thought; if someone should ask me later, I'll be able to tell him: They forgot the way, now they even forgot how to walk. Forget work—they haven't been able to do that for a long time. And we even did them a favor, really; what a terrible road would have been ahead of them, had they not fallen into the ditch just in time! But I'll keep quiet for a moment, just a moment now!, even though I am a messenger and speaking really is my job. The most taciturn among men I'll be and this will be my way of speaking, but hold it now!, this is not what a messenger usually does. Even though I'd still have more to say and deliver; somebody one sent off about six pounds of dental gold and forgot the address for the next fifty, sixty, hundred years, I saw it myself; he addressed it to himself, to our stupid pride of sin, which will arrive as surely as the amen in the prayer, end of story, while he's still on the road, although the show has long been over, all on his own, a complete unknown, so I don't know anymore where he is, that messenger, that's what he called himself; everything made by him and named by him, I know, all things that happen, and those to be, I can also see: Ur-Mother Wala, Erda, warns you: Beware! Three daughters were born to you long before earth was. The things I see, the papers tell us daily, I mean: the Norns report nightly, *die nächtlichen Nornen*, no, those *EU-Normen* tell us nothing but the Richter magnitudes. Just a moment, I said Norns, *Nornen*, not *Normen*, norms, as in standards!, yes, after the weather report it's the Norns' turn, those diviners of futures, the weather report is true, the untruth comes afterwards, no, I haven't heard anything from anyone directly, maybe he kept it all for himself, all that gold, pure gold, (rein Gold), *Das Rheingold*?, Ja? as in Wagner no (as in Gold standard). Let's wait for my report, but I don't know what I should say. What I may say. I have so much to give to you, but the messenger always gets clobbered. So take off my backpack, will you?; I am a wanderer and mountain climber at heart, I do not like the plain, and it seems I can't sit still for long! Can't wait for my own self to finally come back home to me, time to get back to civilian life, without the nasty gossip, that's important to me, I am a sinner and proud of it, I don't need you to tell me that; let me tell you: That's all I have left; I can't even pay the interest they slap on me, yes, now I am talking, the messenger, who always runs ahead and talks his head off, but keeps his ass covered all the time; who reports and returns right away. And through it all I always wanted to be myself. That's important to me, since so many have been others for so long, they can't even remember themselves. It won't happen to me. I will always remember it all as the most exciting time; and remembrance is all that remains. Remembrance and love, and when it comes to love, one shouldn't be shy. There are folks, who want to drag naked men into the forest by force of arms, at least that's what I heard, but that can't be right. I still am supposed to tell you, without passing judgment. I don't see a forest. For all the foreign trees I can't see the forest. Yes, I see the pits, but no forest. They probably cut the forest for the pits. There was one, who wanted to reveal himself as God or to his God, I couldn't really tell which. Thou shalt not rob! Thou shalt not kill! Such words used to be sacred; we wouldn't need a messenger, we wouldn't need a judge, if they still were. But where in the world were there ever better robbers and killers than those sacred words? As so-called sacred words didn't they kill truth itself? No, they didn't. Haven't we admitted everything? We admit we were robbers, killers and dead-beaters, and that should do, once and for all and everyone. Now that we admitted to robbing and killing, we can finally break the old tablets with those words wrought in stone. We don't need them anymore. We can be proud of ourselves. We are *der neue Mensch*, the new man, who doesn't need tablets, he can learn these things by heart, no, he doesn't need a heart, he can commit them to memory. We are the messengers of times to come, we are the message, the media, the market and its truth. We have pity for all that's past, for the things that passed, because as messengers we are the first to see how the past is at the mercy, especially of folks like us. Every messenger tells a different story. A great despot came, but also left again, after he saw the writing on the wall that he would be gone again. Had the new time come, they couldn't have done much with their captives. So all that's passed is at our mercy now, but first we have to determine what it is. What has been done? For what purpose? It is us, after all, who have to report it. Shooting is practical. Whoever returns from the shooting will be dragged back to be slaughtered by the countess and her adjutant in person. Now, that we are at it, we aren't going to stop! Everyone gets a turn. No need to push! But we won't choose a land, where the worst of all trees grows: the cross. That land deserves no praise. It would be overshadowed forever by those trees. Only guns talk. A tree gets us nothing. A tree doesn't lead. A tree is no leader. At best a tree leads to a *Lied*, about a Lindentree.

Off to Switzerland! On we go to Switzerland! No one escapes a banking house, let alone the slaughterhouse. What says the pig, smart phone in its claw? It says: Friday? No, Friday is really bad. I'll be slaughtered on Friday. But first let's pop the champagne and then we pop some more, lets not owe anything to life! Neither money nor oneself, I mean, don't let yourself be owned by the bank. Then they can grow human capital again and bring home the bacon as beacons of culture, as if they'd never been big fat vultures; but I am getting ahead of myself, there is nothing yet to report.

Culture has not arrived yet. I check the time, the collection of paintings must be arriving now. Right! It's already here. We're already here too, but the home for it is still to come, a home for the art, a *Kunsthaus*, it's home to me, the home of Being, if you ask me; such House of Art, this *Kunsthaus* has yet to be built. To the age its art, to art its home. To the house its art and a house we shall build; in the meantime we take this one, it's also nice, all it needs is the art, which is on the way, it will be your favorite, it's a savings bank, that's where we put our money and art, first the money, then the art. No, the brother's name is not Orestes, luckily he has not passed away, he moved on, to Switzerland, where he passed that horrible time with his possessions, amassing even more, his possessions were not decimated, he did not have to be laid to rest, not even placed under surveillance, we know where he is, we know how he spends his time on the one hand, his money with the other and holds out both hands, when his deals get out of hand. No, Orestes isn't his name, this brother's name is Heinrich, Heini or something like that, he is a real pain in the you know where, though not his own, thank you, no problem. In my view he is an ass all right, but right now they are still making a lot of noise on the right, for them a party is a party and they know how to party and raise funds and hell. You can see that yourself. No need for me to tell you. The guns shoot out of the castle, all sound and fury, they frighten the horses, the whole ranch, you can hear it, you can hear them trample and bellow, you see the white of their eyes, no, you don't see it, that's just it, that's what you need me for. Or you can imagine it, if you wanted to. For God's sake! Don't! Don't frighten the horses! All right, the sound is traveling nicely now, as you can hear, so I don't have much to report. The other ladies and gentlemen, please join the dancing and dining and drinking!

I, for one. Hotel room, Capri, night, murd—, uhm, moon, stars. No, Cuba, likewise hotel room, a letter, mistakenly sent to the wrong address, messengers probably aren't trained as well there, I guess, the envelopes were exchanged, somewhere, somehow. A letter to the pope, no—the count received it, a bank statement, Banco di Roma, five-hundred-dollar dividend for a US producer of contraceptives. God's pill be done. No, that's not how it goes. God help us all. But God helps those who help themselves The pope must have misunderstood something, because he also has his lord and master, just like any old messenger. Well, maybe to help prevent an accident. It's not a lot of money, anyway. The count makes more in one hour, in one minute. I think the pope can be forgiven, however, I didn't become a messenger to think but to deliver or pass on information I received from someone else. The count told me he studied at the ETH, the Eidgenössische Technische Hochschule in Zürich and the MIT, in Cambridge, Massachusetts, nevertheless, though he would have much to tell, he won't leave his hotel room ever again. He doesn't have to. He has everything here, he has everything there, Cuban beaches, paintings, artifacts, endlessness, all the loose ends no one will ever put together; hold it now, I didn't see any of it myself, it was only reported to me; but the messenger is authorized to pass on any confidential information he received; still, his way of speaking, the baron's voice on the phone sounded pressured somehow, depressing, I was glad the connection was lost and I got off without a charge. However, the count wasn't charged, his connections were, those in charge were. Well, if you ask me, I'd rather not to be in charge, I don't have it in me. They might hold me accountable later. No. They can't. Only the housekeeping staff had access to the hotel room. No one else. The count, no, another count, no, thanks, that's enough, we have enough already, we have enough counts, too many to count them all, counts, please, stop counting on us!, so, this one lived, I mean, he lived there with wife and grown daughter, and a suitcase with SS uniform and Iron Cross safely locked inside, uniform still neatly pressed, regularly pressed even after his death, pressed to death, to keep the heat on, the uniform stiff as a coffin board, hard as a coffin nail, as if he had just nailed at least twenty people, nailed like an expert, the count, no, of, course he didn't do it himself, why do you keep asking what someone did in person?, that's been slipped to the bottom of deep cases, which can do without pressing; but the count still has to decompress after the stress of getting away with it all. What is he afraid off? There is no reason. I don't see any reason. What I see every day is hundred-plus degrees. Twelve years in Havana, in a hotel. This doesn't mean that you should do the same; you couldn't afford it anyway; you might not even have twelve years left. You wouldn't have them even if you had them handed to you, the years that were taken from others. You'd have to get to be five-hundred-something or so. You couldn't do that, with just you and your daughters, who depended on your sperm donations already before they were born, It's not so simple. You need someone to guide your steps, and you found him herewith. Unfortunately, my steps are also guided by someone else. Too bad for you! At least I already have my pacemaker. Every messenger got one. They can also be implanted, so you can't see who or what is driving the messenger. It's an electric impulse to the heart at the right time, which is good for everyone from time to time. So the three of them, the count, the countess and the daughter have each their own broker, they love playing the market and going for broke again, betting whose bets will yield the highest profit. More later. No, no more later, unfortunately we don't have the time. The time belongs to someone else now and he won't share it.

Why don't I share my report, after I went out of my way to put it together only to put it away again? I saw how one of them trembled and said: I don't want to! Then laughter surrounded him. The countess stepped in front of him with her rifle, but take a look yourself!, drunkenness works real miracles: doors and castles were built by human hand, and can be set on fire or dismantled any time, if they are dismantled they must be taken along; what?, the whole castle?, the ashes?, we must clear out, we can't clean up, no, wrong translation, *Schlösser* for locks, not castles, all the locks of the castle, *jawohl*, especially the *Schlösser* of the *Schloß* must be taken along, or someone else might find the key, the *Schlüssel* to it all; take a look yourself, which hand is falling here! Yes, this one, exactly. It wasn't secured by a castle nut. That one too. Who wouldn't like to torch some castles? Who wouldn't like to catch a disease? Who wouldn't like to pull the plug from the drip of time? So, time has run out now. This is how it works with water: it either floods everything and you can't see anything anymore, or it disappears without a trace, just like time. Then everything rots. But we can't get away with just being rotten, we must first construct a solid foundation again. The fetid rot has to come out somehow, so we can live in clean, healthy air again. Look! Listen! Can you tell me please: which way to greatness? Oh, here it is, this must be it, because it's no way at all. What sort of way is this supposed to be with nothing behind and everything ahead? What? My own foot has erased the way behind me? It's gone, the way has gone away, why? You don't know? Shit! That's not the way, if one has to go it alone. Because you have been there, gone it?, or what? Because you set it up, so no one can creep after you, like gratitude, which is supposed to creep after you forever, but the moment you look away, all that creepy gratitude turns ungrateful before you know it? So now the gentlest in you must become the hardest, that's all it takes, then we don't have to take that stupid way anymore, we can shoot right through the window, the gun is still smoking in the kitchen, reloaded, ready to go. But we can also have it wrapped for takeout.

He who has spared himself much, will in the end become sick of so much consideration. Praised be what hardens. Such miracles men are able to perform, yes, and also the countess and her two minions, Messrs. P. and O., her lovers, one after the other?, next to each other?, whatever, love does not ask, she does not ask where and what, she does not ask for what is hers, it wouldn't be to her advantage, she asks: Where are P. and O. and *wo ist das Klo*, the loo, the water loo; the john!, shithead! well, I don't know, where or whether one after the other or at once; what a word, minion!, not my favorite; to begin with, no one still knows what it means! And they have to wear black uniforms. Or maybe not. Whatever. That's what comes with a queen, that breed of ver-minion, a minionair, oooh, what a thrill, one or two, better two, take two, taste two, so it goes, even as a messenger I am at a loss for words sometimes, who else would have them, if not even I can find them?, let's see, where is my list of words for messengers? The word for the messenger is that the countess stayed in the castle to enjoy the attention of the officers, to enjoy the legendary fame of an art collection, to enjoy herself, to enjoy her treasures, which, however, are someplace else, they had been moved just in time or perhaps they had always been there, no, they never were here, the art stayed in Switzerland, it didn't want to come, what would a Russian make of it?, we're not bringing our treasures, the Russians wouldn't know what to do with them, except steal them, something we Germans would never do, because we have the choice of reflection and reflex, as to how human flexors can further be flected, bent, I mean, we bend and twist everything and everyone into shape!, so then, we are the only ones in the world to turn a mental activity into action, with full force, and what would this task be? What kind of force would it take for this task? And to what end? What's the position of those we want to put into position? How are they positioned for the task? How principled are they? There it is, close to the castle, reasonably principled and with good reason, the special force, our principle of reason, the forces of unreason on their path to the pits, where the storms plunge into the sea, no, the lake, Lake Neusiedlersee, Fertő tó in Hungarian, no, sorry, that one's someplace else, but also not far, where the storms plunge into the sea and the mountain stretches out its trunk for the water, no, I beg your pardon, not there, there everyone shall have his day and night watches for the sake of character and knowledge, no, sorry, the gaining of knowledge is not the messenger's mission, it is the report's recipient's job; here, it's clearly written on the envelope, pushing it is the recipient's task; please sign here. Well, then, the collection is safe, why else would it have been collected piece by piece? For collecting means to bring to safety, which, however, is not the case with the transport of humans, where accidents happen repeatedly, and don't ask what happens then! But the art is safe, I can imagine you were worried about that; no, not at all, that's not what I am saying, the collection wouldn't tell you that either, so that it can't be torn apart again. From the very beginning this collection could develop only by realizing its own potential of self-knowledge; O God, I am talking about a totally different kind of collecting, I beg your pardon, the papers got mixed up, mine says it realized itself, by itself, through self-knowledge and self-reflection all the way to absolute self-identity. But this collection did not realize itself. It did not realize what was going on. Those shapes produced by human hand did not take shape all by themselves. They were taken from others. Collecting oneself and holding one's breath for a moment is good for all valuable objects which have to breathe, and even those who no longer need to breathe might want to think and collect themselves. Humans might find themselves, without looking, in such conditions that, in order to continue breathing, they must first bring themselves to safety. Works of art, by contrast, are required by law to be free of damage, which does not apply to human beings. This is why works of art have eternal validity; we value them much higher and longer than human beings. On my frequent assignments I come across so many who had been sorted out because there was nothing noteworthy about them and I, breathing heavily, I, airborne with flying feet, must always jump aside when I run into those people, who give off a lot of hot air and then suck up every breath of fresh air. I avoid those people, getting out of their way as fast as I can, otherwise I might get shot or beaten up or even inhaled instead of the air, no, wrong play, I jump aside as fast as I can, I throw myself in the bushes, I duck in a ditch, climb every mountain, no, no singing, please!, making myself small will do when their cars zoom by me on their way to Switzerland, at the border they will have to make a quick stop, but only a quickie, it's not yet borderless Schengenland, far from it, but almost, at least for the right people, for all others not a chance, and this land doesn't come for a song of course, one needs an ID and it better be valid and prove who one is; but then they can immediately hit the gas again. It won't take long. From here they can drive nonstop straight to Lugano for all I care. And what about me? As a poor messenger I don't have the right vehicle for the fast track, I'll quickly lose track of them, it'll take too long before I get anywhere with my heavy courier load. I'll lose the track before I found it. The track will be lost forever. The art, though, will be collected forever. What do you mean?, and anyway, what's your name?

I can take it. I better not take on too much. Ah well, so what, someone will take me: Only yesterday those ecstatic revelers amused themselves shooting crap, what?!, THE Trapp, no, sorry, this is not a musical, THAT baron was about to fire Maria, but then they got married; those other merry folk shot lightning bolts from their unconcealed weapons, they merrily rolled along, take a look!, down there, a last breath is exhaled, that's too much, so much breath wasted, vanished in thin air, air to air, just to stay alive, they even breathe used air, which we all usually avoid, they aren't picky, as long as it's air. They didn't really need it before, their breath, if you ask me, they only thought they did, and as a messenger I am an expert in breathing, you better believe it, and I am also somewhat out of breath, because I just burst out of the womb, no, from that woman's castle, the castle collapsed, ashes to ashes, but here I am now, a god, living in Switzerland, it's a tradition, the Gods always reside there when they aren't residing somewhere else—that's their address on the registration form—because they can stay there, undisturbed, among themselves; you'll see, they are all in Switzerland now, where else, huh?, so most of them have already been there before?, well, then I could have stayed there too, I didn't have to run so far. That other messenger, whom I don't know, or is he also a God?, has something to hide in his loins, I didn't see what it was, but he had to protect it from his wife, with whom he lives in a constant state of separation, no wonder, he's never at home, and he's probably living with a few others and for other reasons through various stages of separation, until he also gets too tired to go through all these separations, so this messenger has to hide from his wife what he owns, since messengers in the course of their runs across borders can amass quite a bit, but he won't get away with it, he can't hide anything from his wife, the count with his little courier, who has nothing to deliver this time, because someone else delivered, yes, the sperms are also from someone else, no, I don't know his name, but I know he is the kind who proudly boasts about his *Fang*, his catch; you mean his fang?, well, the catch here is, he cannot show it, because it is still growing; I don't get it. If his fang is still growing, how can it be stuck in his *Fang*?; you mean his catch?, I mean, if it's still growing, how can it be stuck in his catch?, didn't he bury it like gold, his fang, his *Fang*, whatever, *Fang* or fang, it's catch as catch can, so no one can find it, in any case, he made a good *Fang*. You figure it out. Well, that a bull-shaped God should come into the world, whose father is certainly not the baron but someone else, that's the way it's done here, others do the work, a certain count is supposed to be the real father, but it's only a rumor, we don't bother with that. That the child is supposed to have a bull's head is also a rumor; messengers on principle don't deal with rumors, because they'd never stop talking, we'd still be talking today, right now, if we'd also have to pass on rumors! It simply wouldn't work. That's not how it works. And that the countess had her pillows stuffed with the hair of the killed is also just a rumor I won't deal with; and that the countess had a ladder brought to her so she could hang up the head of one of the dead she brought from the hunt—she probably found it attractive, that's also a rumor, it wouldn't have made any sense when the castle was soon to be set on fire anyway. I see and report: the countess put on bushels of ermine, a diamond necklace, diamond earrings and a diamond bracelet, not to mention the diamond ring, before lighting up a cigarette and then the whole castle; life was fun for ten years, that's enough for some people. You can tell they had a gas, and they'll be the first for sure to gas up, clean up and clear out when the Russians are coming, the blood has to go, or the car seats will get dirty, doors and windows might get dirty, or hands will get dirty if they get into the bloody mess by mistake, so let's come clean to the car and hit the gas, this way to the gas, and to hell with it all; thus end the hell-bent. Bending only to their own commandments, which they bent to fit their demands; and those, who are completely bent out of shape look for something to depend on, but they can't find it. So what! Who wants security? Run for your life! Yes, you can, you guys always can, whatever it may be. Upon request, the messenger will lead the party, his partying party into the woods, into the mountains, where perhaps the female host, no, a host of females are ready for some mounting. But for now they are still here in the ballroom. I am to tell you: Although no one can imagine how just two days before the Russians were coming this orgy could happen, without you, no, you are not on my list, sorry!, you are not on the guest list, I got the list of invitations; maybe you are on the victim list?, but that's probably not what you want to know. No one can explain so much ecstatic lust in the face of extinction. The messenger knows that the rich are different, but what he doesn't know: Different from whom?

Boundless misery! Oh shame so great no eye can bear it! Oh bloody murder by ill-fated hands! A sacrifice without compare, slaughtered for the gods, a feast to which you want to invite all of Rechnitz—I exaggerate, half of Rechnitz?, well then, a good part of it, but not the best, no doubt, one half invited as servants, the other half as other servants and myself; no, not all of Rechnitz, one part of it has to serve, the biggest part, all of Rechnitz has to serve, and get what they deserve, while most of us have had enough already. The rest was quickly taken out. Woe, wow, what tragedy, first yours, then mine, no, mine first, then yours! The God has destroyed us, cruelly, but, alas, cheaply, his own family, the bull-horned God, the roaring one. Well, none of it is true. I must be in the wrong play. Short applause, please! We need the blind seers in front of the TV, where you can hear lots of applause, every three minutes or so, sometimes even more often, the TV of course cannot be blind. Anyway, we can do without those scenes. Please put the TV over there, put it on low volume and see if you can get a halfway decent reception and a halfway decent sound, anything is welcome that shows those conditions, as long as they're only the good conditions, the decent and utterly just conditions, which we may finally get to know. Unlike before, this won't be a problem, now that we have a digital receiver. Before, we only had a very narrow spectrum; with HD, however, you can see everything that wasn't in the picture before. So now we can stay on our couch and out of the picture to get a much clearer picture of many things and also of where we got together by chance; don't worry, the castle will soon be freed from all specters, but new specters will come; hands will be free to get everything to safety, which isn't yet in Switzerland and the rest, what's to be done with it, what's the messengers' special word for that, which they had to first invent, which only they are allowed to use? Destroy: the rest. That's a deadly sentence. All right then: Burn the rest, but that's really all the countess told me, though I believe the castle was torched to leave no marks, but all marks were bad anyway, who would want to get those?, you'd never make it to the next grade, if anyone saw those marks. We, however, don't have to do the work, we present ourselves as a little fairy tale and they'll believe us. No need for further evidence. As a messenger I would have certainly liked to provide you with more reliable written records, but that would have made me a witness and possibly liable for prosecution, just because I might have seen what others saw and the emphasis is on others, there were others who saw what I saw, in plain sight even of the Holy See. So what do you want from me? I might not even have gotten the records, and to whom could I have given them? There's no one left. That's not possible! I need all my records for a valid ID before I can report. To deport others, one has to make a report, a mark of distinction for oneself, of extinction for others. Being a messenger proves that one's ancestry was not close enough to call, not even long distance, but far out like the countess's, or he would have come to his end, he could have never joined the race, he would never get his message across as a messenger with a goal, which must of course always come before the end, otherwise the goal would be no big deal, but in this case the goal is quite an ordeal. Without a goal, the messenger would never have anything to say and he would never land. Or he would overshoot the goal, if he doesn't see it. HE would have to have popped out of the ground or descended from a dragon, conceived thousands of years ago. Unfortunately, we messengers have been conceived by earthly humans, the hollow men, yes, that's us too, more or less; only the hollow men's hope can rise, as they are empty and weigh very little, they must be tamed tied to a rope and with a rope, but since we can't see anything in these dark holes, since we are also completely hollow and can't take in anything, since we can't take in anybody, like Switzerland, which already took in many, maybe too many, whom she didn't take a good look at; no, she didn't look into empty eyes, she looked into full eyes, hopeful eyes, but since we can't take in anyone anymore, we rose on our own and we can attest that holes have been dug into the earth of our mothers, I mean into mother earth, so we can stack humans in there, in the ground, as there is no more room above, there are mean mothers, and earth is one of them, but even mean mothers have to bury their children, but where? It's anyone's guess. In suitcases, boxes, in attics, in flower pots?, their ideas, but also their options are limited, and they certainly wouldn't want to stay there, the children of the earth, with pollution all around, those children couldn't have imagined that they'd be poisoned some day, I am to tell you this as well, in short, those children had to leave their friends!, I have no idea who these friends were. All I do is tell. I can't tell what will be, only what was, that is: how I see it, not what I saw.

As a messenger I also noticed the following along the way: one could be like a child, one could have become young too late, or old too late, one could feel shame or not when asked to undress; an old man's weariness, a woman's beauty, the insecurity of youth yet to find security, if there were time for it, could still have been inside oneself, shame or no shame, whoever would become as a child must first overcome his youth. Then laughter surrounded me, the messenger, and then shots, a laughter that could tear up one's entrails, if the shots hadn't torn them already. The countess noticed before me that the fruit is ripe, the intestines torn and the heart slit open. Her fruit was ripe, and she was as ripe for her fruit. People are constantly foaming inside, and they are ripe only after sufficient fermentation, or is it the other way around?, first ripe, then foaming fermentation?, that's when you can do something with them. The alcohol flowed freely. I saw it myself. And the countess laughed again and fled, I saw that too. I saw how she laughed before she fled. Then there was multiple stillness all around, but before that it was very loud and I didn't know what that was all about. To me, the countess looked like a servant to the ungodly godly intoxicator, while she herself drank also like a fish. No one can tell her to do something she doesn't want to do, but that's what she always does to her horses; however, this is just my personal observation, my opinion doesn't count here, an opinion has no place in a messenger's report. Instead, I was put in my place right at the door, where I was frisked for any personal opinion I might have tried to slip in, say, under my belt; and had I had one, they would have taken it before they let me in, so I wouldn't drag it inside like dirt on running shoes. But I what I was able to see with my own eyes—though I am not sure I should tell: Down in the dungeon's darkest night, the countess and her gay young men in their human ur-forms or original form as in original sin, called *un*-form, un-form by some, regarding the position, because it's the uniform that gives form to a man; but that's not what I say, I am not at liberty to speak so freely, I simply can't; I can't look ahead and behind at the same time, still, I can't see an end either way, neither in the front nor in the back and there are some who are finished, others get worked over again, how could they finish so many of them, if they weren't already completely finished themselves?, they aren't my business, those young men, in their unimportant un-form—thank you, Werner, no problem, Elfi, I am dead anyway and can do nothing about it—those men the countess likes to come on to. And if the opportunity comes up, she has the other naked men brought to her, those men she keeps locked up in the castle, one never knows when they might come in handy, all tied up inside the house, in the expansive cellar, or shed of all shame in the shed, that's all I am saying, I already mentioned the shots, more than once, probably too many times, you know all about it by now. That's all I am saying, because in the same dungeon's darkest night they already hold comrades in my line of work, messengers all, who didn't get the message, so now they are up against the wall. Countess, dear, swing yourself up to mount Olympus in Switzerland, swing your ass up there, go west!, okay, go find your vest!, but hurry now, get a move on!, I saw what happens when the Russians are coming, nothing will grow and blossom anymore, so please restrain the Russians' defiance before you can see them coming, because if you can see them, it's too late for women to bloom, there won't be any fruit or wine that year, I am afraid. No, dear, not even *Liebfrauenmilk*. But I am only the messenger. Please, don't hit me! My dad already said that and it didn't help him either.

Lords and masters this way please, next to the chorus of messengers over there, you are safe there, and you will have to shout if you want to be heard. Only the grave is quiet, forever, so quiet it will never be found. The whole village keeps quiet, the folks in the bar with their bright stare, the earth with its bright stars above at night, the lake, the sea, no, sorry, I don't mean those two, they can't be seen from there, oh, this pregnant nocturnal distress, we must do something about it! We must get down again! Deeper down into the pain than they ever descended waiting for the stag; whence come the highest mountains? When I find out, I'll order some, we can't just have them close by in Switzerland, but where else should we go? We need those mountains, so that next to them we look smaller than we are. It is war, after all, hardly anyone will stay neutral, but Switzerland does, oh yes, indeed, it does! Blackest flood, bloody flood, bloody funds flooding the banks of Switzerland! War! There is also war in Austria, land of mountains and riverbanks, run by mountebanks; it will be totally neutral later, but luckily, at least lucky for them, right now it doesn't even exist. It existed earlier, only much bigger, then much smaller, and then not at all. The long and the short of it. Small but mine. We got nothing, we give nothing. That's what it will always claim, this country, and it will have the beauty of truth, whatever it claims. Yes, and it will be the absolute truth. This is why it is the most innocent country ever, because what doesn't exist cannot sin either. Perhaps one can be born again, surely, a free Austria will be born again, rising from the ashes, but at this point I can't yet see it. The past cannot be tracked in report cards, if the student whose past it is does not even exist, or if the student misbehaved. Such tracks are inscribed or rather chiseled in Austria's rocky scenery, I mean its rocky history as a warning, lest someday it suddenly picks up a scent again and takes quick cover in case a stronger country comes along and wants to devour it. My Austria, my fatherland, what did you do to my daddy, you asshole? However, I have come to accept it. What else could I do? It took a long time, but now I can take it somehow. Even so, I am always weary when I walk through this land and ever more desperate for it than before; but since this land has existed for so long and then it no longer existed and I won't exist much longer either, and since this land does not let me be, I cannot simply walk away from it. Yes, I can, now. For all I care, leave the land as it is, where it is, it can stay there, for all I care. What else is left for me to do? This is why I want to leave. This is paradoxical. It does not let me be, it no longer exists for me, but I cannot simply walk away from it. I must get away from it, but I can't do it, I must get over it, but how?, it doesn't even exist, does it? Well, not for me. So then it does exist again? Oh well, maybe it can bear me now. It couldn't bear so many people, but maybe it will bear with me, I am coming without my dead relatives, I am alone, I don't weigh much, please bear me now, dear land!, oh, how nice!, finally!, but now I don't want it anymore! I don't want this land anymore, even though it is so nice to me; its breath is warm, I can feel it, but I don't know what it is that's breathing. What's breathing is a pretty lively country they tell me. And now it stopped breathing. Oh dear! Well, after a while it gets boring to listen to people not breathing. Better to help people not doing anything. But I am afraid my hand isn't strong enough for doing nothing. In any case: Seeking nothing makes more sense, but I am not all that sensuous. Pity. Maybe it'll come back to me some day.

They got a bit shaky, over there, at the masters' hunting party, we must do something about it. As lords of the castle they should know when it's time to hightail it, ideally before setting it on fire, the castle, which is supposed to go to the Russians, but that's not how it goes. It would be stupid vice versa: burning it down, before getting out. Let it live again, this beautiful castle! Live like all of Austria, which applied for a name change, but then changed it back a few years later! Better not try to get in if it's burning, but otherwise ... well, to begin with, and that's something I am supposed to pass on to you from Switzerland, where all of you, as I can see, have arrived again, a headcount, please, one, two, three; three people then, we don't need more in Switzerland, but the three of us have arrived, as this is an absolutely safe third country, a country for third men; first Austria, which doesn't exist, not even a third of it, then Switzerland, which, luckily, has been around longer than people, because it is so absolutely safe, therefore people have squeezed in there, well, as many as could get in; if we let them, even more would be coming, the three of us barely made it in, into the first and second safest third country, loading the bases, but no one remembers how it all began, how my report started, which proceeds in this chronological and ranking order, unfortunately, I don't know either of them well, either of the two countries, wherever home is, wherever one is safe, except if you are a victim, then it won't work, at least not always, therefore you better not ask whether you'll also be safe there or not, it might save you a lot of trouble; in any event, the fiery flame the countess hurled, like lightning's fire, into the house, her castle, cannot be seen all the way to Switzerland, the blaze, which she was quick to pin on the Russians, who also wanted to get in, serves them right, when they finally got there, armed to the teeth, since no one was left to check them for weapons, as everyone knew the Russians were coming, by then the beautiful castle had burnt down completely. Since the Germans had been in the castle, the others naturally wanted to get in there too. Since the Germans got out again, all of us got burnt. But cleaning up takes no time at all. Do something and fear no one is what I always say. The countess, of course—and I can fully understand her—, wanted to destroy the palace, after me the deluge, I mean, the fire, beautiful woman, one of a kind, horse sense and always proved it, after her hell or high water, or both, the castle's special firewater, famous for its high, goes right through you, even a messenger has to go with that flow, especially when he had too much, well, the palace, the castle will get completely smashed, I can see it coming, although the messenger should first take a long hard look and then tell it as if it had just happened; but you have no idea how long it takes to get to Switzerland, and all those borders between!, no God lived in this palace, but the countess was worshipped by her buddies, worshipped, I said and still they shipped out after lighting her fire. They chucked the flames. I don't know how else to put it. They shot those naked gentlemen, no, they didn't tell me their names, and then, as if groping with cowardly hand for a thread that might lead them out again, they got into a car and just shot took off. Lugano, an apartment above a bar, very nice; as an opposite option, they could have loosened their own tongues, as they listened and broke the ice from their hearts, as we messengers do all the time.

What do you want to hear from me? Everyone changed into a serpent, the woman a beast in the shape of a dragon, the cattle car, no, I think it was a Daimler, but I can't see it anywhere, I mean, I couldn't find any description of the car they got away with, the countess plus Podezin plus Oldenburg, P. and O., Podezin was terrible, that much has been documented. This documented citizen was one to be endured and to endure, passionately, during a time of momentous passion. Well, that historic moment has passed. Long, long ago. The castle went up in flames. So, they finally got Phoebos' holy seer's blind, what, the Holy See is blind?, well, that's not what it has always been, it was much later that Phoibus set it on fire, the hunting castle and also our desires; plundered and ignited, there won't ever be any infernal recurrences. It's best we all stay away from there. But the lords and masters, the lady and mistress of the castle, the gentlemen in general and her gentlemen in particular keep transferring to Switzerland, they all want to lord it once in their lives, they go gaga over the lady, who was born this way, beautiful and dirty rich; they keep crossing borders, how could one remember them all?, well then, the respective border crossers are saved by someone, including their harmonies, I mean, including their harmonicas, their Jew's organs and mouth harps, or the other way around, it's all tangled up in Jews, but everything has to run harmoniously, all have to run harmoniously, they are saved before they are in danger, they are saved even before they can see the danger, their Being has been traded to the Islands of the Blessed, even before they are dead. I am saying this as a messenger, no, as the son of an earthly father, no, as the son of a God, all earthlings are sons of God, and I mean all, all of them. Besides myself. Too bad. So it goes. I am beside myself, but the advantage is that no one is here besides me. All are inside me and want out, and all at the same time. But besides myself: no one around. No one listens. No one around to listen. Poor messenger-me. And if those gentlemen, if the lady chose to be humble when they no longer liked it in these beautiful fields, they might have stayed there, and they might have lived happily ever after! What? They did? They were happy, happy all the time? Something is wrong with this story, and not only that. Just a moment, someone just handed me a note—the messenger is allowed to read if he forgot something. I quote: One must not acknowledge anything to not get punished severely. One does not have to acknowledge anything. They fare well and that's not impossible for them as they can always move to another country, where no one will see them, and they will not have to see any bodies or put them in their pipes and smoke them too, and the mountains don't see them and they don't see the mountains and no one looks at them and their eyes don't look to see.

All messengers exit, everything gets dismantled.

A hunting lodge in the mountains.

There are several possibilities. Here is what I have to offer, without any obligations, of course: people in rather disheveled evening clothes are decorating an alpine manger. But the animals are not ox and donkey and lambs but wild animals. The people tear antlers off stags and roebucks and nail them to the walls, along with stuffed birds, etc., etc. When they are ready to leave and open the door, the animals in their soft-toy suits block their way and don't let them out. But, of course, it could be done completely different. The Austrian weather channel (TW 1) would be great, that is, the folksy music, that's always played to underscore the beautiful landscapes and their tourist specials.

Then the actual performers turn to one another, in a conversational tone.

Meet me at the Wolf's Glen at midnight, at the strike of twelve.

At midnight at the Wolf's Glen? No! The glen is condemned and the gates of hell open at twelve.

Forgive me if you stayed up for my sake.

You seem to be in a bad mood. You had no luck again?

No, no, on the contrary! Look! I shot the greatest bird of prey straight down out of the clouds. It won't go for my eyes anymore.

I am sorry. But what's that? Your locks are bloody. Jesus Christ! What happened?

Nothing. It's already healing. It'll be all right.

Did you hear that? The tower clock on the mountain just started to strike and stopped again. You could hardly notice it strike. Usually I notice, when something strikes me I or when I hit someone. As if it shied away from striking. But it isn't usually that shy.

But never made it to three.

Strange. It must have been exactly the time I shot the eagle. Out of the lofty air. (*Shows a bloody human head, which he pulled out of the backpack.*) I shot the eagle out of the lofty air. I cannot turn back, my destiny calls!

Well, then, come on then!

Okay. I'm here. (*He tries to nail the human head into the wall.*)

Did you see the storm clouds cluster? Did you see the weather report? Did you see the gloomy chasm—what horror! And the clouds are looking, no idea where, at any rate high up. Everyone wants to be up there. What did your eyes believe they saw? Tell me, please!

Well, if you insist: they saw the storm clouds gather, they saw the moon give up some of its beams, ghostly mist shapes wavered and hard rock came to life, unbelievable unless you saw it as I did and even I would not believe it. What I can believe and what I also saw were night birds fly up in the bushes.

I knew it! Something had to be in the bushes!

Exactly. And I saw branches, ruddy grey and scarred, stretch out gigantic arms at me. My heart was horrified. But I had to go on despite the horror.

But it was really mean of you to leave me all alone.

I am sorry. But I had to do it. And it wasn't easy.

Would you have preferred the sun stayed in the sky, just this once, and night would not have fallen, just this once? And the world would not serve blind chance? That the eye, forever clear and pure, would lovingly perceive all creatures? Would you really have liked that better?

Nonsense. I wanted to have it exactly the way it was.

And jump into the chasm? Never! That would be the end.

Hush, hush, that none may warn you!

Were you ever so horny you grabbed a syringe, drew blood and drank it?

I take it you liked the taste of your blood. Or you wouldn't have done it.

It was delicious. Once, when I was drilling with a Black & Decker, I let the drill slip and it went right through my hand, it was a real pleasure.

Blood after all is the juice of giving.

Of living.

Has all necessary nutrients.

One can also eat humans. Did that thought ever come to you?

It made me come. But live flesh is somewhat more resistant than when its fried or boiled.

I can do that. Afterwards you have something to decorate the wall with. That's my specialty.

Nice if it were legal.

Who cares! Say no more. I just have to do some shopping. I have to get your side dishes. I mean, I have to get the side dishes to go with you.

I am not nervous at all. Just horny as hell. I can hardly wait.

I picture myself biting into your neck, your shoulders, belly, thighs, which you then will eat with me; the most delicious parts.

But don't just bite, please. I want to see and feel you taking those bites from my neck, my shoulders, my belly, my chest.

Yes, but not all at once!

You can also bite through my cheeks to give you direct access to my mouth, which you then can open wide. Then eat my tongue all the way to the root, please! Take, eat my flesh; this is my body, take and eat it! This is my blood. Take and drink it. I am taking it. I can take everything. And I'll love it, I am sure.

I'd love to have a taste of you. Maybe we can cook and roast some and eat it together?

It'll last us for a while. That's my plan.

I want to eat something of myself too, maybe a bit of the thigh or a bite of ham. If I had a choice.

Generally, there are no discussions with animals up for slaughter.

Right you are. I'll leave it all up to you.

Not the nipple. Even though it protrudes, but there's too much blood. It would go too fast. Better take a piece above or below.

Nipple. Okay. No problem. Though it wouldn't be difficult to first tie it off and then bite it off.

If you don't want to eat anything raw, my mouth will be a happy taker. In case you want to feed me with my own flesh. Maybe you would like that. It's important to me to satisfy your will.

Of course we also have to carve a hole to scoop it all out. Whatever you bite off, keep it hanging from its last tissues connected to the body and eat it very slowly, while it's still attached to me. Don't swallow it right away. Chew it before you bite it off completely. Cut the connection only at the end.

I like a man to keep his lips open while he chews, so I can see the teeth. One should be able to see the teeth working. Raw flesh is much firmer than cooked. Generally speaking.

But don't forget, it should also be a feast for the eyes! It should look beautiful. The sight alone should be a pleasure. Maybe the preparation should come afterwards, it might make the flesh unappealing to look at, but good to eat.

The ribs must be roasted separately. It would be great if the ribcage could stay in one piece. But that depends on the size of the available oven. It would work in a hotel kitchen. After defrosting, the whole arch of ribs gets to be roasted or baked.

Will there be anything left then for the burial?

Yes, and I am not against it being ceremonious. What do you think? How would you like it? This is how I see it: A grave gets dug and everything that hasn't been eaten goes in there.

The hole is dug in the dark and then everything is put in there. Then a reading: Psalm 23. It is beautiful. I think you'll like it too. Then the prayer: Our Father. Then the hole gets filled again.

Will the hole be marked somehow?

No, it would be too conspicuous. A flower maybe, but nothing else, no. The rest of the bones, the leftovers, can be buried somewhere else. But afterwards, no one will know, and even you will forget.

Will the site be marked somehow?

No, it would be too conspicuous and also unnecessary. I know where it is, after all. After a while I won't know anymore. That's the curse, I mean, the course of time; wait, let me see what time it is, yes, the clock is running. If you want to keep up with the time, you better hurry! The bones shall be buried without prayers.

Did the owners mention anything that's off limits, certain rooms that can't be used?

Well, the rooms underground we wouldn't have found anyway. But we could always move freely inside the house. They let us do that. We just had to be careful, since there are many rooms in father's house, he told us we should be careful, since many floors are quite brittle; with our weight we could easily break through. They must have meant the ceilings. That's why we stayed mostly on the first two floors.

I think, the correct way goes like this: In my father's house are many mansions: If it were not so, I would have told you: I go to prepare a place for you; I will come again and receive you unto myself; that where I am there may also be you. And whither I go ye know, ye know the way. And when one says: We know not whither thou goest; how know we the way? The Lord saith unto him, I am the way, the truth, and the life. No man cometh unto the father, but by me. You are all invited. So there was the party, and we watched the movie *Armageddon*. The landlord said, we could come by any time and watch movies with his family.

In each of these mansions, I think, a table will be prepared against the enemies. The roast will be anointed with oil and cups will run over.

Actually, all will run. Everything will be run over. It'll be all over. And that will follow me all my life. It will follow me voluntarily. No, it doesn't. Nothing follows. It was too tough an act to follow, voluntarily at least. And whatever you will ask for in my name, I shall not do.

Acknowledgements start now.

So then:

Special thanks to

David R. L. Litchfield. *The Thyssen Art Macabre*

Friedrich Nietzsche. *Thus Spoke Zarathustra*

Euripides. *The Bacchae*

T. S. Eliot. *The Hollow Men*

Friedrich Kind. *Der Freischütz*

Thanks to Hans Magnus Enzensberger for the beautiful interview!

There are other small things, which I have to be thankful for and which I still have to digest. But that has time. I am still chewing on it.

THE MERCHANT'S CONTRACTS

A Comedy of Economics

This is how it might look here perhaps:

The hall is windowless, dim light, black walls and ceilings, dark gray floor, rows of chairs, also dark gray, the people are dressed in dark colors. A podium all the way in the front, with tables covered in black cloth. Where am I? At the annual convention of Goths? Or of groupies of undertakers? Wouldn't I know better? "Annual General meeting, July 16, 2008, St. Helier, Jersey, or St. Peter Port, Guernsey, wherever our company requests your company." The words are projected on the back wall of the hall. One word is missing: Extraordinary. Extraordinary General Meeting. The subject is a multi-million business. The bank, the mortgage company from a faraway land, inaccessible to us, want to have their resolutions approved. Many investors fear that they will lose even more money. And that is what will happen. With a few thousand voting rights in the bag, they are seated in the hall, representatives of small investors who wouldn't even find their own bathroom without an arrow pointing to it in their homes, from which they will soon be evicted, if they bought any paper from this company. They sold everything to buy paper from this company. What is lying around? MacBook or other notebooks on knees, you too on your knees, three electronic voting machines, bags, blackberry, camera, documents, pads, pencils, a small bottle of mineral water. No table. Everything is on the floor.

The text can start and stop anywhere at random. It doesn't matter how it is staged, I imagine three or four men yelling it out as loudly as possible. They don't have to do it with precision, that is, they don't have to always do it in unison, there can be shifts and inaccuracies, but not intentionally, please! One can also tape it and transmit it to the toilets and check rooms, whatever . . . When it is staged, big papier mâché heads of politicians, the way they are worn at the G8 summit demonstrations, might be quite funny.

Thank you all, ye bloggers, oh come to me, there still is much room in the manger.

PROLOGUE

I play you like an instrument; sooner or later I'll get the right tones out of you. I understand you are neither a psychic nor a speculator, anyway, you are innocent, is there anything you would like to add? So close, and still we blew it, we almost got the bank back on its feet, had we not blown it—that's something that sticks to you for the rest of your life, it'd be easier to get your life unstuck. Would you explain this to me? I can't explain it. I can't figure out how the union owned the Refco Corporation through a few dummy companies, which were incorporated informally to form a foundation in Liechtenstein, that is: Nothing into Nothing, from Nothing to Nothing, smack between Nothing and Nothing!, I can't figure it out: there are the guys who got everything, a union that is, and here are the others, who can't explain where they got it. Go figure! A labor union, which was even the majority shareholder of the Refco Corporation for a few months! How could that have happened? Oops, how did it happen? How can it happen that a union owns an investor or more, oops, I mean, a locust, locusts, that's what those guys are called here, well then, a union owns a locust, which it trains not to sing, though it should know how to sing—like a cricket caught in a hot field?, and then it gets eaten up by another locust, who's already sick to his stomach but still has so much food in front of him? Those crickets, those creatures, those screechers often continue to sing in a cat's stomach! He has to rehearse the range of his capabilities, the locust, he wants to make mincemeat out of this bank, but only in a few years. A bank owned by the union, which is busy transferring the little bit of money of the little people, to the scalpers, that's why he was hired, that's why the union was constructed and it developed fabulously, like us in good, hot weather. This union sits on its little riverbank eating our brownbag lunches (for which we don't dare to take the time anymore) after they sold us down the river. It eats up all our food in the shape of a horrendous whopper, uhm, I mean hopper, at least temporarily; now look, there are fuck-around jobs and there are fake jobs, and in-between there are people, who really work, so they won't lose their real jobs, which, actually, are not really right for them. The fuckers, the fakers can't suppress a faint yawn. Please take note now of due diligence: you work with your own money, which should finally get to work, or you don't work at all, then your money won't work either and not only because you don't have any. You wouldn't be a very good role model but you wouldn't have violated due diligence, since you wouldn't be accountable to your own money, even if the dealer is already closing out your account; your loss!, the bank always wins; but doesn't a bank work with other people's money?, strange money?, the money of strangers? Does the bank always win as well?, no, the bank even gives away its own money!, this bank is too good for us, this bank is good for everything, yes, the union too; the union gives everything it got to become a stranger like money, which is already controlled by too many folks estranged from each other. Better, you throw it away! You, yes, you, will only become a winner when someone else can see something in you, which you are not. Okay. As soon as he sees what you are he runs away. In exchange, well, may be not in exchange for that, the speculator has you in his hand. But only because you handed him something, and then he lost everything, you lost and he lost and he also lost you. But he doesn't miss you at all! You, however, are missing a few things, which, in truth, you never owned anyway. When will you now be able to own the new sofa set and sit on it? Not this year! You stick to your suggestions how to make a profit. Mitigating circumstances? Isn't it somewhat ludicrous that a manager whose earnings in this world are already otherworldly gets a severance pay that's higher than his subordinates' lifetime earnings, and the fact that he had no previous convictions is considered a mitigating factor? Mitigating at sentence? This man was in the position to approve his pay raises and severances more or less single handedly; why would he go through the trouble of committing a crime for his personal enrichment? Committing the crime, for which he was sentenced here, even though he had no need whatsoever for the money, should count as an aggravating rather than an extenuating factor! On the other hand, one has to consider the effort it took for the accused to commit a crime, as this effort cut into his leisure time for which he had plenty of money to gamble away. Everything gambled away. Here it's all a game. The losses are elsewhere. That it's all part of his job can be seen as a mitigating factor. He didn't have to, he didn't have to have others speculate with the money, he didn't even make the effort to blow it himself, he had strangers blowing it with their leaf blowers, that's mitigating, isn't it? Is advanced age also a mitigating factor? Well, I don't know, for if he won't live to the end of his punishment, how can this be punishment? Punishment will be left behind. Poor punishment always pays the price. Ultimately, he got the death penalty, but things are never as bad as they seem. He didn't do what he did for his own enrichment, so it's irrelevant whether or not he needed the money, right? It doesn't hold. The sentence won't hold. It won't even make it to the next level. It'll collapse on the way. The sentence is outrageous. Even people who brutally murder other people or turn them into cripples aren't punished like that! Very disturbing! Where are people who commit the aforementioned crimes not punished? Nowhere are they not punished. No, that's wrong. If you want to mitigate, you can't first aggravate. The truth is aggravating enough, but that can't count as a mitigating factor in your case. Can't you do the math? Well, in court you can't count on the truth. Say yay, here you stay. Say no, home you go. Recollections can at best count as self-protective assertions, as long as they don't really exist, not for self-protection anyway, no, those assertions don't have to be protected; furthermore, memory should fall under resource protection, before it disappears all together. The court will not consider those self-protective assertions, or the suggestion that the principal offender could not have acted alone; that theory is going nowhere, because the accused distributed orders to the lower levels, until they broke through under the weight. The floor just broke through. Not the brokers, they didn't break, only the floor did. And then, of course the upper floors and the penthouse and the pool also crashed into the chasm, which was man-made, not caused by an earthquake or something like that; the shock from falling made them wet themselves, as the crashing pool spilled all over, all that was left in the end was a heap of rubble, a huge field of rubble; the party is over, the party is finished. And all because of money! It's too much! No, not the money. The punishment just for the money is too much, worse people get a lot less, but sometimes they have more and get even more, that's not right. The court has no right to revenge; it should never take vengeance; the avengers play some other place; never heard of it!, unheard of! A judge is always right with his sentence; except when the sentence doesn't hold up; then maybe the ground it stands on will hold up; no?, it won't either?, no, no, it's good!, now look, quite often a hold-up on the street is also for the money; often just for the money. One plays money like a sort of mandolin or guitar or accordion, and you put it away again, and when you want to play it again, you realize it wasn't even an instrument, at any rate not a financial instrument worth its name. Everyone wants to sing, albeit not in court, and not everyone was granted a full voice, some have to share it, a sorrow shared is a sorrow halved, lost money was not shared, and if it had been, I don't know who's got the shares, they are gone, all gone, blown, blowing in the wind. Well, I am blown away. I am that I am. I am where I am. I am that, where I am. Where do they talk that way? I am this, where I am. I am still totally blown away from all that, no, not really blown away, just normally blown away, as they say. It's not been shared, not split, the money, it split all the way. That's why one shouldn't split to begin with, or it will be all blown some day. Blown away. Lost. Lost it, well, not "it" and not that way. Lost, because I lost it all. It's not been shared, the money, it's all blown. That's why one shouldn't share to begin with, or it will all really blow up some day.

THE REAL THING (THE PLOT)

One of several acts, I just don't know where one begins and the next one ends.

As a projection or some other way the following should come up in irregular intervals: "These are only a few of the deeds. The assumption of innocence applies here."

Stripped of everything we, the small investors, guard this site of loss, deserted by our means for meat and drink and clothing and household appliances and homes and gardens, coops and condos in East and West, more in the East; there's property still up for grabs. And now we must rest on the rough bottom of our own weary limbs, since we can no longer afford our new sofa, although it was such a bargain: No way! There's no way out for us, cast out from our own homes, at a loss for what to do, and lost beyond help. For some friends, I see, are neither real nor true, those are not stocks, those are just securities, but even those securities are not our just friends as we thought they were, when that broken piggy bank appeared to us on TV together with a proud woman; nothing could happen to this woman in the forest, no bear could crush her on her way home from the market carrying a big shopping bag stuffed with real values, real estate values that guarantee real status, which comes with a portfolio, and that's where they are now, the values; yes, we've got them, immortal values, mortgage-backed values, for mortgage values last forever, still, our plot isn't bottomless, but it can't walk away either and they weigh little, values weigh little, the plot, however, weighs a lot. Idly, we harness ourselves for work, sheep-like dependents, without the right to vote, we'll just have to work another twenty years, because our retirement fund is gone, gone up in thin air, we bet on the wrong horse, we have the certificates, but we never get the prize, we are priced out; our price is on this tag, but we didn't mark it, so here they are, those prized values, marked down, while we missed some steps, and we are falling, falling, oh!, if only we held our own horses before they fell, before we fell, but we bet, we were set on something else; we sat on nothing, we had no seat, no voice in a boardroom or on a board where our names were listed in chalk; we list our losses and get wiped off; and as I said: No way; no way they let us in, we are wiped out, we wipe ourselves, but only in the bathroom, the only place we had a seat. Though we took a bath some other place. So now we sit here, locked out of our own houses, of all places, our heads locked up our ass, unfortunately, because some friends, what's up with them?, this bag with the coffee and grocery-company logo, the little company moor who was our friend, he promised us a lot, but he unmoored us and now the moor is gone, that cute company logo and so promising, at least until now; hadn't we lived together for so long, best of friends with his mar-malades, cakes, and all sorts of coffee, oh, so many, so vast and diverse his field, the grocer as banker, from rags to riches, promises, promises, none kept!, ever expanding, the smart owner's field, while ours kept shrinking and now it is gone, we have lost our field of activity and didn't get another one; what did I want to say? I knew earlier, as I checked the portfolio, there still was something left in it, something is left in it still, but it's not worth a thing, not as much as we paid for it, we would have paid with our blood for the secu-rities, and they would have taken it for sure. We would have defied the heavens for such security, defiant we would have been in any case, but only to be wounded all the more deeply. For some friends, such as that cute little moor, who departed, if not this life, well, yes, he departed from our lives with our savings, our servant, who became our ruler, what did I want to say, oh yes, some friends are not real or true, the faithful ones without the power to stand by us, the small investors' rep, who represents so many powerless, does all he can to help us, but his power is limited, the bank's certificates are already tied around our neck, they pull us down, our worth is written on them, but whatever is on it, is of no interest, it's the weight of the stone around our necks that counts, the numbers on the stone also count, but the stone counts more, it sinks, it throws up its arms and sinks and we die because we stopped thinking, had we stopped to think we would never have stopped thinking and would still be alive. Our worth is nothing, our value is not ours, we surrendered our value and got nothing in return, we redeemed our value and got nothing, there is no redemption for us, we have no value, and we have no values, our values have no value and our own value is zilch, what did I want to say, those who are on our side, no, I said that already, they are powerless, they can't help us small investors, and that's not even what we are, we the little bitty investors, that's all we have, that's all we own, everything we had we pawned for ourselves, a pawn for something that was worth nothing, and if we owned more, we would of course invest big, not teensy-weensy; this is how misfortune serves us mortals. To prove it, we can kill ourselves now, our retirement money is gone, 15 percent per year guaranteed, at the very least! And what have we now? Now the shit has hit the fan and is steaming up the place, and now we got the pie in our face. Oh wouldst thou that even just half-loved us never . . . . No idea, what he would or wouldn't want, where is he anyway, who half-loved us at least? He took off, I think, there's no one left here who even loves some part of us, we had one earlier, one at the very least, because we were part of a community, the community of small investors, who stuck together, earlier, when we still had CDOs and creditworthiness and mortgage-backed securities, all Nothings, collateralized by a lack—a lack backed by nothing but a sucking vacuum, even when the securities took off, we took the shit, at best we took hold of Nothing, which does not secure us the way the rope secures the mountain climber, his dear and loyal rope—now and forever, so we hope. But we hold on to nothing, we hold up nothing and no one holds us up, it's not worth anyone's trouble and we have enough troubles; we don't want any hold on our pension checks, so we don't have to hold up the bank or anyone else, and what have we got a hold of? Nothing at best; but even this Nothing is tied to claims and if this Nothing finally wants to pay us, because it must, because the one Nothing we own forces us to destroy the other Nothing we are and then still continues making claims, I said it already, someone else said it before me, then, well then, then nothing will happen either, because all that Nothing has been used up, why should anyone give you anything for it? Maybe it was used too much, we need so much, but this Nothing wasn't something we good-for-nothings really needed, this Nothing between nothing and nothing, that big Nothing, that's been invested; it should still be there, that Nothing, between nothing and nothing, that big Nothing, that's been invested, it still should be there; and there it is! The net gain consists only of interest earnings, and nothing else, it should still be there, since nothing flows back from the projects in which we invested; everything that flows always flows downhill, right? But nothing flows back, no gains, nothing comes back, you can't make nothing from nothing, not even nothing can be made of nothing; but it's coming, the big Nothing, where we, the have-nothings are stuck chewing our fingernails, which we've still got, we haven't got anything else, so if that Nothing wants to pay us, we have to realize it paid off only for that Nothing, while for us it didn't pay at all, buying those CDOs, offered to us by an independent trader for the Funds Promotion and Investment Co. This lady had been specifically advised to take out a loan for the fabulous, safe purchase of securities that offered additional securities, a purchase anchored in the ground as solidly as the roots of blackberry twines; this was no simple recommendation, it was an offer impossible to resist! But now those securities have done their job, they've done a lousy job, one can't have enough security, right?— but we have none, so here we are, here we are, stuck, as if we had roots, but the money is some other place, it blossoms and thrives elsewhere, it does not bloom in the securities we bought, those took root some other place, those will only yield themselves, when all claims are fulfilled, one claim follows the other, those claims are our only security, it's easier ripping out a fully grown tree than fulfilling rapidly growing claims and those collaterally insured securities—which they outsourced to so-called securitization special-purpose entities—which already means those securities had no purpose—, to special-purpose entities then, which they in turn financed with short-term certificates of indebtedness, only Nothing can come out of nothing, but all can be got for nothing, if you pull out billions worth of risks and pour them into a foundation, which then holds the horn of plenty, the horn that feeds it, while we slowly grow roots, filled with restlessness that we might never get anything back, those roots however find no fertile ground, after they sucked us dry instead of sucking their ground, their plot, which consists of debts—certified debts then are their securities, the security of the plot, which is no security, that's the ground we stand on; roots keep growing nonetheless but not for our money, that's gone, it vanished long ago but somehow those

claims are holding up, while we aren't, while we lost everything, they hold on somewhere, those claims, the bank holds
on to its claims and we hold on to them too, though we want
to get away!, though we really want to take a look at this
foundation, which doesn't fill anyone's pockets, this foundation does not feed its folks, it doesn't feed its family, its wife
and its children, it doesn't feed anyone, because it consists
of nothing, we, however, we buy, we buy those instruments
like nothing, with nothing like nothing, with a negative
nothing, with a minus-nothing, with claims which are supposed to fill up that nothing, oh dear, where are we supposed
to get that from? Wherever. We still buy those instruments,
because they pampered us with a false sense of security, us
crybabies, crying in our pampers, unable to get out of ourselves that want to find some security but can't get out; their
security, however, is nothing, it doesn't exist, security, they
have no securities, those instruments have claims as securities, and we buy them, we idiots buy them and think we are
secure but it's a false security, a negative security; the shit hit
our pampers, they clean us out, if we think we are secure,
we overshot security by far, we have claims on the securities
which they can't fulfill, we face the greatest insecurity but
we believe in our security, we believe that those securities
are worth something, we couldn't believe it, when our assets,
which we took to be set in stone, our nest egg, which we
believed to last, to last for the future, changed into liabilities
backed by nothing but claims, not just secured by nothing,
but secured by claims, yep, what did I want to say, perhaps
something new regarding our secure claims and unsecured
profits, which we hoped to be able to believe in, the risks of
the credits are coming back, yep, they're coming back to us,
help!, run for your life!, or they'll run us over, that's how low
they sank, all of a sudden our securities are worth nothing

and they'll sink even more, we spent them for insecurity, but as risks they are running us over, in constant danger of dropping, of crashing, not as a loss but as risks, that's more than a loss, because one can only hope and be uncertain, while a loss is a loss, gone, finished, done with. At least it doesn't continue. We however, believing we owned something, did not only own nothing but, rather, owned losses, we are sitting on our losses, right?, only—we don't yet know it, the bank also sits on losses but it doesn't admit them, let alone remit them to us, it's also sitting on its losses, the bank, only, it had planned it exactly that way so that we would believe, we born-again losers would finally be winners with it and in it , when everyone has losses, others win, if not yet all the others, there is unity but no trinity among us about that, because you won't find three of us as winners, Jesus gets lost in us, right?, like at communion, you get a tasteless host out of the can stuck in your mouth, it doesn't even leave a taste, there never was any, but with it we consumed the entire bleeding Jesus, that's the truth, no?, that's right, no!, that's the truth; there we thought we placed our bet on the right horse, and the horse on the right track and where did it get us? Did someone else get it right? But we had nothing to do with it, still—we must pay for it, and that's the truth, no? No! That's the truth; so the crisis is spreading and it affects all segments of the financial market whose winners we thought we were, we, the lucky ones, the poor can stay poor but poor us will get rich now!, yep, poor us will be rich now, though with no sweat pouring down our backs ! We can bank on it that we can't bank on anything, we got bunked already; as they say, bank on others and you'll go bunkers; but we know our bankers and we'll belong to the winners, that's the truth, no? NO! *That's* the truth! Not even the banks buy from other banks anymore, they buy less from other banks, not more, but we are still buying, we can't lose at all, we will win, because we can't lose, because we already lost, and now we simply have to win, we would make such bad losers, they wouldn't even take us on as losers, but we can't really lose, because we would be really bad as losers, but we have to, because we can't tell a good risk from a bad one, that's alright, that's all, right?, the banks can't either anymore, even though they once invented it; being able to tell one risk from another would be the least one should be able to ask from a bank, because you almost never get your money back , and if you do, it's bad money, badly invested, well, but as advised, well advised. Still, a mistake. But as there is little difference between humans, there is a lot between money and money, the money one loses from the money one owns, not to mention the money one wins, that's the money that talks, but now *we* talk, no one talks about us, so now we talk, we are all equal, compared to money, which is not equally distributed, we are all only human, equal and alike like Tweedledum and Tweedledee, and we talk like the common folk we are, we talk ourselves out of the warnings and notices of others, we don't pay attention, we can't pay, we pray, we pray for our spouses, we pray for our children, we die praying; we invested, listen now, we invested and now a song of great lament crosses my lips, it suddenly bursts forth between lips parched and burned from so much throwing up and cracking up, as soon as we open our mouth, we invested in something we thought was safe, we could have just as well burned the money, because what we thought was safe, what they sold us as safe and secure, was not, that's for sure, but there is no security anyway, we invested and we did not invest Nothing, that Nothing is our life; still, there were the occasional highlights of high-risk adventure vacations, thus completing a magnificent project, which our land would never acknowledge, that's why we travel abroad; we take a break to take our risks; not anymore, now we are broke; at best, we take a dive; oh, if only it hadn't been us!, if only it had been others but us!, we invested much, we invested everything in what was not our life, but was supposed to become our life, in retirement, in old age, we invested in the Nothing that was to be our old age, oh, had we not saved ourselves for old age, when life is just beginning, although it's over already. If it has to be Nothing, let it be comfortable!, but old age is worthless anyway, an old person has no value, so then we invested in a dead-on Nothing, we said it already, we invested in CDOs, in pieces of paper, which were secured not only by nothing, but by a negative Nothing, a less than Nothing, in one claim on another one, which we don't know, but the bank knows, naturally, the bank uses only natural cosmetics for its accounting and it knows its Nothing quite well, we, however, don't know the Nothing that will noth us, so we invested in nothing from nothing, but for us it didn't pay off, it was thrown into Nothing, which was made insecure with more than nothing, no, less than Nothing, I mean the negative Nothing, which consists of nothing but carelessly made up claims, yes, claims on us too, on me, a pitiful have-not, why on me, why on us? Didn't we give, whole— and—brave—and—fool-heartedly! And we also have claims, always, anytime, just not on us, how will that end, with nothing but claims? It never ends! It'll never end well. It can only be the end of us all, because we are all secured by claims of Nothing on Nothing, at best by no claims from Nothing on the loss of Nothing. What's that supposed to mean? No, it means nothing. Once again I don't know how to say it. Because it is less than having no security! It is less than nothing. Because insecurity also has claims, yes, insecurity won't just settle for more insecurities, it has claims, also on us, this time on us as well, who have plenty of claims ourselves, but also on Nothing, and first, of course, this Nothing, which has claims on our securities, must be paid, the debt of Nothing to the less than Nothing has to be settled, right, no?, and then finally it's our turn to get paid out our Nothing. Well, that surely paid off! We get nothing. Well, that really paid off! We get nothing! For us it didn't pay off, but there must be someone for whom it paid off, that Nothing, which first must pay off the Nothing and its claims, and the claims of Nothing on us are not nothing, they have it in them, they come with interest, ten years from now they will still squeeze those claims out of that Nothing, which will have to pay interest for unpaid debts, and when that interest is finally paid off, the interest for the actual debt, the original debt certificates will then also have matured, unlike us, who finally can be had for a dime, though no one will take us, for we've been had already. Then they finally can have us for free, and that's still better than not having us at all, because Being and Having are collateralized debt obligations, they are foundations, where debts get parked, not ours, but those made by others—after they got all our capital—were parked there, the parking ticket expired long ago, let it go, they are still standing there, some are lying, and no one asks, no one asks for a reality check. The Nothing, the void is parked in a claim, and then even the Nothing will be nowhere to be found, then the less than Nothing will be nowhere to be found, so the bank will create a nifty foundation, which also considers itself too nifty for us, and what do we have? Nothing. And what do they find?, the new board of directors—elected with great effort by the small investors—a smorgasboard of wild nuts, ripe for the can, the trash of the conned, the scammed, the canned, the conned, the pros and the cons, what?—no, it can't be!, And what do they find, the board, the directors, when they start working for those who elected them, for the hardworking small investors, who counted their pennies, collected coupons for years, small investors, who also have rights but never are right, now then, working for those small investors with their messed up small change, still, they are represented by this new board of directors, elected is elected, small investors electing such a directorate is a small revolution and a revolution needs a directorate, an executive body, that's an old custom, right?, a directorate with two relentless chambers, yes, in both we get threshed like straw; so what do the directors find as they are ready to start working in the service of small investors? They find nothing. This directorate can't even get heads chopped off, no heads will roll, because the directors found nothing, they didn't look for anything either, they simply were there and fueled the inflation, something must keep the engine rolling, the directors hauled us over the coals all right, no, no people were incinerated, no, no people, no heads off!, no heads-up, registered office doesn't exist, no computer, no secretary, no anything, because the company, the small investors are now ashamed of the company, but nevertheless they elected a board for it. The firm, however, which now has hatched directors, new directors, consists of nothing but nothing; all that effort for nothing. For nothing. No, not for nothing, not for free, the effort consists of debts, because the company doesn't exist, whoop-de-doo, we invested in a company, which doesn't exist, we invested in nothing!, which, however, had once been something: our small capital, our savings, our life savings, which we could save up only because for decades we didn't have a life, but we saved, we invested, and now this! We invested in a company that exists only on paper, like its board of directors, which exists, but doesn't direct! A director would have to be paid extra, and from what? From nothing? No wonder, they stage such phony stuff! So then the investments of this company, the one in which we invested, were purchased in turn by management companies and then this company was simply closed down, that is, *that* company parted company with *this* company, well, it's not all that simple, but anyway, it's closed now, and a board of directors won't do any good, but how can something be closed that doesn't even exist?; that had opened wide the doors for our investments, but those were not doors, there was nothing, the Nothing that was kept alive only by the fees for the transactions with our lives?, but unfortunately, that Nothing doesn't keep us alive now, now that we would need it, it can't contribute to our livelihood; we already put our lives into it, for decades we didn't have a life and we saved our money so we could buy those papers, and now this! management companies hired, old directors fired, replaced by new ones after a coup by small investors, let's hope the new board will do better, the old directors didn't even have a working phone, they too had nothing!, they had nothing themselves! Those poor guys! That'll change now; they had nothing, those old directors, but the new ones better give us back some of it, the small investors' directors, elected by us small fry, but finding nothing big enough anymore to chop into mincemeat, so the new ones will get an entirely new telephone service, but no fixed line in a fixed network, that's the very least, the bottom line!, it's a concrete business transaction, a purchase, really, no, it's not the bottom line, well perhaps it is, no, it's not a deal either, and if it is, it's a bad one, Lucky Hans, who got a blank piece of paper for a golden goose; but if the bottom line was our money, for which we purchased these papers, our money that's gone, what's at the bottom, what's our bottom line, our asses are the bottom, our asses are on the line, and we shit, but not money, on other people's pastures, like horses, asses and live stock, which is different from common stock in that it holds no voting rights. But nothing can come from nothing, But if it moves in the right direction, which is not ours—we have no sense of direction, we are senseless, leaderless and without direction in the markets—, then something might come of it still, but what?, we don't know whether to buy pumpkins, lemons or peppers, the main thing is that others know, but, oh dear, what should we put now in our shopping cart, with inflation munching away at it and us crunching the numbers to pay for it, before inflation deflates and implodes?, we must hurry to get our share of the inflation, before it all gets too cheap and caves in! Where do we get the shopping cart, and what do we put in? We can't even find the market, the market avoids us, that's why we don't find it, even though it's marked on every admission ticket, but we don't have such a ticket, we stumble around, without direction and with no interest, without a shopping bag, without a shopping cart, because we lost our interest, it has no value, we didn't earn it, so we don't get any interest or sympathy, they cut all bonds with us, we are no longer part of anything, we can express our condolences to the parted, no, rather to the bereft; Nothing is all we can still be a part of, we still can have our share of Nothing, we still may purchase shares in Nothing and participate in Nothing, we can take part in the Paralympics of Nothingness, we the legless, the headless, the countless, the nameless, the homeless, hopeless, who can't even hope for the consolation prize; yes, we can—take part, that is, but will never get a part of it, never, never, never! So there, and now the inflation is over too, that's what we get for our lessness!

The market took a dive, woe, woe, woe! It makes no difference to us, but maybe to our customers, what will we tell
them now? What do we tell them? But the substance is there
unchanged. That is, it never was there and it isn't now, but it
never was changed to not be there! It was never changed to
be there. It is unchanged, since nothing was ever taken from
the firm—that is to say, we took, so that no one else can take
on our firm, and that's the truth. The truth is: nothing was
ever taken away against the firm's interests! We took in our
own interest, because we are the firm! Nothing was under-
taken without interest, and it was in our interest to take from
you—but also to give it to you! But what is there to give, if
we can't take anymore? Then we wouldn't have anything left
at all. Please give to us, so we can give it to you! What, you
are not giving any more? You don't trust us anymore? Then
we won't give you anything either. Trust against trust! Our
market ratings reflect the overall market and the market is
weak. It is chronically weak. Whenever we ask how it is
doing, it tells us it feels weak. Too weak even to answer. If
we were to follow your logic that you want back what you
put in—plus 15 percent interest, of course, which our firm
promised you firmly—you might as well pack it all up, you
pack ass! You idiot, hopeless moron, who hasn't learned that
all great things are simple, but not all simple things great!
We promised you 15 percent per annum and you really
believed us?! Excuse my small digression, but the quote
doesn't sound right now, then again, what is right?, soon
enough I'll break into your wallet again as we once broke
into Wall Street. For 15 percent you really should give us
everything! And more! Just take out another loan! Then
you'll already have more than you have now! So, if you want
back at least what you put in for the future, since all futures

were blue chip, safe and stable, here is what you have to do, dumb ass: get back to your stable, if you've still got one and shut up! I don't know where you would go from there, but you won't hear me anyway. So now you have the blues and you want those chips off your shoulder; but the chips are already down and out of your computer, so what do you need security for? You want someone to count on instead of counting sheep because you can't sleep? Your shorn sheep is out to pasture, high and dry, it would rather be out in the rain, to get washed off, not washed up like you; the rain won't wash away your debts; or our sins, only a god can do that, no matter what god, so what's left, what's left for the sheep to do? It has no stable, after all, couldn't afford it, huh? So? What is it? Huh? Well? Cat got your tongue? It sure got your brain! So what security do you need for that? What security do you need? You want it for yourself? That's not what we promised you; you want to be safe and secure and sure of your future? That's not what we promised you. We didn't promise you personal safety but a future. But it makes no difference, since you won't get either, there is no safe you can crack, crack you can get in the street, but it's not safe, too much traffic, you might need some safety in your car, if you still have one, so buckle up and don't look at us! You don't get it, because you don't need it. And even if you needed some security, you won't get it, at least not from us. But lets take a closer look at your complaint, which isn't worth looking at; we will explain it to you as a bonus, since we already got the money, your money, you little investor, you! You, who might have been lucky once, with a father who left you, who left you a facsimile home, I mean a family home in the foothills somewhere, under the rainbow, with mountains hidden right in the back of them, so you thought. So we promised you something that wasn't ours to promise?

Sorry, but we missed your point! And there was no way to make sure the mountains wouldn't fall on the house; the threat of the mountains tearing the house off the ground in one swap—I mean swoop—, one momentous rockslide was the only thing it could be sure of!, as you swept us away at the last road show when you conned us into buying those papers, that's called a con job, it's called a deal, though not new, but at least the house has a good foundation and you didn't begrudge it a patio with a small pool in front, this House of Being, which is a negative one, your Being an ever-hungry infant, eager to suck, sucking you dry; you already got over the mountains, they are piled up high on your house—the second mortgage, which you took out with our help for property in the East, it's somewhere in that pile, but now you must face the rainy days in the plains, the bone grinders of your existence, and the mortgages weigh on your house and once again you weigh on your parents, whom you outgrew long ago, as a financial burden, you are not as big a burden to us as to your parents, for whom you are a heck of a load, you can't even make the down payment, or pay off the interest—or did you inherit a home in a cheaper neigh-borhood?, you have to admit, your inheritance was not in an expensive or trendy area, though the construction of a new upscale mall could increase its value, what did I want to say, its value could have increased, had you not sold it to invest in penny stocks, in our stocks, secured by us and that's security!, your insecurity is our security, which you can also purchase from us, with 15 percent per annum guaranteed, which your little house would never have earned you; that little house could never make such a huge profit all on its own, well, not with us either, not in a hundred years, because by then it will be gone, in any event, it won't be there, while in a hundred years you expect your assets to be worth a hundred times 15 percent, someone should do the math, I can't, but in a hundred years we, who made such good investments, the right investments, will own the whole city and we started with our sweet little house, we sold it and used the proceeds to invest in safe asset-backed securities to make a killing and save our asses and redeem our souls, because we still have claims on life, we have several claims on life that have not been redeemed, at least not until now, but since these mean our life's savings, life will pay back a hundred fold, until our savior will finally deliver us from bondage, from all bonds, and deliver the goods: hallelujah! our redeemer will come and redeem us for good, for good money, and once we make our fortune, once we are fortunate enough to sell the house, we will count our blessings and invest them in something better than the house, something much better! And we will quickly be redeemed! Our redeemer will be here in a jiffy, wait and see! No, better not, all you will see at this time are claims, but no redemption; all right then, take a look, after all, there's nothing left for you to look at but your own face in the mirror: A house can't do anything for you, but cost you a bundle for repairs, for the upkeep, it will cost you precious time of your life, which isn't worth it, your life isn't worth anything anyway, your life isn't worth living!, that'll never cut it! But 15 percent per anus, per rectus, per annorectis, that's our offer, that's our guarantee!, well, it didn't quite cut it either, no matter, doesn't matter to us, but maybe to you, well, once you were fortunate to be blessed by the father, and now you are blessed and secured by the great fortune, that is our bank, but only for us, of course, its owners and donors, not of our blood, but yours that's running to our bloodbank, the bank we are running, the bank that is running in our blood, though it had not been our main line of work. Professional background: grocer and merchant with his own grocery chain. It's only natural that something pays off for someone who owns something, in that he doesn't pay out what he owns, he needs to hold on to what he owns, doesn't he?, undiminished, if possible, increased, if necessary; the bank always wins, doesn't it, so now you have matured through misfortune, you are blessed by misfortune, misfortune works, you don't have to climb every mountain to fall from high, misfortune works, now the vast barren orchards belong to you, who used to be able to eat fruit right from the trees, for only our fortunes are still growing here, I figure and I am right, we used up your fortune, what you inherited from your fathers to preserve it, we have it now, it's ours now, and they are ours to keep, highly priced and praised as we are for our fortunes. Ours is the throne, which always is pursued by long and greedy spears, we do not complain, we sue right away, we'll sue you too, we sue everyone, let others complain, it won't do them any good, we are the ones who file the complaints, who go to court if necessary, but we also offer an investor's bill of rights, take a look at our prospectus, go ahead, take a good look at it, take it in your hand, hold it against the light of day, and it will all come out, no, nothing will ever get out, but one day it will come to light, our bill of rights, which we offer for your penny stocks, no, nothing will ever get out, it will stay on the conveyor belt, we have nothing to declare, with this bill you can aim for the heads of the fortunate, our heads, you can aim, but you'll miss, you'll miss us at home, because we had to sell the home; no, it was you who had to sell. You, however, you, no, not you, someone else, you are still aiming at us, you target us, who stay the same, who are always the same, you still target us, the customers, you really dare to aim for our head? Well, you are in for a surprise, you'll see, you can see already, but you can't yet believe it, I enjoy talking my head off, because as long as we speak as a bank, you can't speak as an individual, no, not even as the small-investors' rep. You can't tell us anything! But we have something to tell you! Like a hen, under our wings, we sheltered your money close to our loyal heart. Did I already tell you: All great things are simple and many of them can be described in one word! I think I already told you that, but I did not tell you the word, which lets you finally express what you cannot have or know or name, so, ready—here we go: "Freedom," "Justice," "Honor," "Mercy," "Hope;" that's from the foreword of our brand new annual report that beats everything, it beats, it baits and beats them all, and if already the foreword is so fantastic, how fantastic, how fabulous will the word itself be, the word that was in the beginning and shall be forever and everywhere?, because you can say any word and it is already with God, in the beginning was the word and the word was with God, and you shall also be, delivered from all earthly things, which you don't have anymore anyway, which you haven't had in a long time, you too shall be with him, the child of God you will always be, it won't cost you anything, you just thought you would get it some day during your lifetime, you'd get a word in at the general meeting, GM for short, before the bust, well all right, the word was with God, not with you, remember, but you never remember anything, my word is totally wasted on you, while you already wasted all your money, doesn't matter, our clients and staff represent almost all political viewpoints, well, some are missing, but I am sure they will be replaced in time for things to fall into place, and they also represent many religious communities! We can describe our destiny in a single word: *Europa*. Oh my God, now I just dropped that word and lost it, I just wasted it senselessly on total dimwits! Luckily, I said it, when

I still had it, and no wonder, I miss it now, I got accustomed to that word, but now it is with God, though now it's already returning from this heavenly vacation, it was the last trip, the plane crashed, so did the market, this is why it was the last heavenly vacation on earth, or maybe not, the word won't be coming back from there, because it really likes it there and now it won't back the bank anymore, which once sold us the asset-backed securities. And the word is silent now. Soon we will have no words for it. *Europa*. Money is our God, he is right on the money, God our gold in whom we trust, we are with him there, but we won't find our money there, even though we worshipped it. Europe we did find, eureka, we sit right in the middle of it, though lately without money. *Europa*. A strong border against all others, while your imagined profits are boundless, of course, but we will make sure you know your limits, right now we are showing you the borders of Europe, and those are much more expansive than the limits to your pursuit of profit. It's okay, go on, invest in more debts, we support your debts and we can also support your death, if you like, it won't be easy, though, in a beautiful sanitarium or in the home care of a smart, handsome, hands-on nurse, that's what you thought, but it won't be; it won't be a pricey suicide clinic either, since your priceless life is all you got, and you couldn't afford anything higher than this clinic, huh?, so you are dying for us to finance your debts?, you want to get your fill of life, though you have to already watch what you eat?, well, who do you think you are? Where are your securities? Well?, we are waiting? They aren't secured by debts, are they? The charges on the debts have already completely eaten up your securities. You are completely insecure and unsecured. Well, if that's the case, let us show you your natural limits, which of course don't overlap with those of Europe, you are much smaller.

But your plans for the future will collapse, no matter what plans you had! You will collapse, but not *Europa*! Europe won't collapse, something more would have to happen than your lapsed securities and the return of your leased car. Europe's borderlines are natural, so are yours, only smaller and narrower, but that's okay, since you don't have a car anymore. So you are walking a narrow line, you walk the line, but without cash, Johnny! Let me tell you, the real demarcation between Europa and Asia is not a mountain range, it's not an age range, a price range or a shooting range, it's not a range at all, rather, it is a system of faith and ideas, which we call Western civilization. Well, isn't that a good idea? *Europa* as a spiritual concept? It costs us nothing, it costs you everything! But it is profitable to invest in Europe, perhaps it will come to you some day, if you can't go there, because you will have a problem, because you won't have a car anymore, because the gas will have become too expensive, no, too cheap, no, too expensive, no, too cheap, in any case, lack of money and many other things will make it impossible for you to go there, but now a part of Europe belongs to you anyway, so you don't have to go there anymore, it's enough that we are there already, to finish the big project, which is what our European land, split in small shares, which you can buy, means, this is how much Europe means to us!, just imagine, and you, too, can buy Europe!, the car has been returned, but you can relax, because a part of Europe is yours now, as proven by this share. If you stop carrying the concept of Europe in your heart, it will die! So make sure to get your share! We should proclaim programmatically, that the spiritual concept of *Europa* will not die, as some people predict. Quite the opposite: We declare that it should live and shine and bring light to those parts of the world, where unrest and terror rule. It also says so in our annual report, it says it even in the foreword to our annual report, and it will also be proclaimed in the afterword, though we don't make a big deal of it, and just wait till you see the revised report! And there won't be a sequel in court, and if there were, the script would be the same until our goals are reached and all our hopes fulfilled and there shall be prosperity for us to have and to hold, for richer rather than poorer, yes, and for prosperity to hold on to us, so we can have it all to ourselves, until death, until our debts do part from us. We, for example, receive something, which we give to ourselves, by holding on to a license fee; what for?, for what?, that's what!, by passing on the fee to a firm which we own and earned, which carries our dear, yes, very dear name, but has nothing to do with us, yes sir, it carries our name, our good old merchant's name, but we don't own it, don't you also carry a name, and it weighs heavily on you, a lot comes with it, doesn't it?, but you own nothing, we, however, carry our name and now you too, we haul you along, and we'll also haul you off, in case we can't carry you any longer, our name alone will carry you, it will carry you across everything, our name is like an airplane, it will carry you across anything, but it's not right to let yourself be carried away by our dear name, across Europe, beyond Europe, carrying on with our name as if it belonged to you, you don't even belong to you, not by a long shot, not even by a fraction. You don't even own yourself, not on your life, not in your lifetime, your life belongs to us; so you really believed in the 15 percent abnormalum, *nomen est omen*, and now it's time for congratulations!, you belong to the bank!, but your name is not The First, Bank, of course, or is it? If your name were The First Bank, no, the Last Bank, the last exit, the last breath, you'd be the first to have that name, but you have nothing, you are nothing, we throw you away, because you are not the one I called forth, you are not the chosen one, you are someone who's called something, and we don't give a damn what, the main thing is, you buy the certificates, which have the same name as us, but don't belong to us, they belong to everyone. No, they belong to a company on the island of Guernsey, but you will never get to Guernsey, unless you take out a loan for the trip, which we won't approve, we won't approve your attending our annual meeting to insist on your rights, we won't dump you, of all people, on our institution, which knows all about dumping! A firm, that has our name, but it's not us and it doesn't belong to us, though the name is misleading, as if it were us, but we aren't it, it's just our name, as we said before, pure coincidence that this is our name, generations of merchants before us had that name before us, and now it is us!, it's also pure coincidence that your name is what it is, no coincidence that it is nothing, you can believe what you want, in Europe everyone can believe, they can believe in what they want, that's Europe; Christianity has for centuries shaped and hammered and twisted and bent its history, which it held up against—art, science, diligence, industry, research, influence, success, *Europa*, go ahead, believe in whatever, or don't, it won't affect us, but where would you be, had you not taken advantage of this opportunity to buy these certificates, which bear our name, they bear our name only, but they are barely worth their name, they bear our name, but they can't bear us, these are stern bears, I mean, bear sterns, no, what did I want to say?, what's in a name?, it's full of bull in a bare market. They bear only our good old loyal faithful name, which follows us like a dog. We return him but he comes back again, good dog! Good name. What belongs to us, nevertheless—well, in fact, it's always more than less!— what belongs to us, nevertheless, are the license fees, these

fees fall due every day, they don't fall, they rise again before
they fall and you, of course, are also due, even if you don't
understand a thing, if you don't understand why, they are
due this minute, if you don't keep your due date, what did I
want to say, we are really doing you a favor, but that's not
really what I wanted to say, well then: Our bank, who bears
our name, but is barely worth its name, its name is on these
certificates and supplements that ascertain its undivided
interest and dividends, indivisible and united, like the stars
on the flag for its large lobby; the bank sells you its paper
beautifully bundled and collateralized already by your future
debts, and all these materials indicate that up to 80 percent
of this bank's revenues can finally be delivered by such fees.
Deliverance is all, sins don't count then anymore. Not in this
bank! They don't count in this bank that is us, that is us, as
in U-S, you ass, the bank that's us and has our name!, we are
the bank, but the firm, the family, this great family, just like
our great country which should in fact have our name, the
firm is not us, at least not anymore, those are two totally different things, the bank and the family, you have to understand that, you simply must understand, although it's not
that simple, it's the economy, stupid!, but if it were simple,
you would never have bought into it! It's just by accident that
our papers carry our name, just as we carry our name; both
of us kept our fine name—fine for us, the fines go to you—
on these documents, and doesn't everyone want to keep
refining documents with his name on them?, it makes his
documents so personal, so proprietary, so all one's own,
owing to no one, everyone his own owner, how about that!
But we didn't give you a present, of course, you have to pay
for it, so does the firm, the family, our great country, where
you count the least, the country that counted on us and
counted us out, but not for long, the company that has our

name but doesn't belong to us—just like the country—has to pay, so that it can keep our fine name, like you can keep yours and we can keep all, because you are not a chair, you like to sit in one, nice and easy, you are a follower, you follow us wherever we want to go, wherever our name takes us, you've known our name since childhood, you were allowed to go shopping but not to fuck with it and your mother, the name, I mean, the name on the bag, the shopping bag your mother could go shopping with, with a name given by God, the joy of my youth, he gave us this name at holy baptism and we pass on that name to this company, which is called like us, yes, to this firm, which has our name, which is us, the great Family, which, however, isn't us, that's pretty simple, and the bank, which has our name but isn't us, has earnings of up to 80 percent, and that's the truth, no?, yes, no!, *that's* the truth, yes?, no?, what am I saying, well then, 80 percent earnings from transactions with the firm, which has our name, accidentally, certainly accidentally it has the same name as we, there are worse names, right, no?, no! right!, but we are not them. We are not this firm. We are part of a family, this great Family, our great country, but we are not this firm, we only have the same name, whether the firm exists or not, whatever, it existed and its name shines far and wide. There is a glow to this name, which doesn't come without a price, we promise, we already got the prize. So what's in a name?, like yours?, you've got nothing to your name, that's why you need new papers, you need papers made out to our name, but it's not us; yes, our name stands out in these papers, but they are only paper, you can say anything on paper, and that's the truth!, but it cannot stand up, and we are not it. Watch out: it's not us. You can't know that, of course, because we have the same name but we are not to be confused with our name. Caution, please! The water is only five feet deep here, you cannot dive in, or you'll be paralyzed, so surely, you don't want to take a dive, do you?, no, you don't want to be immobilized, you want a Stimulus! Like us! The bank has the same name as us, a whole bank is named after us!, but our papers also have our name, they are our babies, after all, our smart babies, those papers, but there's nothing to the name. You bought these papers, because they have our name, but what's in it? Nothing! In effect you bought nothing, because you believed in our name, in whose name you bought, but that left you high and dry, because you did not consider, well, you didn't consider anything and we didn't tell you anything, but now we do, because it's too late for you, well, maybe for you, for us, unfortunately, it's too soon, because we would have liked to continue trading with our highly valued name, that's also the name of the firm, which means nothing as there is nothing to its name, this is why we are telling you now that the identical names are coincidental, that the firm's, our great family's name is coincidentally the same as the name of the bank, which is us all right, it rightly belongs to us, so that our days may be long and go well in the great land the Lord our God has given to us, the land that's registered in our firm's name you can pull from the universal trade register of the human family, which pulls out all the stops all by itself, yes, and that includes you too, this register makes sure we get a good tone for our tune and sustain it too, as long as we want to, because we have the majority of voices voting for us and the tone is ours as well, every tone, we call the tune, we register it in the economy's organ, we take care of the good sound of our name, which belongs to the same-named bank but not to the same-named firm, which is listed in the well-prepared register of the island of Guernsey, the rocky island, the isle that rocks, where you will never get to, unless you can afford it, and we'll take care you can't, because you bought our papers, which are called like us but aren't us, but that's okay, the papers are not real either, because the bank, which is named like us and which indeed is us, you are right in that regard, the bank, as you know, is us and it's named like us, that's quite logical, we are this bank, we are not the company, it came about without us doing anything, we have nothing to do with it, absolutely nothing, and if we did, not anymore, we even have a different name, but it's still us, it's not us, it still is us, we are the bank, not the firm, although it has our name, at least in the old days it had the name of us great merchants, but you shouldn't count on that, because now it has another name, it's name is Heracles now, names are sound and smoke, but for us they are capital, that name is our capital, that name is our diversified capital, which we have in stocks and now we send to battle, whatever there is to our name, it will win in our name, whatever we make of your name, we make you bring your money after a long battle to this lovely place of rest, where the bank will take it over, if we take on the costs of care, where your money rests, but grows no more and works no more, at least for you, but surely for us, no more for you, not more for you, not ever more for you, for now it is still our firm, our great family, it just no longer has our name, but it's ours still, there, yes, this is where your capital is sleeping, it even works in its sleep, but not for you, you are supposed to keep buying, not just get something out of here, on the contrary, we'll get out of you everything we can, as long as we can and you got a lot more in you than you think!, take a chance and give us a chance!, you can trust our yearly report that you can trust the chance we give you to take a chance with us, and ours alone are the license fees charged to you from August to the end of 2007 for our dear name alone, alas, I am so alone!, which we milked for you in the stable of Augeas, who for you is identical to us, but is not us, never!, you are not your name either, that's what you are called, okay, but you are so much more than your name!, you are a human being, you are human through and through, that's the highest there is, we are only a bank, right?, we happen to have this name, so we can make sure nothing happens to you in difficult times, and this firm paid a license fee for being allowed to have the same name as us, but we, we have nothing to do with this company, we just told everyone what to do, we certainly can tell this company of unlimited liarbilities whatever we want it to do, because it has nothing but our name, without being us, as we remind it every now and then, and we also remind you as our dear client that the license fee for our name is due and with this license fee we gutted the firm, which has our name, for which it paid, for which it delivered the goods, only you, you caved in, we don't, why did you cave in prematurely?, imagine a roof would do that, you'd never get it under control again!, caved in before you could cash in, cash in like us?, now you can cave in as much as you like, you'll never cash in again, we did it for you, we cashed in for you, now you belong to the bank and you can take a rest or a hike, it won't do you any good, you crashed, you caved in instead of cashing in like us. Had you only done like us! But you didn't, you should be happy someone still likes you. We like you just the way you are, Europe takes you the way you are, now be on your way, take Europe's mission, which we are not, wherever you want to! If we were Europe's mission, Europe would also bear our name and we would get the license fee! A license fee also for the name *Europa*. We'll have to take a closer look, there might be something left for us, there might be something in it for us, something might stick, but what's left for you? At best the IRS comes after you from time to time, from country to country, but the money you once had is with us now, we let it disappear, poof, a magic trick, where would we be today, if we hadn't jumped at the opportunity? Where would we be, if our clients hadn't believed in our ideas of expansion and Eastern Europe? But I am going off on a tangent, I am going as far as Bratislava, where we also have an office, yes, also in Györ and even in Prague and Budapest, what did I want to say?, you weren't supposed to know that, but it just came out, it always comes out, it always comes out. Luckily, too late for you and without consequences for us, more episodes will follow, something always has to follow, there will be a follow up, let it come, we don't mind, right now we are still with episode one, the pilot project, right?, we'll get it right, because we'll be the pilots, you are our dear guests, our guests on board, you can get a good rest with us, your money also takes a rest, right, and the cheers of victory get us all fired up, it's our own cheers that get us all fired up, they pop like champagne corks from our throats! We are the gods, we got all fired up by ourselves, while you got burned. We burned your capital, but it was very small, it didn't burn long, though it still made us happy, your capital, your poor little cappy, which once was yours, has been burned by us. And for the naming of our dear name, which is identical with us, but not with this firm, which only is called like us, which just bought the name, which idiotically is the same, we've got to change that, but as long as our name is our capital, we take your capital too, we have the same name as this unlimited, uninhibited company we do not keep, which isn't us, please, no mix up here!, names are sound and smoke, and the smoke is ours too, 23 Million Euros license fees were taken in by our bank, whose name alone is capital, maybe our biggest, you'll hardly stick out, your cute little cappy won't be noticed at all, it disappears in the license fees we took in, you think they are too high? You are right. Because of accounting in breach of contract the license fee was set too high, but it can't be high enough for our reach, that's the lesson we teach when it comes to our dear name, dear in the truest sense of the word, that's the truth, our bank has to live off something, too, you don't have to live, you are much too small to live, you are a premature birth, we are your incubator, but you fatten us, we stuff ourselves with you, and this incubator is turbo-charged, we charge ahead and flash the big V, we charge interest while you have to charge everything. We already have your capital: It's already been sunk on one of the Channel Islands, well, maybe not on the island, but off-shore, sunk in the sea, your little capital, end of chapter, but our firm, the Family and our great country are alive and well!, this great Family, which is all of us, even if we don't get the money from all of you, but only a part, long live the Family, which is all of us, our great country, and God bless! Oh, Jesus Christ, just let it live, period, that's a lot already! Your capital goes on living, it has eternal life, it lives on beyond your death, it lives in our company, which is every-one's family, you were its host only, you could give it a tem-porary home, your sweet little cappy, but that chapter is closed now, it goes on living with us, and you can file chapter 13. Your lucky number, our lucky strike, let's strike up the band, let them strike in Europe, it's all Greek to us! But your capital is alive and well, so why are you complaining?, it lives on a beautiful island, aren't you happy it's alive?, and will go on living?, while you are dying, your capital lives, it lives with us, and it likes living with us, it has good company with us, it would be all alone with you, but with us it has enter-tainment, fun and games, sports on board with a board that thirsts for your credit and hands you back a debit, our bank has to live off something, that's the truth, no? no? No!, how true!, we've said it so many times already, and it lives off the firms, which bear its name, but they are not it, the firms receive, they receive from you, you are the firm!, you are firm, we are firm, it's all firmly in the Family, it's destiny, manifest destiny!, and the bank takes all, and what's best: We all have the same name! Isn't it lovely, isn't it meaningful and precious the way it was conceived? Precious indeed, even though we didn't have to think for long, which name to borrow from whom. Everything in life is borrowed, life itself and names as well. The name is gone now, but everyone still knows it. No one knows the name Heracles, but soon everyone will know it, soon everyone will know that Heracles is our name now, but it's not us, earlier, we were called like us, but it wasn't us, now we have a different name, but it's not us, and that's us, that's us! Isn't it lovely? Man proposes, God disposes!, but he doesn't dispose of us!, we dispose ourselves, we dispose our firms, which have our name but are not us!, I've said that a few times before, I am still saying it, you still don't believe it, yes, okay, an audit revealed that our legal limit for license fees was a total of 1 million Euros max, now that's the limit!, really now, who says we have to know how to count?, you can count on us, you might want to count us out, but you wouldn't believe how well you could do with us, in our place, with our name and even better, if you were us! But you are not, no, you are not. You do understand, do you, you made a good deal with and under our name and value, you didn't deserve such a deal, no need to make such a big deal out of it, you made nothing, you didn't earn your share, so that's what you get, you got nothing!, you don't deserve us, you sure didn't earn us, we can assure you, but of course there's no insurance for that, the premium would be much too high, but it's a good idea, it would be a good idea to start an insurance company with our name, which, of course, would also not be us, which would insure you in our name against losses, which you had and will have by investing in our name, it's a terrific idea, don't you think so, an insurance that would have our name but wouldn't be us, just as we are not the bank and the firms with our name. It is pure coincidence that the names are the same, though that doesn't prevent us from charging fees, we have to give a name to such coincidence and that's the name of the firm, which isn't us. The child needs a name, isn't that the truth, no, that's the truth. Even a premature birth, which comes to nothing, gets a name before it is carried to its grave. Only the coincidentally identical names of the firms and maybe soon even of the insurance of our bank would be pure happenstance and disregarded for that reason, although we do not disregard any fee, ever, not a single one, we guard them good! We make an estimate. We estimate the costs for the coincidental uniformity of names, I say purely accidental, and that's the truth, no, that's the truth, no accident, we just couldn't think of another name, and our control mechanisms, I meant to say, are firmly in place, as you can see. We control ourselves, and that's enough. Just think how often you couldn't even control yourself, so be thankful we let ourselves be controlled at all, and our in-house control, our self-control is the strongest!, we don't have to submit to any control, but we do. We don't have to allow any degree of control, but we do. We make allowances for all controls. We even allow ourselves to control ourselves. Where would we be, where would we be, where would we be, if our clients hadn't believed in our ideas of expanding ourselves, in the identity of names and ourselves, in our resemblance to a holy twinity?, no, wrong, not even two gods would make a unity of two, let alone three!, a God even our clients resemble more or less, but there is no control, by God, God knows no control, God knows, there's no control under God, there's supposed to be only one nation under God, God controls himself, and that means that no one can control him: He is the ultimate justice on rocky downhill turns from appeal to appeal , he is the highest authority on a rocky downward trail of appeals, for God loves the poor the most, he doesn't care for us, but we don't care, because he can't control us! We control ourselves, just like HE, and he doesn't like it, because HE wants to be the only one in control of himself, and that means, there is no need for control, HE is that HE is, we are, what we are, well, okay, there is unity among our clients, but they have no other option, they are a unity in and of themselves, but that doesn't do them any good, the IRS controls them, the partner controls them, the authorities control them, the parking inspector controls them, since he hasn't learned anything else, isn't that the truth, that's the truth. This prevents you and everyone else from feeling like a little God, without knowing what God really looks like, everyone like a little God, you'll all be like Gods, we promise you, cross my heart and hope you die, after you signed our contracts! Where would we be, where would we be, where on earth would we be if our godlike clients hadn't signed our contracts, our clients, who let it rain Olympic gold, who poured the riches of mount Olymp's gods all over us, for they had faith in the bank that had our name; it sure was gold, man, but it sucks! and now they say our standards were poor, because they thought we were the bank with the same name, while we are only a firm which coincidentally has the same name, a company with limited liability, that should be locked up, lock, stocks and barrel, whose liability is still limited, not entirely eliminated, just limited, and the company, a shitty stock company, should be put in the stocks, if it doesn't stick to its liability, oh dear, that's a shitty glue, and the company can't be basted, I mean busted, though it delivers license fees as a purge to us, but we, we don't shit money, we don't give a shit about taxes, we don't defecate, we deduct, that's how we relieve ourselves, the money keeps flowing in to us, but nothing flows out from us, the money keeps flowing to us from those who have had it, who have been had by us, we have them by the balls, we, the sperm bank, the issuing house, which strokes the market and blows the market, and that costs something, of course, dues for contracts and services are transferred to us, because our name is what we are not, fees for marketing and management services are proffered to us, offered at our altar, for services we don't know what they're supposed to consist of, where they could lead and where they will land, but since we are the service providers, we'll provide, and you will fork out the fees, you'll fork out a whole *Wurst* of fees and in turn will be taken apart by our salami tactics, sausage is our business, we once were grocers, we still are merchants, only now we sell our name, which we are not, so we actually sell nothing, we already sold everything, everything must go, our name must go too, only because we are called what we are not, not anymore, we were, but we are not it, and because we are called what we are not we are doing all this for you!, and you don't even pay your dues, but your losses pay for your dues, all outstanding dues are more than balanced by your outstanding losses, but we, we want to have a balanced budget, and we get it with our services, which consist of us having the name we happen to have, it's not our doing, we can do nothing about having the name we happen to have, but that costs you, and we collect for these services we provided, for the services we promised you with our dear name and in our dear name, just because we happen to be named, what we are not; our name is our game and now we are hot for gaming your money; we are a hot tip, we are hot money, because the name of the game is the bank's, the company's like the bank's, the bank's like the company's, it's one big family just like our great country, which is a bank, so someone's gotta clean up and that's us, yes, U-S, Ace, we collect the fees, we clean up and we clean up good, we don't want an infection to spread, do we?, the fees are feeding on you, they are nesting in your flesh, like a virus, they are eating up your nest egg, but you must scramble it up for the dough, so scram, will you, scramble up some money, we don't want your flesh, it's foul and ours is fair, no use pounding on our doors, the pound is falling, we are busy packing it in and you can pack up and pull out, no, not the gun, the dough, the dough for the dues, you pay the dues, that's best for you, trust us! giving us the money, it's better than a viral infection having the name we've got, and you have nothing to your name, so it's only fitting that you shell out those bucks, but remember, the gun is always pointed in your direction, so go ahead, shoot!, shoot for the sky, so things start moving, so we can swing into action, so that everything goes down again fast, hurry, move it!, even faster, so that everything goes down the drain, get a move on, it's gonna be a bumpy ride, we are not a plane, we are a bank, which has the same name as the great family that is our great country, which it is not, well then, what did I want to say?, where would we be, where would we be, where would we be without you having the guts to accept our project Eastern Europe, had we not adopted you as our child, because your money is as dear to us as our own child, as our own flesh and blood, it really is our own flesh and blood, even though you birthed and took care of it, now it's ours, where would we be, where would we be, if you hadn't gutted us, uhm, if we hadn't gutted you like a Christmas goose, though we also got some we gutted like a chicken for soup, yes, you can get poultry with us too, its wings will pull you up, no, not a bull's, a bull won't do that, and you can also buy all that from our store, from one, the last one that's left from the chain, the rest is Bank, the rest is bunk?, no, *Bank*, as in *Deutsche Bank*, and what's left of you gets in our bank, where they are always ready to serve you, after they put you through the grinder, though you are a bit skinny, but it's all right with us, we still take you, we don't take you, we take in the dues, you smashed your piggy bank into small pieces, it has been butchered for us, but a penny saved is a penny earned, and that ain't no shit either. And before you have a chance to ask: No, we can't accept you as a member of our bank, there are strict rules, and you are no exception. But we'll be happy to sell you our securities, which are meant especially for you, as one of our countless small investors; yes, we can always sell, it's our pleasure. And we even take the shit, we even take your change, it also adds up, just like all of you are teaming up against us right now, at least that's what you are trying to do and it's unfair, unlawful even, because you surely have something else cooking in the back of your head, and it's simmering even further back in the head of your small investors' rep, when he wants to sell you a small plot of swamp for a highway, an airport, a power plant, and you can't even afford the gas to keep it going, no, wrong, the gas is all you can afford, they'll sell you the car dirt cheap, but you won't want it. You'll want to keep your half-finished house, but you won't be able to. You are thinking up some-thing behind your specs, though it's doubtful there are any thoughts anywhere in the back of you. Our small investors' rep, who is not identical to yours, he is another, just as the I is another, our bank is another, even though it has the same name as your investments, as your firm and co's, which are one great family, one great infamy, no, as our firm, but we aren't it, and your small investments rep, your small swamp broker, your small investors' small plots broker, your broke investors' broker got some thoughts behind his specs, he is cooking up a storm in the back, the little backroom of his brain, you can smell it all the way, and he's not only got you, his small fry, eating it all up, he has created quite a stink and this is the kind of guy you trust!, oh well, it's your business, you are the small investors, who are not up front, your rep isn't the straight shooter he pretends to be, he won't stick to his guns either, wait and see, but he won't do much harm, he is a little speck like you, or he would be a big shot specu-lator, right? But behind him there are others, we swear, we swear to anything, we swear at the things he has cooking in the back, let them come up to the fucking front, you can wait that long, just wait!, just a moment!, the small investors' rep, you know about representatives, don't you, the small guys' rep acts at the behest of stronger guys, much stronger guys, and we know it, because we are already much stronger than you, we always were, we always were among ourselves, we didn't need a rep, in any event, this small swamp developers' rep has something in mind, the small investors' rep is a small plot rep, he is plotting something, okay, let him, he doesn't represent us, that's a representative picked by small folks, who don't even have the instruments to play and score, we do have the financial instruments, you, however, have no instrument to make some noise with, to fight back with, but you have a broker, who'll break your neck, who won't break his leg, who'll just stretch his legs and piss on you!, you'll see, you are nothing, you are a nobody, but you want to be represented! That's just like you, having a representative for Nothing, you have-not, whom you let represent you as the small investor, listen now, behind the rep you picked are real big shots, bigger than us, and we are quite big!, he's got a whole army of locusts, of predators, an army of animals standing behind him, who will go after your money even more aggressively than us, much worse than what we could ever do, what we would have been able to do; well, they know what they are doing, not even we could have done it, we only had your best interest in mind, since you took care of our interest, right?, therefore, let us warn you right now: Behind your small investors' rep, there are bigger folk than us, be prepared, be forewarned, we know who's standing there, we can't prove it, but we know it, and we dare to tell you, and that doesn't take much daring, we are also bigger than you, and that's already very, very big, but the hedge funds, the leopard funds, the beef stock funds, they all stand behind your investors' rep, the rep you picked, fourteen different bouillon stock funds or even more, all available in our store, all organic and pure—pure nonsense, that a store can't have other business deals in store—they are all standing there and you don't see them. You see us, you can see us as the speck of sawdust in our eyes, but you can't see the plank in your rep's eye. The funds, the *fonds*, the giant *frondists*, the gigantic frontline soldiers standing behind your small investor, steering him like a car, right behind the man, your rep, who represents you and everything you no longer have; there they stand, those funds, and there are others standing behind those funds, they stand there with other funds like a firewall, like a one with many zeroes, but the zeroes come after the number one, and you come after all those zeroes, you are after them to make you a zero as well, we can see that, you make a good zero, otherwise you would never have entrusted your money to us of all people. How do you like them apples? But you started counting your apples, before the picking was done, didn't you? You picked the wrong apple, you wanted the biggest one, so you banked on the city. You picked the big apple, not the small Mac, someone had taken a bite out of it already, in any case, you probably figured out some profits. But, we already told you who's behind your money, they are predators, so big, you wouldn't believe it, who knows, behind your rep, your reputed rescuer, who, we impute, does not represent you, but just pretends to represent you and won't present a dime to you, he'll break you worse than we, you bet!, we bet he'll break you, as your broker he'll go for broke with you, maybe no, but we believe he'll break your balls, there are bigger ones behind him, we can see them from afar, while you already dropped the ball, we can see who's already on his way, what saviors will save you for good, but you can't see anything, because we are standing in the way, but unlike you, we can at least imagine that in the end he will resent you and us and he will proceed with his proceeds against us all, we are in the same boat, after all, and you should be in row with us instead of him, who has stronger guys behind him and they won't row your boat, why should they, they don't even have to get back on shore, they are doing very well off shore, they let you run ashore; everything you kept running after all your life is gone now and your small investors' reps will put a motor on your money and let it fly away, farther than we could ever throw a stone after you, you didn't see it coming, did you, and now you see it going, and we keep pulling ahead, we're still pulling it in, while you, unfortunately are back-paddling, full speed back, we can understand that you're feeling bad somehow, because you lost your money to us, so it's with us now, aren't you happy you can come and visit your money any time, you can read our balance sheets like the augur, the flight of birds, the screams of birds, no, really, you can see

for yourself that it is doing well, your money, better than
with you, because with us it has friends, fitness, fun and
games on the island, which every man is, but not every man
can have one, he can be, but he can't have, no, we can't give
your money back to you, can't you see, it's on vacation here,
at least it gets a vacation, on an island, why would it want to
come back to you, it doesn't want to, that's a fact, no?, yes,
no?, that's a fact, that's right, it had to deal with the license
agreement, which cost a good deal, which was a great deal
for us, a deal done with your good money, because, be honest now, you only gave us your money because of our good
old vintage brand name to which we attached new tires at
least a hundred times, on the radiator grill, where you poor
little Wieners are stuck, because the company carried that
name and carries us still, maybe not for much longer, but
for now it carries us, because its retreaded or brand new tires
kept the wheels rolling and the show rocking, but it wasn't
us, whoever says we're still it will be sued, our name is
Heracles now or Hercules, whatever you prefer, sometimes
you may express a preference, but it's not us, or are we it
already? Have the contracts already been executed? Yes, of
course, now and then our executions are open to the public,
you want to know, don't you, what happened to your
resources, your capital, which doesn't deserve this name, to
your money, yes, I see, the birds flew, their bloody insides
landed in the books, the insiders understand it all: now we
are it all right, and it makes no sense for you to complain,
we manage your money, you can manage without it;
Hercules or something like that is our name now, it's not us
either, but it's even less us than we were, when we were still
we and had our name, this is something to be looked into,
but not all too closely, right, no?, right!, proud millions we
took in for the brand, which certainly has been damaged by

you for years to come, maybe forever, and that's the truth, isn't it? True!, it's your own fault the brand is damaged now, the brand that was also our name but is no longer now, though we were it and still are now, no?, no longer now, true?, no?, at the close-by annual meeting, it was so close, you couldn't even notice it, and now its already over, right, not many of you could participate, right?, right!, no? that's where we erased our own name, that's how generous we are, taking out our own damaged, half-wrecked, spit out, vomited name, erasing it on the spot, since it wasn't our groceries that made you puke, right, no?, right, can't complain about those, those are A-Okay, you didn't puke because of them, you must have eaten something else, but it didn't come from us, nothing comes from us, besides, is this trademark still a trademark? We are a super trademark, we can assure you. Is our trademark, which trades so well on the market still one? Yes, yes, of course, it marks our margin of profit, which always propelled us to the top of the food chain and earned us many points, discount points?,—no, we don't have those, whatever; whatever there is to our name, whatever we are named after, what's your name anyway? How should we remember everything, right? Whatever, it was a trademark with good reason, a hot brand that rocked, a firebrand that rocked the market, it was our trademark, but our bank had the same name, a coincidence? No coincidence, the company had the same name as our bank, it's not its name anymore, but the bank is our bank, and a man is a man, right? Whatever, it made sense to be a brand, a hot brand that marks profit. A man is a man, no?, people are people, a brand is a brand. It puts its stamp on everything to be sent anywhere as long as the address is known. A man is a man, we'll get back to that as soon as we've been sent off, that's how it always starts, that's just the beginning and the success story goes on, it's coming to us now, but after us it is going nowhere, what we've got we got and what we have, we keep, right?!, and real estate stays put, and real estate is real estate is real, right? And a real estate is static, a man and his money are mobile, and that's a good thing, real estate is not, right?, it has to stay where it is, in old, small towns in the new Europe, in new, modernized, completely rebuilt cities, whatever, they have to stay, some made a mint, others didn't, some put their mint in bourbon, Kentucky bourbon and played the horses — and lost; location, location, location, is what it's all about, right!, we never ran into you, but we ran you down, you couldn't hold your horses, you bet on us, too bad for you, uhm what did I want to say, well, so we invested in realties, in Eastern Europe, where it's still cheap, right?, just at the right time, when the price was right and the times no longer just, while elsewhere the spoiled loans were still sleeping undisturbed in their little beds without any intention of waking up again They are probably dead by now!, but not with us, our realties are still working for us, they represent value to you, to which your value has been added since you invested in our unrealities, those unrealities have a name, which we also have, which we always had, but it's a coincidence, like love, a coincidence, because they aren't it, they aren't us, we just take, can you finally get that into your head?, we just collect the fees for ingesting, uhm, investing your good money!, money you put down so ferociously, you lost it, didn't you, so now it stays put with us and you'll have to put up with us, that's how it goes, so we take the fees for all the money put in the wrong place at the wrong time, though with a charming face that strangely attracted fabulous fees, but not for you, no fee for you, just us and you for us alone for the wrong game with the wrong chips, so picture you on your knees, not ours, those are fees for the money you have put or will continue to put into our unrealties, you'll have to come to us but you won't find us, we are unreal, as everything great, except for example the majestic whale, who at least can get his head out of the water, your money doesn't and if it were great, you wouldn't have it and it wouldn't even want to work for you, because now it works for us, whom else, it's us who have the name and always had it but soon won't have it, but now we still do, your money has our name now, your money has a famous name now, it has celebrity status, you can be proud of your money's career with us, don't you think?, with you it couldn't even work as a domestic, thank you for letting it work for us, be proud!, it was you who gave it to us, you took a shot at it, a big shot, kaboom and your capital dropped dead and now it won't do you any good, but it does us, because it works, it works for the real big shots in the firm which has our name, but nothing to its name, it has a different name, whatever, it works for the firm, the great family, which is our great country, no, it doesn't work for the whole country, just for the company, it stands firm on that, and we cash in on account of a management contract we made with you, even though you don't know that, it's a done deal, somebody has to take care of the money, right, no?, no, yes!, right, because you can't do it, that's why you gave it to us, because you didn't want to take care of your money, well, then we do it, we take care of your money and for starters we collected a license fee and management fees and office fees and parking fees and fees for the use of our money park, where we parked your money, and for the use of our lookout platform, because our outlook is great now, while you missed the step to the platform and it doesn't look good for you at all. It has to get a rest somewhere, your money, otherwise it would keep pushing like you, for tickets to the world cup or world series, it pushes its way to the stadium, to the TV, to the beach, it pushes, it shoves, but no longer for you; it is dying for a new order, it would kill to get some order into this raging current, into those gripping and ripping jaws. Your money is no longer dying to see you, you left it; before your audit, you ripped up all your orders, the kind of rip-off you are; this is how we picture it: as your money is lying in the sun with us, oiling its skin with interest, before you burn like a moth on a light bulb, before you get burnt by us, interest, yes, it yields interest, but not for you, it's not the least bit interested in you, who earns it, huh? Why are you so negative? Why can you only see losses rather than negative interest? Who's supposed to do it? Who will produce a loss if not us? Who is doing anything if we don't do it? If we don't report for a job, which should have been done by you: the management of your money, which is now with us, vacationing on the island, fun, games, sports, beach volleyball, right on target, right on the money, we volley your net assets, that's what we do for diversion, we instantly divert, uhm, diversify your investments, how are we doing it?, wouldn't you like to know! We diversify everything we can get our hands on, anything that slipped through your fingers!, we give those precious investments our precious name, the name of the little piggies that went to the market and found, no, founded a bank, you can't even find a bank anymore, can you, to finance a little house in the country, a vacation home in Mallorca, you can't do any of this because we are already doing it and what we can do, you don't have to undertake or take over, you are not an undertaker, right?, well, you might as well be one, but an entrepreneur you are not, right?, sure, you like to venture new things and so you should, by all means, biking, swimming, computer games, go ahead, do it!, we'll be happy to also take on those ventures for you, it'll be to their profit, we also regularly service your money, which is ours now, for which we charge a service fee, of course, your service station does too, and when enough has been served and the tables have been cleared and everything has disappeared into your greedy little jaws grinding the infinite, in your terms: the unlimited and unprejudiced Nothing, then the shop closes, and even the shop takes more than we do, it would take more than we do, if you still had it, if you had more to invest, we can assure you; we can also spell it out for you: It comes to 160 mill total! And if we figure in the comparative value, God willing, last year's imperative value of money—we figured it was the will of God, when money still had value, except yours, since you no longer had it—then we can rightfully claim that last year the comparative value, including the commission for two stock offers, which we were able to make because of you, right?, well then, it still amounted to 147 mill! So then, within those two years, while your money vacationed on the island, no need to check train schedules, flight schedules, boat schedules, you'll never get to this island!, while your money was serving an internship on the island—because your money is working for us now, were you even aware that your money was doing God's work? Just in case you don't know where and for whom your money is working, it is working for us!,—well then, while working on the island and using its limited free time for a few scenic round trips, always going round in a circle, right?, your money also shed a few pounds!, it shielded you from shedding pounds, true!, but while you took your after-lunch nap on the patio, your money practiced with us and lost some pounds, but all that's lost on you, though we are telling you the truth!, no, your money never sleeps, that's not how it works with us, that's not how we do it!, it might have slept when it was with you, but not with us, there is no sleeping on the job with us! On the island it has to work out after work, it races against you in the company jersey for the firm that has our name but isn't us, now less than ever, because we have a different name, right?, that's right and just, your money took good care of us, why should it care about you, now that you can finally sit on your patio and read the paper, before, you could have never taken the time, and now we are also taking care of your time, this is definitely not your time, maybe your time is still to come, but it isn't this one, now you can finally get some rest, go ahead, read the sports pages, get excited!, read about politics, tiring as they are, isn't it lovely! you could also open the big umbrella, but it won't rain money on you, that's pouring on us!, though it rains no more in the plains of Spain, it reigns here with us, and we let the rain fall as long as it falls, until it all falls, it's a windfall for us, but not for you, you paid it all out to us; should we tell you something? Maybe we shouldn't, but we will anyway: we don't charge for placement, and we won't take your place either; the silverware, linen napkin, a glass of wine, marketing, licensing, the artsy label on the bottle, made by a famous artist, right?, those are extras, gifts for loyalty, that's right!, for loyalty to your money, which in turn wasn't loyal to you, but to us, why?, because!, your fault, your own fault, and now it is so much happier with us, well, yes, sometimes it looks at us quizzically, pensively, but we reassure it right away, we reassure your money, sure, it has to work, but it also is entitled to fun and games and sport on this beautiful island, right? That's why you are no longer entitled to any supplementary retirement funds, isn't that the truth, yes?, no? otherwise it might as well have stayed with you, back home, on the patio, where you take care of your plants and advantage of your retirement, which is all there is, which will never be more, which will be no more, or it wouldn't have had to leave, your money, for which you hunger and thirst, like for justice, but the money is also hungry and wants to devour other monies and grow, getting devoured by other money, stronger money in the process, and that costs!, just the management of your monies, they are flowing to us from everywhere like brooks that merge into rivers that run into the sea that surrounds our island, our gourmet Guernsey, washing 'round our land of cheeses, of hams and jams and wieners, lapping 'round our ankles—the management is costly, of course, it costs a fortune, for as soon as the money arrives on our blessed isle, there are the aforementioned facilities: fun and games and gaming and sports and schmooze with likeminded peers and likeminded money, which has to work whether it wants to or not. You don't have to anymore, but your money must—big relief for you, big relief in your change purse, on the stock exchange, on Wall Street, in your Wall Mart wallet, in your portfoolio, great stress and hard work for us, our pleasure, don't mention it, well, not a great pleasure, but, as they say, a penny saved etcetera, . . . and what it earns is lots of fun and games and gaming and sports, whether or not you want that for your money doesn't make any difference, because it's not yours anymore, it is these loyal, strong and reliable hands that hold your money, which does not have your name anymore, which took our family name, because you entrusted it to our firm, our great family, our great country, to put it in our nimble, tough and trustworthy hands, in our trust— *Treuhand* in German meaning "trusted hand;" it handles your money so lovingly now—which was to yank you up the high bar; but it was only a local bar, which left you high and dry and hungover; well, you wouldn't have gotten very far with it anyway, in any case, it was our *Treuhand*, our nimble trusted hands that brought the bank, which has our name and also is us, while the company no longer has our name, but still is us, which means we brought the bank a handsome two-thirds of its current gains! Well aimed and gamed. Bingo! Isn't that great! Island hopping on the sweet dreams boat—isn't that a hoot? Your money wanted to get away from you, it wanted a vacation, a summer job maybe, an internship with us, and so it happened to get here, so it happened that your money is getting ahead, it's getting much further than it would have with you, well, now you are amazed how far money can travel, you would never have thought your money could do that, it wasn't all that athletic before, you are amazed how your money amassed more money, however, not for you, but for us, who have the same name as your money, while you have nothing to your name because you have no way with money, while we have our ways to get our way with your money, we loved it even before we had seen it, you blame us for heavy losses, but we no longer hear you, we play badminton with your money, because it's light as a birdie and flies away as if by itself, because all those shorted securities are lying around heavy as lead, suddenly they don't want to play anymore, they just want to lie there quietly all around the world, since they are constantly pooled and drained by our fucking, uhm, sucking claims, by all kinds of claims that suck, why is that?, why?, you too do nothing but claim and blame and complain to us, though no one gets anything for their claims anymore, worldwide!, we don't really know anymore what exactly it is we claim, but we still have claims, and we also get nothing, because we already got everything, we got unfeasible fees, we got those securely tucked away, the capital is still inse-cure, it's gone now, we too have claims, mind you, thank you, you handed it to us, and the credit-enhanced instruments bearing our name, they still bear it, soon they will get another name to wear and wash themselves white with, well then, those thus enhanced claims have come, by way of a firm on a Caribbean island, Aruba, Aruba, Aruba, within the reach of our bank, which has our name and is us and so are we, though under a different name, that's a well kept secret, it's the best guarded secret there is, but it seems to have gotten away from the shepherd, since you too know it now, but what can you do anyway? You can do nothing, it is where we are, no matter what name we have, and we put our livestock in the stable, which we don't have to clean anymore, who will do it then, who will reevaluate the stock, which suddenly has become so much more than it was, those animals have multiplied uncontrollably, how did that happen?, we aren't Noah's ark, eh?! If the small animals behave like bulls and mess around and poop all over the place, we didn't keep that from you, we keep a lot of things, but we didn't keep the dough, I mean the doo, which gets collected in small plastic bags, that's the law now, right?, so we collect it, that keeps the land clean, it keeps up the European land, which has our name, but isn't us, which is all of us, but we aren't it, so the land is kept clean. Someone has to do the cleaning up, no matter what his name, someone has to do it, his name is Heracles now, or Hercules, as the common folk call him. All right, then. What's next? Your money isn't next, at least not next to you, next to you it is nothing, but it is much further than you. And not only your money belongs to the firm, the family, the world, no more, no less, yes, you too are the firm, which for a long time had our name, but wasn't us, when you still thought it was, even when we still had the same name as the firm, but were no longer it, which has a different name now anyway, no, one can't say it has nothing to its name, it's just a different name, right? The firm handed us two-thirds of the bank's current profits, which have our name and they are us indeed, because we can completely identify with them. Gotta hand it to us, ask anyone, ask yourself, how come? How come it is all gone? It isn't gone, oh no, no way, it's well on its way to being blown, but not all of it yet. We are blown away by how long your money could last, we didn't think it would, but we gave it great upward mobility, that's the truth, no?!, that's the truth. But since you are asking: No one will answer you. No need to reply. You don't have to wait, your money will never return to you, get used to it!, we'd rather have it get used to us, it likes it much better with us, and that's a no-brainer!, after all, it means a lot more to us than to you, who just threw it at us, it means license fees to us, and trust fees and a few more fees, which we freely invented without anyone contesting this invention, man is free to take it or leave it, we take it, you leave it, two-thirds of our bank's profits are drawn from your capital, which was very small to begin with, it didn't pay off for you, it only pays off when it comes in huge amounts, one has to collect it, so, you paid it out to us and it truly paid off for us, that's the truth, two-thirds of the bank profits and more!, because we think in larger dimensions, right?, no? that's right, in European dimensions, which only we are able to recognize, since we had to first reach those larger dimensions, we had to blow a few things out of proportion, to enlarge these dimensions, fit for us, not you, you would have never recognized those European dimensions, no matter how often you vacation in Hungary, or bike through the Czech Republic or hike through another country you already know, that's something you can still afford, go ahead, treat yourself!, take a hike, you can also run until you are run over, but you will never grasp Europe's dimensions, but we grasp you, we grasp your capital and use it to stake out Europe's dimensions, where you would be stuck forever, since your money doesn't work for you, right, with you it would go nowhere and come to nothing, it only works with us, we have only your and Europe's prosperity in mind and in our pockets, first in the mind, the mint, then in the pockets we filled, we stuffed them with, but not to make us drown, we would have to be in the ocean for that, we, however, are highflyers and we fly over the ocean, to Guernsey, to the island of Guernsey, we gorged ourselves with your money, but we didn't regurgitate it, there never is enough of it, and it was for a good purpose, it was a benefit banquet, a fundraiser, a charity banquet for prominent bankers, it was truly fun to raise all those funds for ourselves, otherwise they might get into the wrong hands, then we'd rather keep it all to ourselves, we can talk openly here, right, no? no, that's right. We can see that all of these things are our roots, but also the crown that tops it all, just as we strive to top all your dreams and never put a stop to ours, we never stop, we never drop!, you do, come on now, where would we be, where would we be, where would we be, if we didn't know where our roots are, aha, here they are, our roots, we already thought we'd never find them, we dug from the top down, well, from where else?, we dug and dug till we were black all over, we even dug in the center of old Vienna, where we really dig our fancy gourmet market, and now we finally know where we come from, we do know where the money came from, but now we know where we are coming from, we found our roots, they have the same name as the bank, but that's just by coincidence, the roots of our bank reach back much further, after all, we have been cleaning you out for years, before we had to close out your account, all right, your account doesn't exist anymore, you wouldn't have gotten one with us anyway, because we close right on time and, as usual, you weren't there. But on the other hand, whose hand?, the other's; you could be there with our firm, if you buy our securities and by doing so, you could pass on to our bank, which has our name and also is us, two-thirds of your income. What are you so pissed about? It was you who wanted it that way when you entrusted your money to us. That money had its roots with you, but now we planted it on our turf, no shit!, you said it, we are not shitting you! Your money is your little rep, and we plant it wherever we send it, you tore out your money by its roots, and now you stand there, duh, and stare, but you don't see a thing; of course you have been rooted out from our roots, nothing grows for you from our roots, look for your own roots, we can't afford to think European or question Europe before we got the last cent out of you, because you are Europe, in case you didn't know that: All of us are Europe, but you especially, you still have a lot in you. Therefore we are offering an easy credit package, look at all the stuff that comes with it! The bank that has our name but isn't us, is now ready to waive the contractually agreed upon payments! Yeah, we believe you that you can't believe it, but it's the truth! We even offer you our easy credit package, because our companies fell far beyond the true worth of our companies, values dropped, but luckily we had none in our portfolios, instead we have real estate, electricity and airports, it can be a lot, it can be a little, it can be nothing, it doesn't matter, because you paid for it, not us, no, we don't have values ourselves. That's why we need yours! Okay. We took over your values, but those aren't values. You call those values? You can't be serious! Well, yes, seen from our end they are values, they could be values. We only represent those values, we stand for those values! While you have no more leg to stand on, we stand for values, great values, the fees for our bank alone come to at least two-thirds of our current profits, if not more, those are values!, and those values don't run away from us the way you, as our customer, are running away from us now, your money is smarter than you, it stays with us, it stays with us, it stays with us. And now in response to the constructive criticism of a few investors, not many, just a few, we tightened the fair credit package, so it unfortunately canceled on us. Well, so it goes. In any case, from now on, in all upcoming cases the company has the name not of the bank we were and still are, there's nothing to our name, I mean, we still have our name, but the name of the company is—listen carefully now: Heracles, also Hercules, because we do such superhuman work for you. Thus all other names are void. In Europe we are called Heracles, because of the jobs we do on, uhm, for you, because of the commitments we fulfill for you, because we fill what's empty; there's nothing unusual about us, nothing is unusual about it, not the fees, not the profits, not the losses nor the firm's home base in Guernsey nor the firm's holdings in Europe, which don't exist as of now, though it's a safe bet they will, although there's no longer any room in Europe anymore, well, maybe still for money, if we all move closer together, but not for people, certainly not for people, no more room for people, only for money, in Europe, because anywhere in Europe is Europe, everywhere in Europe is Europe, no, it's not anywhere else, there might be people anywhere else, but they don't belong to Europe. Everywhere places which you don't own, but you own Europe instead, no, you don't have to buy the people if you want to buy Europe, people are not included; if you want people you have to get them yourself, because you wouldn't take other people, not even for free, you would take Europeans only, and even those you would carefully pre-screen. You, of course, are European and you have values, and you have roots, well-trained roots that no one wants to follow, skimming everything off the top will do, right?, therefore we also own you, at some point you will belong to us, you already are part of our great family of investors, in whose port everyone longs to land, with open hands and land to lend, and when you own a piece of us, you will soon own Europe. It's not Turkey, which produces only the coffee and often not even the right sort, Africa produces the moor, but you are you! No, not the moor, the moor is us, so put thy money in his purse, gimme, gimme, gimme more! You are Europa! Eureka! You gotta be it. The biggest peace project in our times, Europa!, hubba, hubba, you stand strong like us, money never disappears with us, we can show the money upon request, on our quest for more and more, it comes from you, but it goes to us, where it builds a healthy equity base, we are healthy, thank you, thank you, I hope you are too, when the economy is healthy, you are too, you won't need a doctor, even though your appointment with him was set before the due date, but you were set up here in expert financial care, then offered to the public and then issued like a medical prescription that comes with a list of all the drugs one must not take, and you dare to show yourself to the public, who certainly won't be much taken by you? Even before you were plasticized, since now your plastic money no longer works either? Anyway, where are your securities that would allow you to do that? We are amazed you dare such a thing, going public with no cash flow to show for yourself, thanks, but no thanks, our cash flows beneath those banks where rivers stream, whose bed we dug ourselves, we lower our boat into the cash streams, our boat follows them blindly, those cash streams that will converge in wide rivers, which should benefit you alone, once they finally flow into the sea and around the

Caribbean isle of Aruba and the island of Guernsey, so why can't you shut up and leave us alone, so we can do our work, so your money will finally find some peace?, why don't you leave us alone to work with your money, to work with our bank rather than against it, since your part is peace, you are after all a peace project, the greatest in history, the greatest peace object of all times, *Europa! Europa!*, no, not Aruba, that's a misunderstanding, but what do you know about that anyway!, you yourself are stuck deep in the muddy! *Europa!*, it's good for business, for all who will generously contribute to accomplishing the peace project *Europa* will be rewarded, if not by us, certainly not by us, Europe will reward you. We reward ourselves all right, not to worry. Give us your wages to wager, then you too are *Europa*, like us, you are like us, but not us, and you reward us instantly for the good job we are doing and you don't have; you purchased our securitized bonds, our certificates, our triple-A ratings, instead of having to work yourself and now you think you have a claim? That's not what we meant. That's not what we intended. That's not what we tendered. You should remember how it is, making claims and getting nothing back. Nothing comes from nothing. Nothing dead-on against nothing, so let it come, this Nothing, let it come, for all we care, but nothing is coming, nothing is coming to us, maybe you have it coming, this Nothing, but it isn't coming to us, though it may be coming from us, but not to us. Whoever wants to reward himself, rewards us. This *Project Europa* carries its own reward, Europe is its name, but it is not what it is, luckily, because at any moment you could find yourself in the unpleasant situation that the certificates for the stocks you purchased for your portfolio—and that is something everyone needs, everyone needs a portfolio, perhaps not yours,— well then, the situation is such that those aforementioned certificates are not stocks, and furthermore, they are expired: so then, of course, the portfolio needs a meaning of itself and it does find a meaning, namely in itself, because it has content, true, no?!, true, you are looking for content?, here, in your portfolio, you have plenty of contents, but they contain nothing, nevertheless, your portfolio contains them, that sustains them, but it is on the look out, it is quite a looker, your portfolio, that little devil, right?, it is looking for meaning, your money, that's what you taught it, and now, moneyless as you are, you are looking for at least some meaning in it, yes, your money is also looking for meaning, but not with you, it can find no meaning, in itself or in you, but with us your money found its meaning, because its meaning had to be fed to it, its meaning had to be whispered to it, because mortgage-backed paper must be in every portfolio, that's what we told you all along, even on TV, that's what we fed you, as soon as you started breaking your poor little innocent piggy bank, that's what we whispered to you like to a horse run wild; well then, those risk-free stocks, which you purchased as stocks, which they weren't, that was a bit of a shock, huh?, anyway, they are terribly hurt, I am sorry to say, by your attitude, so they simply went away, well, not quite as simple as that, but they are off and running, they don't want to stay with you anymore, they have no more value, and if they do, then not for you, what would you do in Aruba with your money, what would you do in Guernsey with your money, since you are here, but your money isn't, oh dear, your money suffers from retention problems now, but you don't notice, as it is in Aruba in spring training, and it's all your fault, you trained it first, your money, it doesn't flow as it should and if it did, you have no container for it, where is it supposed to go, poor money?, well, it's flowing all right for us, but no longer for you, it flows into Project

Europa, but Project *Europa* flows directly into the Caribbean firm, where it no longer has our name, but it is us just the same, well, okay, it might not flow directly to us in the Caribbean, it makes a few twists and turns along the way, true, no?! right!, after all, it wants to turn away from you, right?, so it flows, it flows away from you, everything flows, it flows through your fingers, it flows away, it resembles us that way, that mega-project, that's much too big for you anyhow, get yourself a smaller one and start small again, from the beginning, as the zero you are—who could doubt its great future, the future of *Project Europa*, which you will be part of, or maybe not? Now the question is: Will this future actually happen?, will all those new ideas you can read about every day in the papers, actually happen? The Peace Project *Europa*—-will it happen or not, that is the question? It will happen, as we happened to find a city, a refuge, a safe haven, but not for the have-not refugees, and also asylum on the island of Guernsey, as we founded a firm in the Caribbean, far, so far away!, and all for you, all on your account, Guernsey is not Europe, of course, no matter, Jersey, Guernsey, or later Aruba, we do need Aruba, it's part of the game, whatever—they are all part of it, those beautiful Icelands, uhm, Irelands, heck no, islands, where we could realize our own big project, with a little help from a bank that proposes and disposes, which at this point stands still firm in the middle of Europe, it stands in for the firm there, that never stands still anywhere,], which is called like us and is us, even though as of right now we are called Heracles, which calls for us to work for you twice as much as before, no, three times, four times, five times, six times!, and we are proud of it. We quickly need new big shareholders, and we must cut ourselves off from the bank, which only yesterday had our name, but today it still has the same name, I mean, there never was nothing to its name, it was always the same today as it was yesterday and the day before yesterday, but it no longer is ours, we have a new name, we couldn't help it, and it helps, our new name, it is Heracles now, names are sound and smoke, it's a free for all after all and sometimes also a free fall, whatever works; hurry up now, we are calling it a day, don't call us, we'll call you, we can call you any names we want, what's in a name?, a stooge is a stooge is a stooge, we don't have another name, uhm, we have the name we always had, only the firm that took us in so kindly, now has another name, it still is us, nevertheless, the name one has is sound and smoke, and Curry and Larry and Moe, isn't it so?, that our name is Heracles now doesn't count, though it pays to our account, for license fees, but it doesn't count, it may count for you, because you liked our old name, because you got accustomed to our name, but for us it's not the names that count but gains; we are not talking about gaining weight, we don't want to get distracted, just because we also have to eat, we want to talk about the work, the working of Heracles, talk, just talk, sure, no no, these are gigantic jobs and you too can participate in our great project, as long as you stay peaceful, as long as you hold your peace, hold it tight!, don't let go, otherwise it might drop on your toes, so keep the peace!, because this is a peace project, right, as long as we don't get off the road, which is also named after us, since the journey is the goal, which also has our name, though it is no longer us, while we still are, we are Heracles, we are Heracles now, and we can make anything happen, we can do anything, even small jobs, the big ones anyway, with the help of your money, which you so bravely entrusted to us, we can always hit it, the new road, that's better than bashing your head, so go ahead, this way leads directly to us, it always does, the way, that's named after us, but isn't us, that is, in a way we are the way as well, the way, the truth and the life, but it only has our name and not even that anymore, but don't worry, hit it, we already did, and we hit it big!, so come you after us and we'll come after you right away . . . ahem . . . I am the way, the truth and the life, says this man, who has our name, but is not us, because his name is Heracles now, but he still is us, we are the way, the truth and the life, if you believe in us, follow us, it won't do any good though, because we already found the man to follow us. We already have a successor, who has the same name as our bank and is it too, we got him already. We can afford another name now, because it is still us! Go ahead, make your own name, it will get as little out of it as you. Only we get something out of it. We already got everything anyway, and we also got a successor. He is our heir. What did I want to say? Yes, our heir, who has our name and also is us. Who now has a different name, but is still us all the same. Everyone has the right to a job. Everyone has the right to do our job for us, anyway he likes, the way we like it, by spending what he earns, by giving us what he earned for himself, owning property, having the government at his service, yes sir, the government as servant, you heard correctly, because the government, which is our servant, we had it first, we trained the government, we drained the government, first come, first saved, the government as your servant won't give you a handout when you need one, why should it?, it works for us!, it is and we serve you, thank you for choosing us as your nest egg, your children and grandchildren will still have a nest, though they won't have an apartment, not to mention a house, not even a small one, at best it might fit in some public shelter, but not a tax shelter, that's for us, you can file for as much relief as you like. We, however, don't give anything either, we are not here to give any handouts, that's the government's job, because the government serves us, it serves all earnings to us, oops, something's not right here, whatever. You don't deserve any better than us making money off you, as you committed yourself, body and soul, in other words, all your money, to us, don't you worry, we are your worries now, give us your worries, we take them, we take everything, we are the lamb of God, but we are everything else as well, we don't give anything, we don't even give the basic support to your undernourished capital, that's less, in any case—and what a case it will be!, the worst case scenario is bound to happen—, than you gave us!, that's not much, it's only natural; Jesus Christ gave a lot more, naturally, you give what you have, that's not much, that's normal, the rest is for the government to give, our loyal servant of his master, true?, no?, we are Mr. M., that's our name, which is us, no, that's the truth. The government is also important somehow, because the Government oversees us, it oversees us even overseas, we are looked over, we are looked into, we are on the look out; and what is the outlook? We are overlooked, nothing was found because everything had already found its way home to us; Nothing was found, nothing got out, because everything already had come in, to us, home to us; they found nothing, those worthless wretches in our government who are not worth the dirt under our stomping feet, not even worth smashing their bodies to a pulp, those bloody nobodies, not worth the bullet to blow their brains out, they got no brain and that's a no-brainer; the government, it is the helping hand under our boots, trying to hold on to our bootstraps, because it is also strapped for cash; and now we should get the boot, because we did not deliver the booty, but we stood firm in our bootlegs; the government is also us, although we don't have its name, as we now have a completely different name, but it's still us, all the same! Yes, the government leans heavy on us; it leaned on us while it fed on our loans; while it learned from us how to run on the nation's reserves, uh, to run the nation's banks, uh, the nation's federal reserve bank, uh, to reign in the nation's banks, which gave the Fed a run for its money, the main thing is that nothing will be government-run, the main thing is that the government won't be government-run, then we'll be okay; because then we will have prevented the worst, because the states have competences, the government has the competences of the nation as long as it is not nationalized, that would be very bad for everyone, uh, not for us, not for us, nothing would be bad for us, but we did not confer any competences on the government, we don't have any, how could we confer what we don't have?, but it has them, nonetheless, the government has competences, as long as it isn't government-run, it should only be nationalized when it is broke, a nation can only be nationalized when it is broke, one can nationalize a nation only when it is totally bankrupt, as bankrupt as you will be soon, or already are, weren't you in a hurry! Now you too are the nation, I mean, now you are finally quiet, because you are dumbfounded, even though now that you are the nation you also are its politician, the representative of the people. Weren't you a bit hasty choosing your way, the way of having nothing, of having nothing left? So we'll have to nationalize the nation sooner than planned, true, no?! True! Why not apply your logic to us, go ahead, give it a try!, if you were to take as hard a look at us as we had to look at hard times, uh, you would find, no, not the money you gave us, what you would find is that even the biggest mortgage companies, which are listed, say, in Vienna, had losses of eight billions, yes, sir, if they can lose eight billions without anyone noticing, how much more then can get lost with us!, and that can be looked into, but that's not happening. The government has the competence, that's the least one can expect, but we have it too, we have competence, whatever it may be, we have more competence than you, we even have more competence than the government, which can't touch us, so why should we keep in touch, we can keep our cool, we don't even have to keep our clothes on, the emperor was also naked, though all had seen his clothes, right, you bought our guaranteed insecurities, but we sold them as absolutely safe securities, that's obvious, that's understood, you need some security, that's as good a reason, we can explain it anytime, the reason for us selling you insecurity as security, right, selling you the emperor's new clothes, the clothes everyone sees although there aren't any, and it is us who gave you the competence to do so, you, the people as government were given by us the competence to compliment us, uh, to compromise us, no, to compose us, uh, to control us, yes, that's it!, that's what I wanted to say!, Control! That's the word we needed! No, we don't need anything else, thank you. We are happy we could sell you those securities!, that we had anything to sell to you!, others would have sold the shirt off their backs to get our securities, we, on the other hand, would take your last shirt off your back, your burial shirt, for which you had to take out an additional loan to qualify for eternal life with the help of our certificates, which can attest to your innocence of mind and spirit, all natural, pure, and unprocessed throughout your life, that's what you thought!, securities, certificates, which will also prove your existence to your creator, that's what you thought, certificates which we dressed up in the wrong and as it turned out, toxic stocks, it makes no difference, God sees through all clothes, which will be torn off your body when the time has come and you will be sucked into the vacuum, because the loan for the last shirt has not been paid off, has it?, you still owe us for our securities and you will be sucked from the bank straight into Nothingness like an aborted fetus, how far? that far!, quite a feat, huh? go ahead, please, take off whatever you like, you can leave everything with us, so take it all off, if you want to multiply, you will have to, anyway, before your lord, the Invisible one, who will suddenly show up right in front of you, you can't take it with you, the burial shirt has no pockets, as they say , but you can entrust everything to us, even what isn't there, what you no longer own; we are more important than your parents, we are more important than your leaders, we will take care of you for a long time, after you have come of age, and before you could become a leader, we take you at your full value and prop it up artificially for a while, until our hands start trembling, a job for Heracles you'll get to hear about, since you never heard of it, you'll also hear about his other jobs, we support you, because the government has the competence, we, however, dispose of it, government proposes, we dispose, by ourselves, for ourselves!, the way we see it, these are no competences, this little steering wheel we turn—that's no competence!, but the government bravely keeps up with us, we chart the course and the government follows our strategic competence, which even the chancellor tried, but failed to gain, we got it, this competence, there are no audit reports just lying around here in some drawer inviting anyone to read them; no, no, they are not inviting, we would surely know about an invitation to a reading, after all, we are the catering service, we, after all, are setting the table for you, which up to now was set only for us, we would be notified first about an invitation to a reading of audit reports, we would take care of the buffet, we'll be happy to do that, it all comes out of the same pot and goes right back into it anyway! Is that the media heading our way?, to our investors' party in our investment home? Press hacks! Printing every piece of crap that's directed against us, that column of hacks prints more crap than the paper we could ever press others to buy, their crap gets in the press, but we must press flesh, we do that much better, we can beat them at any roadshow with our good—and forward looking former finance minister!—sure, he looks good, that's his best investment, but we cannot invest in his looks, we can't have his looks, we can have a lot, but not that, so how can we be like him and also sell our paper?, how to con people into buying our paper? We can't paper ourselves with the fallacious face of our former minister, can we now?—well, yes, that man once was somebody, he invested wisely in his face, and now he doesn't have to be anybody, because he already was somebody, because he looks as if he could be somebody again anytime, and how does that make us look, who can't be ministers and don't even look like one?, what do we lack? Anything he could do we can do much better, we sell better, after all, we've been sold out and were sell-outs once before, we know how that is! The minister was just a straw man, the merchant's straw man, the media's straw man, we made him our man, yes, ultimately he was just pushed to the front so that our dark envious faces couldn't be seen, only his, but really just the face, it is the face of capital, it is the handsome face of the born and native-born car salesman, who went to the capital, and a car salesman can sell anything, from cars that make us greedier to oil companies, we are him too, now we are also the former minister, who under-represents us, but nevertheless, he would represent us, if we could look as good as he, he is our handsome handpicked rep, just the right majority of one, we don't need more, we are also right, even righter than right, far to the right, the extreme right, that's us—as in u. s.—that's right!, but he isn't called like us, he doesn't even like us, but he is us, he isn't like us, but he is us, who are now also running under a different name to make people think we still got something to our name. No, we now have another name, but it's still us. We're still the same and we stay the same, because we have to, but we have nothing to our name. The ex-minister with his extremely flashy face amidst the flashing flashlights, so much energy wasted on him!, enough to supply a one family home with gas and electricity!, he served us well, the ex, the husband of somebody, of some woman, who isn't just anybody, and we served him well as well, he has to work like money does, right? No, not that bad! He has to work for our money, but our money works on its own, he has nothing to worry about, nothing to look after, though he has to look for future investors, whose investments don't look as good as ours, their looks alone have nothing much to offer, right?, so we better get ready that he won't offer anything, he'll offer nothing in our name, he'll only offer our name in case someone makes him an offer, but who cares, we take anything, we'll nickel and dime anyone to debts; many mickles also make a muckle, as George Washington learned from the Scotts, you might hear this the first time, you'll hear it from me a hundred times. So now the ward wants to be guardian, as we said before, and someone said before us, someone bigger, whatever, the ward doesn't want to have his foot thrown in his mouth, but money, major money, and some wouldn't even manage to hit it in, even if his mouth were bigger than a barn door or even bigger. Minors, bigmouths, all of you, so, dear bigmouthed minors, why don't you use your mouths and say what you want, you won't get it, use your mouths which you don't have, just as the emperor has no clothes. Your mouth is for eating, not speaking, all speaking is done by our speaker, he takes care of your speech, so don't speak, eat, come to our general meeting, where you'll hardly be able to meet, because at the same time you would have to also meet at our company headquarters, according to company by-laws, and you can't split yourself in two, you don't want to split anything, be honest now!, that's why you are so stuck on our stuff, so we can stuff ourselves and put on an awful lot of pounds, which is all right with us; which is us all right, getting fatter all the time, gaining in the shortest time, uhm, what did we want to say, so you are stuck for good in the place you wanted your money come back to, back home, right, at home with you, but what was your money supposed to do there with you? You wouldn't expect your money to settle for that, you are not that kind of slipper animal, although you slouch in your slippers on the couch in front of the TV all day, what else is left for you to do, you can't split yourself like some single-celled organism that has to stay in its cell, because there's no money left to go out, because his money ran out, and money is indivisible, because we don't want to share, we want the whole thing, don't we?, you could not be at our company headquarters and in Guernsey simultaneously, you will have to decide where to go, getting to Jersey or Guernsey is definitely quite difficult, due to the bad weather there year round, you better stay at home, do nothing, do it secretly, the main thing is, you can't be seen. In fact, you can't be seen right now, we didn't even notice that you can't be seen, so we won't be able to see you at our annual meeting either! What a pity! We would have given you something to look at! Here we go shoving money down your throat, safe money, which you first stuffed in our mouths, the money which you left with us, so we would watch it, so it would be safer with us, don't worry, we are watching, we are watching out, because it's no longer here, it's not here for you, we are still here for you, but your money isn't, it isn't—your money, because you lost it, because you lost, that's why it might, perhaps, be safer with you, because it's no longer there, your money is no longer at home with you, you can be sure!, you threw it down our jaws, and now you don't join us on this beautiful island! Though we invited you! Your money got ahead of you! Go ahead, take a look, it's gone!, Your money is gone!, the loan too, which you took out against your income, puff, all gone!, it prefers being with us, you can be sure!, and your small capital, against which you took out an advance so you wouldn't have to shoot yourself, it wants to get bigger, it is quite sure that it is safer with us than with you, in your home with padlocked doors and pads in the crotch to catch the dribbles, ahem, and padding between window sills to catch the draft; your curtains are drawn, the blinds are down, so no one can watch you banging, banging the woe drum, the woe-is-me drum. You, full of woe—wow—now!, bang it all out, how now? You can't? well then, go on a binge, pig out, eat all you can!, what? On what? You can't? You can't pig out anymore? At least you can still pick our catering service and products, all pure and natural, our all-natural jellies and juices, yes, sir, all of them!, so pig out on our juices and jellies, then out into nature to pick fresh cherries!, that's where you belong, not to us, you belong out in nature, we are the wrong place for you, we came out in the open with our binges, now you can move out into open spaces, you won't need to shell out money there, you'll just need shells to trade, shells picked up at the shore, berries picked from a raspberry bush, you won't need your money there, we traded it for you, there you'll find nature pure, just like in our dear loyal marmalades, what did I want to say, now it's raining safe, risk-free money, it pours right into your wide open mouth, whoops, here it comes!, that's what you thought, huh?, we gave you all natural stuff and a lot of security, lots of securities, we fed and raised you on our grocery chain so you'd later be able to give back to us, to the chain, which originally had our name and also was us, I said "was," because it no longer is us, our name is Hercules now, we have your CDOs, we have happy CEOs, and we have very busy CFOs, quite naturally, there are expenses for our natural, risk free food products, which will all be passed on to you, but our various jams and coffees still earn their good name, whatever it is, they have our name, but that's not who they are, they are not us, we have been tested and all contents are out in the open, so how do you like them apples?, the purity of all contents is guaranteed by our name, by our honor we no longer have, nor are we it anymore, there's nothing to it anymore, its name is Heracles now and we are it, we are still it, we still are a credit to you anytime, just make sure you don't forget our new precious name!, otherwise we won't know in which name your money has been credited to us, yes, with your ID!, everything the legal way!, no, we won't forget it, your name, don't you worry!, the government has to guarantee the security even of your heirs and it does, big deal!, the obnoxious Mr. X Minister, blossoming from having so much fun working for us now, expressly, expertly and exclusively after he was expelled from the administration, don't expect them to make him an ex-ex, a minister again; that man's like a roly-poly, look here, he always stands up again, but he never really stands up straight, he never stands still, he has to keep working, but we don't see on what, no, you never know what to expect, but he won't stand up again!, because he's always standing, well, yes, he keeps bouncing back and forth, but he stands, and when he falls, he always lands on his feet, never on his pretty face, this minister is the opposite of no way, he has his ways, he's on his way, way to go, go for it, have your way! We'll find out soon enough with whom, I mean what he is going for; it's the first time in his life he is working by not working, by letting the money do the work, driving it on like a soft, cuddly Goose Girl, hitting the money's calves with a crop to make it run and it runs to find some security with us; that money doesn't have any securities, but at least it is secure with us, it sought refuge with us, yes, he too, the ex-Minister, once and never more!, he once was more before, now he is more once more, he drove on, though his motor isn't all that strong, though he is not a car, he gets moved by himself, he has to follow his own calling, since no one else is calling anymore, he is motionless now, all he is now is the motor of the economy, can you beat that?, we don't beat, we cheat, we let the economy take us for a ride, the engine's humming, it's all tuned up for us to take a ride, we are taken for a ride, that's not what we had in mind and after it's taken us for a long bumpy ride, it drags us through the dirt instead of us taking it, because it's people who drive the economy, not the economy the people, how lucky that's not us, we aren't human, we are the fine thorns that prick the economy's tires until they blow up with anger, but one can't see the cause, what did we want to say?, so then the ex—minister made his tutor his auditor, his "uncle" of choice, who made the darling nephew—a screaming bundle in his baby bunting, another bundle and another, they came with a lot of securities, which he passed on to us all bundled, such bundles can be used in many ways, there are enough for several generations, they come in bands, who rob, no, rock, they rock the nephew in his carriage to make him feel secure, what did I want to say?, so, this former minister— you followed me so far, yes?—continue with the script!, he got—and it didn't cost him a penny!,—so this had-been and has-had-it-once-and-for-all-ex-and-axed minister got the auditor, the well-tutored auditor, into the regulatory bank to supersede the band of directors, he personally got him in, the exile minister—once a ministrant, always a ministrant, our little altar boy serving a higher cause with pomp and circumstance, he got his hand-picked uncle auditor on board to audit him!, and that's where he still sits, the auditor. Yes, take a good look at him, he doesn't age, he was replaced by a statue, at least that's what he looks like, he doesn't move. That's not one we can move. The born auditor, this uncle. Makes everyone cry "uncle." He got some band to play along with him. Those bands stick together, we can see that. We swear: They still sit there, he and his band. Well, maybe not for much longer, but now he does, in spite of everything, to spite us all. He's got balls, he's better endowed than you, than all of us. Oh yes! No, he won't have to sit in jail, he might be sent to Yale, no, Harvard, they're even better endowed, to audit some courses. He'll never have to go to jail for something he didn't do, for what he did by not doing anything, he just was the right person in the right place, that's a lot, he might as well stand, but that's not what he does, he sits, he hangs, no, they won't hang him, he's too well hung, he's got balls, he's hanging in, he won't let it all hang out, he's made of stone, though he keeps checking. The ex-minister's cheeky chum even checks himself. And then he checks us, how well we are endowed. He checks our dough, he checks the Dow. Of course, we lose against him! Our dough won't make the kind of cake we can eat too. He checks what's left of our dough gone sour, and what does he do with it? He wipes his butt with it. Great butt. Nice and shiny. But that's our inheritance!, No, not his butt, our assets, checked and secured by him, they were to be safe and secure for our kids, maybe even make good uncles, for what are we going to eat without those bundled pension funds, when the future breaks out all around us with hail and thunder and lightening, but not for us, for us the kid's not yet secure enough, though a real minister made him his nephew with the kind of security he offered us as those futures, which was to be our future, which we don't have, that's not the way to play it; poor baby has to pay for it, this kid won't even make it to the pay-offs, I mean the play-offs, well we won't pay, but the kid should start playing to get some pay, we aren't kidding, time to take off the kid gloves, here, what I hold here in the palm of my hand is his whole inheritance, that's all he got, our son, whose name is the same as ours, and that's who he is and will be. He is Heracles, he is like Heracles, he works the most difficult jobs, the biggest jobs, he seals leaks, clears all in-and-outflows, our son, a real Hercules, but his name is the same as ours, and what did it get him? Killing his own kids, because there wasn't enough left for them, and he didn't spare us any of it, he is some kind of a guy, that Hercules, you better believe it, he is our guy and he has our name too! Go ahead, give us your inheritance, we have ours, you've got your own, we'll make sure your heirs won't inherit a thing! We guarantee it with our name! That's our free service, exclusively for you, all extras excluded! We'll make you so careless you'll even forget your name, the main thing is, we still know ours, we have the same name as the bank and all the firms by that name, which, in God's name promise us, uh— you a huge profit, profit is our God, let him promise you whatever he wants, even nothing if he likes, we have another name, we want your name, because you really did it this time, you outdid yourself all right undoing our pension fund, and now you are done in and your name is also different somehow, you no longer have the same name as the bank and neither are you the same, oh dear, what's the bank going to do now, what's the bank getting out of it now? It got away by the skin of its gold teeth, that's more than we got, but we promise you not stability but the stables of Augeas, where we shall hook up all the cattle that are now patiently standing around, gazing, while sucking away on their blades of grass, to milk and honey pumps, which shall suck them dry, day after day, early in the morning, as the fog drifts off, we can already see it drifting off. You get the drift of riches all around, but the fog won't lift in front of your eyes, it won't leave our firms, which all have our name, so it's easier to remember their names, but there's nothing to their name, not even us and now not even our name, but we still exist, here to stay, we no longer have your name nor are we you, but we still are. And you are who you are. You want to be who you are not. How could we ever be anything with nothing to its name? It would be impossible! Our bank has our name and that's what it is. Our firms have the name of the bank, but that's not what they are. Phew! Just a moment!, they also have another name now, but they're still us, we are it still. Not to worry, we still are it. Maybe we'll present an overview, but I don't think so. Too much overview would only be harmful. You wouldn't know what to make of it all. You can trust our overview, we got it! It has our name, but is not us, it got another name now, but is us. But it is not for you, this overview will soon overlook you. Every viewing will overlook you, you and almost everyone else, no idea, why we would need an overview, there's no need for it, we already got it. We've been overlooked already, and an overview is no longer necessary. Phew, I am afraid, we'll have to say this again in completely different words. As can be seen, we do not lack the stuff whereof to speak, though we may ill-versed be in words.

Labor is the source of all wealth and all culture, and since profitable labor is possible only in society and through society, the yield of labor belongs wholly, with equal rights for all, to all members of society None of this is true, not true, any of it, none of it true, where is the Angel of Contentment to set this right? I am just the Angel of Justice, I don't have to be content, I can only rectify, this one is a wandering rock, take one look—rock unchanged! Look away, then take another look—rock still unchanged, but someplace else. But you can object any time, because labor is not the source of all things, of all wealth. Nature is also the source of great practical values, of gray values, uh... what should material wealth consist of, if not of practical values?, what did I want to say?, would you please also use your brain, because I lost mine, I misplaced it, it is less mobile than a wandering rock, really!

ANGEL AND ROCK

In Death Valley there are pieces of fifty-pound rocks, real rocks, wandering about, cross my heart, some even move uphill! No one knows why or how, because at first sight there is stasis, and that's how it goes with our money; my brain didn't wander off, my brain isn't dead either, nonsense, my brain is gone, there's a strange dynamic in my brain, but you can't see it, nothing moves in my head, and yet the rocks are wandering, the rocks keep wandering, why shouldn't my brain also go to work?

No one has ever seen those rocks wander, no one has ever seen my brain working, my head, my head, my heart, my heart, well now, my heart is working, I am sure it's still working, no, yes, I know it, there are hundreds of yards of tracks indicating that it's working, there is no such indication with regard to your money, and yet it worked, in foreign hands, not in yours, that's good, you put it in foreign hands just in time! Even rocks, once they start moving, can get up to a speed of three miles per hour. And what did your money accomplish when it was with you? Nothing! And what did it accomplish in the Caribbean? It rocked! But it didn't roll back to you, it didn't roll over you, it left no tracks, which even rocks leave, in Death Valley, though they can't be seen, one cannot see rocks wander through the Valley of Death! That would even melt a heart of stone.

Just about now the rock could start speaking on his own, with the Angel cutting in again and again and vice versa.

No, they don't melt, they just wander and wander and wander, those rocks, it is true, even rocks are more mobile than your small capital was in your hands, take Karen as an example, Karen is the biggest, with 700 lbs the heaviest rock of all, yet she moved only 59 feet in the same time period. You say 'only', but try being a rock and come that far!, watching you do it would melt a heart of stone, no, Karen won't melt as she wanders through the Valley of Death, but still, she wanders, she wanders quite nicely and relatively fast, they all wander, those rocks, they wander on dry or wet grounds, every theory so far has failed to explain them, except monetary theory, no, it always falls short when it comes to rocks, it's not made for rocks, it's made for what you produced through your labor—a special theory, to melt hearts of stone. You wonder why you don't have your money anymore? Because it wandered, it wandered like a rock, but even a 700-lb rock leaves traces of its wandering and the biggest mystery is, yes, I know, everything is a mystery to you, but this one is the biggest, why, why, why even some

neighboring stones, and those are good, welcoming neighbors!, why some of those very close-by stones take completely different ways. The Lord moves in mysterious ways,
so are the ways of money, we'll never be able to backtrack
them, until we get our capital back, until we're back inside
our minds, when even stones, which are so close to each
other, which might even be close friends, take such different
ways, some even move in circles! Circles! And you wonder,
why our company's money could grow, naturally because it
was passed on in our name and we also passed on to you
that it could move in circles, as if a tornado had sucked you
up, and you were waiting for it: some sucker to blow you,
but nothing is coming, no wind to blow us away, yes, something is blowing us up like balloons now, lots of gas we must
pass and it blows us away, perhaps to the loony bin and from
there to skid row, to shit row, passed like a buck and
dropped, because the firm dropped our pension plan, the
buck stopped right there, but even a buck, stopped or not,
is worth something and can start moving again, all you have
left to move is your bowels, nature is so mysterious, even a
rock can move in a circle, like you got our money moving
in a circle, no, that was us after all, no, it was you, it was a
different circle, it wasn't a gifting circle, gifts don't come for
free anymore. You sent our money in the ring, so it would
win for you, so it would pay off for you that we sent you our
money, we sent it as an intern so it would return to us as a
pro and as what did it return? It didn't return! Even empires
can crumble. Even kingdoms can fall. Commonwealths also
can disappear, and wealth can even be lost by the wealthy!
They can have partial losses, but they still have more parts.
Others have nothing. They have nothing, and they get nothing. Even rocks can wander, but those who don't have anything don't get anything, they can run around as much as

they like. Our money, however, was sent around in circles and now it is back with us, only it's worth more now, no, just a moment, please, it's worth nothing now, it is exhausted, it's nothing, it's down to nothing, we can see that right away, we know it well after all, but we don't recognize it anymore, after wandering for so long it's no longer worth anything. Clinging to the broker between worlds, between buyers and sellers of stock it expired, it died a miserable death, our money, after it's been sent around in a circle forever, it started to wander, the money, to make sure that the ethical standards that supposedly were the hallmark of your firm, which sent all that money on this tedious, tenuous trip, were firmly in place. Way to go!, that leaves no wishes unfulfilled, no open questions, no, some questions are still open, there's a terrible draught, and who will close the door now? Well then, the money is wandering now, okay, it's also wondering, when it'll get there, it won't get anywhere, because it's running in a circle, like in a fog, around and around and every time it gets less; one money is running ahead, okay, to pay the next money, which also wants to have its fitness sport, can't avoid that, money wants to be paid, even if it's with the nothing one still has, but one shouldn't pay with money, which doesn't even exist! But that's how it goes. Now we know. Too late. You promise us something, which doesn't even exist, which only exists on paper, like the money, which is supposed to pay for new money, but somehow can no longer do it, because something cracked, and now there is a hole, and everything falls into that hole. We can demand to get back as much as we want, there's nothing to be had, the money no longer exists. The money existed as long as you were there to be had, well, I don't know, I understand, but I don't know, I just don't know! Bullshit! The profit then is the giddy money, which was just staggering around in circles instead of multiplying in a straight line because if it keeps going in a circle, that stupid money, if it's sent around in circles, it has no goal, it doesn't know where to start and where it ends, it won't make it to the finish line, it will make no profit, it will have to pay instead, yes, it must pay, even money must pay, it must pay with itself and also be paid; but the money doesn't want to always be used only for paying with it, it wants to do it itself, it wants to pay with itself, but caught up in a circle, how can it spend itself?, it has known the way for so long now, it knows all the stores and every business, it can't spend anymore, it can only spend itself, for someone else, who, alas, won't be us much longer, and this someone will be paid with the next one's money, with ours, of course, we are always next in line, but it's never our turn; one money pays the other, another pays for the other, money can be quite a big spender and gets all spent itself, it is, that it is, it is God, it is nothing but what it is, and one money pays, while it's still panting and running in circles, the money that went first pays the one coming next, no, the one coming next pays for the one that went before, the phony profits of some investors get played, I mean paid with the bull, no: the bills of others, one money gets paid with the other, which once belonged to us, and that's no bull, but it's gone to shit now; you can see that yourself; one's money exists only in and of itself, it works only for itself, but unfortunately, that's not how it works, it works for the other one too. This money is that money at one and the same time, because it bought the other one with itself, it is God, it is that it is. Empires can fall, commonwealths can collapse, it can hit even the wealthy, it can hit even those who are rolling in money, and fall, like rolling rocks, something isn't right here, oh yes, it is, one money pays for the other that's made to run in a never-ending circle, so it can no longer buy anything for itself. This money, which one no longer owns, was paid with the other money, which is still owned by someone else, just wait until he demands it back, then everything is up shit creek, then money doesn't pay anymore, money doesn't keep anyone free, money won't make anyone free anymore, one doesn't own it anymore, and it's not owned by someone else anymore, it is no more and what's more, without it getting more, it has been sent in a circle until it got sick of it, it got sick of you and, sadly, also of us, it had to puke, it made us puke, until nothing was left, we'd even take the puke, but nothing's coming out, no shit!, they even took our puke, well, why not?, but it's not worth a dime, even rocks can wander, and they aren't worth anything, it's such a mystery how they can do that, in Death Valley, in the Valley of Death, where they are taken care of nevertheless, while we can't even pay for a caregiver for ourselves, even rocks can wander, even puke makes a muckle, but its tracks, like the tracks of those rocks, remain a mystery, the result is a mystery, how rocks wander, how money becomes more, but not with us, though it does some place else, why did it walk away from us for good, without reason, it's a mystery, the result is a fascinating mystery, because there is none. Nature can make even rocks wander, but not our capital, our capital is dead now, it paid for another capital, and now it's gone, and what's gone isn't always dead, but this time it is, the rich fell, the *Reich* fell, how do I feel?, I don't feel anything anymore, I do feel good, when even the rich fall, that's only right and just . . .

The Angel finally manages to push the Rock off stage and continues to talk alone.

Nature is as much the source of wealth as labor, which is only the expression or rather expulsion of a natural force, and although nature is stronger than you, always stronger than you, it can even make rocks wander, if only in the Valley of Death, where even you might be able to wander around, if you had a wind energy power of, say, 500 miles per hour, which we would love to have for our cars, they go down to the river all by themselves, but there is no such power, let alone a natural one, human labor is no natural force!, oh yes, it is!, as I was saying, although nature is stronger than you, you'll show her! Stronger than you? You'll get her weak enough, simply by getting to work. Work as a natural energy, which would like to express itself to you, if you had any? Oh yes, that's what it is, as it is a natural energy, if only a small one, a minimal one, to be employed only minimally, as compared to nature, which is always stronger and will get even stronger after the climate change, after such a change we won't be able to climb all over nature anymore, because we might get burnt, unlike the rocks in the Valley of Death, no, no, at first glance they are static, look again, and there was movement, but your money doesn't move, at least not where we are. And you don't move anything through your labor! What? Useful labor is possible only in society and through society? First labor was supposed to be the source of all wealth, which is totally stupid to begin with, because then the money would be the source of our wealth, and we don't have the money anymore, we gave it to you, don't you remember?, you can't remember everyone?!, and then? And then? I don't remember what was happening then and who is supposed to talk now, but you can decide that, there should be something you can decide, even where to invest your money, but wherever, it's gone now, it's not worth anything now, it's been destroyed, the work has been destroyed and the earnings too, and it was you who did it, how can a society be possible without work, since money can and should work all on its own, if not with you and completely without us, who keep sending the money around in circles, and how should we deal with the suggestion that no useful work is possible without society, without everyone of us? We can deal with it very well, we have your money, the money you worked for! You might as well have said that useless and even harmful labor only becomes possible in society and it frequently does, that only in society can one make a living from idleness. What's in it for us? Nothing's in it for us. We can't even bring in our own crops. Something might be in it for others, but for us: nothing. A big, fat zero. And what are they saying in conclusion, am I hearing this right? If useful labor is possible only in society and through society, the proceeds of labor belong to society—and the worker gets only as much as is needed to keep up the prerequisite for labor, which is society. First come the demands, then everything else. There's no more to demand from us, we have already passed on everything to you, we posted three letters with detailed answers to your questions, and now we have run out of answers to what has become of the fruit of your, as well as our labor, since they are the same, right, no?, well, you are working, yes, and your money works for us, so what became of it?, we ask and we are short of answers about your money's whereabouts now, because, Chorus of working folks, please start singing now: We passed on to you the fruit of our labor, our money, our savings, which we were finally saved from, and now the super test to pass would be the question: Where have our riches gone? Thank you, dear Chorus! That's enough! That'll do. I mean, we already know they are with you, we passed them on to you. And that was our response and you, once you had them, our riches, you did not respond to our request of such and such a date. First the government makes demands, because it is supposed to get things back in order. And what are you getting back? You get zilch, no, the government won't get you back on your feet either, God help us, well, maybe he will, he'll get us sooner or later, but otherwise, no one will get us going again, and there was this tiny percentage, to which you never belonged, they naturally wanted to get something out of it, since everyone got something, if only to get themselves out of it, so they had it coming, those one percent, they had it coming all by itself, they got it all, where did it come from?, just dropping on them, a windfall, and there you have it, yes, you too, the little you once had, gone to the wind, it now it belongs to us, one hundred percent, otherwise we wouldn't be and always have been the one percent, we are used to it, we know it all, we do with it whatever we want, because you can't be trusted with it anyway, you'd just do with it what you want, so it's better we deal with it, we'll deal with it, we make the deals. Because the different kinds of the one percent, the dealmakers, the job creators, the God creators, are the foundation of society. There you go. The fount of all wealth is bubbling so nicely just now, look here!, the rocks wander, they don't wonder where they're coming from, don't you want to take a picture with your new cell phone, the smart phone that's smarter than you? But you'll never catch them in motion, even if you waited for days, you can only take a picture of the result, that those rocks will again have moved a few yards. Then you at least will have gotten the picture, and we can also picture who still got something, and who doesn't and who went where, as a rock, as a rolling rock. We make conditions, you make demands. And both conditions and demands are taking positions, but they won't get anywhere. You just don't get it, do you, you get nothing.

You didn't consider that justice originates, I said *originates,* not *ends,* which would take us to a completely different place, you got that, yes?!, with the more or less equally powerful. It must not weigh heavier to one side or the other. There must not be a clearly recognizable superpower, or every fight would result in futile mutual damages, it would lead to damages like a flash flood, a flesh-filled flood, you wouldn't want that, right, no? No! That's right. Everyone satisfies the other, as everyone gets what he values more than the other. Give everyone what he wants and receive in return what you want.

Second Angel can't go on speaking. He keeps having fits of laughter and stumbles off; as he staggers out, he manages to utter only sentence fragments.

I see the noble man never wants for topics whereof to speak, though words may fail him still, what's in a word?, so then, rise up against us with proud words, let them speak daggers, we shall raise ours against them, send men into the glens to cut me logs of oak (*cries laughing*) and when they are brought to town, (*sobs*) pile up a stack of wood all 'round the altar, where we will roast them nice and crisp, set your own sacrificial fires in the pits, where you will sizzle, where you will piss, but you won't extinguish the fire. And so they all get burnt, scorch them all, but first drag in the wood, (*twitching helplessly on the ground now*) or do you think we should get our own wood to the cabin, where we will butter you up to sear you? Ha ha ha ha! Go get it yourself, you want

to get a nice tan, don't you? Get the wood and then get yourself nicely burnt, but not too much, it takes away the taste,
get a good fire going and we'll put some fire under your butt
so you know that in this country it's not the politicians but
us, us, us, who are running it.

Second Angel collapses completely and lies there, twitching.

THIRD ANGEL OF JUSTICE

*Bends down graciously, like a funerary statue, with a white
lily in her hand, to Second Angel on the floor.*

Money isn't everything. Money isn't everything. It's not that
bad we lost it. Our blessed city can easily survive the losses
you caused us with the foul papers you conned us into buying. What's a million, compared to the forty I invested, verily, verily, I say unto you, as the mayor who has no partly
paid shares, but instead acquired certificates scantily disguised as stocks, which are already in tatters, verifying that
he bought and then lost them, that's how easy it is. Verily,
verily, I say unto you! No. I say nothing. I'd rather give you
the heads up: a new fountain goes over there, around it we'll
build a cafe with a sundeck! The free public pool is filthy,
unusable and dried up, but you aren't free either!, you aren't
even free enough to live freely, but the civic center gets a new
outside terrine, no, latrine, no, a terrace and also completely
new chairs. In a year or two, the project will be finished.
Then the last ugly spot in the inner city is gone. Money's not
everything. Money isn't all. More than a million has vanished into thin air together with your certificates, ashes to
ashes, but money isn't everything. But as long as people don't
know that, it isn't true either, no?, right? No, that's right.
And people don't know. No one knows anything. You have
nothing, but you know that money isn't all. It's just all gone

now. Money isn't all. Nothing at all. Just all gone. And that's
all she wrote.

THE FIRST ANGEL OF JUSTICE

Enters rather unwillingly; he is pushed out by invisible hands.

A social condition is just, if it can be reconstructed as the
result of rules, according to which each individual is treated
equally. The differences start with the construction of these
rules, for example, a head tax—and by head and tax I mean
that everyone pays the same amount, irrespective of
income—can be justified as just, as can a progressive tax that
is determined by a person's productivity. Uh . . .

(*Takes off discreetly.*)

SEVERAL ANGELS OF INJUSTICE

*Pushing out Second and Third Angel of Justice with sheaves
of wheat while talking.*

What hope, what path, old man or whoever you are, can you
source for your fortune now? When your resources are
exhausted, you are exhausted, how only man can be
exhausted, an old one even sooner, maybe livestock, yes,
livestock too. Living creatures get exhausted, quite frequently, that's how they've been created, they are exhausted
as long as they live, their resources, we said it already, are
exhausted. Exhausted. I look at you, old man, whoever you
are, this country's marches and Europe's borders, we showed
them earlier, in the school of life, alas, we can't secretly over-
step those marks, the watchdogs are stronger there than
here. Our friends' protective resources can no longer be
counted on, as they are securitized only with claims, they
are clinging heavily like grapes to the old men's canes. What

is your opinion now?, stranger, not unknown to the bank, for you want loans, but do not get them, since your loans, which alas, you did receive back then, in great need, before the purchase of your house, loans before the vacation in the Caribbean, where your money had its main residence for quite a while—and you wanted to see your money, to visit it, be with it, before it's all over, before the dangerous surgery, without any security, there is no security in life, by the way— anyway, since those loans got together to form a chain, no one wants to be alone, why should those loans?, chains which hold together better than life with your body, oh stranger, whose body already has become a stranger to him, a stranger among strangers, inside every stranger is another stranger, those chains, which always hold together, those chains of loans, locked together, daisy chains, they'll hold up somehow, they hold on and yield nothing!, because it is Nothing that holds those loans together, those loans, which you once received, my dear stranger, my dear, dear to some- one, I am sure, just not to me!, to me you are dead!, well then, those loans you wouldn't get anymore either today, too late for those loans you won't get, what would a stranger know, at least he knows he's a stranger and those loans are in a terrible state, no, this state is not terrible at all, it's good old solid handiwork, what's the difference between Bad and Good? You know it well, and you, stranger, also know it, so I don't have to carry it out, I'm getting tired of it anyway. But does the bank know it, the difference, now I forgot which one? Between who and who? Between Nothing and Nothing? It doesn't have to know, the bank doesn't have to know the difference, it has to make differences, because it has its executive organs, which never fail, they could star in a circus as finance acrobats, with a safety net, of course, yes, they could, no, oh no, the organs are also failing now, where's the doctor, please, call for a doctor, he must come, immediately! He's coming, he's coming! The doctor will be coming when he comes. Oil will go higher until it breaks the market. This big doctor is going to the market, until it goes belly up. And who will cut the pork?, who?, which state?, makes no difference, the states privatize your income and socialize, no, no, democratize your losses. I never said such bull, and I've said a lot of bull, as you know, luckily someone else said it, before silly me could come up with it! And then they are done with you, the states, the government, the government enterprise, in which we all participate, uhm . . . and if you feel sick now, you may also call a doctor now, everyone can call a doctor, everyone is free to call the doctor of his choice as everyone is free to call his representative of choice, but also free to choose anyone else. Then everyone will have time for everyone right away again and the doctor will also have time for you. For men's pain also tires over time, the wind's breath doesn't always blow so strong, and those blessèd with fortune will not always be: for all things change and nothing lasts forever. The bravest is he who always relieth on hope: despair is the sign of the loser.

ANGEL OF JUSTICE, BUT I DON'T KNOW WHICH ONE

It is time to speak about contents, it is time to speak about great deeds, let us rise with our proud words, we do not lack the stuff whereof to speak, though we may ill versed be in words, we can send men, hunks like trunks of oak, but first we must take out a liability insurance, and that means twenty million euros, we must take care of this once and for all, or it will never go away, so we can go on lying, we must take out a liability insurance policy, as long as we're still likeable, before the police takes us to jail, so we won't be liable, it's surely understandable that we must be able to rely on a liability policy to protect us against the police, against being libeled, against our old name being dragged through the mire, our good name, we acquired with coffee, jams, cheese, ham, and wieners, etcetera, thus our name has a reach beyond ourselves, it made us rich, our name, the reach of our name is far enough to make you rich too, to let you be our face on TV, to further capitalize on the capital of our name, to add another, bigger chapter to the capital of our name, namely a bank that lives off the capital of our cheese and sausage and marmalade empire. We dissolve the empire and when an empire falls, it makes big waves, the foam sizzles, oh yes, it does, you can't make an omelet without breaking eggs, the eggs scramble, this one got egg on his face, that one keeps egging them on, here one sits on the wall, there another makes a great fall, you must peel this egg, you must peel that melon, you must peel this cheese, the wiener too, yes, why not, the wiener too, and you should peel those certificates before you eat them, you should peel them to see what we are able to see what painstaking efforts we take, what pain you will go through on account of us, what pain your painstaking payments will go through on account of our pay rates and you slip on the peels, uhm, deals, our deals that caused you so much pain, when we, the bank which has our name and which is us, took everything from you, as opposed to what we sold you, which also has our name and is also us, but isn't us, or we would have to sell ourselves, you won't seriously expect that from us now, though you wouldn't get us, you'd get our dear, precious name that's what you bought, no, you can't buy us, only our name. We can't be bought, just our name. Because now it's our turn to buy. We do the buying now. Why should we buy what we already have? There you go. We shouldn't and, what's more, you should, you should make sure that we get much more than we had. We are insured, we paid on time to make sure we won't be liable and locked up in jail, we've got that assurance, we are not liable, and should we be, it's no longer us, it's the insurance company we paid to keep us out of jail. And so we buy at our country's, uhm, company's expense, which has our name, but is not us, it's made up of you, but it's not you either, we buy millions and zillions, but one million isn't a lot, right, no? No, that's right, that's why we refer to the millions really as zillions now, we call them zillions, almost ninety of them, zillions of millions, okay, but those are millions too!, baloney, we buy it all back from the market, where we stirred things up not long ago, when we all had the name which was our name, and it still was us, we buy all those millions off the market, on the spot, which we always could count on before the time which in the meantime has shrunk to our time, in our big time, well, and big it still is. Good for us. But now time can do with just a small branch, and that's where it takes place. Time has time now. Before it had lots of branches, and lots of lots to build on, our time, which always was ours, for which we always were ready, weren't we? Indeed, in word and deed we were, verily we say unto you, what's more, what's more is more!, and now it has only one branch to sit on, time has time now, but it also has its own bank, down by the river, there is room for anyone who wants to sit and rest now. Only your money has no place at our bank, it thought it just could come along and sit with us, but we take it away right away. Others take it from you, but we take it far away. We relocate it to where it's no longer in your way. No more disturbances! We understand that you don't want to be bothered by your money anymore, you'd rather sit down comfortably with us at the bank, this is why we take the money, which would only take your last breath away, which would drive you out of your mind, if you'd let it, which would take the beautiful air at sea, in the mountains, at the blue lake, which you think you need so badly, but don't really need, the money, which would only constrain you if you wanted to let loose for once; it would also take your customary place at the bank, we'll send it off, we'll ship it all the way to the Caribbean, all of it?, yes, all of it, a veritably Herculean task, verily, verily, that's what we say to you, and this is why we named our company after Hercules, that's what we call it, but of course another name would also work perfectly well, it would be perfect everywhere, the money, the main thing is, it's gone and doesn't bother you anymore at our bank, now you can sit down and relax instead of your money, it will no longer bother you, we subdued it, we rescued it in a rescue company, and this is how, for better or worse, I mean, before things would get worse, bought it right off the market and moved the investors' money, which sat all nice and quiet down by our little river bank, soaking up the sun, so we moved it out of the sun, out of its dangerous rays, which might wreck your money's skin, no, not your oilskin. God made it, but we have made it. We made sure to get your money away from our bank as gently as possible. But suddenly, as soon as this place became available at our bank, because we bought up our certificates, which had our name but weren't us, money with money, moneys to moneys, certificates for money, that's less than money, it's less than a share, but it isn't nothing, for you it's a lot, for us too little, what did we want to say?, so then, the bank suddenly felt, like, liberated from your money, which we spent for our own name and for the certificates, which we dispensed on our own, right?, which raised a huge outcry, of course, someone always has to make a noise. We had to rescue our speculations somehow, and how does one rescue money? With more money. Money must be rescued with more money. And since we have too little, we take yours, it all goes in the same pot, right, no?, no, that's right, it all goes in the same pot, it comes from your pot and goes into ours, right, no?, right!, money has been rescued by money, the one money in the form of money, the other money in the form of paper, but money still, it's a paper that represents money and for which you also paid money, since we issued certificates in our name, but there actually was nothing to their name, but you couldn't know that, right, no? Right, how are we to sell those papers, which are less now than the money you spent for them, the papers, which we issued, right, no? No, that's right, how are we to sell those papers, so that you can continue to spend your money for us? Those papers must be issued, so that you are worth the paper on which they are printed, that's why we dispensed them so you can spend your money on them, right, no?, right!, so those papers went out first, which had our name but weren't us, that's the name of the game, those papers had to be issued by our bank and then be bought back again, so first they hit the ground running and when they hit rock bottom, it was man who got hit; the Lord gave it and the Lord took it away, who else?, or else it's humans who'd take it right away, right, no? right!, people would love to take it all, no matter from whom, well, so we just beat them to it and take it from them, we take it from the living, three for one, no, three in one God, well, either way it's a good deal!, Jesus fucking Christ, we don't take it from God, and we don't deal with God, and there's absolutely no dealing with you, we just take what life has dealt us and what a life it is!, we live it and we have to defend a name, which is ours and which is us; you might get hit while we hit it big at our bank, which has helped us so often, helped us like Heracles, a man not of many words but deeds, and now we bundle those papers we couldn't sell, even though they had the same name as us, even though they were shown on TV and that's the farthest you'll be able to see, those papers which had our name and also were us, no, sorry, we might have been our all-natural products, but that's not our true nature either, still, the truth is in our pudding, but beware, *veritas* is not a ware, is not the truth, not even truthy, not everything is a ware, and you can't buy every ware anywhere you want, but this one you can, it has our name, it stands for quality, and we stand for us with our name, which is the same as ours and it is us, we are something, finally, we are not something else, which might have our name but isn't us, and these papers, whose name is ours, but is no longer us, they are off to the Caribbean and that's that. The Caribbean, where people are lolling about in the sun and pounding on washboards, which are their own bellies, go ahead, lie down right next to them, people don't work there, you don't want to work either, that's why you understand those folks so well, everyone takes a vacation if he can't get anything else, we take anything we can get, how often do we have to tell you about the mickle and muckle, and the company in the Caribbean could send your money for diving lessons, the money you gave us, you gave to our bank believing it would turn into more, but we believe it got to be rather less, you don't seriously believe we would tell you that, even if we knew it, right, no? No, that's right, so we pay for the papers, which are dizzy already from all that traveling around in circles, from all that merry-go-round, the money, which was real with you, which got dizzy only with us, the money, which once was so healthy, it's sick now, the money, it's got nothing to its name, but we still take it, this money has our name, it doesn't matter if it's not us, we won't tell, we won't tell anyone, but with what money should we now buy the papers that have our name but nothing to their name?, well, then, the papers will buy themselves! Isn't that great! We don't need a Hercules to lift those papers, to make room for them at the bank again, if need be by force, the papers are proceeding to attack, they take in the proceeds, which you once generated so generously, but no longer do, we got it all, so that now those papers can buy themselves! They had our name, they have our name, but they are not us, though they are well on the way to be us, to become us, so now those papers got something to their name, because they purchased themselves, no pain, no gain, so now we sign loans for certificates, uhm, so we sign in our name, which is the same as ours, but isn't us, it's the certificates that certify that we can buy ourselves anytime, just not our name, which also belongs to us, but isn't us, we buy these papers, which no longer sit at some river bank but lie at the Caribbean shore, not doing much of anything, a bit of sports, vacationing, they earned it, after all, and now we buy them all up, they always shared our name, and now we are those shares, no? We aren't? Well, no matter what's their name, what's in a name, it's us, and if we try to sign those papers in your name, you won't have any luck, we don't sit on our papers, you can't sit on your papers any longer either, we know you are tired, but you can't retire now, not if you just sit on your papers, right?, they aren't even there anymore, right?, you relied on your papers, you wanted to retire, to rest on your papers, and suddenly you don't sit, you fall on your ass, you hit your bottom!, because there are no more papers to cushion the crash, right, no?, right, but now we've got a problem, we've got a big problem. It's not that we got nothing to our name or that we're called names, but. But. What did we want to say? Well, at any rate, those papers are very special! They stay on course. They stay in the Caribbean. They don't need a crash course in ratings to know what they have to do, they aren't moody, they don't have to know how to play any instruments and analyze instruments, they know Poor's standards, they set their own, they are a credit to their name, and credit is our name, which is the name of these papers, but it's not us, it isn't us and it wasn't us, we were only at our bank, the one you may not sit on, but pay into, forced, yes, we were forced, to buy back papers which had our name and also were us, so that you can quickly go on buying them again and again at their newest and therefore ever higher rates, keep going, so there won't be a bottleneck for buyers, what are you saying?, if we also kept selling? Of course!, we kept selling your papers to you, so that you could quickly go on buying at the rate that's supported by our precious name that comes at a price which was to stay on course, which we didn't have to take, the course, but you did, you took it to take a look if the ratings held up, they didn't do so well, and now you are on welfare, but it would be good for you to take our course at any rate, it's low now anyway, as it is supported by us, we fully support this rate, we do it all by ourselves and we do it all to, I mean, for you!, the labors of Hercules are nothing compared to ours, if necessary we offer ourselves as supportive columns for those rates, it was necessary!, some job!, worthy of a Hercules, a Heracles, you should appreciate this kind of labor, because it generously supported not only our priceless name, priceless to us, pricey for you, as it was artificially kept up high by us, who carry a name like ours and carry it like Hercules carries the heavy balcony of our bank, which has our name and is us, and thus we hold up our own bank, our hands shaking from the effort, as it gets heavier of course, because there's so much in it, it's for our bank we keep the rates sky high, we support them for our bank, where only you can't count on sitting, you are supposed to count on us, right, no?, right , but at any rate you can't sit at our bank, that's where we sit, not just anybody can sit around here, you gave us this place, which didn't even belong to you, you'd be out of place using a name that's not yours, you did the right thing, because this name wasn't yours, it was ours, but you bought it, which doesn't mean you've got anything to your name, at any rate, it won't be your name, just because you bought our name and did it in our name, you paid with our marmalade's good name, you bought securities under value, but with a good name, you bought under our but above your worth and what do you demand now? What do you want from us now? We are insured, so you do whatever you like. You should have made sure that our name is really us, and it is, it is us, and it is also it!, we are sitting on the certificates like you sit at a bank, if not at ours, you came to our bank to buy something, no, you even went to other banks to buy us!, anything from us, the dirt under the fingernail, our dirt, something that had our name, but wasn't us, because we never were black like our blood sausages, never, ever! No, we are we, we, wowee!, and we are insured even against ourselves, and of course we are also insured against you, in short, against everything, also against the law, oh yes, we can assure you, no matter what you do, you won't get anywhere, because our stabilization policy was all that was needed, that's all we needed, you think you need more? Forget it! You won't get it! You want our name? You won't ever have anything to your name! So there. So far, so good. What do you want to do now? Everything went well so far. But only that far, not further. It didn't go well further on. The whole world did better by far than ever before. It couldn't go any further. What do you want? What do you want from us? You got our name, but you can't carry it, and you aren't it either, you might be, but you are not us, even though our name is on your papers— you aren't we and you'll never be!

Those are the essences, those are the essentials of a truly free country, all our freedoms depend upon this freedom. We want a totally free economy, not only because it guarantees freedoms, but because it is the best way to create wealth and prosperity for the entire country, for Europe, for the country which has our name and is us! Wealth is the single resource for our growth, no, for your growth, no, for everyone's growth, for wealth in itself is thriving, but only when it grows, when it increases, when it grows, right, no? Right!, and it grows from the little patch of land, which had our name, but which we never were, from this small European country, but only relatively small, great in reality, from this little big country, right, no? right!, we can get better results, results that will result in better services for those especially close to our heart and wallet, isn't it wonderful, better benefits for the needy, who need our help, who need our papers and they are getting them, those papers! Pick up your papers! Now you can get your papers from life itself, from your children's life, from your own life in old age, but even better for the children, for whom these papers were intended, those were your savings, after all, now they are our savings. Oh, we see, they are beyond saving, but we are insured! We are insured against you, that's understood. We won't lose your savings the way you lost them! To us. But that's as if you still had them. You don't have them anymore, but they are fine with us, who have saved you a lot, they are doing well. We promoted the entrepreneurial spirit and we will keep it moving, always in a circle until it gets back to us, the spirit, the free private entrepreneurial spirit, beware when you see it! That's our advice. We take everything and we don't give you anything back for it, that's what makes us free entrepreneurs, we freed ourselves from you as well, you bought our certificates, that's how we could free ourselves from you, then we freed ourselves from our name, which we never were, though it was our name, look!, the money is coming back to you, here it runs, it's running!, there it goes!, quick!, maybe you can catch up with it!, that's what we promised you, it'll return some time from the Caribbean, that's what it says on its luggage ticket, it's always coming around in a circle, because it's a heavy load, quite a lot, and the ticket never wins, quite some baggage your money carries around, and for this heavy baggage we gave you a check which you can cash in now. Your money will come back to you, no question, the conveyor belt is moving, it will come some time, it's coming, it's coming, well, aren't you coming already at the thought of your money coming back to you? And how it hurries!, where's the motor of your money?, you can't even see it! Isn't that moving! Aren't you moved at all, how quickly your money wants to get back to you? It's coming back! Yes, it's coming! When it becomes so small that you can't see it anymore, it will come back to you, maybe not on its own feet, maybe in a baby carriage, maybe not straight to you, but it's coming back, so we don't get the blame, what we got instead is inner satisfaction, we played your invested money and we won inner satisfaction, and what did you win? Did you win the lottery? No? What a shame. Shame for you. Not on us. The sham's on you. But don't be ashamed. Your money is good for the old, the sick, the handicapped, and it's good for us, but we don't count, we only count the money you once gave us, that's what we count, we don't count, we counted on our name on our account. You did too, but now you don't count anymore and you have nothing to count, you can't count on a vacation, you can only dream about the Caribbean, where did it go, all that money? Oh, there it is. Everything's okay. We have the gains in our pockets, we have the dues for our services, which we also deserve, in our pockets, it was us, after all, who taught the money to work, it couldn't do it before, it could only waste its strengths, rather than invest them, but now it's pulling its own weight and still gained weight along the way, our gains, which weigh so heavily on you, everybody has a weight problem, everyone weighs in on behalf of the old, the sick, the handicapped, there must also be enough for them, to that end all of us must pull together, that leads to higher investments in the economy, because no gain means no investments, it means death, not debt, death, valley of death, migrating stones, ashes, it means a world gone by and fewer jobs. Ashes, ashes, ashes. Sacrifice, ashes, the ax. We must never become numbers in the government's computer! We'd rather be a nothing among ourselves than a number in a government computer. Rather a next to nothing among ourselves than a number in a soulless government computer! We are all individuals. You too are individuals, that's what you should be. Therefore you trust individuals like us, maybe because our name is what we are not? Maybe because you were wrong about us? Without you there would be no nation. Without you there would only be soulless computers, without you, the shame of a nation, there'd only be nation, nationalization, socialism!, uhm . . . something's wrong with that! I guess we got lost somewhere, we got lost in this deal we cannot win. The freedom to vote is something we took as a given, therefore you gave it to us, you gave us your vote, you took it as a given that we would give you more than you gave us, meaning: up to the moment we were about to take it, take all, lose all, yes, lose too, we are individuals, not soulless government computers, uhm, fortunately we have the freedom to lose, without us you would lose this freedom to the government, but with us you won't win either, you'll never win, you'll win nothing except your freedom to win nothing, but you'll win that much! You'll certainly win that, the freedom to win nothing. That's something you will win. One can't even call that a win, because first of all you still don't win, and second, you'll only win when you have won the freedom to win. We won't be responsible for it, and if we were, we'd be insured against it. You, however, will be a responsible citizen, we call all the shots, we call for shut-downs, we don't have to put up with any hotshots. We are hot ourselves. We got all the hot stuff. It's all good. Finally we got all the goodies. So far, so good. Good.

The Labors of Hercules make some sort of a neat little entrance. They can be symbolized by household stuff, but also by packaged food, teapots, bags of coffee, etc., shown on sandwich boards the actors have tied around them, like those guys in the street, or like walking advertisement pillars. But there are other ways, I am sure. We always have ways, as always, we have our own ways.

We now sing a little song to our Lord, a blessed song, we won't complain, we won't file a complaint against anyone, and no one will file one against us, why should they? It would make no sense. We can't raise the dead and dead capital cannot resurrect itself, capital must work, how lucky we don't have it, but then, who does? Who has capital now?

Where does it work now? Where does it stand? No idea, no idea. The crisis got it, we get the crisis, and then we restore the public trust, and then we take it away again, we can deregulate entire markets like rivers, and then we regulate them again as we wish, and when they lie peacefully in their little beds, those markets, then we deregulate them again and they get thrown off again, and they splash in our face like milk out of udders, which we hold up, so that not only the cattle get it. The market has hardly recovered and it is thrown out again, out of a red light pay-by-the-hour hotel, where it changes rooms every hour, so that no one can touch it while it just lies there, open to anything. Well then. The market will now voluntarily lie down for a bit, well, maybe not quite voluntarily, but you can't force it, you can't squeeze it into a pigeonhole just so you can better estimate your risk. In the night of the earth, the vulture's shadow rises, his croaking crowning his toils, a specter of bankruptcy he returns, emaciated beyond recognition, a skeleton, and still he sings his song of praise to the market, the prize for noble toils is the market, that's where we are driving you now, you old pig, hedgehogger, pork-barrel pol! Because the prize for magnanimous deeds adorns only the dead. Because they don't need anything anymore. As long as they live, they want something from the market, but when they are dead, they are done wanting. The dead don't bother us anymore, they don't bother to sue us anymore, they aren't bothered, that Hercules once cleared a lion from the grove of Zeus, we can highly recommend clearing the market of wild beasts, they bother us quite a bit, those animals, one animal bothers the other, please set the market free as Hercules did for the God, so that at long last it can really be free!, because once it is freed, we'll already be someplace else and gorge ourselves and sell, sell, sell. We'll buy too, of course, that's part of it, buying is the absolution for selling, as the sacrifice at the altar is the absolution for the killer. Politics will happily pick up on the suggestion to free the market from us, and then it'll drop it again. It already punishes the sins. That's only a small step. Politics will submit to a rating agency, it can't do everything by itself, right, no?, no, that's right, it can't; it outsources itself to an agency, which grades the papers, good grades for ours, bad ones for yours. So then, the sacred grove is cleared and already our heads, our multi-headed heads are covered—hold it, the stuff with the serpent comes later or it might not come at all—our head is covered by the lion's skin which we distributed before we had the lion, too late, now we keep it, we throw the lion's skin that we will not share and never wanted to share, on our own backs. Meanwhile, you, dear customer, are roaming the mountains and cursing your head off, but no one can hear you up in the mountains, where the market won't offer any crash courses at any rate, so we can't even sound out your echo, which should resound in the mountains, right?, right now the market wants to stay sound on the ground, it will stay its course on the ground, the crash course will be held there at low rates, it won't take the low rates off the ground, no, that's not what it does, the market, not that, and while they are lying there, poor things, we buy, while you are roaming the mountains and want to recover, that's legitimate, quite legitimate, perfectly legal, you may do that, what you may not do is cutting down the tribe of centaurs that capsized in the middle of the market, they capsized because of the market, it wasn't our fault, so then this tribe of centaurs, those blind men among whom the one-eyed man is king, you may not cut them down with bloody bows, sending them to their death with winged arrows, you may not do that, only we can finish that job, since you lost the skin off your back, and the

lion's skin, and the bear's, the bull's, the minotaur's, plus all
your shares of nothing, nothing, nothing. Weren't there also
horses in that Nothing? Your vast but fruitless fields can see
that, your fields see your fruitless efforts, because we already
fileted your firm before you could blink, and we've got the
filets, we got them, you can't even find those fields, for hardly
any area in your fruitless fields is—heck, I have no idea what
it is, it is not, is not, has not, has been authorized, it has not
been authorized for deregulation and also not for regulation.
This gigantic torrent has not been authorized at all. You have
not been authorized to enter the market, did you forget your
authorization? Then you can't buy, you must regulate yourself, just like the market self-regulates and then it self-dereg-
ulates, as we wish, then we take matters in our hands, and
now it's our business. Then even fir trees can move their
arms, they won't get us, let firs wiggle their little arms: This
way!, this way!, who wants more, who hasn't yet?, you can
come around on your high horse, you can come in your car,
you can come any way you want, even on a mountain bike,
if you want to rough it up, you get nothing, you won't get
us!, never, ever will you get us, just as you didn't get the hind
with the golden antlers, you won't get us, you won't get any
Olympic gold either, and should the river regulation
threaten to fail, should all regulation systems fail, then we
just change the rules. We tell politics to change the rules and
changed they are, and on our high horse we beat the hind,
which we kill, no, that one we keep alive, tied up for the ride,
the speckled she-robber of the fields, and we glorify robbers,
we adore hoods, Robin Hood's deeds are legendary. They
aren't a fable, they are just fab. So are we. It wasn't Hercules,
we just made him our front man, he stands for us now, that's
now the name of our mortgage funds, which are finally
moving, but not in your direction, they no longer have our

name, but they are still us, no, which we are no longer, what is it now?, now we are confused, even about ourselves, how could you see through any of this? And we can easily beat your car, it's a five years old model, that's ancient history, get yourself a new car, so we get some life into the car market, before it dies on us!, the make is not unimportant, neither is the car market, smaller vehicles are preferred these days, we, however, go for the Mercedes Benz. And we'll take you for a ride that'll get us an even bigger model, always the bigger model, the horses under our three-pointed star easily beat the horses under your hood, we have more horsepower under our hood than you ever had hoodies, we dine in five-star restaurants, while you picnic in the park under the stars and the wind rips your hood off when you have to make a turn, we rip you off, we chew you up and you don't notice, we eat you out of house and home and you think it's fate and termites that put you on the street?, that's a joke, I'm not joking. Our horses storm, howling and braying, heads tossing— and it's not our heads they are tossing—jockeying for the job that would earn them their keep in the killer's stable, that's where our horses jockey—no infant lies in that manger, what's lying there is bloody fare at a bloody cost, which we couldn't get down, hard as we tried, our horse power couldn't do it either, those are very strong horses under our hoods, but they can't do everything, not even our new fund, Heracles, Hercules could manage that, horses devouring human flesh! Horse powers just running people down!! Terrible, the things that happen every day, terrible, terrible, terrible. So much flesh! That's so gross! No more gross, no growth! So we watch for the wave of silver, then we watch for the wave of gold, the price of gold rises, oh no, now it's already falling again, but we rode it just in time, so now, after we saddle, no, after we set the price of gold, no, set out for this golden prize, those waves of gold shimmering in the evening sun, which we won, we visited those singing maidens, come evening we come to those singing saws, those Western maidens, right, no?, yes, to pick the golden fruit between golden leaves, an apple of gold is also good money, that's what we think, yes, the main thing is, we find the golden apples, they are real beauties, really, and then we'll kill a dragon, we'll knock out the Security and Exchange Commission, and before that we'll knock out all controlling agencies, we won't knock down the lowest level, we go straight for the next one, we'll knock that one down, that's what we tell them already at the first level, we'll knock off heads; but we won't knock in every door, well, not quite, we'll knock on every door, that might take a while, we already took out the dragon, who guarded the golden apples, we got around the control by getting it out of the way, all the way, and there, those steep ocean bays, the silence of the sea, that's how far we got, so far, so good. But what do we do now? What do we do? Are those amazons riding toward us, raging females, terrifying women, could be it's them, maybe not, they still have both breasts, plumped up like diapers their breasts, clogged like plumbing, their breasts, what could still come out of there? Come out where? Nothing will come out anywhere. So we can calmly withdraw our troops and withdraw our papers and draw them up under a different name, names are but sound and smoke, and how shall we deal with the sound and the smoke?, fury won't help, not even a dealer can deal with it. Where do we take the sound and the smoke? To the Environmental Protection Agency, which is in a permanent fog? What do we do with the sound and the smoke of our name? We do nothing. We don't do anything! We haven't done anything and aren't doing anything, we do the work of Hercules, yes, we do that much, but otherwise we do nothing. We haven't done anything! Have we done anything to you? What are you saying? We did you in? We cut into your savings, we cut the best parts out of it, we cut it by its full amount? Where do you see any money we would like to see cut by anyone? We would never cut our money! We could never hurt our money. We can do the labors of Hercules, yes, we can, but we can't hurt our money, that's when we get weak. When it's about money, we get soft. We could no longer slay the thousand-headed killer dog, Lerna's Hydra, we wouldn't know what to do with it, we could throw it in the fire, but the fire wasn't our doing, we didn't start it, so we didn't do it, it was you, you did it yourself, you once had fire, no idea who brought it to you, but now you no longer have fire for your poor cave, isn't that a shepherd with three bodies, three executive bodies, no, three corporate bodies? So then, this is one shepherd who represents three such bodies in one, we also represent three bodies, three corporate bodies, this shepherd is one of us, he has the same name as us, but isn't us, those corporate bodies, who have our name, well, one no longer does, the other two won't much longer, but for the time being they still do, they'll do; this one is one of us, the Lord is his shepherd and we are the lords of the shepherds, we don't control any mortgage banks, we control the mortgages themselves, while the banks collapse all around us, one bank was able to save itself, but this doesn't go to our credit. One is saved as of today, a mortgage bank, no, now both of them are rescued!, so, it won't be all that bad, it won't get so bad that we can no longer run more winning races, everyone can strike out once, you just have to deal with it, and as long as we can make a deal, it's not so bad, on average we always win. And so forth and so on. Left without friends, your house is in mourning. Nothing can be done about that on death's path whence no one does return, Charon is waiting in his boat, he waits for the hero's sons. They fought a good battle but they could not win. You fought a good battle against us, but you couldn't win. You'd have to be a Hercules to win against us and you aren't. Your single family home keeps looking but you aren't coming. You don't come. We are coming. You don't. Maybe the house is waiting for the wrong guy, that's you, who never gets all six numbers right, not even five, not four, at best three. That's too little. Your house won't wait for someone like that. That's all it would need! It is waiting for the bank, which is us, we are everything, things picked up, we are the berry pickers in the golden fields, youth still blossoms in us though we are old. Old, so old, we can no longer protect you, dear children, you can't protect your property and we can't protect you. Your dog might be able to protect it, but the dog was stolen, and now you are totally unprotected, like Charon, the ferry man in his little boat. You, after all, acted at your own risk, while we carried ours, and what a heavy load it is. Alright, so now the spring of your happy youth is also leaving you. So, where does that leave you? You can't see? You can't see any way out? So you offer to slaughter your children for us, but what are we to do with the flesh of your children? Are we to make mincemeat of them? Burgers? Big Macs? We chose to be vegetarians. What for would we need the flesh of your children? What for would we need your rotting mortgages? Your fresh, new, funny credits? What do we need? First let's think what we need and then let's get it. We get us the victims, who are ready to meet their death; huh?, me?, how ready are we to meet our death? That's a misunderstanding. Of course it isn't us. We don't have to go, the victims must go, they must go to be sacrificed, that's obvious. First the sacrifices, one after the other, no pushing, please! We'll be the lords, we'll be the masters, while you must sacrifice, your children, your car, your God-knows-what, you know better what you still have to offer, you offer us something just so you can keep something? You can't keep up and you offer us junk, us of all people? What are we supposed to do with it? What are we to do with junk bonds? We put them out, we put you on, so you put up with them. We can't do anything with them, but you can, you do, you can do anything if you just put your mind to it. We, at any rate, put our minds where your money is, you must be out of your mind, if you want all your money back and more, lo and behold, woe oh woe! Shaken by the storm the house trembles, the roof collapses! Oh dear, it's down. Misery's dark cloud enfolds you, right, no?, oh no!, far be it from us to bemoan your misfortune, it was your own mad-ness that wrecked the house, slaughtered the children, sold the car, it was you, who took the children out of private school before you had them slaughtered and now you feel horrible. We know all that. We know you are unhappy and can never be happy again. Yes, the children too. The children most of all. They are dead, after all. And now? Where has your raging gone? Where did it start? Do you remember? Where did your rage begin, do you still know? Where will you end in old age, can you tell? Not at all? Not so soon? Whatever. Where did you get so messed up to play for broke, lose the game and slaughter the children or at least that one child, what, you don't have more?, you don't have more, or more would have been killed; slaughtering the child, was that really necessary?, yes, it was necessary, covering it nicely afterwards, putting its teddy next to it, slaying the wife with an ax, the cheapest brand, not even ten euros, that's the way!, ax handle pressed brutally against the victim's mouth, because you couldn't bear her groans?, I can see it coming, this won't be just one murder, this will be multiple murders, this will be an overkill, some are still alive, who also want a turn, maybe they don't really want it, but they will get their turn nonetheless!, both parents must be massacred, that was necessary, absolutely necessary, the mother is groaning too, groaning from afar, as if in her heaven she could not keep her head above water either, the father-in-law, sleeping in front of the TV, bludgeoned with the ax, enough!, you are not a common killer, are you?, you are a special killer!, enough already!, enough, the father-in-law was the last anyway, beat already by old age and illness, no, he was still in good shape for his age, he had set aside a bit for his old age, he thought!, typical case of dream on!, he'd be able to sit back and relax in front of the TV and now he's beaten to a pulp? Where were you when that happened? Oh, you did it all by yourself!, a job worthy of Hercules, can't argue with that. It was not driven by base motives as hatred, jealousy or greed, the motive rather was a matter of thrift, all those people, little and big, all killed for the sake of thrift, because one gets short thrift no matter what. That was worth it. They had it coming, since we had no money coming in and we lost the income we had! It shouldn't all come down to us! It wasn't only our speculations that didn't pay off, on the contrary, the assets of the whole family are gone, gambled away on the stock exchange, right out of the change purse, so the whole family had it coming. So off with the family, off, off, off! It should be quite logical to the very end, the killer can see no other option, I don't either, all his money down the drain, he must free his daughter, his wife, his parents and his wife's father. Free from what? The disgrace the killer brought upon them with his failure, at least he won't fail them, he and his faithful ax, those two won't fail, they belong together like the fist in the jaw, one doesn't blow all the family's money, the nuclear family's money, because every family has a nucleus of hope, while the killer, the nucleus of this whole thing did not blow his slaughter, he did blow it, however, at the stock market, all blown, the investors' money, who were invested in the hope only money can bring, all that money had to be invested, 500K invested, piled up hope, piled up the Nothing that was to become of it, all that hope, such invested interest—all gone!, all this would have caused the family boundless sadness, no doubt, therefore off with the family, let them follow the money, the lost money, no more family, it shall go the way of the money, it shall go the way of all flesh, off and away!, one after the other, one behind the other, losses thrown after the great loss, tragic losses of human lives thrown after the tragic loss of money, better dead than hearing about our great loss, better, parents and father-in-law are also dead, the loss of such a loss—the loss of their family, a loss added, piled on top of all other losses, so actually a gain—the loss of such a loss would have been too much for them to bear. Dead, all dead. The nuclear family, dead. It's tough luck, when a particular sperm meets a particular egg, but it can still be corrected, if late, late, but not too, stock market losses can't be easily corrected. They are no accident. Conception happens by chance, unless it is immaculate and that happened just once, by divine intervention, for which there is no public record. Record losses do not happen by chance, they are man-made. This child's conception should have been avoided, which could be said of all humans, just as records should be voided or altogether avoided. Putting a child into this world is a crime, which can only be compensated for by the destruction of the child, wanna bet?, only the killing of the child can make up for a lost bet, a lost kill. But those losses cannot be recovered, they cannot be undone. Lives can be undone, by force, if necessary, but losses remain, no matter what one does. Owning is better than renting, property is half the rent, but if it's lost, lost in a bet, it's nothing. Then one doesn't own it anymore and then it's no longer a property, or it is someone else's property, that's even worse. Made possible by the selling and buying and the investment in smaller real estate, all piled up with great effort, which made it possible to buy a luxury property, so we can live comfortably, so that the family feels comfortable. It was their gain, but our loss, we lost it all, we lost the right to have a family, lost it once and for all, all's lost, more irrevocably than death, well, let's say, equally so. Well then, after we swooped down on them with our axes, on our victims, our later victims, all our later victims, covered with comforters, symbolically buried; our debts, unfortunately, aren't covered, the losses not covered, so then, swooped down on the victims like a swarm of crows, but without a sound, quiet, quiet, not a peep coming from us!, so the neighbors wouldn't hear us, they all lay there, under their comforter clouds, buried symbolically; it was the best we could do for them, sparing them the loss of all their means, we spared them quite a bit, that was our goal. The goal. Total extinction. Sure, one puts in more effort for oneself, it's the main character, after all, a backpack packed with knives, an entire backpack packed with knives, which we put on our shoulders, good idea, for my money, duh!, lots of money, no more money!, tip of the ax put on the mouth so it can cut right in, knives arranged around the chest—that's an awful lot of work!, all for nothing, nada, like the investments, all for nothing, and then we drive it into the wall, that living vehicle, ourselves, we drive ourselves and those knives into the wall in such a way that the knives will pierce us, penetrate us, the ax, its tip put in our mouth like a word should cut through the mouth and split us apart and then the wall will smash our heads and that's it. But the slow deaths, especially mother's, were not a pretty sight, it wasn't good to see that, that's why we distance ourselves from the idea to kill ourselves, we keep the car in some distance from the wall, we keep the distance between the wall and the car, between the knife and the chest, between the blade of the ax and the mouth, please keep the distance between us and the backpack and the knives!, we better keep a safe distance from ourselves, yes, from the ax too, we better keep the distance, we'll be glad to, now that we saw how painful and drawn out dying is and how much effort it takes to kill, we could see it with our own mother, our child, our wife, we could watch our parents and our father-in-law in the process. Now they are all dead, we can't reverse that, death has only one gear, and that's not always the fastest, that wouldn't take us far. So, now they're all dead, some faster, some slower. Woe, woe to them! Interest rates shot up, while we couldn't even shoot ourselves, tried to hit the wall, not full strength anyway, the survival drive was too strong, too bad!, interest rates grew over the hedges, they should be sprayed some time; the once shiny ax, brand new, straight from the store, the famous brand store, with which you killed your family and did it like a machine, no need for a spray to polish that ax, you won't need it anymore, no one is left. Nothing is left of your money either, nothing left of any kind of money, no CDOs, no paper, no shares, no interest paid to you, but plenty charged to you, a give and take, for it is more blessèd to give than to receive, that's how it was supposed to be, but that's not their game, that's not what they are playing, no show today. You are all alone. Alone. Why did you spare your own life after you murdered all your loved ones whom you now must mourn?, all the good times you had with them!, all right, it's none of our business, we only ask, because we are interested. Why did you spare your own life, why didn't you throw yourself off a cliff? That's what we would like to know. Why didn't you burn your own flesh in the flames? That's what we would really like to know. Bludgeoning yourself, okay, we understand that in the end you didn't have the nerve to do that, though you managed all the other jobs. But, loyal friend of capital, who killed his family like Hercules the serpent and other animals, some of them caught alive and transported tied up in ropes, which made the task more difficult, as they were kicking up a storm, pinioned as they were, grim lions, three-bodied Typhon and giants and four-legged centaurs, a hydra in her hydraculture, no, without any hydraculture, wild, very wild, this hydra with her hundred heads, mean!, really mean!, and all that with one single ax!, how about that, buddy?, now what? Straight to the kingdom of the dead, with the ax and with its harvest!, you're absolutely right, you might still need it, the tool, for the three headed watchdog in front of Hades' door, and you also killed the children, *Herr* Cules, Hercules, Heracles, we see you and the horror of your child's murder in the papers, on TV, what do your best friends have to say about that? They can't understand? That's understandable. Where to start now? It makes no sense to start something new since you already put an end to everything. That makes no sense. No, you can't escape your sorrow either, not on wings nor in the night of earth, night comes by itself, nothing you can do about that, nothing you can do against it, you can do nothing. We are not against you doing nothing. You already did everything possible, and your loved ones' bodies are covering the grounds which no longer belong to you, the little house, half finished, up for auction, the condo sold, there's no one left to live there anyway; you can come off your high horse now, get down, or we'll show you how to get back on your feet. And once you get your feet back our way, you won't need the high horse anymore. You don't know where to go? Well, then, why not back into earth's womb, where you came from. Above the earth, everything belongs to us, but below the earth, you can have it, we don't mind. You can take it, except, if you find gold or gas or oil. You can go there and dig in—except if you should find something. No one will disturb you there. The treasures of the earth will not disturb you. But should they be down there, treasures of the earth, oil, gas, electricity, uranium, flowerpots, running water, then the earth below our grounds will no longer belong to you either, then the dirt under your nails won't belong to you anymore, then nothing belongs to you anymore, nothing at all, absolutely nothing, nothing.

Acknowledgements: Thank you, *merci*, mercy,

all you newspapers and magazines, thank you, too, dear Internet!

Thank you Helene Schuberth, thank you, Europe, uhm, Euripides

Thank you, Meinl Bank, for the truth and the preface to the annual report of 2006.

Below are the first additional sequences, *Bad Rap* and *You Bet*, which Elfriede Jelinek wrote for the performances of Nicolas Stemann's production of *The Merchant's Contracts* in Cologne and Hamburg respectively. The sections Stemann selected and interwove in the performances are indicated in bold lettering. These texts are not part of the German publication by Rowohlt Verlag, which I followed in my translation for this edition. They are included in this volume as examples of Jelinek's open dramaturgy, which allows her directors and dramaturgs to pick, choose and assemble their specific performance texts. The German originals are posted on Jelinek's homepage: http://www.elfriedejelinek.com

Gitta Honegger

Bad Rap
Now What?

Already we can see people gathering angrily in front of this building, shoulder to shoulder they want to drag the gentlemen on the executive floors out of their bunkers, and take them out with one shot in the neck. Thus they shout in the streets, stomping their feet on the hard stone pavement. They rage. Knowing that no one would approach

even their graves with compassion. They shout. They stomp. They don't want to inquire, they just want to scream, because their lungs still work, though they themselves no longer do. But even from this herd young lambs, unadvised, are pulling away all on their own, their lips pursed once again for mother's breast, that strong bond they had barely been weaned off. Just waiting for *the* opportunity. Can't wait to lose again what they had lost long ago. The breast denied to them forever, as well as the womb, but perhaps there is a way back into it? Any time they would snatch that breast of gold again, the spring of all their riches, only to invest and lose it all again. Oh, if this mother would only take them on, if she could just let her darling little ram bounce happily around her once again! Alas, the bank would yield no more. They always had to yield, being constantly yelled at by strong folk leads to resentment. Sure. That old, long-preserved treasure, now irretrievably lost and completely out of reach for them. How sweetly it smelled, while it felt so safe and secure. Safe and secure: Those words taste so good, what's safe on earth?! Nothing. Not the silver coin's hallmark glow, nor dead presidents' famous glare. Who steals a purse steals trash, 'tis something, nothing, much ado about you know what. No problem. Instead of mother's breast, a cup was handed to them, for their hand-to-mouth lives, not worth the steam of their piss. Not enough for a valid check. Let's get foreigners into the house and us out. Let's get the foreign owner in, let's yield to him and get our credits out. **Just now we can see them in front of the home, where we thought they were safe, the credits we don't have anymore. Not good. Now they are coming out, hostages of bigger powers, with raised arms our credits are coming; they surrender, but they yield nothing for us. Everything comes out into the** open. The money has come a long way, all the way to the **Caribbean**, the money we took such good care of, but liked as much to take away again, with a small gesture, that nonetheless tears the community apart, **the rest of us will never again have such carefree cash-free lives, so free of cash we never had.** At our wit's end let's dry the tears that wet our cheeks. Oh dear! Our eyes are bathed in tears! We wouldn't have thought we had that much left to waste! An example: No, no example!, we won't get it. Let us talk as befits wise men! No, don't know how. So let's speak frankly. We can do that. But it's a foreign language. It is because of our need for security that we will never get any security. Let's shape our destiny, but it won't be ours! So many had it before us! They spit it out, that kind of destiny! And that's what we should swallow? Let's shape it now, though we don't know what shape we'll be in! Index finger's last pull on the trigger. Let's pull out! At least let's pull some strings! Let's pull a fast one, before it's too late! **For only the fortunate are taken to the house of fortune. No one takes us in and no one takes us out, even if we were dogs. Were we investments, we would already have been taken out of the country!** Trade: Taken care off! Thank you for your trust. There is no reason. So we're losing our minds as well. We never are what we should be. Now let me tell you, who won't be happy with things short of big, there is no cure for you: This certificate, praised as a safe investment by the bank who is happy to open the security gate for you and close it again right under your nose, a trap for men, for money and for your mice, the bank always wins, what is it selling to you now, what has it been selling to you? Just an example, oh, I can't even explain it to you with the help of an example, forgive me, it's not my fault, I don't understand it, but it's not my fault, it's definitely not my fault, that this discount certificate is actually a bearer security, because it is always the bearer's fault, who will always default, it can't be helped, it was your default, your own fault, your most grievous fault! **Because all options go to the bank, that's a safe bet, that's what they have always been. And now? Are they? Are they really? Are they safe? What on earth did you buy? Did you really buy security, did you say you wanted security, when you bought this junk? You should have said so, how could we guess you wanted security. You wanted security, they all want security right away, but now you sink, you are underwater now and that means insecurity. Speculation. Stocks. Crash. Kaboom!** No, I can't explain it. I am trying, but I can't. Your heart still throbs with cheers, but do not cheer too soon! Your need for security literally drove you into the arms of speculation, into the dear multimillipeded arms of stocks, which rise and fall, but hardly move forward. Good job on our part, no?, you don't see it. You don't see it coming. It's overcoming you, but you can't see it. You can't even see that it's a stock! Which will get you under the earth. Which will even take your shroud off your body.

Because: The bank, this shelter that welcomed you so kindly and sold you instantly, yes, sold you, the bank is doing well again, thank you. It suffered for a long time, but now it is doing well again. Thank you for asking! Thanks to you asking for more! Yes, of course, the bank sells, what else it is supposed to do?, and the bank buys back, because no one else does it, and the bank buys you, and it sells you out and it leads you and it leads you on. The bank—the blind seer. But all it can see is the nearest bank. It doesn't have to go any further. Because the bank, only the bank, bank, oh bank, only you!, it sees everything, it takes in and it spends, and whatever we want to spend, we don't have it and we won't get it anymore. If you like it that way, it's okay, but there's no know-it-all old man to whom you could report it! You buy from the bank and you sell it back to the bank, because no one else will take it, **yes, man's art of foreseeing comes down to nothing, and that's exactly what you will get. Had you practiced seeing, you would have become Apollo and let people worship you. But the way it is, the way it is . . . What you see is Nothing. In this bank you looked the nothing right in the eye.** You looked into the eye of the hurricane. And there you have the silence at the teller's window, for reasons of discretion, please, keep some distance from the line of losers in front of it, but there are also other reasons—so you can fully enjoy the silence of tallying and winnowing, while you are being turned on and off like a dim light, your life's shaky little light. You still have to close out and shut down this and that before you can finally shoot yourself. Your fate could have been warmed by joy, if you had shaped it yourself, but you left its shape up to the bank, which produces nothing but schemes, shadows, mirages, fata morganas, father's organs?, no!. And shame, because it will have always been your fault. You didn't know that, did you? You are safe from us now, since we bought them for you and sold them to you for a hefty surcharge, those bearer securities with the charge that you will have always been at fault, herewith we hand it to you in writing: Yes, you may be safe from us, but not from our conditions, according to which you can get everything you want, even before you have received it, taken away again. What do you say? We can take everything else, we can shove it all up our ass, except the money! That's what you're telling us? And you still want something from us?

What does this bank promise, and that one too, bolder still than this one? The bank misspoke before, it promised us five percent, but guaranteed it is not. Oh. What did you just say? You said, we wait until the value drops, the interest payments flee as long as they are still children and then we take everything you could have had but never got.

Look here, the nature of Gods is rooted in force, while our money has been routed off shore, where it is nice and quiet though exposed to the force of strangers. The prophetic goes hand in hand with power, that's the way it is, people like to be foretold: this stock rises, that one too, this one doesn't, that one plunges. All that frenzy, that thing, that how shall I put it, extra sense, that's simply part of power, don't you think?, you sell us something, you are selling us, you take and you sell us more; which all of a sudden we no longer have . Where has it gone? Save and keep looking, my child! **They take our money and produce nothing but crimes.** The bank a sacred site of Dionysian ecstasy? Am I reading this right or am I making it up? Could this be my own text? Wow! I never made up anything as beautiful! We never saw it like that! **The Bank as church that's going gaga! A church of passion, a church of lunatics! Yes, there is your money raving, and people are watching and cheering. People with hot glowing cheeks! Go on, go on in!**; you'll get fucked there, there is unanimity in that all want more than they had before, all want more than they ever had, but there is also pusillanimity, will they really get it?, **don't we all know: Money leads to violence, because it always wants to be more,** but how to get it without stealing? And how to get *lebensraum*, more space to live, without killing? No idea. **Well then, let's start with a small human sacrifice.**

All we must find now is one person, and it's a go. We need a violent death to let off steam. We don't care who, but die he must. And if it were our little savings account. Yes, we could send our account to be sacrificed in place of us. Robbing ourselves?, sure, why not.

Our world protects itself from violence, that is its principle, only the violence of Dionysian banking gets protected, no, of the bank of Dionysus, no, of Mr. Dionysus, who drops in every now and then just for our execution at the bank, no, no need for this bank to run wild and gorge itself and kill and tear apart, we can do that ourselves, we storm into the bank and rant and rage and tear ourselves apart. We sacrifice ourselves. That Dionysian stuff is slowly becoming some kind of a joke in a world that should be free from violence. We can agree on that, yes? It's going around like crazy, and it makes no sense at all. Capitalism as Dionysus, well, he'll now sit down nicely on his little bench in his little bank and start planning. He has time. He has plenty of time until you have nothing. That much time is necessary. Capitalism is the only power we must acknowledge. We don't exist without it. How else should we distinguish ourselves from the other? How else to use ourselves as weapons? Wouldn't that mean even more violence? That without capitalism we would not be? This banking palace will be destroyed any moment. No, not yet. It's going to fall now! No. It didn't. The money has left the palace! No, it didn't. Yes! It's gone! Didn't you see it run out just now? Would you please honor the god of money! That's what we are doing! We honor him. We can't honor him any more, because we don't have anything anymore, but whatever we have we will give, so it would become more, but it never does, a principle of sacrifice. The animal also gets knocked down, throat cut and bled, drained completely, so that we get more from the sacrifice than we had before. We could also try that on ourselves, but then we would have to sacrifice ourselves. Death, bringer of good fortune, our little lucky charm death, a pendant on the chain around the neck, replacing the cross. But no luck. Death just won't bring it. It never does. Look, this bank has a pillared hall of marble, can you see it shake and fall? No, I don't. It's still standing, no one runs a subway through it from below! That might be the only decent action, but no one does it. Too much effort. Can you hear the cheers of victory inside, about those handsome bonuses? Oh yes, I do, I can hear them now! That's right! I hear screams, but I don't know what they are screaming about! All those blows! Bills hitting us unprepared, we didn't deserve them, but they're coming, we have it coming from everywhere, hitting us over the head, ouch! No one is waiting for bills. Even so, payments must be effected. Even though one's efforts were so ineffective. If just one of, let's say, twelve values in this pretty, well-endowed package that we bought, happens to come across some threshold we never saw, which no one had shown us, over which we will trip on the road to fame and fortune, (okay, fortune will do), which seemed already close enough to touch, right on the mark, right on the money, the market, the bull market, which turned out to be nothing but bull, that's right, those dollar bills and euro trash, all bull—well then, if a value slips on the shit on the stairs and falls below the threshold, if just one single value drops, if it trips over the threshold and drops into your arms, worthless suddenly and light as a feather, then what?, well, what then?, then the yield is out the window. It's been cut. It cut out to the bank. Passed right by you. A deadly bypass just for you. Who led you to this house of fortune? Who led you on? At any rate, the yield's all gone. How quickly it all went! What can we say? And we have no way to estimate the value of the charges the bank is in charge of, but we still must pay. Pay those, who are sitting inside and trick I mean track our bad fortune to burn it with our good money. Good at least for kindling us, the sacrificial victims. Can you hear the cheers of victory inside? No, I don't. This bank went bust and won't be bailed out. The one over there is also broke but it will get a break, it will be bailed out. No, I just heard, the other one will also be bailed out, yes, the one from before. Bailed out. The last moment. We wouldn't want to lose our bonuses! No bank—no bonus! You can understand that, no? And no bank—no bonus, neither for you nor for us. And if you let our bank die, that's bad, even though the community wants this murder. But if it dies—who would pay us our bonus? Strange sacrificial cult! Dying in order to get even more! Sacrifices are thrown in, so we finally get some order. So in order to get some order, let's first create some chaos.

The stars' heavenly chorus enters and exits again. Morrow is dawning and it is getting better. Tomorrow and tomorrow and tomorrow, things will get better tomorrow. The sun's coming up tomorrow and then it goes down again. Helios's glowing disc lights up the shield's center and fades away again. The stars of rain, Hyads and also Pleiades, such terror to Hector's eye, enter and exit again. Your money enters and disappears. It enters only to disappear, though you did not imagine it that way. Quite a production! We invest so much in it only to see it disappear. Bet your bottom dollar, as the cute little orphan sings to us. Now back to the classics. On the helmet, no matter whose—let's stay with Helios for now, so, on the helmet's golden images sphinxes carry the infamous loot, in their claws and carry it off again. All that drama, the charges, the hopes, the desire to ease the house's misfortune, all those dreams just for a little security! It was different in the old times. Back then, on the tank, the lioness with fire on her heavy breath runs in and out again, in pursuit of something for her paws, I forgot what and you can forget it too, so forget it. **And all that just for security! The universe just for security, and for whom, only for those who can bring us only insecurity! And that's supposed to be a sacrifice? For that, you put down everything you had? For securities that don't exist? Killing for securities? Murder for a little more security? No more speed guns for a little more security in traffic? Absurd!** And then, as soon as you felt absolutely safe, four-legged horses are storming in and run you over. Black dust, distilled from deceased human beings, billows in their wake. Whence this rush? A rush for security? I don't get it! Intoxicating derivatives, uhm, distillates, for security? Security for small investors? The Gods will send all those to their deaths, who feel smug as a bug bundled up in their securities. **Let them all die! That would be the greatest security.** And that's what will happen right now. But maybe just insisting it's all good and secure will be enough? Why are your eyes flooded with tears, old hag, you want to be a seer and can't even see with your glasses on?, you and your retirement plans, which make you look even older now, because those plans get no supplements? But it was you who added the supplements to this type of plan! None other than you! Why do you look so old now? Is it because you are old? You wouldn't have to look like that, even if you were old! Look, we are bringing you a lamb from our flock, you dear old granny you! Or should we bring you something else? Just tell us! We bring you everything you want after you gave us everything, even more than everything you had. You can say what you want and have what you want. We'll take it from you later anyway. The organization of your execution doesn't come for free! The planning of your execution also costs some money, it will not pay for itself. We will have to invest something in it. And now we have to cook up a ritual for your sacrifice. And then we have to make sure you pay for the loan, which you once took out to make your sacrifice even bigger.

What we once sold you has crumbled. The steps to our bank are too steep, too much for you to climb, at least for you, the old and the dumb! For the old man's tired foot. Too much. Too much. Commissions: not too much. That is, not for us. For us it's no more than a small advance from your small capital, your little cappy we'll take it, our pleasure, it's no trouble for us! Not at all, banish the thought. We can take it. No more for you, all gone, swallowed, emptied the cup of Bacchus's long-held treasure, deliciously fragrant, not much, but even just one cup, mixed into the weaker potion yielded a heady drink. Your small cup merged with the great whole. The weaker drink merged with the strong, which you are not, old man. Stronger stuff: already bought. Bought up and used up too. Why are your eyes awash in tears, old woman? Oh, yes, I already said why and you are still crying? Even though I already explained it, you are crying? They are running in circles with banners and signs, running after their supplementary pension funds, which in any event would have been more than they are entitled to. A supplement is a supplement. A present. A gift. Not an entitlement. Done. Gone. Finished.

As soon as the bank is dead, the community realizes it didn't want that either! Stupid commies! Cunning isn't enough, well, it was enough for us but it won't be enough for you. Not quite. There never is quite enough. The sacrifice is torn apart by exactly the same hands that once fed it. It is an organized execution. The public is admitted and will be cured. The public was ill but now it is cured. This bank will be executed now. At first the crowd is peaceful, but not for long. It happens very quickly. We don't see any reason why this otherwise peaceful mass of investors starts moving now, we can't see a thing, it's all foggy. We don't see the reason and there is no reason for us to know. The crowd will lunge at someone. Wanna bet? Usually it's the wrong one. And this is also why we locked the main entrance and lead the masses driven by their creed, uhm, greed, to the side entrance, where they can only go in one after the other and can't gang up. But now that one gets walled up as well. The sacrifice is closed to the public. So. The public is shut out again. We open and shut people at our pleasure. Only the flow of money must not be interrupted. The doors for money must not be shut. We'll now have to open new doors for capital, doors that were locked before. Their capital's violent death offers the crowd a valve to blow off steam; but it calms down quickly and invests again, one just has to be careful not to get in the way when the crowd invests again. There, it is calm now and invests again, with much more, well somewhat more confidence than before. We conned, uhm, calmed it down all right. The point is it invests. And you? You want to investigate? That won't help your investment. IRAs, idiot retired assholes, that's the words the bank invented for people like you. For the sacrificial lambs. Well, can't call them "lambs" anymore. They emerge from their dens, where dreams of bigger homes sleep. They buy everything! They buy whatever we tell them! Their problem! Ignite the thunder club's blazing flame and let it burn, baby, burn, burn down this banking palace. Retirees and assholes preferred. They are allowed to go first to the sacrifice so they can sit and watch themselves getting burnt. So they have good seats when their money gets burnt in front of their eyes. Then they will get their turn to burn, just be patient, all lambs will be fleeced, yes, you go first, you have preference, the preference of your very special preferred stock in being a retired ass. Everyone will be fleeced. Don't push now. Most of all, don't you push us! It's not our fault that the market always comes back home to itself, but has nothing to sell. At least not to you. You have already been sold. So, now you want to burn down our banking palace! You can't be serious! There they come, they're coming, I can see them already, I can see them, on the broad street, near the great wall my eyes behold the sheep, what, so many?, we would not have expected so many, black wool their sacrificial offering, freshly spilled blood and shorn locks too, we fleeced it ourselves, your lamb! We should know whom we fleeced! Now that it's too late you are showing up! Unfortunately, we already burnt your money some other place, for which we received a pretty bonus. We wouldn't have missed that opportunity! Now let's turn away for a moment from your grave and your dollar or euro grave, we'll put a couple of branches there, whatever, but no, we won't lie down there ourselves. We still must be at our winning best. There are so many others coming up right behind you. CDOs are beyond the reach of law. So, please, just come closer, where legal rights apply! What, you no longer have any rights? You are no longer right? You never were! Private investors please use the door next door, which, however, doesn't lead into a bank, but into our private abode! No pushing! Everyone gets a turn! All those years they didn't get it, they never went into the bank, they took the wrong turn with their money, which also took a wrong turn. This bank was not secured. Why are you in such need of security that you entrusted your money to a bank, of all places? What? You got trust? That's completely out of place. Oh, so now all of a sudden security is an issue! No problem! That just means we can rip you off again! We wouldn't have thought it would work. And you'll pay extra for security, we can assure you! In order for us to secure enough securities to profit once again from your need for security, you get to pay extra! This time we'll also rip off your need for security. It was you who gave us the idea! Your need for security is legitimate, but you don't have the time to turn it into a legitimate child. It is legitimate and legitimized. Until you've got nothing left again. Duped again. You think you are buying something more or less safe with whatever you had left, but now you also get the banks thrown into the deal! Didn't we do a fabulous job? When you came to burn us, you got burnt by us instead! You give us your need for security and in return you get burnt right next to your money. You can watch it all. But it won't become more. As it keeps burning, it will become less and less. It all goes into one urn anyway. There it will intermingle with you. All comes to dust. Just take a look at your need for security: hidden options in this beautiful discount certificate. Yes. That's why we won't let you in through the main entrance again, you can push us as much as you want for the right to even set foot in our bank, you've got no business here, whatever business you are looking for, you are already lost, you'd give everything for the right to enter, to entertain us there's no business like show business, but we are stealing the show and you will have to pay us for taking your money!, because if you drop below a certain threshold, you are gone. Then you get stocks, and then you're gone forever. Then the stocks are gone too. So there. You get a certificate with an eight percent prescription fee, uhm, subscription fee. That's only right, because it has to get by so many restrictions, and this has to be paid with more subscriptions. And you needed so many prescriptions for your ailing funds, so now you can no longer pay for drugs. Yes, and the overtime hours the money is resting with us do not come for free.

Who else can do it but this certificate?, who else would do the hard work, promising security, but not giving any? We sell you shares and you must sell them back to us. There are no buyers other then those who sold them to you. Only the fees are gone. A lot of dirt collected in those fees, with which you paid for it all. Crumbs. Everything that fell out of our mouths, which was enough for you. How greedily you snatched it. The cleaners will find it after your death. Don't worry!

Well now, to you. Not a shred of your pants will be left after your death on the tracks. Wanna bet? Your betting got you in this bind, wanna bet? Bets are absolutely spontaneous but the rites of money serve to fix this spontaneity. Paradoxical, huh? Though absolutely fleeting, betting, the sudden intuition, gets fixed and falls apart, landing on your head. What was meant to bring an end to chaos led up to it. Man, oh man! Yes, you! You too are only human. For us it's crumbs that you got for those fees, peanuts, but it adds up. **There is no market for what we sold you, the market is us alone.**

We give and we take. That's what the market is all about. You pay for what we give, and for what we take, we take again from you. This market is crooked but it still holds its ground. One bank supports the other. Who else should support it? Only if someone were to build a subway underneath, would it most likely not hold up. If just one of your values drops below the threshold, just like you, who should not kill yourself or another, well, you can't do that even on the threshold to the back door, well then, **if just one of your values goes off track, the returns are gone. Then you can throw yourself on the railroad tracks but it won't get you much.**

The branch makes money on everything. It makes something up and then it makes money with it. It makes something up to make money. And now it fulfills our need for security by taking the rest from us. Once we have nothing, we surely are safe and perfectly secure. Then we can be sure of the security that comes with nothing. First it gives us security, our bank, but it costs and right away it's paid. The bank makes up products in order to take our returns from us. Don't you worry! If you want such a product, it will be here right away. The bank could never make up as many products as you in turn will get no returns and no security. Just one value has to drop and no security. Just one value has to drop and it's all gone. You couldn't ever give us more than we can take. **OD: old and dumb. Our preferred target group. Hitting the bull between the eyes while the shit is hitting our fans. We could never build the number of trains it would take to move all those bodies on shiny wet tracks towards their final processing. We couldn't count the miles of railroad wagons we could fill with still more** human sacrifices. Trains as grills for the bodies we sacrifice or who even sacrifice themselves. Our sacrifices can't run fast enough to offer themselves up on the tracks, in the retirement home, in the nursing home. They are still twitching, but soon they will lie still. There is never enough of anything. There is never anything not enough for us not to possibly still sacrifice ourselves. Our sacrifice comes on top of what we have. And more so of what we don't have. And from their blood new ones shoot up already. I mean: from your sacrifice. We'll take even you as a sacrifice. No need to thank us. Sacrifices of the old and dumb don't count, they were already cast out before they could offer themselves up. Those aren't real sacrifices! No one wants them! If there must be a sacrifice, then a real one, please. Let a stranger filled with compassion approach the grave and in he goes before he knows what is happening. It was meant to happen to him. He will not leave this house with winged steps. He is no longer among us, that's just between us. He wasn't one of us. He made his dwelling among us, but he didn't do so well with us. He, who makes the faraway his goal, will not win what is near. Running blindly, he will always miss it.

Who can hate the wise man, who never banked on smart phones?, no, I meant to say, hate the smart ass, who never stopped being the wise guy, the whiz kid. As long as the nation considers minimal thinking a God-given custom, we have nothing to worry about. It has our blessing. We bless our nation. Because we are doing God's work. The cleverer give in. The cleverest give nothing. Just remember, in case you want to picket us with your ludicrous signs, circling our buildings, remember now!, there is no knowledge, none whatsoever we don't have. Yes, it's about time you remember! Yes, the time is now! Go ahead, rise up against us with proud words! It is too late to put out the fire. Go get some wood, and start burning yourselves, but not too much—it diminishes the pleasure, get a nice fire going in the oven and then we'll turn the heat up on you, just so you know that in this country it's not some politician but us, it is us, who rule!

Ha! I knew it! I knew I would find something I can discredit and devalue like money: René Girard: Violence and the Sacred.

In addition, something classic: The Electra *by Euripides.*

And for modernity: Professor Max Otte, 44.

You Bet! (A Sequel)

I OR ANOTHER ANIMAL

Quite unfamiliar am I with this matter, without knowledge of the case, as I arrived much later, a stranger in this city in search of its killer not knowing it got him already. Houses wither under the weather, people are leaving, copper pipes, the source of warmth are torn out. Report to me if you stole the toilet and the sink or report the person who did and now fears a suit against his head, for taking something. The rug on the floor in the hallway was still good, good enough for him, if he fears a suit let him be calm no harm will meet him. It will all be torn down anyway says the man from the bank says another man say our masters. I only want to know who the man was who spoke before. All the copper that once was filled with good water for heating and warming yes, also for the body which also disappeared, staying in tents, in campers, in the park, under the bridge, above him the humming of better vehicles than his. That take others out of danger zones?, all that stuff , copper, iron, sanitary equipment, gets sold by weight. That's worth something, more than the people who now live in tents or with kin, but that's not forever. I see their desert. I look for the mountains. Others attack me from behind, their screams over lost things howling in my ear. For no one takes them into their home. As much as we try to persuade him, no man would take in strangers, they could kill him, fuck his wife, marry her even, and stay in his house, where the other gets pampered by everyone else here, who now are family to the intruder, the one who wasn't here before. Lost the house he once owned, which is deserted now, vandalized, gutted, who would buy it now? Without pipes, without warmth and water and electricity and sewer connection?, no one will buy something like that and if anyone did, he'd buy another better house, without the poor homeless one in front of the door polluting the air with himself, the dispossessed, whose ground is sacred, but only since he left it. It is I. Fever devoured my marrow which I stuffed into my bones as reserve, the way so many refugees did it. Murderer without shape, money without a goal, investment not vested, without any vestige. Chase me, go on, hunt me down, push me down, can't tell head from tail anymore anyway. Down the cliffs, what are you waiting for? Yes, I kept saving, now down the river, down the slope into the lake, into the foaming sea, push me down. Who hurries here to help me, no one's in a hurry, many are fired in a hurry, but no one hurries here. Abandoned houses are under water, the water long cut off. Payments are due, but we are falling, we have fallen already, no one's falling for us anymore. Gods brandish their beams, banks brandish their claims like weapons.

Hurry , help us! As long as we still belong to us! But who would want us anyway? Everywhere the look on people: woe, terrible knowledge! Painful staring at bank statements! Foreclosed real estates! Evictions! Moving out! Down and out with no way out. We said it already, how big a burden the current crisis is for us, alas, we knew that before and could forget it, now we can no longer forget it, we can forget about it: to live in our beautiful house ever again, or in another, smaller one, but we are living in none and forget it, forgetting everything, and never ever coming back to this place. But he who never loses his mind over losses, his account on account of debts, his life for his guilt, comes out the strongest. I don't yet see him, but a strong man must come, who will stand firm, like the firm, firmer than our house, in a jungle of weed, with leaks in its beautiful roof, every shingle carried up the ladder by us, the earth abused by rubbers that stuck too long in fluids and will never carry seeds again, still births; they have been carrying on in some other place for some time now, those with rubbers at their service. Empty cans, plastic bowls, rice still in it and some sauce, two, three bones, the rats are happy and don't want to rest until they polished off what was left. And we, beaten by fate, have been good men, but are no longer. Beaten. Beat up. No, it wasn't him, that one over there, that's him, no, he didn't do it either. Strength doesn't help at all. Nothing helps anymore. Are you feeling better? Would you like some water? Should you talk about it? Talk with your assigned consultant, he will certainly be on your side. No, I am not feeling any better. But you should be okay now!, your firm is up and running again, and if you are a bank, you are up to speed again, and if you are a car, you are back in the race, if not, you'll be beaten up, locked up or banished like a regicide, except that you are innocent, this is my word, whoever acts against it, shall be cursed, whoever likes it, shall be blessed, no, the credit will not be extended again you haven't paid your mortgage in three months, we also have to look after ourselves, we do not look out for you.

So now, as a bank, they got you up to speed again. You always have the right of way. As of this moment you are up and going again. You got the money from us. From us. U-S. Respect! That was quick! What the heavens breed and the earth bears, you penetrate with inner light you, our government, you oh you, the savior, and we—our own saviors, but nothing can save us or you anymore. We leave it up to the government, when rescue is supposed to come, to the administration, who leaves us, because we are not banks, they sold us down the river, and no one was on our side when the torrent tore us underwater. Say, didn't you marry my sister?, why me, I am not a bank. If a bank, do not abandon. If not, abandon. Else, already abandoned. Unseeing seeing is the government. Our misery does not remain hidden from it, for the bank tells the government what there is to save, and the government saves the bank, it does not save us, our dear government, and we don't save ourselves, where would we go to be safe, there are already people living everywhere, no place for us poor folks, we better get a ride with an ambulance, all others would run over us, no one saves us, this car doesn't take us either. This is why we turn to someone else to rescue us, someone who knows everything, a god, who knows us, the government— a god, who knows everything, from us and about us, nothing slipped through the cracks. Our word still lives, but it will also die away soon. We call for help and we don't get it if we aren't a bank. We are no bank. We get nothing. The government receives our small shipment disgustedly, it signs our invoice, which is blank, and does not respond to it. There is no answer. We are handed over to our murderers, who are the kind we are. On the outside I can't yet see a difference. We don't yet know it, but we are our own murderers. As the self-blinded king was a murderer and didn't know it, we too are self-blinded, our own murderers. Our unforgiven debts flash across the monitor, they are high, too high, we were blinded, blinded by ourselves, therefore such sky high debts, blinded by us and by what was possible for us, which is no longer possible, now we see our debts were our fault, our own fault, our most grievous fault, to you oh lord, uhm, no, to us, who suddenly became debtors, all at once, unexpectedly, and we weren't even blind yet!, to us then, thy kingdom come to us, but no, it won't come, our home, our castle, our little kingdom, gone, gone, gone! Expelled from our home, from our land, for we are not a bank, for only banks get saved, who must in turn help other banks, that's what is really going on, that's what is behind the rescue operation, though covered by silence, the way you spread a piece of paper over the pile of crap you just produced, so save, if you can, but not yourself, it's always someone else who must be saved, everyone saved but ourselves, only he who can save, in the midst of danger, shall receive. This also is where saving graces bloom. Not we, not us. Nothing grows for us. We are we and we only have us. Do not begrudge us the advisors at our banks, for what is more rewarding, what befits a man more than helping where he can. We were helped to ourselves. Here you are being helped. In this bank you get helped. You ghoulish ghost, will you look at your shoes!, completely worn out, not polished in months, the T-shirt stinks, pants are loose, boxers filthy, your number disconnected, cell without SIM,

worthless, that's what you would need now, huh? A module that gives you a worthy identity again. How can you even enter this house, in your condition, closed, like your house, where only the rain gets in, where rain only may come in, where there used to be a beautiful roof, where there used to be your son's tricycle, right next to his Matchbox-Cars. Poor us! We were helped to fall, we were shown out, we were shown the small print, but we did not read the large print either, small as we are, we should have read them, those ground rules, as if they were our friends. But we did not do it. Strong as our souls, that small print, where our murder was registered, a murder of ourselves, on our father's property, mom was already dead at that time, cancer, you know!, it hurts, we could no longer marry her, otherwise the story's right on the money. What are you saying?

You are saying: Our corporation is like a city, a bleeding city, no, others must bleed, everything grown carries already the seed of passing and trespassing. This firm is a city, which has the greatest power everywhere, the world trusts us, it relies on us, we have the seal of approval, but only because we can seal any deal, because we know how to wheel and deal and win every appeal. We conquered Europe, we were active in cross-border leasing with German municipalities, we were active everywhere, we also were buying, we bought everything we could get, wheat fields in Brandenburg, water supply lines in Southern Germany, power plants in Austria, vineyards in France, pastures in Africa, where no one else has anything to eat, people everywhere, we bought people, we didn't need any sports arenas for that, we are always on hand to insure any investment, we were always there, we were passive, but always there, we put our stamp on a thousand contracts, we have the government's stamp of approval, we stand for proper business procedures, the main thing is that business still proceeds, the world leaves us, the world leaves everything up to us, and now it is gone, the world, let it be, leave oh world leave it be, leave us alone, leave us be, but where, oh where? There's no room here, the boat is full, the tent is full, the port-a-pottie bubbles over, well, I'll just have to keep looking, I look for the world, I am its horror, but it doesn't know it, for people have always been horrific, a bloodstained horror. The world doesn't like its people, but people like the world even less, tearing the bowels out of her—copper: very popular, expensive non-ferrous metal, where there is copper there is a way, where there is a will to profit, there is also a way. I, specter of horror that nauseates the world, it chokes on me, it won't swallow me and yet I would be glad right now if it accepted me. I lost the world, but it counts on me! Now it is looking for me, where could it be? Now I am looking for it, where am I? The world can't just disappear like that! We guaranteed it too! What sense would it all have made otherwise?, I am asking you, blind seer, you idiot. We scoff at you, blind man, you, who saw something we didn't even know existed, you argued against us, but we did not see you, we don't need anyone to protect us, let alone a cripple!, we would have used someone, who could have read our contracts at the right time, not a blind idiot, although a blind man with a cane could have felt the snare. We couldn't even see it. We are civic employees, at this time we are on the deserted playground, looking around. We would like to live here, someone planted trees and bushes here and also put up a sandbox. But nothing for us. And now we must clear out, they cleaned us out, blind man, could it be us who are blind? No, we are not blind, not cripples, us blinder than the blind man, the seer, who unfortunately cannot read, not the small print, nor the biggest?, nothing at all, no, we did not see this coming, no one could have seen it coming!, no dough coming in for anyone. *Nada*. We didn't think we'd need a seer to protect us from something no one else could see, least of all us, no one could have foreseen this, blind or not, no one could have even guessed it! Least of all the government we always floffed at and scouted, that we always scoffed at and flouted, now we are crawling to it, blind mice, without visionary instructions, without vision, digging for money, only dirt in front of us, digging, digging, we can't see, but we are digging for natural resources for our portfolio. We are digging for the Barbie doll of our youngest, who says, she was hiding it in the front yard when the men came for the furniture, and now we can't find it, the child is crying, but that doesn't help finding the doll. Can't see those, who are now living with us, all homeless! Like us, like us. We want to hear that our credit has been rolled over, its time on the treadmill increased, more and more increased, our heart beat too, it beats more and more, it beats everything, our heart, that's how good it is, but what should it propel?, us?, where to, what for, why?, here in this tent-city, unprotected, can't leave the children alone for a moment, so many child abusers, stalking the homeless, mine are gone, but other children are still here, we say they should piss off, those abusers, we've been already abused, all of us, not only the children, everyone, everything abused. Do you want to say anything before we sign? A lot, we can say as much as we want. It's like empty air, whatever we say. People here, much too close to each other, right in the next tent, they only get in the way! My wife lives with her sister now and that's where she will stay, I assume, yes, with her children, at her sister's, which doesn't have any room either, but she is the sister, right, her husband split, so she has a little room for the sister. The women don't know the depth of the horror we live in. The women know nothing. They don't know us or anything else. No one beside us. No one beside, below or above us. Only us, beside ourselves. We don't say where we are from. We don't know it ourselves. We just stammer something we don't understand ourselves, we don't know the depth of horror, we only know that we live in it. Already strangers and foes to family back home, also estranged from family here, strangers everywhere, that is us. We lived in the light, now we are lost in the night. Not much longer will we live in our penthouse. Not much longer will we be on our estate, in a calm state, before it all has to go.

We bend over contracts, we bend over this sewage canal system, which we leased for ninety-nine years to the investor who signed here, here on the dotted line, who doesn't know us anymore, who has no need to know us, though he leased our sewage-canal system. He did well, the foreigner, that man from overseas, he did really well, terrible was the swiftness of his steps as he approached—a curse, but we only saw our savior. Saving us and himself by beating his father to death, then fucking his mother and finally fucking himself, he brought us the advantages of cash values, which meant great advances back then!, and now we shit in foreign sewage canals; no gondolier dips his oar into the foreign matter that is us, more foreign to us than to other foreigners. You'll see, says he, the foreigner, from overseas, who is clean, his waterways are clean, ours are sewers, but what can you do?, we need them too!, and we can see, we are sitting with him in the same boat, but we don't see him, he is with us, but it won't do us any good now, all the same.

The sewage canal he is rowing through no longer belongs to us, that's okay, you are welcome!, well, it belongs to us but others reap the benefits, that was the deal: others benefit from our shit. We can use the system, and all the others also make good use of it, each to his own benefit, that is the economy, that is how it has to be, that is how it was explained to us: it is to everyone's benefit; terrifying are the steps of its curse coming over us, but, look, it is to everyone's benefit, it fits everyone's personal needs, otherwise it would not exist! That is the curse; we knew it would come one day, we knew it, but we did not foresee it, yet we knew, though we were blind, always blind like the seer, a blind seer, an absurdity, no?, and now with terrible swiftness the curse has come, pow!, wham!, the curse, of father and mother, who left us this little house, which no longer belongs to us, we wanted a bigger, more beautiful one, with a pool and we bought it, but not even the mortgage is ours anymore, it belongs to the bank, before we even had a chance to pay it, which we couldn't anyway, but the curse, the curse came instead just now, it didn't have to come here just for that, but, since you are here: hello, for God's sake, please no blasphemy in this context!, the curse, let me tell you, it is hunting you down, and then you are devoured by the night, for which you don't have a home anymore, when you no longer have a home, the mountains are howling, the bays have been waling after you, woe, woe, ouch! Where has it all gone? Something was here! And now it's all gone! No. Not all is gone. The sewage-treatment plant still belongs to us, it belongs to the public, it belongs to us, but at the same time it doesn't belong to us. How shall I put it? What does it still have to do with us, the plant, here with us, what harm can it still do those who dwell in the light? How does that work? How is this supposed to work? But it shouldn't be working!

It should rest, it should take a rest, it shouldn't be working. Who wants to work nowadays? We'd rather take off, on a cheap flight.

We fly over the sold, leased, deserted canals, which carry our shit, we fly along, we fly away, we fly off the handle, we are out, we seal the deal, we settle for a lump sum compensation, fine with us, and the sewer's lessee immediately gets a terrific tax break, the buyer might get an even better one, that's why he did it, he's fine too, every break is fine for the one who took it, he can see it, his break, he took it, he got it. That way both get their share. The one taking and the other taken in. Neither one gets away with it, that's what they get, that's all they get, but who could have foreseen that only the bank gets away with it and no one else?

Who feeds us, who? The Bank. Who kills us, who? The Bank. Mistress over life and death. Who, I ask you? You know it anyway! Only dead matter is certain. Only edifications, that is, edifices can be guaranteed. No one can carry them away, they stay, they stay where they are told to. They don't go away. They sway but they stay, buildings, they might be besieged by claims, but they don't cede and cease, buildings, that's how they are, buildings, they don't cede, they don't cease like we must cede and cease, but our house stays, the sewer stays, yes, and the water main stays, so, don't worry, you won't be left hung out to dry!, it doesn't belong to us anymore, but it stays, the subway stays, it no longer belongs to us, but it stays, and the hydroelectric plants, they belong to someone else, but they also stay here. It makes things easier that way.

You belong to us, you are useful for us, you once were useful to others, the fence sitters, small fry filling the holes, sitting tight, renting the holes, renting the wood around them too, to an investor, a cash advance, no doubt, a crash advance, mercy! Taxes, mercy, we are already overtaxed, give us a break! Not a chance. A chance. Here's a chance. A guaranteed chance, and the insurance pays, in case the owner has to pay, which he doesn't, because the insurance pays. So all of us get something out of it. So all of us get away with it, from the get-go, so let's go, is what I've got to say. The contract comes with a limited warranty. The sewer system gets an unlimited flow warranty; it gets a warranted flow, a cash flow gets piped into it, our shit is piped in and out of it, it still stinks, every time, again and again, but one can't smell it amidst all the other stink in this area, where they save on taxes and savings magically disappear in ways we choose, we no longer notice the stink of whatever came out of us in the dark of night to dwell in the light and earn and save money elsewhere, earned money is not saved money, but in this case it is, because we save on taxes that saves us some money, isn't that swell! And whatever the ruler does, we do not see, which head do we stick out? Not that one, something could burst forth, a thought might come out of us. There is nothing we need to hear, what we did speaks for itself. And the insurance pays in case we'd have to pay anything, which we won't have to, those who have nothing, don't pay either, because there is nothing to pay, the insurance pays, if anyone pays it's the insurance, in case, in any case, what?, it won't either?, did I hear you right? What did we do that it doesn't want to pay all of a sudden? But he who ordered me to send a messenger to the seer, who will finally see what this is all about, sent to a seer, one of them should be free, free to see and speak his mind, speaking the truth, saying sooth, he'll know what he has to say, so then: bring in the seer, what does he say?, what does he say?, well you

didn't have to get him here for that, the seer, what is he saying? Nobody pays, on principle, no one, as there is nothing
to pay, how could there be something to pay for?, since
everybody already paid for it, more than they owed, it is
absolutely clear: there is nothing to pay, let the sphinx, that
bitch, sing as much as she likes on her rock, the latest hits,
but there are no due amounts, no declared accounts, no
defrauded amounts, no advanced amounts, it's only logical
that no one pays, isn't it?, why make a down payment, if we
don't have the rest? We have to pay our installments, and the
insurance must assure its ratings, that's logical, otherwise it
could not even guarantee the value of our sewers. Someone
worth nothing can't be liable for others, can't guarantee a
thing, can't vouch, can't vouch for the warranty; however, it
can guarantee that the sewer will be filled, the insurance,
that is, but the contract cannot be fulfilled; that's an entirely
different matter. Okay, it would have to pay, if the owner of
the shit processing plant would have to pay, but he doesn't
have to either, he has to take a shit, but he doesn't have to
pay. We all have to shit, but no one wants to pay for it and
no one has to, if he's already taken his shit and making a shit-
load, he doesn't have to take any more shit, he won't poop
or pay, it's been paid for, it paid for itself, and now no one
will pay, least of all an insurance company that never loses
face. What does it have to lose? We are the ones who lost.
How could we lose?, we, who own nothing! Ask the insurance company, it also owns nothing and loses everything,
because it can't pay. It owns everything and loses nothing,
because it pays nothing. It's lost. The insurance is lost. It
didn't insure itself, and now it is lost. It doesn't matter.

Oh well, the buck has to stop somewhere, and that's at
the insurance. It says, it pays, but if it has to pay, it doesn't,
because it can't. But we, but we, who are passed on by banks

like harmless change, though our debt never changes, it never changes its owner, debt is the debtor's fault, but we, but we, yes, what, what? We don't even have the dough to buy the debts of others, so we have to make some ourselves. We poor suckers who get sucked into everything, We make our own debts. We craft our home-made debts from nothing and what's left is nothing again. We can't bundle them up, our debts, for a walk on the wild side, down by the shadowy river banks, we have no shadow banks, we can't ship anything off shore. Everything stays with us. Our lies stay with us and so do our liabilities. So this insurance company issues guarantees for everything, even before it happens. Well, that's its principle. It became a habit. Isn't that swell? This insurance guarantees my world, the other one yours, call it right away, had we not called that blind seer, that all understanding one, it would have never come, behold: this insurance insures subprime mortgages, and when it does insure that kind of thing, it will insure anything, even things that don't exist, even claims for things that don't exist. It even insures the Nothing we are. What's non-existing is of no use to anyone, but it gets insured and therefore benefits us. Nonsense. We assure you that we insure even whatever doesn't exist. Nonsense, but it doesn't matter. The main thing is it guarantees something and also for something, this insurance, it insures something for us, but we don't know what. It even insures debts, it loves debts, because it is easier to deal with nothing than with *the* Nothing and this insurance company has been assured: no risk with these numbers, no outage with this number, no outrage during this telephone conversation! Who would want a risk? Who would take it on? Out of stock. Sorry. There is no risk. The Nothing, debts, let alone guilt are not risks, at least not for the insurance company. Who's still looking for one, who still needs a risk? Nobody! This insurance alone carries the risk, which isn't one, because if there were any risks, it wouldn't insure them.

So, here we are. May we guide you, seer? So that you can lead us on again? No? You only trust your blindness, but not our leadership? Your blindness seems more reassuring to you than our insurance that assures your blindness? The blind seer, who only has eyes for his advantage, nothing else, but he doesn't have any advantage! Where do you see your advantage, blind man? Say, where did you ever have to prove yourself? You get all the credit you want from the people! Where were you when that dog howled all night? Blind, yes, okay, but one ought to see something if there is something to sign. Here, I guide your hand, but I would not guide a blind man—too risky. This insurance doesn't yet know it would do best to assure us of nothing, to insure *the Nothing*, but what does it do?, it merrily rolls along insuring and assuring; it would never insure anything that stumbles, right? wrong, it would!, and with great pleasure!, whatever stumbles, will fall and then we fall due. It would only insure something solid, wouldn't it?, but only if it holds up, right? This dam, for instance, it would only insure it as long as it holds up, this house only as long as it doesn't slide into the chasm, it would insure your health only, as long as it holds up, not the insurance, the health of course. It wouldn't insure anything dubious, no, we assure ourselves that we are healthy, and then we insure our health, nothing dubious about that, that's the last thing, the insurance would never insure anything dubious, as it only insures what it can be sure of, what cannot fail, what cannot fall. But now what? The more dubious the creditor, the greater, of course, the demand. They'll break down our door to insure our dubious credit, the falling house, the thirsty lake, the sick liver, the already half-dead—life itself, because in this insurance company they know: they don't have to pay. They won't have to pay. Somebody will pay, but not this insurance company. Never. They don't have to pay, because they cannot pay. But they won't pay anyway, even if they could, not even then. It doesn't matter, as long as nothing happens, as long as everything still stands strong and healthy. Whatever. The insurance broker is still here, please come to the meeting, you will see him here, there he stands, straight as a pin, don't you see him?, you aren't blind, are you?, well that one ain't a blind seer, don't you see him?, even if he were blind, you would have to see him!, there he is, assuring you that he's still there, he assures you ahead of time that he will come like Jesus, come over us in a cloudy cliché, in shady wording, rolled out into dough by a thousand lawyers so that it looks bigger, whatever they are doing, and yes, the payments will come, we can assure you, as surely as this insurance will twist the word in our bodies and that's a lot of words, let me tell you, produced by people whose tool is the empty word, the resounding slap in the face, because the arm of this insurance has a long reach, but it doesn't reach us and it doesn't want to reach us, poor arm, all of a sudden it is too short. Because they won't pay. They won't pay. Not us. Maybe others, but not us. We have no securities and we don't get insurance. Others have debts and get insurance. We have nothing and therefore we get no insurance. But no matter what one doesn't have: it won't be possible to pay, so nothing will be paid. Our shit was taken for a ride, in this sewer system, just as I said, and it no longer belongs to us, the shit or the sewer, it did, just for a moment, but not even our shit belonged to us as long as someone could make money from it and that was not the case as long as it was warm and happy inside our bodies. Now it belongs to an investment fund, which can save on taxes with our shit in our sewers, because it leased our sewage system; was it bought? no, something else was bought, this system was leased only, so was—well wherever all that shit is taken. Our shit is our own, but then again it no longer is, not where it is now, not were we flushed it; it flushed all over from the excitement to make it into the sewer, okay, so be it, the sewer has been leased, we have no authority over our shit. Let them have our river-run power plant too, and the transformer, let them have it all. We don't even notice they have it, we don't mind. You are welcome—it's our pleasure! Whoever leaves us we can do without. It is still warm when it comes out of us and already it no longer belongs to us. Kings! They sit on thrones and stools and banks, and humans don't see what their rulers are doing. Don't they consider, up there on top, that some day we might mix ourselves into the concrete, so we would finally be solidly in place, inside ourselves, concrete at last, no longer excreted and flushed away? Did they really believe we would not notice, we would not find out?, did they actually think we would not miss our sewer, when we are about to pass water, and all of a sudden we just lost it?; we couldn't hold it? Didn't it occur to them, that we could—fingers clawing for their crown—find out something that isn't meant for them?, or did they not care, did they think we would forget the sewage system?, forget that it has been let?, to foreigners? Huh? Or should we tear it up in a fury, that network of sewers, tear up that stinking system as soon as we see it? And who are we?, obsessed with themselves, those lords of our sewers, as they once were obsessed with us, who created the system, who built the dam. Huh? Sitting on shady banks and far away shores, those guys, lording it over us, in shadow banks, where they started tailoring debts into value, they are tailoring already, the debts have hardly appeared and there they are tailoring, there they are, bundling sheaves of debts, and here we sit and watch them hacking and slicing and tranching and making bundles—from online business—also gone bust in the meantime, where they filed us, in order to ship us so we'd become better shoppers, but those guys are doing mail order business with our shit, or rather, they would, if they weren't bankrupt, you bet someone will still buy it, just wait, the sewer has already been leased, the shit we can sell like our subway system, a one time only event, but it also comes out only once, right, like the subway, it comes and then it goes again, betcha someone will buy it too!, someone will buy our shit. We just have to wait. We start an online business with our shit, the stream of paybacks collides with the (cash) flow pouring out of our pipelines together with the shit below, it all goes into the same pot, the streams rose up, they met unexpectedly, they crashed, those streams of capital and shit, the current streams, the streams of currencies crashed into each other like the concrete walls that started to move before they could talk to us. Everyone rich before, now all are beggars, that's how it goes, up and down from the high horse, all of us beggars, out on the street, under the bridges, beggars with their canes feeling their way into misery, seeing nothing. Later we will be fictionalized as beggars who killed their fathers and fucked their mothers, what else remains for a beggar to do, he has nothing, he just has fun, that costs nothing, he dwells with his children as their brother and also their father, it doesn't matter, he has nothing, no one has anything, all is lost. We go in and start to think. Then we come out again, as if we'd have never thought that we would think one day! We would have never thought that this would happen!

So they collide, those streams, the spray rises high, delicate papers sway on top, no, nothing is written on them, the streams meander, without direction, but moving ahead, the debts are passed on and bundled anew into rods meant to bat us, they'll never beat us, since security papers are made out of them, debts turn into value, Nothing turns into something, the ego turns into the id, the it turns into nothing, the debts will be well hidden, so that no one can see them, except the one who has them. That costs, of course, it costs something, we don't do that for nothing, turning debts into values, we guarantee that the debts will be paid, they are worth something, after all!, yes, your debts are our values. Your Nothing is our plus, your void goes into our fill, and because that has been guaranteed to us, we can continue to go into debt, no, not you, you just sold us your debts and now you don't have them anymore, you don't even have debts anymore, we, however, can turn your debts into more debts, we can turn your debts into a plus, since they will turn into values, your debts, won't they, they'll amount to something!, we guarantee that'll cost us nothing, you have our guarantee!, the insurer helps to minimize the credit risk, that's his job and he sticks to it, because he is liable for the debts that became values for us, because the values are guaranteed in turn by the insurer, right, otherwise he guarantees nothing but the value coming from the Nothing, that is, what he guarantees, right? No, that's not what he guarantees, because the debts will be hidden, they will be swapped, no, they will be bundled and sold, coughed up and flushed down the sewer, which we luckily leased back just in time for our crap not to drop into nothing, in our hands they become values, those debts, out of nothing, of less than nothing, that Nothing will profit the city, because she literally made a profit out of nothing, value is created out of the

Nothing, values guaranteed by those, who own them, who own them as debts. It doesn't matter in what form values are owned, no one knows who owes what to whom, what counts is that he owns something he still can sell. Insurance companies jumped at the opportunity to buy the debts, the debts were made values, the debt remained and turned into nothing, every day begets a debt, begets it and annihilates the debtor, as soon as he thinks he no longer is; the debts simply keep growing, who conceived them?, the father who conceived them—killed long ago, if that's not guilt—kept from the seer, who never remains in the dark—I don't know what is. But then it's the parents, who come to light, who make clubs out of children's feet, so they can never get away, those children. The debts, however, they rose so high, they gained a lot in value, they were not sold short, their lives were cut short, the children's, who are the parents of those debts?, who conceived them, who in this dark world could create so many debts?, that it was worth buying them? Who created so much of the Nothing, that buying them would produce a profit? Why so much Nothing to begin with? Where did all that Nothing suddenly come from? It wouldn't have come all at once, it probably sneaked in, one after the other, nice and easy. That's my guess. Every day produces new debts and we are their children, who hit our plates with our forks, because our feet were tied so we can't get into the kitchen, what do I know, because we wanted more and still want more and at the same time we are their fathers. We conceive and we receive. We conceive the debts and at the same time the insurance receives the benefits for them, which includes us. It insures the Nothing, which is the most secure, because the Nothing does not exist. Nothing cannot be. Nothing cannot exist. Everyone and everything shies away from the Nothing. The debts produced today will be bigger tomorrow and the day after tomorrow they will have become so big that they are worth buying. But those who create us also crush us. That's how it goes. And no one notices that the insurer cannot insure, he can assure us, but he cannot really, he can't guarantee anything, because he has nothing, he is that he is, the insurer, but he creates value out of nothing, the Nothing is already a value when it is nicely wrapped, so let's tie a rope around it and be done, debts all bundled, the debts become values as soon as they are told so, and they must be told, they must be encouraged, those debts, they have to be explained that in the meantime they have become values and guaranteed as such, the risk is minimal for sure, it is almost zero, it even is beyond zero, beyond reach for us zeroes, but it still is a value, it has to stand in the back of the line, then it is a value, the Nothing is also a value, so there. The debt will be paid anyway, as will guilt, someone will do it, all will do it or none, no matter what happens, no big deal, there is no guilt, the dead father, the fucked mother, guilt is a value, Jesus, bless our guilt, the debt we gave to us, fully insured, so that we are worth something again, so that we are of value to the bank again, to whom we sold our debts, the debt has been certified, securitized and will now be sold, so there. Our shit leaves us and falls into foreign territory in a foreign world, that cannot find me, which I can't find, not anymore, I had it earlier, where is it, this world is completely foreign to me!, where the heck is the other one, where my debt has value, and my guilt, where daddy rises again and Mom stays behind to clean up until he returns again? Unbelievable. How could that have happened so quickly? Such people would ruin, in the shortest time, an entire city, which had just leased—sold?—her entire waste water system, no, not sold, just leased, but still—there, over there, far away, lots of water in between, yes, there is water beyond your short range of vision, take a look at the sewer system's owner! Wouldn't you want to meet him in person?, the investor, who bought your waste water system, to generate even more stuff, to buy more, still more and drag it all home, there is the person who sold his own waste water and the sewer too, that is a person, who does not know now where to throw herself on hot summer days. This city is finished. Done. It's a deal. How much Nothing as been insured, if I may ask? It seems I am shocked. Fifty to sixty billion? That's a whole lot, but it's not everything. That's not all there is. But it is a lot. So then we won't need any more bombing attacks, no more wars, no plagues, no plots! We finished the city ourselves. This city has had it. Peacefulness can no longer hold up in a city which one no longer owns, which was rotten solid and sold or leased, because it was lazy, had it worked, we wouldn't have leased it, would shit not vanish completely, if one pulls a string, or pushes a button, we wouldn't have sold it, we would have made use of it ourselves, so there, we wait for a broker and we wait for a buyer, or we wait for a leaser, because in this kind of world, which we no longer own, which no one owns anymore, whose debts however belong to others, which we don't have to bother with anymore, not with the debts nor with anyone else, we are lost, despite annual vacations and travels abroad, from where we nicely come back again, but even if we were great seers, we would get lost and recognize nothing.

Well now, how about initiative, what about that, that's what it's all about, no doubt about that! Don't let such citizens seduce you! Who? Who are they? Tell us who they are, so we can stay away from them! But it was you who approved it. What did we approve? What have we supposedly approved because we thought we've got to deal with it or that we'll get an even better deal. We wanted everything to be a deal, but we did not approve any steal, others will have to do that, for us everything only gets more expensive. We are the third party, the left out third party, how can that be, we are no lefties, we couldn't be!, oh yes, we can, we share no power, not with anyone, that wasn't part of the bargain, we don't offer bargain prices, power does not get shared, we are always the third, the expendables, the ones no one needs, but we are not third party funds which we would need, but we don't have any, and wouldn't the third one be the one closest to the other two, wouldn't that be me? Oh, who knows! Daddy and Mom are one and two and they share everything, but the third should be closest to them and get something too. No. Oh, I don't know!

A sort of bondage has developed, I think, we submitted ourselves to the banks, a form of dependency that came over us like a disease, ouch, the only event that really exceeded our expectations is that the bank needs less capital, which is a big relief, as the insurance takes on the risk, yes, the one I was just talking about, can you tell me how long it is valid?, what is it, who has it?, how high is its coverage for middle range missiles, for middle-class credit?, how high is it?, how solid the cover up?, tell us right now, how solid is the protection for the middle class?, no, only for its credits?! How much does it cost, how much does it cost, a rock solid milieu, the middle class which always arranged itself in the middle, how much is it and for how long is the coverage of this insurance? How much time do we still have? And after that? How long will it be until we've got nothing again? How long till we get something again? What do we get out of it anyway?

The light breaks through, the light breaks a tooth, the light adds another tooth, and the insurance staggers to the nudist beach, because everything was taken from it, even its Imperial clothes. How long will it be protected? How does it cover itself? With what does it cover itself? It isn't covered, it is naked, the insurance, a naked man has no pockets to reach in. How long will this protection be valid? We do want to know that much, we need to know, thank you, okay. It's rock solid, okay, that milieu of the middle class, the most solid there is, otherwise the above and below would drop out, wouldn't they, if there were no middle which we made extra sticky, the middle class wouldn't really need insurance, it is supported from above and below, they also pay without, without what?, they pay with without, they all pay without, and those who've got something, they don't pay at all, they all don't pay, not because they can't but because they don't want to, but the bank needs less capital for that, less capital to insure itself, to also not pay, the bank only pays so that it doesn't have to pay. Sending messengers to the seer, do you think that's possible?, do you think we can take this risk now?, he'll just say, the capital is enough, enough for him, in that case he won't have to see anything, that's enough, no?, it covers the insurance, we can be satisfied, that is covered in any event, we all can be pleased, for successes, even those that come unexpectedly are successes, aren't they, such an attitude has always been tradition in this city, yes, also in this bank, which is a small world unto itself, in case you are looking for your world, incidentally or intentionally, small sized we can offer it immediately, without a discount, your world is so small that with any more reductions it would no longer exist; we also ordered the big size but it hasn't come in yet; if you want big, very well, a double-whopper world, a bank, here you go, makes no difference, it is financially weak anyway, you can have it. It has already been delivered, and just needs to be picked up, it'll go quickly, but it's no longer a bank, it is empty, it has nothing, but that doesn't matter, the insurance is liable for it, since the insurance is liable for everything, it can also be liable for nothing, can't it?, and it makes absolutely sure there are no values to insure, or it would have to pay, the insurance. Okay, the bank needs less capital, which it wouldn't have anyway and the insurance takes care of the rest, which it doesn't have, it takes it out on us, it gives us nothing, it doesn't give a shit, we can keep ours, because, actually, there is no risk, the middle class is rock-solid, it might sink, but its shit swims, it stays on top, smooth and shiny, like this bank, so, actually, we don't really need the insurance, but it's good to have it, because it comes with a guarantee, because it guarantees, it guarantees, it guarantees what wouldn't even need a guarantee, because we can guarantee it will be here when it's not needed. Oops, now I am confused. But that's how it is. That's it. It is not here. But it is there. There is nothing here. How come nothing is here now? Isn't it clever, isn't it great, the insurance in its great building, where everything goes in and nothing comes out? Through gorges and chasms climbs our swelling foot. Actually, we don't need it, we don't need the insurance, nevertheless, that's all we needed. But okay, since it's here, let it be, let it guarantee us whatever. We believe it. But we really don't need it. We don't need these debts either, but we already have them anyway. They are ours, for sure. No matter. They can be turned into values by turning the debtor's back-payments into a value, into a valuable instrument, there, done, through the wild forest he roams, the debtor, his foot climbs up, he slips, he vanishes, okay, the debtor has finally vanished, he's been going downhill for a long time, doesn't matter, he gets nothing anyway, even when the

Nothing turns into something again, he won't get anything, the debtor, in our hands the shit in canals, in blue grottos, in sewage canals turns into high-rises, we turn out guarantors that don't even exist, we turn nothing into something, we work in the dark, we can work with Nothing, but we don't work for nothing, we work the Nothing until it breaks, we devour the Nothing, we'll cut it down to size, it'll make something out of itself, out of Nothing, it'll be something only the blind man can look into, only the deaf will listen to, on waves that still belong to us, though they have been leased, leased back to us, that is where something like that Nothing lives, which finally made something out of itself. We move the canals back and forth like poker chips, that's not good, their waves get all mixed up, shit gets into the bath salt and body lotion and perfume, things get mixed up that should be kept apart, like well-sorted garbage, doesn't matter, it's only the Nothing, even if it looks like something, it makes no difference for us little shits, because we'll still make some money with this shit, and we'll even shit on the money, with us nothing turns into money, we turn the Nothing into money, the Nothing, what did I want to say about it, what haven't I said already?, there it rages, like water, there it stands still in the fight for dominance, fortified like a wall with a name inscribed in it, that is supposed to bring us to our senses. But we cannot read it. Pity. And then we produced this sucking Nothing, which thanks to us became a value at long last, the value of poverty, of poverty as the essence of being as repossession, of wealth as the essence of being as dispossession, of possession as the essence of being, whatever, we are turning Nothing into a higher value, that's all, don't worry, if you don't get to the highest shelf!, what we find we'll turn into a much higher value: our essence, that's not just a reversal of wealth. What's left to us is poverty, nothing is left to us but poverty, which is a gift, which must be kept safe, at a safe distance, a gift, we resist, because we know nothing about it, but we do know it is always imminent, an imminent threat we avoid, the threat of poverty, which isn't one, always a threat is as good as no threat!, not a noteworthy threat, it is a gift, impoverishment is a present to keep, and as far at a safe distance we keep it, it is a present, always present, and after all that has already happened to us, poverty will really be a present. There is worse to come. On the other hand, if the debtor is solid, rock solid, secure, lock-stock-and-barrel secured, as the middle class is, wealth can also be a gift. Under certain circumstances: wealth is also a gift! Wealth can be a gift of heaven, believe it or not! In the meantime, something has happened, oh, if only I knew, what it was and wealth made its entrance. The middle class is the in-the-meantime, not the in-between. The in-the-meantime. When wealth happens, while others do something or nothing, on the top nothing, down below everything, the hustle is on. Can't even see the check-outs in the crowds on the ground floor, can't see the projectiles flying at us amidst the masses, all want a place in the story of being, please tell us this beautiful story! It is a story of want, not of lack of means—that does not define the Nothing, no, no!, it is defined through want. A wanting thread to a denied other, while the thread is not yet, no thread after all? What thread to what, threat to whom, not thread and not lack, but need for the withdrawn needle!, of course not, no, not just a simple reversal of wealth, but the big bang of the eminent universe of being, which unfolds herewith, which I herewith declare as unfolded, although I can't yet see the rain. The essence of being has opened and is unfolding right now. Take a look! Poverty and property, period. That's all. That's our essence. The in-the-meantime has thus become our essence, because in the meantime we can do something else or nothing. In the meantime wealth will also come to us, you betcha! Because we know nothing. Because we know nothing, we don't dare to keep the gift of poverty, we keep giving it away whenever someone wants it. And in the meantime we keep standing between forever.

But we also can produce value from worse ventures, sure, that'll work, we can make it work, forget everything I said before, and produce value from a business that doesn't look like it, like it could do it, produce value, if not, then the risk is bigger, sure, but so is the profit. The bigger the risk, the bigger the profit. Go ahead, buy this pretty risk, we prepared it so nicely, cooked it up, dressed it, grilled it and poured a hot sauce over it, so one can't see what's underneath, what's lurking underneath, but rather, since grilled, it lies there quietly underneath the sauce, so one can't smell the lie, it no longer looks like a risk, whatever lies there for others to swallow, since we've had enough already, but someone will take it alright, so then we get something for it, we get more than the risk's worth, since it was us who made it worth a lot! A lot worse! The riskier, the worsier, no question! What do you desire? You desire this debt, you want guilt? There, you can have it! What, you don't want this guilt, you reject it out of hand? You didn't want to kill daddy and fuck mommy? So why did you do it? You didn't know? If you had known before, you wouldn't have done it? Well, you should have thought of that before. It was a good idea, no? Out with the eyes! That goes very quickly, one moment you can still see, the next one you are blind! That's a great idea, isn't it! Then you can fight in the dark, you can cause misery in the darkness, where everything all around groans in great pain, but at least they don't have to see anymore, only listen! Go back to your house, led by a nice dog! Stick your white cane wherever, it won't lead you, it will live its own life, which you can't do anymore. It will beat everything, that cane. Produce misery, create even more misery! Go through pain yourself, then you'll know what it is. Work it so that everything will be miserable and everyone is sorry. Then you won't stand out anymore! Grab your share, it'll still be less than the one others have to deal with, that is the principle. The unfathomable you created and then became yourself, impose it on others. Screaming everywhere: Justice! Everyone is looking for it, rummaging through your poor empty pockets, where is it, where is justice and if it existed, could we buy it? But even the blindest one pushes us away. He pushes us away. Won't restrain his wrath in front of the other men, who also stand in the dark. Instead he beats his seeing-eye dog, who walks so nicely in his harness. And now you have wrecked that too!

So. Here you go. Here are the packages, you can pick them up at the counter, we have packed them already, we packed all your stuff, you can pick it up there. I hope you could find a parking spot nearby, while your money hasn't been parked, it's been gone for a long time, gone in the blink of an eye, so, it is gone, gone, gone. We calculated the risk, we even insured it all, which wouldn't have been necessary, the insurance won't pay anyway, after all, insurances are there to insure, aren't they? That is all they do, you can't ask for more. We insure what's foolproof anyway, right?, otherwise we wouldn't insure it and then we sell what we just insured, we guarantee you, there is no risk whatsoever, otherwise we wouldn't insure it, would we?, we wouldn't insure anything that would need an insurance, we would insure the Nothing, love to insure the Nothing, as no one can see it, the Nothing above all. For if it weren't insured, who would buy it?, he wouldn't see it, the Nothing, it looks completely different than back then, when it still consisted of debts, the Nothing, which we don't have anymore, looked different then, when it was even less than Nothing, that is, a debt, a guilt, a fault, an uncertain, a most grievous fault, an enormous debt, debts XXX-Large!, no, a fault, for sure, a certain guilt, that's pretty certain, but unconscious, about unpaid debts leading to death and a deadly sin, all in the family, that's guilty, riddled with debt for sure, to die at the hand of your own son, and that's not something to pay for?, I ask you, if that's not a real debt, then I don't have any either. Those were foreign robbers killing the king at night, that wasn't you, that wasn't his son, no, he couldn't have been, he was on vacation, in the mountains, at survival training, which he won, not even unconsciously could he have been the one, even though, who knows, what consciousness does when you turn your back to it, when you pay no attention to it, because you know less than your consciousness, which should know everything, so what is it?, bundle the debts, bundle the feet of the little son, bundle everything and throw it out into the wilderness? Who would do a thing like that? There's always a servant, who'd do it, for a small fee, but everybody collects fees, that's nothing special; into desolate wilderness, no one sets foot on, the son, the guilt, the debt, all of it bundled and tied, the foot of the son tied into a bundle, pierce the feet and tie them into a bundle, a silent bundle of papers that speak to only a few, that means something to only a few, no, not papers, not contracts, not loan defaults, no, a human being, a man, someone will kill him alright, but not us, not us, others, those are other animals!, let other animals take care of it, wild animals should take him out, other animals, that sort of being cannot grow up, let me tell you, that sort of being cannot grow up like your debts, but it can be killed off, wiped off the earth, and it grows up nonetheless, then we insure it and bundle it all the more, then we bundle the insured debt, we guarantee you, we tie it together and then we throw it out, somehow, somewhere, your debt will be liquidated; und you can gouge your eyes out, you can, blinded by us, become blind yourself. We turn a man into a bundle, the way we turn his debt into a bundle, everyone makes a bundle of debts, that's normal, here, if you please, here you can buy it, no risk involved, and then we insure it once more, and then we guarantee you whatever you want, we guarantee it once again. If the Gods want to unveil fate, they will swiftly tear off the darkest veils. Therefore you cannot be at fault, you can't have any debts, because we have them now, you want them back to pay your debts, to pay for your guilt?, that's not possible, we already bundled and sold them, you won't get your debts back from us, we sold them and now they are free, free, free. They are free of guilt and free of debts, and as to all that crap—since none belongs to anyone, since nothing belongs to anyone, someone will buy it, you betcha! You wouldn't have thought so, would you? Horrid thoughts fly around the brain, but nothing comes out but more debts, but you can still sell them too, again and again, yes. And on and on. And on. And on. Yes!

How much time might have passed since that deed? Did anything happen in that time? What could have happened in that lost time? Didn't it create a new risk since I fucked daddy and killed mom?, no, you can do that only once, it must have been the other way around, since I've been married to mom for many years! She isn't dead, nonono, Dad is dead, not mom, I still can use mom, I can use her very well. And if I were to kill mom too, just like dad? You can also buy insurance against that remaining risk, I will take care of the rest. I told you already, what no blind seer can do: we insure you against every risk, even against that one, simply against everything! Even against anything you have not yet done. Whatever the shape, whatever the age, how grievous the fault might be—we insure everything! We can assure you, we insure everything!

It's not enough, that this venture is risk free and that other one too, dad is dead, mom is fucked, all this has already happened, what could become a risk now?, that is why we loved to insure you, right?, no risk in sight, but that's not enough either, we understand that you hate even the tiniest risk, which, however—thanks to us—doesn't even exist, because we found it, no, because we did not want to find anything, no risk available, we guarantee, and should it be, we'll insure it right away, it's all the same, before it raises its serpent's head, before the pit has been dug, before you fall in. We guarantee that we simply insure everything, all and everything. What can happen? No risk can happen. When we guarantee it, there is no risk and if there is no risk, we will certainly insure it. What's in it? Do you mean the pit or the reason for it being the pits, for the pit's being there, there was no other way, since a mountain has been piled up there?!

Do you mean the pit on the lake, that your house with all your kids slid into? Do you mean the bundled guilt you are carrying, or do you mean the bundled debts you were saddled with, which you bought later? Why are you asking us? We don't know. Not we! We only insure something, because it is risk-free and then it will certainly be risk-free, but we don't know what it is. Only you know that, only you know what's in it, but all that time you did not know either! Admit it! How should we know? What's in it? We don't know, but we insure it and we assure you that if we insure something, it does not come with a risk, otherwise we would never do it. And if we do, the risk is gone right away. Get it? We also hate even the tiniest risk, which, however, doesn't exist, after all, you only have one dad to kill and only one mom you can fuck, so then, risk versus zero! All gone. Deed done. We resell, if it can't be done any other way, we securitize the debts and resell them, we resell the risk, even if it is small, so small, that it can't be seen anymore, we still resell it, then it is gone, gone like your guilt, the debt that has bothered you for so long. You didn't even know about any guilt, a debt you burdened yourself with!, not even the shadow of a risk can fall on you, terrific, no? We invented that. Now it is gone, and when its gone, we can still resell the sold risks, and for the remaining risk, which doesn't exist anyway, which can't exist, we can resell our insurance policies, isn't that dandy, something is coming from nothing, nothing is coming from something, whatever. The shit's coming too, there it is, it always comes, that's only human that debts turn into shit, that everything turns into shit, that most of all money turns into shit, that money already IS shit before it's even there, but it's never there when it's needed, so now the shit goes into the sewer, which we still own, I better look. No, just a moment, it doesn't belong to us anymore, we leased it out, no, we didn't after all, but leasing in our case is as good as buying, buying across borders and selling, now Europe has been conquered, instead of us, as before, makes no difference, across the border it goes, it goes on, cross-border leasing,

Europe doesn't belong to itself anymore, that's not proper, that it's not its property, but now Europe belongs to others, well, of course we leased it out, the sewer, otherwise no one gets anything out of it, it has been leased out or sold and leased back, we should be making shitloads of money with our poop, we'd be real idiots if we didn't!, weren't we clever! From beyond the world we once conquered, the folks who leased our sewage canal are looking at us, our beautiful, useful canal, otherwise we might have to eat our own shit, that's a scary thought, it's stuff that's already been eaten, this shit!, the seer might not have seen it right, he himself believes not having seen this right!, but it doesn't matter, it's all the same, it still belongs to us, the sewer, no, it doesn't, oh yes, it still does, it has only been leased out, well, I don't know myself, where I am, but others, who leased it, those poopsters, parasites, people from the edge of the world, they surely bought into it, they'll quickly fall into it, they'll take a great dive together with their buildings, right into the lake of our shit. No, it won't happen. The ones who drown will always be us and we are always the other. Nope, not this time. Is this an other talking? Then no one told me. It's always an other who talks, haven't known for a long time which one, talking and talking and talking, it's convenient, won't hurt anyone. I'd love to get to the open country, but it's not possible. I fear for me and I want out! Please, may I finally go? I want to so much. I fear for me, that I talked too much, most of all that I said the wrong thing, I apologize, I beg your pardon! Look, it's not about your shit, the point is: to sell as much insurance as possible, are you with me so far?, okay, but in case of damage, which is out of the picture, because it hasn't happened, in case of damage we pay nothing, whoever we are, we the faceless, the tasteless, the odorless, the ruthless, we don't pay, then we don't know from Adam, not the father, whom we are supposed to kill, not the mother we could fuck, we don't know them from Adam and we don't pay. We do know, however, those dear losses, unfortunately!, we got to know them, wasn't pleasant!, the father here, the mother there, we know where our parents are, even when they are dead, father killed, mother fucked, well, she's still alive somehow, not much, anyway, yesterday she was still alive, but in that case, at any rate, we don't know ourselves, but we do know the rates for damage all the better, because we are the damage, the damage is always also us! In that case, we don't know you, you don't know your parents anymore, well, we do know ours, after all, we killed daddy and fucked mommy, who should know them better than we?, but besides us, no one knows anyone anymore, we are beside ourselves, I am beside myself!, and in the case of damage, there's no standing up for anything, there's no sitting down, you're knocked out, and no one gets up again! Insurance is sold, as much as possible, but in case of damage, who's gonna pay? No one's gonna pay, as usual. And no one had anything to do with it. No one pays for it, it's nobody's fault, after all. No one pays, least of all for what he was paid for, no, no, no one pays for anything, which he never got, which he took, that's beyond any price, such a debt can't ever be paid and no one pays, if he has no respect, no fear of people and who does?, no respect, no fear of anyone, respect for money, but not for people and their deeds, have no fear, don't be shy!, step inside, no matter, whatever it was you stepped into before, step inside, we show you this without a name, this One without a name, there is no name for your debts, for your guilt, there is no name, you were born nameless, and then you killed your daddy too soon and fucked your mommy too soon, and now we don't know your name and we'll never find out, from whom could we?, from whom?, up there something's sparkling up there, it wouldn't be the sun, would it now?, well we haven't yet insured the sun, no, nor God, we insure everything, even what we don't know, how could we ever get to know everything about a European sewage system?, that's impossible!, but somehow we missed those two, we missed that credit, pity, the sun, God, both look down to the earth now, to this horror, that twists and turns, because the earth does not want to be touched by someone guilty, it has to be someone, the earth does not want him, the light does not want him either, the rain does not want to drip on him, nothing's dripping, maybe blood, which the bank squeezed out from under your fingernails, without effect, since nothing comes from nothing, it trickles, it flows, we all are the salt of the earth, we are Daddy's blood, we are Mommy's cunt, that's where we got out that's where we must get in, like money, out there, in there, we'll show it, who's God around here, we'll show it, we'll show it to the money and then we'll show the money, this is our blood, take it and eat!, we are His life blood, take it and drink, take everything, that's all you get, take it! So, it's come down to us, sharing a house with our money, oh horror, nameless, but there are some who baptize it, they give him a name, the son, who killed his father, before he got his name, he knows his guilt now, he knows he now has debts he can never pay back. He has more of a chance paying for his guilt than repaying his debts. They are his blood now. Everyone's the architect of his own fortune, everyone his debts' debtor. They weigh him down, and his misery—having come into so much debt, so much guilt through no fault of his own, beholding the passion of the blood, is weighing us down, it's all come down to us.

To the point. Don't waste your time pushing this debtor into the Nothing, to a place, where he will never again be greeted by a human voice, don't bother, it doesn't pay! No one pays for what he would have to pay someone else, and all that credit default insurance, which was senseless, since credits don't just jump ship and if they do, it is a natural disaster and that is not a sure thing. It cannot be insured. Nothing is sure. **We, all of us, will pay for it. The government will pay for it. The risk is zero, because the government will pay for it.** In the end the government will pay for it. **And somebody will buy for sure.** That much is sure. What all others spit out and throw up, someone will still buy. Wanna bet? **But is there someone to first answer any questions?** There is no one. There is no one. No more questions, only extinction is all he wants, the man burdened with so much guilt! Now this! That's all we need! That's what we needed, yes, that *is* what we needed all that time. End of questions. An ending with questions? No more questions. Don't ask, don't tell. That site, where my parents, not knowing they were my parents, abandoned me, who did not know these were my parents, there, all right, it was there, where my grave was meant to be, I did not contribute to the yearly rent, I did not know about the grave, there, right there, something is standing there, in the dark, uncanny, some kind of thing without a name, for if it had a name, I would not know it, would I, and for this thing I do not know, or against it, depends how you look at it, they sold me insurance, they assured me that I was insured, yes, sure, nameless, why not, in an anonymous bundle that someone tied, as someone tied my foot, all tied up, and terribly swollen in the meantime, my foot that is, and also my poor little bankbook, which, however, is not swollen, the bank book doesn't pay, not even tied up it pays, it pays as little as crime, no, crimes do pay, my debts pay, but not me, my debts don't pay me, on the contrary, they take, they keep taking, they take us all, kindly they take us to the cleaners, they take us on so lovingly, no one else does. No one used to eating at our table, no one used to scooping up the scraps that dropped from our table and eating them too, no one used to sharing a bite, no matter with whom, give me shelter! Give me shelter! Don't shelter any one not used to it! No one could endure your shelter if he doesn't know you! No one would accept your shelter, if he knew where you are coming from! Let yourselves be touched, let yourself be moved, just once, please, let yourself be touched. I can't see you anymore, but for once I want to be allowed to move you, to remove you, at least once.

CHARGES
(The Supplicants)

TRANSLATOR'S PREFACE

A group of asylum seekers from Central Asia and the Middle East leave a large holding facility in a small town on the outskirts of the capital city. To draw attention to their plight, they march into the city's beautiful, historic center and set up camp without permission of the municipal authorities in the small park in front of a well-known church. A couple of weeks later some of the refugees move inside the church. The Interior Ministry and the media get involved. The refugees go on a hunger strike. There are public demonstrations in support of the undocumented migrants. They trigger impassioned public arguments for and against granting asylum to the people who escaped life-threatening situations and mourn the extinction of their families. One month after the arrival of the migrants the police clear the park of the campers. Others remain in the church for ten more weeks, while politicians either scramble or attack each other trying to finesse a way out of the embarrassing situation. The asylum seekers are finally transferred to a nearby monastery, a secluded temporary refuge to keep them out of public sight. Not long before the refugees arrived in the city, a world-famous opera singer and the daughter of a former powerful politician, both from privileged backgrounds in another country, had been awarded citizenship with the help of a powerful industrialist who also founded a new populist political party which won a number of seats in parliament at around the same time. Sadly, this story of precarity and privilege is happening around the world. Countries, victims, celebrities and moneyed power brokers are exchangeable.

As usual, Elfriede Jelinek's performance text was triggered by a specific event that began in Vienna in November 2012, as outlined in the above narrative.

The actual asylum seekers were from Afghanistan and Pakistan. They occupied the Votiv-*Kirche* on Vienna's splendid Ringstrasse that encircles the historic core of the city. The prominent singer stands for Anna Netrebko, the Russian star of the Salzburg Festival and leading opera houses worldwide. The other Russian woman is Tatyana Yumesheva the daughter of the first free-market president of the newly created Russian Soviet Federative Republic, Boris Yeltsin. The entrepreneur refers to Austrian-Canadian Frank Stronach, who strategized Yumesheva's naturalization as an Austrian citizen. For this he won the support of the *Sberbank of Russia* to finance the acquisition of an Opel plant in Vienna. The deal was eventually vetoed by General Motors, the American owner of the Opel corporation.

The "real life" personalities are referred to by the choral speakers in archetypical terms, such as the singer, the industrialist turned politician, the daughter of a former Russian president. They never enter as stage characters, though they are the driving forces, the plotters, as it were, of the "plot" of the "drama" emerging from the choral passages. Accordingly, the actual places of events are referred to in general terms: a church, a monastery, a lake, a city famous for its international summer festival. This indicates that the urgent issues raised by the local event have universal relevance.

In Jelinek's characteristic dramaturgical approach the text features no designated speakers and at first suggests a Chorus. Reading the text and its musical undertones out loud will reveal that the voices of the speakers change, even in the middle of a sentence. Punctuations in the long run-on sentences function as musical notations rather than in accordance with grammatical rules. The rhythm often suggests the breathless anguish, confusion and hurry of the refugees and the writer's own deeply conflicted response to the situation. Jelinek's method allows directors, dramaturgs and actors to discover individual characters/speakers or the representative voice of a social group a given text passage or sentence represents. Referring to some of her defining directors (as well as translators) as "co-authors," she has also given her directors the freedom to "carve out" their text. She has given me as her authorized translator the freedom to change her long chain of intricate word-games into equivalent American-English idioms and colloquialisms.

Jelinek characteristically interweaves texts from the Western canon with trivia from media and social networks into immediate concerns. Aeschylus's *The Supplicants* introduces the motif of daughters (the fifty daughters of Danaus) fleeing from their homeland (to avoid forced marriages), and echoes the heightened language of Greek tragedy.

Martin Heidegger's tracking of word roots and their transformations in his philosophical investigations of origin and meaning serves as a target of mockery that exposes the dangerous nativism and populism deeply embedded in his thinking and convoluted language. T. S. Eliot's poem "The Hollow Men" provides the leitmotif of hollowness— the literal, physical hollowness of the emaciated victims and perpetrators' mental/spiritual hollowness. Nietzsche's Zarathustra adds his mocking worldview.

Jelinek had already mulled over writing a text in response to the refugees' drama while it was still unrav-eling in Vienna at that time, when one of her favorite directors, Nicolas Stemann inquired whether she would be interested in contributing a short text for his *Commune of Truth. Reality Machine* project. He was already in the process of devising this performance with his company for the Vienna Festival 2013. Jelinek considered this the perfect opportunity to draw renewed attention to the refugees' predicament. In his signature method of directing Jelinek's plays (most prominently *The Merchant's Contracts*) Stemann usually requested additional topical material from Elfriede Jelinek that applied specifically to the cities and international festivals where his productions toured. Frequently, when Jelinek is asked to provide a text for a specific occasion, her contribution develops into an autonomous performance text, too long and too compact and too tightly woven to extract a few passages for just another sketch in a collaboratively devised hi-tech spec-tacle of improvisations on the daily news in the framework of original soundtracks and video clips of the daily news interspersed with songs appropriated from both popular culture and classical music.

Although the text had lost its immediate site-specific context, its primary concerns and circumstances—streams of displaced people, xenophobia, political corruption and favoritism are an urgent global concern. Streams of refugees from Africa continue to try to reach Europe in ramshackle overcrowded boats. If they survive the precarious crossing, they first land on the Italian island of Lampedusa. According to European Union law, undocumented refugees must stay in the country of their first arrival until their asylum request is either granted or denied. However, the Italian government frequently offers them (short-term) tourist visas in order to pass on the overflow to other European countries. For many Germany is a desired destination. At one point, 80 of around 300 African refugees found accommodation in Hamburg's St. Paul Lutheran Church. The presence of these refugees inspired a staged reading of *Charges* in the church, co-sponsored by its pastor Sieghard Wilm, and Joachim Lux, the artistic director of Hamburg's Thalia Theatre. The presentation included the refugees and actors from the theatre's resident company. At the time of the reading in September 2013, the refugees' fate was not yet decided. The following year, in May 2014, a full production of the play, now directed by Nicolas Stemann, premiered at the quadrennial Theatre of the World Festival (Theater der Welt) in Mannheim. It was co-produced by the Festival and the Thalia Theatre and included local refugees along naturalized or first- generation German professional actors and some stalwart Jelinek performers from the Thalia ensemble. *Charges* was the 'keynote' production introducing the Festival's focus on cultural diversity and precarity at a time when political crises, religious conflicts and local wars further intensified the tragedies of migrants and refugees around the world. As I am writing this preface (April 2015), reports of the drown ing of refugees on their way to Lampedusa or the Greek Islands continue to make news on a nearly daily basis. At the same time, the plight of unaccompanied children crossing from Mexico to the United States was gaining increasing attention in the media. Furthermore, the explosive conditions in Gaza, Syria, the Ukraine, Iraq and ongoing conflicts around the world continue to turn millions of people into migrants and refugees.

As with her previous play *The Merchant's Contracts* which dealt with the ongoing global economic crisis, Jelinek continued to add sequels to the main text of *Charges* titled

Coda and *Appendix*. *Coda* was written in response to the many reports of the drowning or bare survival of African refugees packed by irresponsible smugglers into overcrowded, ramshackle boats. The speakers draw from the countless media reports and images of such tragedies. One image gone viral showed a smuggler in green swim trunks pushing the crowded boat into the water and then swimming back to the shore. The irony was not lost on Jelinek. She refers to him in the *Coda* as the "dolphin man." In her signature style Jelinek also inserts herself into the text. The occasional interjections of the author's voice suggest a woman surrounded by television screens, smartphones, newspapers and magazines in dialog with the unfolding events. Such personal interjections become more frequent and intense in the second addendum *Appendix*. As she clarifies the title with characteristic self-deprecating irony, it should indicate that the piece is not a direct continuation of the preceding texts but rather attached to them like the anatomical appendix—a small thin extension without a specific function of a long continuous tube. Though not indicated in a stage direction, the scenario emerging from the text's musical composition suggests the author obsessively following the unstoppable refugee crisis, struggling to come to terms with the absurdity of her own position: the writer as a solitary but intensely engaged observer, driven by the need to intervene in the events as they happen. Though fully aware of the futility of any such attempt Jelinek compulsively tries to catch up with them. Therefore her performance texts cannot reach a closure. They remain open to history in action. Needless to say, this presents enormous challenges to the stage director—in this case her frequent collaborator Nicolas Stemann—and to the translator. In order to preserve the dynamic of the evolving texts they are published and

introduced here in the chronological order of their devel-
opment. A series of conversations with Elfriede Jelinek, who
has not granted a personal interview in over ten years, con-
cludes the ongoing work on this publication in tandem with
the close observation of the production process for the texts'
word premiere.

Gitta Honegger
May 2016

CHARGES

(The Supplicants)

We are alive. We are alive. The main thing is we live and it hardly is more than that after leaving the sacred homeland. No one looks down with mercy at our train, but everyone looks down on us. We fled, not convicted by any court in the world, convicted by all, there and here. All things knowable about our lives are gone, choked beneath a layer of appearances, nothing is an object of knowledge anymore, there is no more. No more need to try to grasp anything. We try to read foreign laws. They tell us nothing, we find out nothing. We are summoned but not seen, we must appear here, then there; but which land that's lovelier than this— and we don't know of any—, which land can we set foot on? None. We stand around unsettled. We are sent away again. We lie down on the cold church floor. We get up again. We don't eat. We should eat, at least drink something again. We have some branches here, for peace, from the oil palm, no, we tore them off the olive tree, and this here too, all filled with writing; we have nothing else, whom may we hand this, this pile, we filled two tons of paper with our writing, we had help with that, of course, now we hold it up suppliantly, all that paper, no, we don't have papers, only paper, to whom may we give it? You? Please, here it is, but if you do nothing with it, we have to make another copy, print it all again, surely you are aware of that? Oh, you celestial ones above, devoutly we clasp our hands, yes, we mean you, look down, we are praying to you, yes you, who surely own the city and the land and the Danube's glistening waters and even more surely you, the harsh punishers in the bureaucracy: you tell us this and you tell us that, and there is nothing we can do right, but you are not right and just either, you angels, plus you, dear father in heaven. What could we do against you?, you can do anything, there is nothing you cannot do. You there, can you tell us please, who, what God lives here and is in charge, here in this church we know who, but maybe there are others, some other place, there is a president, a lady chancellor, a minister, okay, and of course there are also those punishing ones we noticed, not down in Hades, they are right next door, you, whoever, you, whoever you are, you, you, Jesus, Messiah, Messi, doesn't matter, who protects the house, the family line, you did not admit us, we came on our own, to your church, a train of supplicants, please help us, God, please help us, we set foot on your shore, our foot also stepped on quite different shores, when it was lucky, but how will it go from here? The sea almost destroyed us, the mountains almost destroyed us, now we are in the church, tomorrow we will be in the monastery, thanks to our Lord God, thanks to our Mr. President, they were called upon, they heeded the call, but where will we be the day after tomorrow and after that? Where will a bed be denied to us, where will we prevail, where will they kick us out again, where will we be able to bury our own bones, that is to say, who will do all that, who will do that for us? Who will make sure that we will also be seen as *beings*, and without disgust? Those chased away from the brook's banks, the ocean's shore, the forest's brush, mourning the lost homeland, bewildered by their ancient mothers' wrath, those are the ones you are seeing here, no one claims his descent from anyone here, little good would it do him here, and why are they angry with us here too? We don't understand. We have long been acquainted with pain, yes, but what have we done here that you keep us in fear, fear everywhere, fear of my people, whom I left, fear that I must go back again, yet still more fear of you, that I am forced to stay, that I cannot stay, and on this you will surely agree with me: If you are fear-filled everywhere, you will say, why did you come here? To have new fears so soon again? But now it is the local barbarians' language, speech we do not know; is it always like this in a different place, among foreign people, what will happen now? What could possibly happen? We call out to you suppliantly in this language we do not know and cannot speak, which you are in perfect control of, like of yourself, except when you are standing on a railway platform and see us coming, please try to experience just some of the things you can never know! Please!

Look at us, Sir, yes, you!, as supplicants we turn to you, someone conceived us, someone gave birth to us, we can understand that you want to check that, but you will not be able to. Wherever there is a somewhere else, we don't know anything, for whatever there is might be something else and always elsewhere anyway and whatever there is for us to recognize is Nothing. They sent us videos, to my family, when I still had one, they are dead now, all of them, dead, not one single one left there, my old horizon no longer a given, that's now a given, they are all gone, except myself, I am still here and what do they do with me? The horizon turns into nothing, it ends at the mountains, the sea is a hole, a gorge, no one there anymore, no one here, only me who is here and not there, but here, left with my memories, all dead, dead somewhere else, dead for sure, I am the last one, a hard lot, I loudly lament it, I drew the saddest lot. Here, look, two of my folks getting their heads cut off, a few relatives were still left after that, they shot it with the smart phone as long as there still was time, now that's no longer the case, they are no more, now there is only me, but this hard to unravel lot— for why are people doing that?—won't let me stay here, look here, that is me cutting up the jeans given to me, the donated sweater, I cut up the donated backpack right away, I must be crazy, those things belong to me now, after all!, I let myself be swept away by invisible waves, but does it do me any good? It doesn't. Two of my cousins beheaded, I beseech you, I know, you would not do that to me, you could never do that, but don't my two cousins speak for me? With their cut throats, their heads off? Doesn't it count in my favor, that I experienced such horror, don't you want us?, yes, you! Us, a dark, sun-raised group, we then turned around, but: where to? To other peoples, blooming on the night-side of the world, bombing the daylight out of the world, booming at the world's end. Everything in the earth's night, in the end's night, night everywhere where we are not, but should go and also want to, we, strangers in the night, is there a Mr. President, of one nation, under God, an all-accepting one? No, there isn't. There is no one all-accepting. There might be someone to sooner accept all the universe than us, nothing, no one will accept us. It is unheard of! And unheard is what we are.

We will remember you in angry speeches, but you won't care, we know that, for our being here will not be legal, and that is your favorite world, legal, legal, not legal your being here, no matter the testimony we give, the births, the care our women give, no matter how we break our backs for you, you couldn't care less, you turned your backs on us, despite our supplications, you turned your backs on us, we scratched them, it didn't help ours, still, we implore, we supplicate, we implore you up there, hello, if you don't want us, we'll still stay with you, as your charges, on the already discussed grounds no one lets us stand on. And even the decision as to the direction of our relocation, our retreat, which we don't even request, which you require, the return, no matter in what direction, out, just out of here, is denied to us. This paper, this signed paper orders our return into the bombed, the bummed-out land, where we came from: Where were you last? You must file your request there! This is what you want from us, you do want something after all! The head, they cut the heads off my two cousins, there is no one to testify, there is one thing to testify: the camera, no one, no place without it nowadays, hanging everywhere, attached to anything, everything can be proven on the spot, here you can see it, see the proof, in this video, how two men are getting their heads cut off, isn't that horrifying? You don't believe it, but you can see it, you see it right there, my family has the video, but they don't exist anymore, the family, they are all dead now, only the video is left, no one feels any shame about it, only you are ashamed for me, your imagination can't deal with that, there is no dealing with you, you are the one dealing out, dealing everyone out, that is the deal, get them out of here, people conceived and born, chasing them away, you do that well. And chopping off heads, which is nothing compared to all the ways of suffering, which have gone on forever and everywhere and those methods took much longer, for obvious reasons. Only suffering lasts. No one gets worked up about that. It won't get anyone out of the woodwork. Father, mother, children murdered, but that's nothing. All our thoughts are focused on objects, subjects don't count, the dead don't count, they don't exist. We can't refer to the dead to make folks here convert our status. No, what they want is to divert us, (the 'them' into them), like rivers, streaming into a Nowhere they cannot flood, or an ocean they cross illegally, those streams, where they can no longer cut through or out, where they won't cut throats and we couldn't cut it either. Divert, deport, good riddance to them and nothing to ride on us. All dead, why should I, the last one, still be alive? You can't understand that. I don't understand it either. But if time, that three-parts-in-one, the tri-unity, if it also includes us, no, not God, not the trinity, they never were a unity, I am talking about the three tenses of time in one time which never united anything, which united us, as a group, which threw us together, a bunch of nobodies and nothings, have-nothings for sure, well then, if time, as I just said, I can't really say it, if time is this tri-unified whole of presentness, past-presentness and future, and if the thinker—hide-egg—something like that, I don't know him, but he thinks, the thinker, if he now added to the two modi, which have been proven to produce time, so then, if the thinker added to the two a third modus—but which?, which one?,—that would enable us to stay and thus be outside of time, so that we also can get out again, well, an additional modus, how come, there are already three, past, present and the future, whatever, if it were the way I said, actually, it wasn't me, it was that Heidegghead, but if I were to say it, if I could think that way, I don't know what this *that way* means, in any case, if we think of all ways of imagining that includes think-ing—and you don't give a damn, uh, penny for our thoughts, which yield nothing, they don't make a killing—, so then, if this thinking, your thinking is also subject to time, then this third modus of the synthesis must shape, inform, enlighten the future, no future for the unenlightened, but nothing for the enlightened either, nothing for anyone, time then must make the future like a dress. And? And, now what? Will this land's bosses, the heads of states, who, unlike my cousins still have their heads attached to their bodies, will they, alerted by this fast urgent mission, that slow foreign mission, whatever, will they come in person to see us? They won't. We would tell the bosses in this land and the representatives of the bosses in this land and the representatives of the representatives of the bosses in this land, we would, we aren't allowed to, but we would, as it befits aliens, we would speak understandingly, understandably of our bloodguilt- free flight, we would be happy to tell anyone, it would not have to be a representative, we would do it, we promise; we tell everyone, we would tell anyone who would want to hear it, but no one does, not even a representative's representative wants to hear it, no one, but we would tell of our crimeless flight without guilt, which you always present as a flight from debts, thus the flight of the guilt-free-on-all-counts is what we would speak of, our voice will be free of insolence, of falsehood, we will be calm, courteous, composed, and understandable, understandably so, but you will not understand, how could you, as you don't even want to hear it, thus our voice will fall into a void, into weightlessness, our lot that weighs so heavily on us will suddenly be weightless, because it will fall into Nothingness, into a vacuum, into the absolute Nothing, where it will hover, where we will try to hang on, in the water, in the void, yes. Through our unassuming eyes we will look at you softly and ask for a blanket, for food; now look, your reps' representatives will say: Your eyes are not unassuming at all, even though you say so they assume certain things—that you deserve blankets, water and food, what will you think you deserve tomorrow? Our wives, our children, our jobs, our homes? What will you ask for tomorrow? Today you might not ask for a lot, but tomorrow it will be a lot, we already know, and that is why we are the deputies of deputies of deputies, they all know it, everyone knows it, and now we know too, even though we knew it before. We knew. What? What are you saying? We are careful not to be bold or long-winded or too detailed or dull, or too fast or too slow when we talk. We must not be any of it, unfortunately, we don't speak your language, where is the interpreter? where did he go?, you promised us one, so where is he, where is the man who tells us we should not talk too slowly or too fast. Who says so? Doesn't matter, for creatures like us are all too odious to you, we can tell. That much is clear. You should give in as we gave in when we went from the church to the monastery, where it is warm and we will rot faster, decompose more quickly, our selves scurrying away like mice. We gave in and now we are gone, taken out of your sight, out of the public's eye, taken away, they told us, we did it: You must give in, they told us and after some time we did: You must give in, we were told, we are told all the time, told now too, you must give in, fugitive, foreign, in need, as you are here, you must give in just as you are, you must give in, there, you see, now you got it, you gave in; fugitive, foreign and needy, someone like that is not permitted to speak here, someone like that is not permitted to be here. For forward speech never befits the unfortunate. How unbecoming! How could we be coming, when we are always kept going? We will be reasonable and you will tell someone that you reasoned with us and we have finally been brought to reason, ready to move from the church to the monastery, which stands empty right now, they are already showing it on TV, they already talk about it on the radio, it will soon be in the papers, the church is also empty, but it stands, it stands its ground even better, every follower invested in his God should be able to enter, and we would stand in the way, we can understand that, as we have heavily invested in our God, who yields exclusively to the debt-free guiltless. Yes, and? What does that get us now? Have pity on us, before danger crushes us, please!, please!, please! No? That's what we thought. So there is your light-wingèd god hanging, standing everywhere, thousands of statues, gold, glitter, flush of colors, bling, bling, please, we say tentatively, maybe this one will help us, though he is not responsible for us, but that deputy of a deputy of a deputy of a God, whom you just hung there so we would hang here too, no, not for that, so there he hangs, poor fellow, didn't have much luck in his life either, whatever, to this light-winged eagle is where it gets us now, no, that doesn't nail it, this is not an eagle, the eagle is that little thing up there, above him, look, you can see it quite well from here, up there, so that's not an eagle you say, that's supposed to be a dove?, what can you expect from a dove? Just as little. Duh!, a dove, a female bird, a deputress?, debutrix, a lady rep of a lady rep of a lady rep, whatever, the lady is a bird, so she can fly and it is her I call upon in prayer, my call is a prayer, I have to call someone, okay, and then I call my lawyer, but right now I call out a prayer to that dove on the roof, imploring her, suppliantly, you, sun's first responding eye inside the triangle, eye of the sun, hitting the cathedral ceiling, you, yes, we mean you!, you heard right, we implore you of all godly things! There's no one else around. No reason to suddenly hit the ceiling mad with anger! Now the sh* *t got stuck in the ceiling fan, what can we do?

The fact that they are all dead now, the whole family, won't get you anywhere here. We sit here, we greet politely, we don't care whom, we don't care what God it is, they told us, we forgot, but civility dictates us to devoutly greet all the high powers in these pictures and that one out front, alone on his altar, *Grüß Gott*, "God bless" is what you say here or how shall I say it. We huddled in this sacred place like a flock of doves, but folks here only know this one dove up there on the roof, that one is too high up, there is no hawk that dove must fear, and we? We must fear everything and everyone. That's just the way it is. All fell victim to kindred foes. But who accepts such sacrifices? It would take a lot of gods to accept this many sacrificial victims! There is no one left, no one for all I care, not one of ours. They killed them all. I fled, by now the last, the very last of my big, beloved family, one resister killing another until only one side is left, supposedly that's our custom, our tradition, but that's only boasting. And still there are always more left of the ones than the others, especially the ones, the others they kill, but what will happen once no one is left? Well, we can't go through the whole sequence of imagining, you wouldn't be able to imagine it anyway, no one could, except if he had a video; the sequence of memories broken like my family, torn apart, murdered, and here, may I, as the last one, sit here at least? Just sit down? I don't even have to lie down. Or rather there? Would you rather have me sit there?, then I will! I have no position here, so you could easily point me to an opening, a place I may settle down. The freedom to settle is the law here, but not for us. It does not include the dead either, and except for myself everyone is dead, all dead. So you can easily count me among them. I can already hear you laugh, you know that the dead no longer ask for anything, but I am still asking, turned to you suppliantly, some clothes, a bit of food, water, a place. We even have proof that all others are dead, no, no one else will come, don't you worry!, no one except us, no one except us will bother you, we have videos, the murderers have modern equipment for everything. We are not modern, but the murderers are, they are modern and not modern at the same time, they are everything, for murderers are everything and they can do anything. We are in possession of knowledge, but who is interested in that, who cares about knowledge, it's not interesting, nothing that cannot be shown is interesting. Not to us either. Look, now you can see it too: Resistance against us appears on the horizon. We hide in churches, in monasteries, but we are not supposed to stay or it wouldn't be a hideout. This church is an open hiding place, TV was already here, they bring everything to light, the lights they are bringing themselves. There is someone lying right here, another one over there, doomed forever for being foreign. He won't be the only one. He won't be the last one left, the one to leave alive, but he won't be allowed to live here either, says the opposition whose headlines are blinding us, he better dim them. Even if someone drove toward him on the highway, in the opposite direction, a "ghost-driver," as they call it here, he mustn't try to get out of your way, and he mustn't try to get around us either, he must back away from us. Backing away from a ghost driver is difficult. Only getting around him works sometimes. No. Sure! It doesn't work. They all back off from us, a swarm of barbarians. All people, no matter were they live, back away inadvertently from foreign clothes and veils, from us swarming savages, their reflex reaction to make room for random action. That is what they bring in for help these days. It would have been simpler to help us, it would even be simpler not to help us, but so be it. You are backing off, well then, randomness take over, do as you wish! We have no veils to suit your customs or taste, we are simply veiled, like everyone else, but we know, even if we were to look like you: you would spot us, you would recognize us among thousands, you would spot us anywhere, you would know we don't belong here.

Appeal is no longer possible, not even with reference to the dead, no need to appear. Harmonious togetherness is requested, no, not from the dead, they are gone, from us, because we are supposed to contribute to the common prosperity. How does that work? What prosperity? We've heard about it, we have even seen it, we aren't stupid, we look around, but how does prosperity work? If it is that common, shouldn't we have it too? At least be able to obtain it? After those monstrous killers back home, no, that isn't your fault, we aren't throwing that in your face, we are throwing ourselves in front of you, after they took everything from us we should be able to get something, anything back, no? Something should be accessible to us, we should get something, instead you call us a cursèd raging brood, brood, brood! Like animals! Brood of foreigners! That's what you call us and apply local means of atonement, where no sin was committed and the land has no more means. No one can be freed from ancient bloodguilt that horrifically escaped earth's womb, to us of all people, to my family, no exception made, besides me, I am beside myself, all dead, all dead, horrifically escaped guilt, but you don't care, you don't give a damn, all destroying—I can't read that: murdergene? No, we know nothing about genes, we were farmers, we were engineers, we were doctors, men and women, nurses, scientists, we've been something, yes, whatever it was, and now we must follow this brochure, which exists in several languages, while we must not exist even once, now we must read through this brochure and read it again and again. That is why we gratefully praise our memory, in whose service we are, since we can always only see the dead and get distracted like drivers by a cellphone call, and therefore we don't understand this brochure. As much as we try, please be patient, someone will tell us who the people are we are so different from and the ones who just showed up here unexpectedly; and what you see in us that makes us so alien to you; and why we and not our enemies have been marked for bloodguilt and so forth!, but you don't want to know any of that, and yet, over time one learns to even understand it, whatever it may be. The point is: one gets it at some point. Or not. Forgive me, please, we know, of course, that people are not fond of wordy speeches such as mine. Thank you very much. The brochure is brief and clear and not limited only to the specific circumstances, it is limitless, it applies to all, thus your superiority over us. What you say applies to all, to all, all and everyone, therefore also to me, you have poured all your intentions into one formula and now you can't get your intentions out of this formula. You pull and you pull on your intentions but no one can see a thing, the visibility is restricted, and that ghost driver approaches too fast in the fog. We feel really sorry for you! The specific circumstances, the deputies, the representatives of your circumstances are still too limiting for you, besides the awful limitations set by traffic regulations. Mustn't take the high road in the wrong direction. We can see that.

Besides, it is written right here, yes, here. We lie on the cold stone floor, but this comes hot off the press, here it is, irrefutably, irreconcilably, poured into this brochure like water that instantly runs down and out instantly, like water thrown from cliff to cliff, turned into water as well, sinking like statues, almost elegantly, with raised hands, no, no, from dam to dam, into the bottomless, into the micro power plant, down, down it goes for years, we vanish, we vanish as we become more and more, funny, we still vanish, though our numbers increase, our courage does not vanish, there

are ever more, though also fewer and fewer of us, many don't
even arrive, the suffering people are falling like water off the
cliff, down the butte, into the chute, over the mountains,
through the sea, over the sea, into the sea, always thrown,
always driven, for years they swim, they drown, they crash,
they suffocate in cold storage wagons, die in aircraft wheel
wells, fall into highway toilets, fall from balconies, yes, people like us!, they are all like us!, most of them plunge into
unconsciousness, right past your unconscience, honorable
hosts, dear motorists, often oppressed by speed limits, oh,
would those not exist! They are such a pain! Sorry, I must
have already said that somewhere. Equal in honor, it is the
basis of action, no, what are you saying? So this is what you
think of us! You say we don't care about honor, about dignity, we just want to come here, to come all the time never
to leave; you are saying: Once they are here, they are a drain
on our pocket, we'll prevent that and we are doing it right
now, oh dear, they are falling, they are untouchable, we don't
catch them, they drown, they drop, they dread, they quake,
earth quakes, regardless of lineage, gender, age and education, cut loose from everything, they are on their way to us,
no matter how they look or where they come from, future
pointless, past expired, here you have it black on white and
it is right!,—looks, discrimination and racism have no place
here with us, origin has no place here, at least none it would
give up, origin does not give up anything, it doesn't give, it
doesn't pay, racism has not found a place either, it must
stand, serves it right, serves everyone right, doesn't matter
that so many have to stand, that way more people can
squeeze into the wagon, oh, and men and women are on
equal footing, I am sorry, I forgot to mention that before,
their votes count the same, one like the other, their voices
sound, no, count the same, one like the other, it's written

right here, when they cast their votes they count the same, children also have rights, but they don't count, they don't know how, not yet, but once they can count they don't count either, they are protected, they are protected by us, such attention, attention!, requires non-violent handling, they topple, they fall, yes, children too, they also become people after all, which we should prevent unless they are ours; in any case: Everything falls, there is nobody left to reset the trap after it has snapped shut, no one to stop the falling, to shoot the falling, though everyone has a smartphone at hand, ready to shoot, always ready, a must for any human interaction: gotta be ready to capture anyone, with our smartphones, which are smarter than us, which doesn't take much; everyone can capture everyone else, everyone stays, everything sticks and will be held onto, we hold them up high, our phones, like the government upholds the equal treatment of all citizens, everyone holds something, up high, what are you are holding up high here? Oh, I see, everybody holds the iCam, it guides your decision where to fly, drive or eat. Great. All are equal in front of the camera, even if not all have the same camera, but they all have one, children too, children also have rights and the iCam too and also the swipe screen, they'll be great thieves some day, whatever they see, swipe it and gone, and now they also take pictures with it!, attention, human dignity! Watch out, human dignity is also coming. Here it comes!, take a picture, quick, before it's gone again. Dignity, attention!, you should pay attention to it, or you'll miss it!, request that the State treat people who are in the same situation the same way!, okay, then why did that one, that foreigner get a seat in the subway and I didn't, how come he got in sooner than I?, he should always only get out!, how about values?, about falling?, how about anything?, how about it all? Well I'll push that one from the platform first chance I have I'll push him down, and it's like he's never been, if he isn't rescued. If he is rescued, he is free again, but not I, oh no!, was that rescue really necessary? I understand, freedom can be a feeling, I am telling you, a feeling, not everyone has it, sports know that feeling, nature does too, the skier in the mountains knows it, that is, everybody knows the feeling of freedom, everyone knows the feeling, everybody knows it, freedom!, that's all we need now!, yes, that is what we need, let us get out, unforced, undefeated, from the cleaned-up desk let's make a clean break, we need the freedom for free time, freedom is what we need, yes, that one there, sorry, nothing's left, I wanted to save some for you and suddenly it's all gone. I take this freedom and that freedom and suddenly nothing is left, I left no freedom for myself, bad deal, no, that other one's better, I'll take it, what?, someone else got it already? That's outrageous! Well, then I take the freedom next to it, even though someone has already reserved it, I take the liberty to use other people, no, to put them to good use, uh, wrong, it's freedom I put to good use, I use it so I can condemn, uh, condone the freedom of others, but not other people, I have no use for them, it's freedom I can use, yes!, to acknowledge, respect and honor freedom, which can also be taken as freedom of opinion and squeezed like a lemon, nothing left once everything's been pressed out; but not much was there to begin with; I have taken the liberty of having my own opinion, but now nothing's left, all gone, my opinion too, oh dear, pardon me, did I take all the liberties? But here are some I just threw out, you can have those! There must also be some in the trashcan. I am not so bad, you can have them, they must still be good. You can drown, suffocate, freeze, starve, be beaten to death, all beautiful liberties, if not yours, but maybe you are generous enough to pass them on? Thank

you. Thank you much. You know you are free not to share
my opinion. Great. I wouldn't share it anyway, at least not
with you! For no one decides over me, my opinion and my
life, except myself, and I certainly won't decide to let you
decide that I share my opinion with you, you won't even get
a small bite from it, I certainly can decide with whom I
share! You should have expected that, when the light twin-
kled before it went out. I am going now too. They call for
me everywhere. No one called you, forever benighted as you
are, go back to your God with your stupid olive branch, get
out with your whole tribe, just die, dangle from a noose, in
New Zealand, wherever, or, if you prefer, get lost online, plug
yourself in. That's too loud, can't you turn it down? You
can't? Unheard of! You Gods up there, pull the plugs! And
what about that cruel hatred here? What does it want here?
It is wrong here. It's written right here, it's wrong. Freedom
ends where yours begins, yes indeed, but yours doesn't
begin, I'll take care of that, and mine doesn't end. That's that.
Yours ends before it begins and mine doesn't end. And that's
that. No. Not that! Come on now! Don't give me that.

But you can see it right here, really, right in this paragraph which includes us too, can't you see us?, don't you see
us lying where we dropped?, we are lying down, but we are
right in here too, we must read it: that we are not allowed to
lie down, maybe some other place, but not here. Here lying
is *verboten*, it ruins the lawn, it soils the water, if we had any,
it pollutes the ocean, if it were here it would make sure it
isn't!, it must be *verboten* wherever we lie, we have to lie
somewhere, and that ultimately harms humans as such. You
wrote it, it means something, now stand up for it! No, you
don't have to stand, but you don't have to lie down either,
okay, we lied down on the church floor, because God is there
for everyone, lawmakers have defined that border, your God

ends where ours begins, that's like freedom, no one can intervene not even the State, except when he has the urge to intervene in our areas of freedom, oh no, now he has the urge, he wants to cleanse us, so now the state opens his floodgates and passes his water all over us, still more water, thanks a lot, that's all we needed!, well, he had the urge, and just now it's really urgent, he has to let go, he just has to, he has to, he respects living together, but he decides with whom, he says who can live together and who can't, and then he respects that, but only within certain limits, beyond those he doesn't have to respect it, he is the only one who doesn't. For example, while swimming. This example has been chosen expressly, but what does it want to express? No, that's too stupid. What's with swimming? A neck-to-neck race? So that we can express our mutual respect afterwards? Why must we first get into the water, slippery from spilled diesel, sinking, slithering through foreign fingers like fish in order to be recognized? We could just as easily drown right away, get bludgeoned already in the boat, get sick, or just die, have a still birth and the dead stuff gets thrown out, yes, that happens occasionally, be pushed off a platform, get hammered, no, wrong region, wrong religion, we could just as well get clobbered, all at once or individually, but why do we have to get into the water for that? Yes, some of us are getting out of the water, where accidentally, they did not starve to death, die of thirst or drown. But they don't want to get back into it. They don't want to go back. Once you have seen that much water, you don't want to get back in again just to fight by the same rules as the other one who made the rules, yes, I acknowledge your accomplishment, it wasn't bad, your accomplishments are always bigger than mine, I admit, it is important for our coexistence, in sports, in the family, in day-to-day life, that your accomplishments are always bigger than mine, I can see that. How come? Simply because you are bigger than I, your accomplishments are also bigger. This fair play of living so that one can die any time, the other one too, not any time but in his time, everything in its time, yes, living that way is the precondition of justice. We are all for harmonious togetherness, certainly, it is up to everyone's individual responsibility, we are like each and everyone, we are not yet dead, and therefore all set to stand on the same ground, if it's not too small, we are not a statue, we are not a state, not even of mind, no one here uses his mind, we just stand there, on our common ground, it is a foundation of values, called equivalency, yes, that's how values are put together. Why should I even stand up, if all have equal value? I lie here in the church, on the cold stone floor and I am worth as much as you! Believe it or not. You respect our diversity, we respect your exceptionality, though you are not particularly exceptional, except when it comes to making exceptions and exemptions, that is enlightened exceptionalism, which is exceptionally bright, though you are not, it is a blinding light, from one source only, that is the exceptional freedom of light, it has been calculated, the result was exceptionally unanimous, it has been frequently confirmed, it is being proven again right now and will soon be again, you'll see!, you'll see the light!, how bright it is, especially the unanimosity, sorry, unanimousness of our time!, which also applies to us, the time, not the light, for in-between it always gets dark again, this information is free, yes, time also applies to us, that's only fair and just, count me in when it comes to justice, I am in all the way, and even if it were possible to get a clear picture of someone else's death by being there, the way it got to that end would not be captured. You would not really get my end. You might bring it about, but you wouldn't get it. You can experience death on other folks, your own, sadly, only on yourself, and that's no longer an experience, well, I don't know, I could tell you things about death, about cutting off heads, about shooting, bludgeoning, knifing, it would ruin the fun of your own death, so then, end of referring to the death of others, now to yours: there is absolutely nothing you can do with your own death, no, nothing can be done about that, you can't get anything out of it, don't even try telling anyone about it, no one would believe you how it works, dying. You could never understand our endangerment, up there on your cliff, on your mountain, because the moment you are in such danger yourself, oops, it's too late. You don't understand it, but that would be the first step in creating a way for all of us being together, okay. But there can be no to be or not to be, just because you had to pee and didn't look to see if someone already stood there. We have no peers to stand up for us, but we are pissed on and told to piss off, though judged by the same rules, we are sentenced, we don't understand a line, we stand in line, we answer questions, we sign something, we write something, it makes no difference, all men are the same before the law, but law or not, it's all the same to you, same difference with the law that makes you the same, you just don't know: same as who. You only made it to Sesame Street. Real Estate. That was important to you. But then you ran out of money. Why everyone likes running so much is beyond us, we would love to stay.

Well now, does no one want to step on this foundation, up this cliff, from which we were meant to be thrown for years?, will no one climb in this boat, so we're not all alone here, we are all set to step on this foundation made of people, which is us, compacted, so many of us, you'd need an axe to split us apart again, piece by piece off our pile. Baked together, like bread, how can they pull us out again, through portholes, from the hulk that is us?, incredible, but not that one, we human lumps, no longer individuals, a human cake, a crude human block under your crude human wedge. All things imaginable exist in different ways, but we are fundamentally different existences who became one thing, which no longer insists on anything, as it must persist here, for nothing can tear us apart anymore, nothing can tear us away from each other anymore. For he who abides in foreign lands has lost his ties to his homeland. What does that mean? Who says that? The lack of those ties as such constitutes the unique intimacy of this relationship, which is homesickness. Home what? We didn't even know that home makes sick, no, that's all we knew, nothing else. In another homeland, a foreign land, no sickness, that's what we thought. That's how we imagined it. And the lack of ties to the homeland no one binds us to, what ties?, we are no neckties, we just stuck our poor necks out—so the lack of homeland can still exist on account of this relationship. Just about. That's it. Who says so? No one answers. The divers are coming to get us. Now they are looking after us, many thanks! We stand together, what else can we do, before they separate us. We only come in bulk, no longer individually, never again, even though they pull us out one by one. When will we be somebody again? We are all and nothing. We embrace each other forever. It is the foundation of living together and we do want to live together, with whoever it is, even with you if need be, if they let us, I mean, if it is permitted, that's what we want, it means everything to us, to be, to be something, to be a something in front of this clear horizon, upon this foundation on which we build each other up, on which we build, on which we are not allowed to build but still do, so what, the permit will come later. You conveyed your values to us, thank you very much, we can read up on them, so now we step on this foundation of shared values, we want to get to know the fundament of this society, please tell us how we can get to this foundation, so that we can step on the fundament of values, that value base, before the values can step on us. They might want to climb higher. We must get to the first cliff, we must hang on to that. Otherwise it would be too high a step for us, from us, the unknown and ignorant folks, to you; we want to be a part of it, we want to be a part of this society, yes!, exactly!, we want to be cordially invited, and we most definitely will not think it's just for kicks, so we can be kicked off the fundament of your values again, like from a cliff, we, cliff-hangers on the evening news, that wasn't necessary, we've been kicked around and off elsewhere and that was something else, we know all about it, those fundamentalists, they want to throw us down, sure thing. A kick-off is what we need, if not this one, no, but with a ball, otherwise we stand still, we get stuck, we want to stand for your values, absolutely, in the workplace, in school, in vocational schools and in the family, which I no longer have, they are all dead, we have videos of two of them as they were beheaded, we'd love to stand up for your values wherever you like, for we know you wouldn't behead any one, you wouldn't behead us or anyone else, except if someone's coming on to you the wrong way, but then it must have gone really wrong, because that's a lot of work, that's a tall order, but in the end it's a success, for no one can live without a head, that's a sustainable success and sustainability is important to you; we also want to get into your public swimming pools and if you don't kill us in time we'll be there, we'll dive in headlong and then we'll start swimming, and then we'll observe the rules of the swimming competition, and then other rules, then the right of way, we can do that too, we can do that, that's not dangerous, we want it all, we really want it, we want to fill work, school, leisure time with life though not with ours, we have too little of it and gave too much already, we couldn't even get an old-fashioned whirligig going with it, not a single one, and how many are left anyway. We, the dead, the relatives of the dead who lived with the dead, we want to fill your values with life, so at least they can live, we want to fill the base with life, which rests on diversity, by all means, by any means, that's what we want. They are all dead, but we want to fill the base with a life that has value, we want to fill values with life, so that they have a base, we want, we want, we are wanting. We want to be. We want to get rid of our inner problematic, and then we want to stand tall on your values, by all means, they already mean a lot to us too, yes, they mean our lot, no doubt. Especially to us, the dead, your values mean a lot, it's all we have. We have no choice. What base other than human dignity have we got? All dead. All dead. Equal in value, but dead, beheaded in front of a camera, those are small and light, easy to handle, smaller and lighter than the earth above or under us, everything becomes light and easy, the earth too, also the water above us, from where they pull us, we don't resist, we are light, everything is made light and easy for everyone in case it's not light enough, that's why we won't lie down underneath, because maybe whatever will come down on us won't be as light and easy as we thought. But our relatives, they faced it all, they were put in front of a camera, it clicked, it was turned on and aimed at them and then their heads were cut off. The boat was full and then we made a quick exit on it. Which regulation tells us how to find our way in this opaqueness, this mass of water? You see, no, luckily you don't see and still it is true: Human dignity, important at the beginning and the end of life is not a property, a quality, no, not a property, it is the result of our existence as humans, and if we are not human, we have no dignity, if we have no dignity, we are not human, oh no, no one human is one of us, how lucky for him!, but that's exactly what we were dying to be! Every one of us, to be! That is not the question anymore. The clearest eyes shine also in the dark and you can see: not possible. We want to be here, yes, we have different talents, which we offer like gifts, like the heads of the dead, of our dead, we offer our talents, they are our mode of payment, we don't have any other. And that method is outdated, it has expired long ago, like our breath.

Our existence is our currency, it's all we have, in other words, we have nothing, we have our existence as payment, but we are no cash cow, not by any means, that is Mrs. Yumasheva, her name is written right here, spelled correctly I hope, daughter of Yeltsin, yes, a daughter, instantly naturalized, she had it made, she made all the payments, and if not herself, then someone else did it for her, the recognition and acceptance of the uniqueness of a human being has been paid for, it must always be paid for, this daughter has been paid for, maybe not by herself, someone must have paid to make justice possible on the large and not only on the small scale, so she may live here, this daughter of Yeltsin—he has faded in the meantime, back then he might have still been rosy, no rather reddish in full bloom, but I don't think so, I'd have to check, I don't have the time, to get that checked someone probably will have to pay for that too—fixing up an Opel plant with a Russian bank must be paid for, fixing and making cars must be paid for and when someone buys the car, it's time to pay again. I respect any form of payment that's been made so that this daughter can live here, I respect it by forming my own action accordingly: I don't pay, I could not pay anyway, therefore I have no right to be here, I do not pay and I cannot do so, I can't pay and I won't pay. Or the other one, the Russian soprano, Anna, not Tony, we dedicate her to all foreigners, we are happy to share, though she is not. Laurel crowned, she shares neither fruit nor fright: a well-rounded body of sound, as that of the other daughter takes a lot of voices but only one invoice, and that in turn was covered by her voice, we all want to sound harmonious, don't we, and for that voice we need a lot of voices, which we don't have anyway, but also the voice of this second daughter, yes, her, who comes from far away; her homeland's mountain forest no longer stares at her, she is with us now, she has arrived, or not? Not yet? All fees have been paid for her and she came, not enwrapped in fugacious fumes, not spit out of gathering clouds, not sprayed by dew-covered mountain forests, let alone with lots of noise, no, she would not have wanted that, loud and tiring noise. Better quiet. Her residence is here now and her suite, her chambers are here, just another old shack in the borderland, not even the owner ever saw her, not once; then, probably later, something blurs my vision, couldn't be fear, a burglar-proof—whatever—flat, villa, mansion, all paid, that's later, when she's actually there; first she dwelled there, alone or not alone, with spouse, with child, without, with without, whatever, she isn't even here, but that's where she'll be riding in after having ridden out the battle fought in the father-land's customary fashion and the fatherland's citizens' deci-sion, that's where she'll be surfing in on her fatherland's con- verging streams of money, doubtful whether she'd find comfort with her father, he might already be dead, congrat-ulations, that certainly wouldn't get to her, instead she'll get here on account of the man who paid, but she isn't here yet, please be patient for a moment, first there, soon here, with us, where she wanted to be, where she just felt like being, always standing on legal grounds no one ever had against her, there she is, where wild desire carried her, no idea why, she is there, that's all, but now she suddenly is here, in a flash, we are amazed, no, no hot flash, she still is in the heat of her youth, in the company of husband and child and in the meantime she might not even be here anymore, whatever. She has been paid for and now she's here or maybe gone already, the lost one, the found one, I speak of shadows, I speak to the water, it spits at me in response and also spits me out again some time, I know, I know, she is one of those in our homeland's holy groves, who must not become one of ours, no, we don't mean this woman, we don't know anymore whom we mean, yes, now we know again, we mean a secure homeland which we don't get, which that woman already has and already left again, just left it, maybe without having ever been there. A God, deep in secret darkness, no, not in a dungeon, he is not endangered like us, has paid for her, but there's only one God, our God won't pay, not for us at any rate, not for a homeland, happy the daughter, the lucky one!, who still has hers, perhaps she already moved away, the new homeland stamped into her passport, paid and stamped, the lucky one, it was bought for her, the new homeland, that's also hard work!, however, it is the work of others, no matter, the main thing is it will get paid and has been paid. Do not flee from me! Why should I, says the daughter: *Wehe dem Fliehenden, Welt hinaus Ziehenden! Fremde durchmessenden, Heimat vergessenden, Mutterhaus hassenden*, uh, woe to the runaway, traversing worlds away, forsaking his native land, hating his motherhouse— motherhouse?—, a monastery?, *Mutterhaus* for parent company ?, nonsense, it's all in a song, sorry, Franz, all lost in translation, I am not one of those runaways, if I hadn't had that *Mutterhaus*, I certainly wouldn't be here now, and I am also sure that my security has been insured and paid for; mother's house, father's house? Blossoming with no ground to stand on? Properties not proper for us? Not there to prop us up? Memories, gathered in a school, a gym, a community center, a church? Uniqueness, uncomfortable for everyone? We, comforted by no one, except with blankets, sleeping bags and jogging suits. Yeltsin. A ruler. And that's good. That one: don't know her, not the other one either, no, don't know her, never heard of her, what's this all about? *Freunde verlassende folget kein Segen, ach, auf ihren Wegen nach.* Forsaking friends no blessing will follow, oh! on the ways they later will go!—On the contrary! Don't know anything about it, didn't happen to me, no god hinders my flight, I am not a cow, I am not Europa, not Io, nothing hinders me, one or another fucks me or not, he has a choice, it's been paid, and here I am now, exactly where I wanted to be. If I am not completely mistaken, I am getting insulted! No, I am not the one who is speaking here, and no one is insulting me either.

Behold the one who was has been paid for, here she is, the new one, from heaven high she came to earth, on eagles' wings, no, sorry, by plane, she arrived on an airplane, out of her homeland's darkest night into her new homeland's bright light of day, this land that's your land, that cannot be mine, but is already hers. No word that drives the fog away from us, we can see her bright and clear, this woman who came to earth by plane, no word from us can drive the fog away, every one of her words drives everyone else away, only the money stays, the money she pays off with, stays. Even as a cow she would still be beautiful, even transformed, traversing our meadows, even as a cow!, what pasture, pray tell, what cattle track do you belong to, woman? She likes to tell: created from earth, but here now, legally here, supported by

sponsors, how suspicious! But no one cares, shame—
unknown to anyone here—always yields to love, because it
was paid for, lump sum, no lumps taken, and now she is
here, she'd rather not be seen as a cow, which she is not,
though her flanks are the softest. That this woman is allowed
to harmonize with us, well, not with us, we could get in
harm's way, we must not whisper, we must not wail, we can't
do anything, not even be here, but that woman can, maybe
we could sing too, with her body of sound, in her body of
sound, maybe we can do it that way, let's try, body masses
sliding into each other like mountains, the earth quakes,
buildings collapse, relatives die, are dug out of the ground
barehanded, then back into the ground, but this woman's
sounds resound, the hills are alive with her sound, this
seduced beauty, who instantly had the land at her feet, what
a sound! She sounds as if lit by hundred eyes, I mean the
other one, both daughters of another land, both bright and
therefore here, both can trust us, ever vigilantly, the land
spies on us, but it leaves out those two, those daughters don't
have to show any papers, because they have something to
show, those two, yes, money the one, voice the other, her
wonderful voice, here she is, she simply belongs here, can't
do without her, imagine this voice resounding some other
place, which it does, but she belongs to us, the daughter and
her soapy soprano, beg your pardon, that was even lower
than usual, I don't care, I don't have to listen to it, okay, so
she got the residence permit, she can rest wherever she
wants, she gets in anywhere, the other one too, of course.
They may graze during the day, but once the sun drops from
the sky, the guards do not lock them up either, not like us,
the two daughters can do what they want, no humiliating
rope holds them back by the neck, so they can't drink from
the muddy brook, or drown in the ocean like us, the dear

one, the precious one, neither daughter shall suffer, let them stay here and keep quiet or sing, that's up to them, it's all paid for already, paid for one, the other climbs the hills resounding with music and sings, fantastic, no one ever saw such horns, heard such music!, here, go ahead, feel it, if you don't want to hear it, but you definitely want to hear her, we swear! You want to hear her, everybody approaches her admiringly, we, however, we, however, a talking train into nothingness, we, however, our foot marks in the sand, but no traces remain, we are marked, marked by dust, sticky from sea water and gasoline, stuck together by the narrowness, welded together by too much closeness, but we, a pain in the snow-white neck of the groaning cow, seeing the breakneck champs in the deep snow, untouched, everything untouched, everything whiter than white, but we, we touch no one, and no one would touch us, okay, we must remain silent and that stands to reason, for everyone denies us an answer. Our words, only sighs, squeezed from the depth of the heart, are denied an answer, we give everything to the spokesman, we give him every information, but no one wants any, everyone wants to hear only the one daughter singing and not hear the other at all, that one has been paid for, oh, unknowing us!, okay. That daughter now sings here in a choir, be happy! We'll be happy for you if you don't want to be happy. You want to hear it? Wonderful! Enjoy! But we? The locked doors of death expand our sorrow from eternity to eternity. Hear the song, brief and clear, listen to it, it is our song and thus you probably can't hear it, that might be the reason: we may not pride ourselves as foreigners, while the granddaughter of that ecstatic cow, oh well, some kinship must be there, I'm sure, I just forgot which, daughter?, dragged to remote, if hearty pastures? And no guard sitting there, not one who watches from the mountaintop what she is doing, what she is up to, what she wears; we, on the other hand, they follow us, they watch us, because we slipped through the ocean's nets, because we shipped ourselves to the wrong address where we never arrived, where we would have put our stamp on a house, a room of our own, where we would have moved in and moved things around, we are under surveillance, because we messed up the lawn in front of the church with our junk, destroyed its pretty green coif, forever. For once, please, just once pay attention to me, who saw to it that, truth be told, that the truth of this report is being made up as we speak, all lies, for a small fee, that's more than enough for that fee-fi-fo humbug, believe it or not. Of course you believe it. Men-weaned, human-blood-craving amazons is not what we'd take you for, says a politician who knows, who's been to famous Babel more than once, who knows a thing or two, the politician, he talks, many are talking, that one's also talking, I don't know his name, we wouldn't take you for women, he says, first off, because you are men, you are men as well, whatever you are, yes, women too, children too, let the little ones come to me, we swiftly revoke their being if they call for their mommy, we drown them and on top of each coffin we put a little teddy bear. Yes, we top it off with more! Five coffins, five teddies! That'll do. They probably never had those before. They had no coffins to play with and no teddy bears. We withdraw them and they withdraw from us, we swiftly avoid what was sent to us. Delivery refused. If you were archers, you would be just archers, if this woman weren't Yeltsin's daughter, she'd just be a daughter that's all, just anybody, not one struck by lightening, or drowned in the sea, basically she would be like one of our relatives, just different, not beheaded like my cousins, that's what I mean, a naturalized immigrant, that's how it works, that's how it goes, a citizen,

not a supplicant, she doesn't need protection, she doesn't
need surveillance, no need for a shepherd herding her
running wild through hallways, she is already a citizen,
became a citizen just recently, but forever, masterminded by
the CEO who abducted her on her way here, blowing
through taut blades of grass, no whistle blower he, he just
blows through blades, and also through tubes; he fetched
the daughter, not his, a daughter, not any daughter and not
his, just: the daughter, because he wanted the car company,
not at any price, but at one he can pay. His own company,
the subcontractor, which is far from contracting, on the contrary, it's not enough for him anymore, everybody wants
more, many want it all, he does too, he wants it all, we can
see that, he brought her here and paid for her, for nowhere
is the grass greener and the shepherd enjoys any shadow that
falls on him, no, he does not enjoy this one, he doesn't care,
the company guy, who's in the can now, candied, for his life
is sweet, no, sorry, he is a candidate, the candidate cherry
on a humongous cake, which is him, which he built himself, a man in the middle of wedding cake buildings, isn't
his apartment in *Zug*, what?, on a train?, a *Zug* to Zug?,
Switzerland?,—who can stand it so long in either *Zug*?,
whatever!, —*Zug* also stands for draught, so that's where it
is, an apartment on the *Zug*, in *Zug*, in the *Zug*, in the
draught, wherever!, the answer is blowing in the *Zug*, you
said it!, it sucks, that makes slumber shy away even from us,
there is his place, but that's not a home, he's never there, his
softly cradled slumber never guarded, never shadowed, that
man is everywhere and nowhere, but he definitely isn't there,
not anymore, probably never, above that supermarket in
Zug, he had never been seen there, like the daughter who is
to bring the company here has never been sighted in her
squalid little house, she has a better one, I've been told by a

god, whose hundred eyes—out of numbness and boredom, because the same thing keeps happening over and over again—are already drooping in part, always the same, always the same, but elsewhere it's always elsewhere, where another part keeps watch, but none in Zug, Zug has no part of this man, but Zug has it coming, its share, it will get its own little share, and that one he won't share, because he'd have to pay more with us here, it's very little there, ask him, go ahead, ask him, whoever finds him, ask him how he was discovered, he was found, we, however, nobody cares where we are, they couldn't care less about anything, there, where it says Zug, there, on the *Zug*, no, not our pitiful, freezing *Zug*—our train, our column, also called *Zug* in that land—, there in that beautiful train there are many, but again, no one's in the apartment, at least not that man, he must leave the land, he may return, but only for a short time, we aren't worried, we know he'll be back; so he'll come, here he is, on TV, teeing on the golf course, on the race track, racing, no, but he's there too, and then gone again, at the right time, that takes some figuring, and all for him, that figures!, the finance guys want it that way, they even require it, why not, in, out, in, out, why not, it's great to have some variety, fairness is more important, but variety also counts, a band, yes, our entire state orchestra has been enriched by this cool player and it's the same in many other areas of daily life. The man is loaded and now he gets us loaded, onto a draughty old train we don't belong here, we are not entitled to your mountains, your lakes, there is no sea and the people here don't want to see us either. He could do something else too, that man who brought the cow down from cold mountains, where else would gods want to dwell but in the shady woods when it gets hot, and in shady orchards, when they get hungry? Where? Where to dwell? That one? Dwelling? Well, here and there, you can look in Zug, on the *Zug*, you can look in Canada, in Russia, you can look everywhere and he will be everywhere, he does everything for us, well, not for us but for all the others here, those he wants to enrich with himself so he can enrich himself, but not those, no, not those, who fled to us through impassable deserts, calm streams, sandy lands and impossibly deep oceans. We, however, we. We, yes, we.

The man who talks such high-blown talk and has all talk reported to him like a fire, is really valuable as a fellow human being, he is incredibly valuable, which no one can imagine but he, that man and what he does is as valuable as a Hershey's bar, as valuable as a glass of milk, a very small one, invaluable, depends what for and to whom, valuable to us all, to the community, any contribution is valuable and if the man is not elsewhere but here, he is valuable to us and when he is elsewhere, he is valuable to others, maybe to himself, who knows, why not, why not? We don't know any corporate bosses, we don't know anyone, not even ourselves, does anyone know himself?, who knows the ropes? It won't do, nothing will do, even though we make do with so little, no one naturalizes us, we have no one behind us, no one with a corporation, we don't even have someone behind us with a single-family house, well yes, sure, maybe we do have that one, he also wants his role in this environment, wait a minute, he's still looking for it, he'll find it any moment, maybe he finds it with us, who knows? This corporate king found his part in ostracizing, no, sorry Austrocizing this daughter of a cow, no, of a bull, no, there's no bull, no red one in all this bull either, anyway, a star was born. Or did this cow come about some other way? A metamorphosis? Who knows. All that's left is to report the talk, to report this nymph, for us to report at homeland, not ours, at homeland security, the buck stops there, that's where we end, like the cow cut off from water on her flight. But why would she do that? She is already here. Why flee? Once a womb's young sprout, now a womb herself. That's her! Hello! Though once you fugitives seemed to have had a share of this land, oh no, those were others, now we are being questioned and we can't blame others now, it would just be excuses, they ask, snatching up answers like gasping for air, for the answer means nothing to them, it is like the wind sighing above them, like the water they are under, which is crashing above them, until they are revealed again, pulled out, wrung out, laid out, no thoughts of them passed on, although those thoughts were there. Now they are things, same as other things, adjusted to the void, the water, an unequal fight with this element, to swim or not to swim, that is the question, and so they ask: But what caused you to flee the house of the fathers? Yes, that's what we ask ourselves. Not only you ask us this, we ask too, only whom? All dead. They are all dead now, and when there was time to ask, we didn't have any questions. We still don't. Time we do have, but nothing, no one else. Now. For example, we have, it is just an example, that is all we have, we don't even have a phony residence in the safe haven of Zug, a tax haven, above the supermarket, lots of people there, no one in the apartment, they should spread out better! But we spread out here, where alms are handed out, that's not how we imagined it, but that's what happened. While a god listens ecstatically to the newly invented musical art of this singer who became a citizen, she already was a singer before, she was lucky, wasn't she?!, our soft whisper does not reach his ear, of course not, our lisped lament does not reach his desk, how could it, how? We are not sitting at the hearth of our palace, which was a hut, which was a little house, not that little, which was something, whatever, which does not count here, we are no longer sitting there, where we were, so the whole city bears the guilt of our lot.

The water bears the guilt, the water carries the debt, bless you both, that you pay me more than the interest, that you pay with your capital, with people who came here as the method of payment for themselves, I'll take them, do you have more of them? Or have you already enough of them? This question surges up in me, and so I am on my way, the path that follows me, the dear water, or is it the other way around? Do I follow a path? Could be, since so many are riding my waves and rise like suns and then go out. I vaporize them. Good riddance. They rise above me and away. The city bears the guilt, God bless, dear guilt, I am the city, I am happy you exist and happy to be your carrier. Nothing to speculate here, not electricity, not telephone wires, not fiber optic cables. Nothing to carry from or to, nothing to carry on about, no one gets carried away and no one cares anyway. Well, I could also say something altogether different. Nothing to be conducted except that woman and she has long been naturalized, yes, we've already said it and, yes, that other one too, because the art of music should be brought— and kept—in close contact with the people, yes, I've said that before, but no one's interested. After the fight according to the fatherland's custom, which means, none at all, she is already naturalized, the other one too, done deal, we are not, that's dead certain. She has been made a citizen, naturalized against payment, the other for a song, the first one a citizen as per payment and amortization of a certain lump sum, the other for payment by voice and real estate. She has been naturalized and paid, that woman, the daughter, that maiden's name I don't recall, I am afraid I never knew it, no, I did, I wrote it down but now I can't find it—Neb—Neb—no, not nebbish, that lovely name, doesn't matter, she is here now and may stay as long as she wants to, even though she is no longer here, she may stay, with passport and stamp, not collapsed in front of our eyes, she can stand her ground, for never did she hold legal grounds against this land. She really didn't. Not like us, we have grounds, but those are not legal grounds. Where the law starts the ground ends, any ground, any property, that's the so-called legal-property boundary and it runs: exactly here. Exactly! According to the law, pass judgment on me, on the gods' protection here and on those who can bypass the law. We can't. Pass judgment on us. We can do nothing. The daughter, however, Yeltsin's daughter, that much we do know, her name, you can see it right here, we forgot it, sorry, but she was here for a short time only, until she had her passport and the fun that comes with it, but you also can look up her name elsewhere, if you like, I've had enough of looking things up, in my case others are looking for lots of things, yes, the one who had the right to legal residence, even the law itself paid for her, paid by the corporate king, yes, he, who now runs for some higher office, we don't yet know exactly what, but he must know, you, corporate king, you?, this land's chancellor?, why not, from our perspective, we don't have a say anyway, but your name— Yeltsin—no, not that one for once, you, man of Now and man to come, it's your name I know, you produce sound and smoke, and at a high price at that, mind you: the production is difficult and complicated, the sales price therefore all the higher, but still, no Opelia, and no soprano for you. Forgive me, I get carried away some times, but the cow stays, for the time being she'll stay, don't you want to take care of us? Yes, care, you! Take care of an insurance policy. You and your vassals, make sure we are feeling good, as good as the daughter in the empty house in the Burgenland border villages of Upper Wart or Lower Wart, she waits out the qualifying period in a place far away from the refugee quarters in Upper Wait or Lower Wait, she isn't stupid, she waits in Between Waits, in the waiting area, but in a nicer place, and if the Swiss apartment is too small, too empty, too much above the supermarket, then we just won't stay there, that's obvious. Why should we?

You, Sir, in Switzerland, in Canada, in Austria, lord of spare parts, lord of all stocks, I mean of the entire stock, unfortunately you didn't get it all, it surely isn't our fault you couldn't transform the maiden into a cow, uh, I mean the body parts into one big cash cow: one whole car, all those operations for the Opel for nothing, futile I think, as futility is the lot of us all, sadly, because participatory democracy does not just mean casting one's vote in elections, better not having a vote, then one wouldn't have to go there, because democracy is so much more than that, you recognized that with your party, we recognized nothing, but it doesn't matter, we can't vote anyway, we can't even vote where we put up our bed, you lord of the failed car purchase, I mean the purchase of the car factory, you didn't get it, you didn't get the Opel plant, despite all the offerings, none of those a gift, except one, a gift for the Yeltsin daughter, a great gift, and still you are our overlord, even though you give us nothing, nada, not like Jesus, but still lording it over us to a tune we can't sing but that woman can. Quickly listen to the nodding woman, who nods everything through, even the tyrant, also when it's a go, because the point where the head is attached to the neck, that is where her tones originate, her wonderful singing, and we, the bleeding ones, are blown away, thrown off the cliff, out of awe when we hear her sing, off the cliff with us that reddens all the while until we get down into the water. You, lord of the empty flat in Zug, of the wedding-cake castle some other place, where all that sweetness lives:

grace us with your omnipresent justice as you did for that woman you transformed into a fellow-country-woman in this countryside by a *blitz* ruling you took care of, the *blitz* was your doing, Lord Almighty!, you took care of the ruling in the special interest of the land, which exactly suits your interests. This land is you, no, that's a bit too much, the land allows you to introduce your ideas any time, but only you, well, not quite the only one, but you as well, and especially you, the land allows us nothing, we are nothing and it allows us nothing, even though we would like to participate, it's better than watching, no?, so that the law also comes from us, so that the law also goes for the people, which we will be then too, but the law does not come and go, and when it goes out, it dresses up, it gets all decked out, but we may not come along, we can't even get into the restaurant, that's not justice, even though justice would also come to us, at least it would if it could get some time off for once, and our dream act, unfortunately, passed far away, no, it's been shot here, the dream pass, by a soccer hero, local off-shoot of foreign parentage, he passed with flying colors, but now its no longer here, I mean the dream pass, it's been shot, and the hero does his dream act in Munich now with his passport of our dreams, but justice, which could also come to us, if we belonged to this dream-*Volk*, the people who shoot dream passes and have the passports we want so much, but don't get, but you, you, lord, you, man, king, you could not pin down the Opel either, no Sir, you wanted to, with the Russian Bank, that was supposed to work, deep in slumber's shadow you are still making money, even when you do nothing you are making money, but of course that's not true, you must work your butt off, we would too, but they won't let us. You moved the daughter of Zeus, no, the Czar's, you moved her in here and then you had her naturalized, you wanted to buy, well, at least we can buy pita bread, though we don't have to, we get it for nothing, we get food for free, good to be free, even if it's rotten, it rotted and, quite naturally, citizens are outraged about us getting spoiled bread, we shouldn't get anything, of course, but you for once were not spoiled rotten, your plan was spoiled, because you don't make five-year plans, no, that's not why, you couldn't be spoiled, though rotten, because Mommy Dearest, the dear corporate mother, General Motors, the general of motors, the top gun of the entire military, of the entire world with all the motors, all of them, well, almost all of them, she didn't allow it, oh lord, here you can see for once how it is and how it can happen even though the daughter is a citizen now, you paid but you got nothing for it, oh no, you'd never do such a thing, you don't invest in uncertain things, in objectionable objects, you invest with perfect wrath only when it's worth it, the daughter might have paid something too, we don't know, we wouldn't know, amidst the sparks of her precious stones she must have paid, they all pay, they can, everyone pays for what they can get, we, however, do not pay, nor are we methods of payment, but you, lord, master of all methods of payment, please pay for us too, be the State, lead it, pay for us, but no, you don't do that, you could pull off a blitz-naturalization, but you could not obtain the Opel, you see, oh lord, we pay, no, pray that you won't get the Opel, that's total nonsense, we know that of course, we've said it at least three times before, but it still isn't just. It drives the sting of madness deep into our chest, oh no!, that will drive us wildly around the globe. Nothing is just, you, State, are you at least just?, here, with us, you would have an object, you could practice justice on us, please, any time, we are ready, maybe you can finally master it and will no longer have to practice, but you are not, and you don't want to practice either. Be all just, as you are almighty, State, okay, just just will also do, all just even better, then he would be just to us all, pious and loyal, dear State, where we all want to be, our refuge, which you should become! Please help us!

Do not betray us refugees, please, please don't!, like, yes, exactly, like you did not betray that fugitive woman, daughter, with money, you did not betray how much, the way she stood there, knees bent, neck tilted backwards, but bought her, for how much!, you don't tell!, for how much you wanted to buy yourself with the bank into the car business, the plant, the greatest, the biggest ever, I think, okay, almost, but very big at any rate, from far away the nice giant GM looks at you benevolently, but he doesn't want to come here himself, unlike us, who were happy to come, and then he drops you, he, the biggest, much bigger than you, there always is someone bigger, you see, that's what also happens to us, except no one looks at us benevolently, no one looks at all, they don't want to see us, or the crap they feed us, the donated worn-out sofas, no, it's not yet straw-filled sacks we rest on, they don't see any of it, nothing at all—the way we prepare ourselves for participation in the democracy, if we could see it just once, just get a look at it!, withered our shoulders and hands, our hands dried out from doing nothing, a democracy, its hooves racing over us, nevertheless, it would be nice, at least we could see what's ahead of us and what we should prepare for, oh lord, lord of spare parts, for you never got the whole thing even though you paid a pretty penny, in addition to the all new citizenova, the cow, nothing left of the cow now, just the pure white shape, wherever she is, no idea, oh lord, so then do not betray us fugitives, as you did not betray that fugitive, the nymph, now happily naturalized, it's only natural that we like beautiful women, that nymph too, with her fast-climbing legs, our nationalized treasure, she hesitates to talk, we do not see her, who knows where she is, this land's new national, but we don't know where she stands out these days and how she looks, her bovine roar does not reach us here, we, however —our words cut off by fear—do not betray us fleeing ones, who are on earth but fleetingly, there isn't much to fork out for us, we won't stay too long either, we promise, even though we would like to, naturally, we, the expelled, please fork some over for us too, as you once forked over for the cow, your talk lots of dung, your wealth loads of it, please fork it out, not just for forklifts, please pay the price for us also, that's nothing for you, compared to the car plant, not to mention its mommy, the corporation in the USA, that would be too expensive even for you, can't buy that one, but us you can, as you could buy citizen- and sponsorship for the cow, in the shortest time, trying again and again, good man that you are, no, it works right away, with the right amount of money, everything works right away, that's the way to bring the goddess to the people. But as for the daughter company, the sons' company, whatever, lord, are we cheap compared to that, and you might even get a massive discount, we can handle massive workloads, as soon as more are coming, hundreds of thousands are coming, they are already here, they arrived, even if not right here, but they might come here, maybe all of them will come, that's the goal, at least theirs, come on in all of you, please, let the little children come to me! Hundreds of thousands, please come!, into the ocean if need be, there is still room, plenty of it, room for many more, let the little ones come to me, says the ocean, which is already big, come and go with the tide, though it could be a bumpy ride. Here they come to be taken for that ride and there they are coming together, now they stop, everything does, as a pasted-together, glued-together thing, one huge human chunk, in the water, we already bought the crude wedges; they are still coming as we speak, they are coming in droves, we can see them bright and clear, not dark and dirty, they are coming to mass, no, en masse, fear still tames them, but we can't guarantee they will come in the future, because here everything rests upon—it's written right here, let's say it right now, everything rests upon cooperation, participation, discussion, decision making, action taking, policy shaping and sharing accountability. And for all that there are quite a few more than a few and what's more is a lot more than less, that's obvious: the more the merrier. Yeah, well, in America they decided you don't get the plant, even though you wanted it so much, indeed, you've already done one good deed for it, planting good seed, so then, even though you wanted it, the plant, wanted it so bad, really bad, you raised your face to heaven and prayed and paid and put in a good word and had good words thrown into the pressure cooker, where they are boiling with rage now, oh lord, give us rubber to burn, give us Opel, I am the right boss for it, said you, we understand you well, and with your fundamental understanding of the Opel operation, you got it, you don't have to learn anything else for it, you got the understanding for the Opel world, we only for the *Opfer*–, the victim world, you, boss, for the Opel-world, for which you laid the foundation, on which to build the foundation for a new Opel plant: there is, however, more to turning a profit, profit alone won't do, there are too many plants, especially those, they will be shut down now, we, however, don't want to be shut down, we don't want to be shut up and in and deported, we want to grapple with background reports and backroom deals, before they grab us and separate us, because we gabbed too much during class. We want to get to the bottom of it, not the ocean, we just got out of there, but the whole deal, backroom deals, up-front cash, global connections, before they disconnect us, because we have not paid for the call. We don't stop talking, even though we should, this is a church!, we should be allowed to at least point out problems and solutions, no, we aren't, because we are not one of them and never will be, we can see that, even though we've already formed an opinion, but who wants to hear it and what does it look like anyway? We are not given to biases and prejudice, do you think we want to take over and that's the reason we are taken to hearings, frequently, constantly, mostly unexpectedly, taken like animals, driven like crazy through the hallways of the home that isn't ours. But here it says we should express ourselves openly and unprejudiced—oh, unprejudiced—not unperjured, that we are somebody, we are somebody who have an opinion and express it most expressively, we should not be afraid to express ourselves, the sighs, the tears, the nagging melancholy, we should leave it all behind, now we should express ourselves freely and openly, because an open mind will lead to a better understanding and that means making democracy possible, but it doesn't mean making the Opel purchase possible for you, Sir, not even with the Russian bank, not even with the savings bank that saves our money we don't have, but not theirs, not the bank's money, no expense spared there and not even if we get a Russian bank which was naturalized thanks to you and not even if we can bank on a new Russian neighbor on account of your express transfers, yes, the fantastic soprano, the beauty, that one too, of course, she really sings beautifully, like velvet, she really earned it, who if not her, also for the future, she deserves it forever and gets it too, oh, could we lie there for just a moment—no, not on top of her, not under her, what are you thinking—soft like that for an hour, where we could bed down, until we might possibly get a real bed some time. We are waiting, we are lining up, we keep in line, we stay on the line, our life is always on the line, countless Opel parts also get moved on an assembly line, excuse me, that also fits in here, doesn't it?, we wait unquestioningly for our questioning, we are looking for the wrong answers, we are told, we are constantly told, we are telling ourselves just now, because it was told to us. No question, they say, if we hadn't listened to the wrong side our trials would be over now, but we don't believe it, we have kept silent so often, and what happened?, nothing happened, we must all be on the same page, they say, so we can't turn the page either, then how can we check if we got the right answer? Which one is the right side, you think, oh Lord, excuse me, Lord Almighty, are you perhaps the wrong side to listen to? No, you cannot be, the lord is everything, he is every side, he is on every page, he is above everything, he can be turned anytime and there he will show us his real face and interests and critical insight, and he will acquisition something—it says so right here, so you can read up on it too—after he has already acquisitioned everything else, the good lord, he can also acquire art and culture, who cares. Not he. He'd be the last. He is not interested in art and culture, even though he says so. No way. Round eyes just get narrower, legs no longer aim to kick, screams no longer resound, if art were to resound, it would really be a problem, you'd hear nothing and no one anymore. If fear cut off the word, we'd just try again. You, Sir, are you open for the new, the foreign? No, you are not. But we are supposed to be, you, Sir, hear this: You are not president, but verily, we say unto you, ask what you can do for others, not what others can do for you! It says so right here. Isn't that old stuff? Maybe, but it says it right here. We do not have the words. We do not need them anyway, because that much has been answered, it has been answered all by itself, it has been answered without a hearing, and truthfully of course: you naturalized the Russian princess, and others were also supposed to do something for it, no idea what, but those others are in America, and they have done absolutely nothing for you. You wrapped your arms around the Russian presi-princess whom we had never heard of and brought her, got her here, she still hesitates to speak, she says nothing, doesn't live here, where she should live, she only rented, someone else rented it for her, she did not have to come for it in person, she isn't even here, has never been here and now she's gone again anyway. No one saw her. If anyone did, he should report it immediately.

We, however, we could do something, we would love to do something, though it might be the wrong thing, but we would do something, for we could not stop the flight of this maiden, who by now is surely somewhere else. Okay. Everything always starts with rain. No, not the one in Spain, that one makes people sing along, we are not allowed to sing, we are not allowed to do anything, not even for a song, we, of all people!, who would love to do things, good things for you too; and that rain at that time, the rain of the century was proof that we could not do anything, such rain is not always a good thing, no matter whether we are doing something or not, so then we cast a wider net, but we did not get a hold of anyone: Homeland Security, fire department, national guard, neighbors helping neighbors, yes, you can read it right here, they are all on their way, everything is running at full speed, there is an outpour in the downpour to stop the flood—yes, also of people like us, we would, we'd downright flood you if they'd let us, but we would also clean up the flood, honestly, with our hair if necessary, and rubber boots we'd surely get somewhere, and if the water came down through the ether, we would turn off the gas taps and stop the cash flow, you are quite right, everything, everything has been mobilized to prevent floods, to prevent worse, to prevent us, to prevent people, throngs of people from flooding you, a veritable sea, a sea of troubles, sea to sea, sea into sea, where they end, where they finally end up and already there are fewer of them around, so then more and more are coming, whole trainloads, in overloaded sinking boats, they are coming and that must be prevented, we can see that, folks like us must be barred, put in bars, no, behind them, we don't drink, so that we won't flood you, no, no, that must not be, that goes to show the importance of assistance, of solidary collaboration against us, especially in times of crises, that is when the floods of us must be prevented, when you must be in solidarity with yourself, that's a must, with whom else, first of all with yourself, yes and this is when you help your neighbors, so we won't overrun you like water, that's solidarity for you, readiness is all, for action, naturally, because that is anything but natural, not a gift of nature, yes and there it is, the readiness, bravo!, because you apparently are always on duty, when it comes to breaking, jailing and finally shutting us in and remove us by plane, which always rattles, because they keep shooting, no, shutting us up, gagging one, then another and so those choked to death, and others too, for sure. That's what happens when you can't breathe, simple as that, can't do it in the water either, anyone can see that. So you have to be solidary and ready, always ready to stand your ground, and if there still is strength left in you, you energy bar filled with oats, nuts and valuable grains, you, a product yourself, we just can't see by whom or what kind, if there's still strength in you, then go ahead, help each other throwing us out, it is crucial for your social harmony and society's cohesion. We can understand that too. We can see that. You have seen it long ago. We can see it now too. It requires readiness for action and you've got it. No need to talk about it. Who would hear it anyway? Not even the waters of the Stygian swamp would hear us, and they hear everything, everyone who wants to get in and that's whom they hold on to. Here with you it's the other way around, you throw everyone out. The cow should also watch out not to step into the swamp; with the shoes she's wearing she won't get far. Won't make her curves more human, it says here, in this magazine.

We are many, but also just a few, we are the trickle that later runs out of freezer trucks, when we are finally frozen and then thaw again, smuggled, washed, no, not washed but spinning on the autobahn between those beautiful walls of your culture, always higher, always longer, for noise protection, not ours, that wouldn't have been necessary!, constructing walls we cannot see, wow, this car has walls all around, can't look out, can't see a thing, nada, and yet there are so many of us, and yet, we can't be seen either, they are all ready to fight, but not for us, for—yes, it's written right here—in this sacred book, I am God, your Lord, no, I am your God, your Lord, no, it's not him either, you shall believe in one God, yes, okay, but which one? There is one who has us in his hands, who has our fall in his hands and probably fells us himself. One. Okay. But we, we must spread ourselves, we must spread the Lord among many, for many want to lord it over us and have us taken away, they want to show us who is in charge, we never saw him, we are not allowed to see him, how should we recognize him?, this car has no side windows, so many want to show him to us, this Lord, and that one there too; but there is only one, that one Lord and that is the one they want to show us. How can he be sufficient for all? What is he saying? Did you get what he just said? I am the beginning who made heaven and earth, yes, sorry, and the water too, of course! that's also needed, we need it as a wet grave, that's what it is called by folks headed for drowning, they'll make it!, oh well, peace is more important than making, whatever it may be, that's our personal opinion, otherwise everything made will be hacked to pulp again, it has happened to us, often in the countries we come from, where they kill us, for he who makes shall also unmake, everyone shall make and get rid of his own mess, that's logical, even we can understand it, that we must be gotten rid of, since we made ourselves come here, accusing our Lord of harshness we dragged ourselves here, snuggled together, yes, maybe also smuggled ourselves, to here, until something carries us away again, maybe another flood, which in the end turned out to be us, and often we even chilled ourselves in order to arrive fresh and ready to go, some didn't get up anymore, what for. But the State protects the rights, everywhere and everyone's, except ours. The State issues a ruling, but that rule does not apply to us, we do not belong to him, that precious State we had to apply to, but nothing applies to us. The public hand that protects and provides, we would bite into it, that is, we would bite it, if we'd ever get to see it, if it would make a contribution to our health in case we get moldy, expired, spoiled food on the alp, that sow, that sow of an alp, but sorry, we are in a church here, no, not anymore, there we also almost froze to death, like in the refrigerated car, but we did not defile your Lord, and we did not damage your healthcare system, we did not damage anyone and did not get anything, maybe we damaged a lawn, we only took what was offered to us, crap, crap, crap, but we were glad, well, more or less, after all it came from you, we complained, but we took the crap, that's all we got and we froze when the sighing wind drove through the pipes, not unlike whispered lamentations, but no warmth. Let's start all over again, it makes no sense for you to scream No!, we are starting again, and we won't get anywhere anyway: cohesion and cooperation from the basis to the top must exist, must persist, you insist, it's on this list, it already exists here, you insist on that, we are all for it, that is what distinguishes this republic, *wunderbar*, it is a wonderful country. Its water: also *wunderbar*! But we don't have that much of it, so we could not let great numbers of people in, that won't work, they'll have to go some place else if they want it so badly, if they want to get away at all costs. We, however, we however, hardly did we board reason, are drifting under water again, driven like animals, one following the other, but we don't want to follow any leader, we don't even know them, we don't know who is lord of the moment, no idea, doesn't matter, we however, we do not belong, we belong to no one, we belong nowhere, we don't belong to the community, we cannot contribute, we cannot pay the dues, we are responsible for ourselves, oh lord! We aren't even responsible for this fire-extinguisher, it isn't even here, what should we do if we were on fire, we couldn't extinguish it, it's already been tried many times, that nothing can be done about it and we are also irresponsible, because we did not find anyone else for it, you can't find someone irresponsible and someone responsible, who responds as such in a believable way is also hard to find; we would have been so happy, happy like a God about the newly invented art of singing and the innovative kidnapping of women, we would have really enjoyed it, we pay our dues every day, which consist of our own flesh, luckily not the meat we are given, you don't want to cut anything out of us, since there is nothing, can't squeeze blood out of a turnip, not even your government can cut it, so they cut to the chase, chasing us out, we are many, but we count little, we have nothing to count and no account, which creates little interest for the bank or in us, you, however, you can pay, you certainly proved it on a female, who fled from ungodly shame, a cow, no, that can't be right, so what!, she did flee from something, whatever, that Russian, who could get neither Opel nor the bank over here, that is, one could not move the other, the bank the Opel, not vice versa, well, sure, the Opel can't play games with you, you drive it wherever you want and that's where it wants to go too, but by then she was already a citizen, not the bank, no, the sacred, glorious cow, with the help of that man she became a citizen, I swear, she now is your fellow citizen, she would have come anyway; her eyes touched gently by the State's magic van and in an instant she was one of yours, ready to get going, and you to get it on, in this church, if necessary, exactly, just like that fabulous, perfectly coiffed, perfectly tuned singer, exquisitely dressed, always, expensively adorned, yes, that one does not need to serve as tuning fork, her voice is a force of its own. No need to fork her legs, no need to fuck anyone issuing her a short-term visa, you must beg her, on your knees, for she comes with the gift of this unique soprano voice, for which you've been looking for so long, a voice to vote for, to make her come more than once, no, what are you thinking, you won't find something like that in your purse. Nothing can stop this voice, it withstands any drugs, you can hear that, it just gets stronger that way. No one has that kind of voice, no one gets to voice it like her, there isn't any voice next to her and we too get neither voice nor vote here. None whatsoever, not even a weak one. We might have had a voice once, but now it is gone, we almost had it, but nobody knows that, so we don't get a second voice to the one we already have. No say, no stay. Not one of us, no one in our crowd owns anymore whatever he owns. No one has that voice, not even one. No voice, no vote. We would like to but we don't have it; we would like to use our voices for this land's common good, altogether we would like to be useful to this land, which feels comfortable inside itself, like a pig in shit or like that cow who is no longer here, so we can't actually see what she is doing, maybe she also wallows in shit, in good shit at any rate, relaxing in some kind of light her passport brought her under, she rests well, rests, she beams, she shines, and gets turned off again, frolicking in the night that veils the hundred eyes, well, well, we never saw such general wellbeing, we don't see it now either, she already left, she should have been here at least for a short time, but now she is gone, who knows?, maybe she stands right next to you, who knows?, she shall be our role model and though she might have experienced terrible things, we don't believe it, well, yes, we are not the only ones experiencing terrible things, we admit it, oh, but could we just also be admitted, we want to be, oh, so much, to belong here too, to you, well that's what you thought right away, huh?, so you thought up something to prevent that, even though we want it as much as that fantastic singer. Exactly as much, at least as much as her!, she has the natural gift to—, no, not us, the daughter, her fellow citizen, the daughter of the cow Europa—I still have to come up with something for that one—but sorry to say, nothing comes to mind, I should at least have Zeus—Jupiter as a Roman and Io on my mind, and a gadfly, which was sent, sent unlike us, we came voluntarily, yes a gadfly, a nasty bug or is it buck?, stops us here, it does not admit us, the buck is to blame, oh no, I am mixing up something again, the daughter, whichever, seeing her dragged away as we do, by the precious curls crowning her head, by her gown, by her grandiose voice! No, I got totally lost here, lost even in this poor little

line, at least at the beginning, which will be like the end anyway, I beg your pardon. Whatever I can accomplish myself,
I should do on my own the best I can, we can read here,
everyone can read it who knows how, but I can't, whatever
it is, I can do nothing, I cannot possibly include all the
Greeks, the Egyptians, Europa, Io, not the big bug that keeps
us here and made us dig this hole, no, this mudhole, no, this
pit, this ground we break, out of bucks and without breaks,
I mean, brakes, we slammed on the brakes so hard that the
wheels dug into the ground, as we dug ourselves deep into
a hole, oh no, where can we get the twigs now, the olive
branches, whatever, to get going again, to set our fleet afloat
again, our little boat, wood would be best, so the radar won't
spot us, but that won't do us any good, we can see it already,
before it sees us; it won't help, our starry heavens will be
available soon, as per satellite radar, you can see the smallest
thing, the smallest wooden thing, oak veneer or laminate,
a paper boat?, no, plastic junk—same difference, we'll be
seen, we'll be seen! We'll be seen everywhere. We hide, but
it doesn't work, we duck, so the dolphin won't see us, the dear
little playful DOLPHIN, who is supposed to track us down,
to guard us, so that poor us cannot be put down and put out
by ground positioning systems, so that we can be detected
promptly and clearly on the open seas by Earth-observation
satellite-based systems, ouch, that could blow up in your face,
but not to worry, they monitor poor us, so that we can be
rescued in case of stupid accidents at sea. We only came so
he can locate us, whoever, so that he catches us, so he can see
us clearly, there must be someone who can look us in the
face, up there, who always optimizes the services in the
area of Border Surveillance, the combination of information
from cooperative positioning systems (VTS/AIS, VMS, and
LRIT) and remote-sensing observation systems (radar in

particular), always successful. Never makes a mistake. Good thing we got them, good thing we got them all, yes, also the humming drones so that they guard us, observe us, keep watch over us, yes, that's it, so they watch over us on our way of all *being*? The sea has no sieve for our being, no strainer retains us when we must go down, no run-off grid, we just run off, just like that, there's no other way; after us, the ocean will instantly be smooth and even again, until the next ones are coming, or it tosses its curling waves, no, I won't say now it waved us in so we'd sink into its bottom, that would be too cheap, we have sunk low enough, we can't get any cheaper, but anything but the cheapest has not been available to us for a long time; never has been, no matter!, people are still cheaper, I am cheap enough to deal with them, you don't do that. You don't think we are such a deal and you don't want to deal with us, because we can't pay for ourselves and we don't have names and no one pays for us either. We do have names, but what are they good for? You don't want to know them and you are our yardstick. And you won't trade us for anything, no matter what. Our being has no currency, that's correct, we have been through many currents, but not on the exchange. We stand in the clearing of *being*, says the thinker, that Heidegg-man, no, say I, of water, which is clearing per se, which is a gigantic clearing, bounded by nothing but our death, that is to say our un-being, yes, one could put it that way, look at it that way; we crashed there, it was no party, currently we are swimming around in it, uninvited, among the sharks, not so swimmingly, but brazen, we have no choice, we are the uncalled for, the crashed, we will crush that shaky boat, the crooked one, yes, so many of us will not arrive to hack around in the clearing of being. We are the hacks in the endless clearing of un-being, stacked in the stocks of being and time, tiny holes in the infinite. What are we talking about? It's all according to the book. Come, have a look!

Children helping their mother in old age? An additional wife? No, thanks! No wife is enough. Even the cow was more than enough. Those guys also killed our mother, our brothers and sisters, our more distant relatives, furthermore, the most distant relatives, all of them, all, and they cut off the heads of our cousins and sent us the DVD of it, we already said that? We've said everything at least fifty times, give or take, yes, yes, I know, you can't take anymore, though you haven't heard anything yet. Again, we beg your pardon. We were and still are talking about mothers and children in old age, no, about children who never get to be old and their mothers who are dead, no, no, psychologically we have reached our limit and must get professional help, those are the employees of this church and now of the monastery, where you saw us lying on the floor, yes, nice people, helpful, you can spread the word! Distribution of tasks and support are important, not only in the family, which we don't have anymore, no wonder you call us irresponsible, parasites on your body that's ready any time to report freeloaders smearing their snot across this beautiful land, yes, us, they'll still report us when we're already down on the ground, they'll still report us just for being here, although we'd have responsibilities to our families, but all we have in terms of family is here, here with us, which is nothing, no one, nada and all we got is also nothing. Foreigners for foreigners. Measure for measure. Flashlight for night.

Precious curls, we've said it already several times, too many times, as always too many, doesn't matter, a fabulous soprano, she shows others than us who is wearing the pants, she shows Mister Putin, she puts on quite a show and tells Mr. Putin to show his pants; Mister Putin, show me what you've got, this goldilocks says, charmingly disarming papa bear, her teeth flashing, you'd think she might kill or blind you. Well, to see this woman dragged away by her dress!, we'd never want that, we couldn't even imagine it; seeing what happened to our mothers and sisters, we would never want to even imagine it happening to this incredible soprano, who produces sounds where the head rests on the neck, we talked about it before, we can't say it often enough and we can't imagine it either. This princess and that other princess, everything in Russian, by our command everyone goes Russian now, we all go for it, we go for the make of car and we get here in a car that functions, or only those who speak it go all the way with it, even in Kitzbühel, on the golf course, they can speak Russian everywhere, we can't even speak German, that's what they blame us for, with good reason, thank you for telling us again, we also say everything too many times and we don't know anything new. Those princesses know it naturally of course, Russian, that's all they need, even though many know a lot more, good for you, we are glad. Those two! Naturalized in a flash, they were naturals from the get go and so they got to be nationals. Please explain, but never mind, you already did, more than once: both are natural women, both natural-born winners, dressed to kill, and we have plenty more of them, in Kitzbühel, in Vienna, supplies everywhere in the world, even though there aren't hundreds of thousands like us, but they are wherever it's beautiful and there are many such places and those women are everywhere, maybe quite a few, especially conspicuous are their accompanying circumstances, I mean their Russian accompanists, no, not on the piano, their daughters' companions in the house on the busy, dusty lakeside road, no sign of life inside, she is not there, that woman, she'd never think of living in that shack, but at least no one's dead, we assure you, all alive, no lone ranger in the night here, everyone is elsewhere, no one ranging there either, the one trace of life here, us, is of no interest to anyone, no trace on the lake either, in the outlived house no one should live in anymore, on the contrary, it might collapse, who'd want to live there, well certainly not that one!, so then, she isn't dead, we guarantee you, you can bet our lives, how could she become a citizen?, alright then, we guarantee you no one died there, in that dump, not the daughter either, the European cow, excuse me, she turned into one only now, an official main residence has been registered here, which we don't have, she does, but she does not live there either, you are here to stay, you have a say, you have the voters, at least on your side, you have the sponsors but no trace of those— now I don't know myself whom I mean. Those others. Them. They are not where they are supposed to be, they are just gone, those Russians, yes, that's what they are called, they took off, probably as soon as they saw the house, no, they never saw it, they are bye-bye, it wasn't necessary any- way, they are gone and that's that. We are here, but then again we are not, we have nothing, but we aren't dead either. The distribution of tasks is important, life or death, everyone has to do his part, we can see that, it means some are dead, others are not, we are not, but many of us are, you might manage even more if you try really hard, for the State's dis- tribution of tasks requires that you not be dead, we, however should be whenever possible, then we'll finally be gone or at least decimated, out of sight, out of mind, at any rate fewer than before, then there will be enough light, the bright light will be enough for more people, there will be enough for more when there will be fewer, that's obvious. We try, we are trying, a little patience, we beg you, this gadfly still bugs us, unfortunately, we can't move forward, we don't dare, that bugger's got a god's bite and that always draws the most blood, yes, you, good lord!, it's you we are talking about!

This house is empty, no corpses in there either, it has been rented, but stands empty. This flat above the supermarket, in Switzerland, is occupied, but also empty. Full and empty all at once. It seems to be a custom we don't yet know. Always ready to report, but no one lying there faint and pained whom one could look in the eye. But the hireling, what does God have to say about that?—can't look it up now, I don't have time, I have to write,—[*And I have to translate!*]—but the hireling—[*What is a "hireling"?!*]—alright, I will look it up. 'The hireling, who is not a shepherd, and not the owner of the sheep, sees the wolf,' aha, *wunderbar!* the wolf comes in handy, [*oh now I see, a pun, punted in translation, hiring = renting in biblical German*], the hireling flees, because he just came for the money and does not guard the sheep, because he is a hireling, he does not care about the sheep, the foreigner does not care much for sheep, he might eat them and bury the bones next to his house, where unfortunately they will be found, but he does not care for them, sheep, no, not for the bones either, because he took on shepherding for pay. Nobody pays us, even though we would be happy to take good care of sheep, uh, no, of anything and anyone who wants our service! It's not really about service, not even about the rental, oh, how we wish that someone would rent, uh, hire us!

Well then, those in the house at the lake, those renting hirelings, those border-cruising boarders, then naturalized neo-nationals, naturalized, without ever having to show their deeply shadowed eyes, the Russian cow and the other one, I forgot her name, that one now also bought her home, just in time before it collapsed, yes the house, not she, I mean, seriously, are you living there or aren't you living yet?, what have they got, those women, that we don't? Is being women what they've got? Those could be men too, well, not the women, but men can come here too, then they would be businessmen, and they surely are coming, we cannot speak their names out loud, it would bring bad luck. The racer is now running at their expense, I mean, he drives, oh dear, not anymore and never again, he never spent time in a cockpit before, he never did time, still, the businessman shelled out for it all, the racer paid nothing, so now no one is driving anymore, and no one dwells in the stadium for suckers, I mean soccer, a game our suckers don't understand, they've got the ball constantly in front of their feet, but don't know what to do with it and so no one lives there anymore, he is alive, what, he kicked the bucket?, what a shame! If anyone should still be kicking, it's him and now all of a sudden, no more, his powerful hand dropped from the steering wheel, from the stick? Not even the driver races anymore? That's a shame, but now back to the question: How come they can and we cannot? They've got something and aren't here. We've got nothing and are here. And there are no receipts, though we lie here right in front of you, can't you see that?, well, there still are no receipts, no records of anything, because it's not about us, thus no need for any records, no records either of activities in that house, the one over there, the other house, we are not talking of the house of God, of course, no record of the daughter stopping for a moment in her main residence, which she needs, which we don't have, nothing could ever stop that one! No one knows her, not even the landlord, no one knows her, no one knows any names, pardon me, her name is known, it's ours that isn't, no one knows our names, back home everyone is dead and now here too, what a mess, a real bummer! No one knows us anymore, that doesn't speak for us at all, not even a little, because we are the last to speak, we are not the ones who get the last laugh. The daughter has a voice to speak for her, she isn't here, but a voice speaks for her and she also gets to vote; it comes with her voice. She can't be seen but she's got a voice that makes her an instant citizen, with all the rights and duties to promote and demote the general welfare, sorry, wrong constitution, but if you are a woman and pretty, everything is easier right away, which must feel pretty good, but not to us and I don't even know right now what feeling I mean, we promote all freedoms, though not for free, but any contribution, however much, I said it before, and with pleasure, because it says so right here, is valuable for our fellow human beings, even if you can't see them, valuable for the common good, even if it doesn't do any good, like in this community, even if we are not commonly referred to as a community, it's all valuable, it enriches everything, everybody enriches himself, sure, this voice has been bought and that vote too, it is now among us, one of many, but one that counts!, it liveth among us, she hath lived among us, but she hasn't been seen, now she lives above us in a loft, but she still can't be seen. But she can vote, she has a voice, she's always had her voice, the voice, right!, she got it all, but doesn't all flesh have an expiration date, like the grass in front of the church? Now look, this woman has even two, a voice and a vote, but no decay, she just got it all. She got it right. I said it right. Because joining is better than watching.

We chose a church and then a church chose us, so now this is the place we stay for real, feel free to come and take a look, we could also be staying some other place, we have options. We could stay at the bottom of the sea, in the water, in the desert, without water for a change. Our experiences will be sent to us in time to have them while we are having them and then they will have become superfluous. We don't need them anymore. Let alone in water, forget experience, it is totally superfluous! You might not be able to still come today, and we might once again not even be staying here anymore. We were not used to having a place to stay and now we are living here for a bit, which interests no one, we are the forgotten, no one knows us anymore after we showed up here, they took us in and now we are out, out of the church, that's the main thing, we all worked on that, it took some wrangling by quite a few and they pushed it through!, and we don't have a phony residence in some house either, let alone a phony flat in Switzerland, what are you thinking!, we said we did, but we don't live there, God lives there, the new lord and master, the citizenmaker, automobile mover and shaker, deal faker and breaker, who likes tightening screws, but whatever he does: it's shaky, and we know it. He lives on heavily trafficked thoroughfares, but that's not where he lives, of course, he doesn't live above supermarkets with thousands of people and goods inside, all without him, pity on them!, they might feel orphaned without him, who knows, but no, he certainly doesn't live there, everything empty, house empty, address full, here it says full address in Switzerland, residence in Switzerland, Canton Zug, done, filed and saved, naturalized, from the secured residence into security, top security that is, not one hair on his still full head gets hurt or torn out there, because never has anyone seen anyone there, but this citizen is a natural, like in his natural habitat which he inhabits sight unseen like any other inhabitant there, for that's the habit there, and it all goes so fast, no one dwells on it, dwelling somewhere one is not, we think that in principle everybody there is a naturalized, sorry we mean, a natural inhabitant, because even he cannot be naturalized thrice; he who dwells is the monocot, I mean monogod times three, three in one, who would embrace a morass, unfortunately we don't remember what we meant by "morass," surely not what it means to you; who would disappear there?, who can be here as well as not be here?, no records of a reviewing process, only the woman has been naturalized, yes, indeed, the Russian, a not- quite-legally legalized, free citizen, if not for free, even a dual citizen, two is better than one, organized by the company god father, who now has organized a party, his own political party, why not, he has a ball, he's on the ball, somebody has to be the kicker, even we, the living dead still must be kicked around, into the church, into the monastery, into the balls, no matter, there must be a kick in it for everyone, the heavenly goalie hangs on the wall, but the ball is still in the game. We, how-ever, want to know who calls the shots, not of schnapps, the boss!, and the answer is already coming in, because every-thing gets divided up, the way people were sent everywhere to spread the word of God, because they did not have their own, just as people are distributed to all countries, just as this country is split up into nine states, his people also have their fields of work, where they can reap big profits or not, it is completely up to them, they are down on us, but up to getting rich or not. They have every right and every respon-sibility; they've got it all, because their special qualities and skills are paid attention to. They don't know ours, maybe we also have skills, we don't know ourselves. We are blinded by them and troubled by us, because our skills sprout some-where else where we have no access to them. We are not still, but no one wants to hear us. If you hesitate to set up camp all alone you can always bed down some other place. You have the choice. No god sticks the heavenly scepter in your face: this far and no further, he does not reside where we looked him up. We looked for him, on the map, with the GPS, with the route planner, which can calculate even the walking time between trains, depending on how you walk, slow, medium or fast, and you keep going and going or swimming and swimming, you drive and drive, you are sinking and you are almost all the way down, and you are rescued, no, you are dead! Not rescued. Depends what you are, if a No is your fate and no more procedure needed, then all processing, any proceedings would be superfluous like the water above you, the answer is no. You are looking for the lord your master, but he is not where you are looking for him, the invincible master, who is the city, the people, who is everything, he calls the altar his, the hearth of the land, okay, okay, we do not doubt it, it's just that where the letterhead says he is, he is not, not resident, not visiting, not visionary, we can attest to that meanwhile. We are stuck in the Nowhere and that god's stupid fly still keeps us there, it stings and stings and Europa pops out, no, I still have to look that up, it was entirely different, we could tell you, were we not rolling in the mud so lazily. Why don't you tell us!, you won't?, even though you could google it like anyone else, if you had the device for it, which you do, oh yes, you do. In the ocean you don't need a GPS, no one has a clue there, not even a machine, wrong, only machines do!, no one else, the ocean is too big for you? We could have told you so right away. We know from our own experience. It simply is too big. Can't see the end. We know, we've been there, close to the end. It did not support us, the sea. No wonder, it does not have any supporting structures either, no, no foundation, what for, for us it is bottomless anyway. It is as everything is. It has been laid down where building is permitted, because the land knows best whom it can count on and whom it can build on. And it does, because it is important to create living spaces. Eating is important too, but we don't want to ask for too much. We are tired, we went as far as the capital, we lied down in a church, our few belongings, our donated junk, our crap, which is us too, which we are supposed to clean up, at least part of that pitiful crap was pushed together by a bulldozer in a few seconds, done, finished. We did not have to do anymore. We did not have to help. All over.

No more area of activity to be filled. No more area the area manager admits us to. We are the ones to admit: Every person is illegal. That is true. Every one of us. No insurance we could trust. No assurance we would believe, no regional specialty we could taste, no influences which could lead to diversity, well, you prevent that, of course, no unique diversity and no small individual unit. That's what we could be in a pinch, yes, we could, exactly, we could do our duty, but you don't see that at all, no task that could be accomplished, possibly by us, but you don't care, no distribution of tasks, and so we can't take on, over or under anything. In contrast to you and your connection, I can't think now of the lady's name, Europa, no, Io, I, from the South, the *Südländer*, well, it is I, just I, but that is not enough, my name is not enough. Poor me, she says, bugged and impregnated, not guarded by a god, but goaded by a gadfly, no, wrong, that God impregnates everyone but me, not the cow, what would be the outcome! We'd rather come in than out, but that is a no go. Out you go, not in. You hear noise and arguing from the apartment next to you? There is a conflict? We come and that is what we do, we make noise, we argue, we create the conflict, we do that easily. For you can always call for help, the police are always there for you. Not for us, not for us. For us too, but in another way. From the other side they are here for us, they already managed to break through to us, they kicked in the door, the water pushed right through, they stepped right through the water, well, it's not solid, no harm done.

Through various exchanges we found out that the police were there for us, they came especially for us. Only to get us out and avoid panic. To intervene ourselves is *verboten*. No intervention for us. We are the ones to be prevented, the ones picked out, padded down or just picked over on the fly, just in case, okay, here's the fly, go for it. If you find something, keep it. We are not allowed to, here comes the bulldozer! This rickety table was a donation! It's not ours! The dozer doesn't give a damn. Don't stay out of this conflict out of fear, which one?, that one, right here!, grab the opportunity, grab what you can! It'll be worth it for you. If you see someone in need, take heart and do something! If you see us, grab us! Size us up, seize us and provide security, a little bit of security for your state, your fellow citizens, your neighbors, throw us out. Remove us like a grease stain. Remove us, do away with us! Save yourself from us! Yes, that's good. It's the only way for a society where human rights are raided, raked up, thrown on a pile and run over by a bulldozer, I mean, where rights are respected, especially that one farthest to the right. What? Forget it. I mean one society of course, it first has to become one. That's what you want, don't you? Becoming one with you and with itself, then you won't have to flee, across deserts and over the mountains. We just aren't a society, or just a small one, meaning not yet, maybe that has something to do with the hired shepherd, who does not belong to his herd, who was just hired? And hired just for animals? We are just a lot, not as many as the animals, but quite a few, at least some, but not a society and this is the only way to create a secure society: by removing us. Just get us out! We are thinking how we were discovered to begin with, it was dogs who found us, the shepherd's dogs, the loyal helpers. Now you help too! Our things have been thrown out already, we don't mind following them, like we follow you too, your orders, we are gone! Get rid of us. You must assure the security of the land, the police have to too, you see, that makes already two, take care of security and get us out. However you proceed, proceeding or no proceedings, whatever, chase us away! Get us out! Whatever the outcome of the proceeding against us, drive us out! Or just let us glide into the water! Yes, where we are right now. Let go of us, no big deal, and off we go. Or not? Let's leave together for once, that would be kind of nice, why don't you flee with us!, but no, you wouldn't want to, you want to drive off, but not like that, no, not like you can't imagine from where. Our spirit perturbed you, strange, we don't even have any, our lawn- and law-abusing feet, we forgot all about it, no, we didn't, we did—several times, probably too many times, at least a hundred people had called—we did report that now the grass in front of the church is all gone too, flattened, ruined, kicked into the dust, for good. And it had just been freshly seeded last spring, only so the dust can settle on it now, our donated belongings removed by the bagger, all gone, our gross human malformations are not a sight for you to behold, our bodies, half-animal, half-human, like that Europa or Io, well, which one of the two is it now, half-maiden, half-cow, gazed at in wonder for millennia, people don't do that anymore, but they do love to stare, in peace and quiet, because the Atlantic god sits next to them, no, not the Atlantic, we don't need that big an ocean, a small one will do! That's plenty for all of us, promises this god and he protects them, his speeches save the day and take life out of us. You want us gone? You bet, right now! Out! Oh, God, who takes pity on ours, on us, unfortunates, driven to mad- ness, right into madness, half-animal, half-human, not human at all, nothing at all, who takes pity on us? Do you also want to draw a lot and show some feeling perhaps? You don't want to? We understand.

The daughter, the shame-free maiden, no, that she definitely is not, in that house, in the deserted house, legalized, naturally, hush, hush, in a flash and a crash, the Russian occupant, never seen, unknown, but us you can see, you can come and see us any time you want to, but you don't want to. We are not value, we are extraneous to the values produced by others, promoted by the corporation, set in motion by the concern, by the daughter's naturalization, the one who sings in concerts, no, we mean the other one, who can't do anything, but maybe that's a prejudice, we have already been judged, so why not some prejudice for others? We always have some left, no problem, no harm done. The Opel firm has not been bought, though that man certainly wanted to buy it, the parent company prevented it, the corporation, the endless eternal times' ruler over all of us did not release him, God, our lord, was not released from his divine breath, he still is needed, needed to start a whole party, if he is not allowed to build whole cars, he, the supplier, the go-between, but the goners are always us; this plant, the corporation's pawn, God's pawn, a god greater than God, there is always a greater one, greater even than any god—and the desire for MORE, people's best desire, the one that makes something of them, well, not of us, but of all the others—this pawn of God to make more of oneself, the one carried carefully in the womb, like Io carried Europa, unlike the sea that didn't want to carry us, unfortunately, it just didn't want to, neither did the boat, what can you do about that?, we are doing nothing, the boat does not carry us, it does not care for us, the sea doesn't carry us either, we rise in it like dough, our fat swells, if no one comes right away we will be hidden forever like Io and Europa, it's high time, and the two don't even exist!, never did!, just as well!, what doesn't exist can't get lost, something like that, not even close, I am sure—so something is conceived, something gets constructed, which unfortunately was not allowed to be constructed or it got lost before it was conceived, or broken up in parts and shared, as common stock, but not with us. So nothing comes of it. No cars. And cars are the highest of anything, the boat the lowest, but necessary nonetheless, also for us. It just didn't do us any good. Our stuff, our junk is gone, our donated things pushed together, broken and taken away, only we are left and now all around the land is cheering and telling the truth, word of honor, though they wouldn't have to tell, we knew it anyway, but they do tell nevertheless.

We cannot be the sons of that god, it must be others, we don't know who, we are to get lost, perhaps not killed, but out for good, good. This house can boast: They are finally gone, and I've had enough too, don't thank me, no need for it. Maybe you don't feel like coming anymore either, crashing through the door, blasting a hole through the wall, denting the ocean, if only in passing, but without a pass, throwing teargas, shedding tears, getting rid of all the junk, don't feel like it anymore, just don't want to anymore, for all the good intentions went into the plant and many have been naturalized by now; Yeltsin's daughter transplanted, great!, we didn't think it would work, but sadly, it won't do us any good! The firm naturalized, the bank already here, bank at hand or no naturalizing. But it didn't work out. Doesn't matter. Well, maybe not to you, we don't doubt that, but maybe it does to the gentlemen from the firm. So then, this naturalization has already happened, too soon, but done is done, it didn't get us anything, a bad investment, naturalizing Yeltsin's daughter a job well done, there she lies, nature surrounds her, no beasts, no hunters dare to come near her, no,

not here, she must be elsewhere, she must be lying elsewhere, we don't know where, the curtain is closed, the
insights gained narrowly defined, adding up to only a few
pages, who'd write about that, who'd sing about that, who
does what, who acts how, who forces the folks here and their
daze-crazed smiles, dazed from the bull they concocted for
us, who forces them to join the other dead victims, we would
have also fit right in with them, well, maybe not all that well,
but still? Never mind. Pay no mind. We set the horizon for
something that could end happily too, but doesn't. We set
up nothing, we upset no one, we are dead anyway, at least
we look like it. And it says so right here, no, it doesn't, not
right here, that the dead can also be naturalized, no, and
there's nothing about the living dead either, nothing said
about the living dead, nothing, nothing about those whose
dead are still so much alive and whose living are dead, none
of that, we don't want to hear it. The last one does not see
the light, he turned it off. And the last thing is us.

    Yet, it's not our fault. We have respect, we show respect,
we like respect and here it comes, we want it to meet ours
right away, they meet halfway, but ours is not accepted, we
cannot pay respect, we bring different talents and strengths,
but, unfortunately, no money, and those don't get accepted.
Nothing gets accepted, at least not when it comes from us.
They only take from us. The bulldozer takes care of that. We
are not accepted, in our case the word does not have to stand
for any firm or work for us, we have to walk their talk and
rather fast, the firm stands firmly on its own, it doesn't
belong to anyone, certainly not to us; whatever we did,
before, is now in secret darkness, and there is no one anymore to lift us in his mighty hands. Because we do not offer
a Russian bank, we do not crank up the car industry, we
don't even crank up cars, we keep our foot always on the

brake, we can't let go of it, otherwise we would be stuck in nowhere, on the contrary, we might actually be driving, but we have dug ourselves too deeply into your mother soil, that bug—no, not the car—the gadfly has put the brakes on us, otherwise we would not stand here, we would be driving, don't flee from us; we would flee ourselves if we could. We have no merit and no earnings, we also have weaknesses, that's all we have, we do not and never will have citizenship, and we don't have anyone's sponsorship, the only ship we had was an old, sinking boat, we have nothing, no one speaks for us and we don't speak either, nor do our dead speak, least of all for us, like our deeds, they might speak, but not for us, how could they, they are far away, our deeds and our dead are far away, can't go any further, they had their heads cut off, no, not their deeds, that recently happened to my cousins, not quite by accident it was captured on video, nowadays everything comes with a video or a picture. The Russian princess wasn't stopped anywhere, not in her house on the much trafficked road in the borderland region, she is, after all, a citizen now, nobody saw her, maybe she doesn't exist, no, she must, for she is a citizen now, the *Herr* God made it happen, for he rules with almighty power, the highest of all and he does not look up humbly to anyone above him, only his values look at him, and his valves, bolts, brakes, exhausts and other body parts, from valves to values, but they don't belong to anyone, not even the good lord, yes, that one who wanted to create values got them, sure, whatever sprouts in his mind is a done deed in a flash, no, not this time, pity!

We have not been set up by anyone, we are just here, just so, all others dead, we'll soon be too, you'll see, don't hesitate to celebrate too soon, although there is time, plenty of time to celebrate later, for he who laughs last must really have something to laugh about. And when we are gone, you can rejoice and rejoice some more that we are gone, that you could solve this conflict without force, because another force solved it in your name, which you don't want to admit. We would like to take on this task, but around here there always is—and we really mean: always—some deputy putting in a day's work before putting on the green, putting his foot down when it comes to the rights of others, smashing the donated folding table with the plastic cups, squashing the camping chairs, also donated, trashing and removing our few belongings, which aren't even ours, the bagger takes care of it—makes it easier for you, and even though those aren't living things: this is lived civil courage, even though you might have to fear disadvantages on account of it. But you don't, you don't have to fear anything, let alone disadvantages, you have nothing to be afraid of, come on in, please, and trample down everything, it has a short-term effect, which you can easily extend by crushing us as well, we are not even as hard as this wobbly plastic table, not as hard as this outdoor furniture, for which someone somewhere had no more use, because it had already been used too long. If all of us did that, if all of us did all of that, we'd live in a safe country, well, safe from us at least, that's something. The existential possibilities of coexistence, we said it already, we are saying it again in case you didn't get it, require indisputably that one can step on, no, step in for another. But of course you don't want us to step in for you, you don't even want us to step out to stretch our legs in front of the church, that would ruin the beautiful lawn even more, and more every time, we already said it because you said it, the lawn that had just been freshly seeded (who said: last spring?), like a mother's womb because—listen now: stepping out into the world, stepping up the manifold ways of being-in-the-world, we've said it before, but it's so much fun, is not limited to the polished possibilities of public being-togetherness, it equally pertains to those in restricted spaces, with restricted possibilities, us, yes, it pertains to us too, because we too are possible, even though you don't believe it, we are human, after all, we are also others, we might be some of the ones and some of the others, we also have professions, no, not anymore, status, states, no, we have no more states, how could we, states of mind, yes, we have that, so then, the possibilities tailored to all of this, the possibilities of—what is the word?—*besorgen*, taking care of, what about it? oh, yes, it pertains to everything I just mentioned, period; it pertains and applies to . . . Take your pick! This sentence never ends, it isn't mine, it's by that Heidegghead, just as your power never ends, which comes from you and returns to you, which knows where it belongs, caution, high voltage!, here it comes! Please step back from the edge.

We pay respect to others fair and square as is required from us, we shall treat others as we want to be treated ourselves. And this is what we do, we pay respect, it even tries to get ahead of us and pay in advance, respect, but it is out of cash, so it pays more attention to us, which suits our intention, as we intend to pay it something, we will pay its dues one more time, we pay it more respect even though we already paid our dues more than once, we can't remember the last time, but we got something for it, I think it was a thermos because it was so cold in the church, and that is exactly how we want to be treated, that is how we want to be treated ourselves, not like the Russian President's daughter, she does not need respect but gets it all, we on the other hand pay open-handedly and with an open heart, we came with respect, where shall we put it, we took heart and brought you respect, since we got some too, where shall we lay it down, the respect? And where can we lie down ourselves then?

Respect spread out too much. There is no more room. Should we put it next to our talents and strengths, so we have it at hand whenever we want to fall back on our talents and strengths, so it will lie right there as well, the respect we got, or not? Well, we did not steal it! Honestly. We paid. Respect. Indeed. We paid for it. So, let's do it, let's do it now. Right now. Let's get respect and fairness together, yes, our talents and strengths, which are lying there next to each other, already laid to rest, we wanted to have our hands free, we don't need them here, we don't need those things, that camping table, we could have used it, sometimes folks want to hang with each other, right?, but that's collapsed now, no one needs them here, fairness, no, or respect, or us, but maybe it'll pay off. We'll put it together, okay, here we go, everything together, it takes up less room that way. Let's pile up everything we have, maybe we can buy something with it? Let's hope so! I hope they let us in wherever we are supposed to be, added to all those other Dicks and Toms and Harrys who we are supposed to be too. But we cannot be. We can't. We put together what we have and there is the bulldozer, still dozing in the icy cold in front of the church, in the frozen grass, frozen as well, all of us frozen, though inside, in the house of God, then everything will be done away with. All done and gone. We wanted to dwell in this kingdom, but we don't have permission. Having a home, leak-proof and quiet, with the others would be nice, but you don't like it. No small houses ready for us to move into, only this monastery, we can stay here because we can be thrown out again any time, maybe we have been already, since getting thrown out means staying for us, just elsewhere, and yes, we still are at your service, just say the word, use your voice, vote, maybe even for us! Be selective! What else are elections for? You don't want to give us shelter. So now all the citizens who decided to get us out of their sight, to cast us out, are going to cast their vote, for their own God and good; their scale in delicate balance, the parties look at us, they want to be just, no, they don't, and anyway, no one does us justice either. So, are you now expecting better friends than us? What do you expect? Better than us? Not shame would we have brought you, we would have taken on the shame, would have felt ashamed whenever you wanted us to, as for those in need of protection every word said quickly adds up to a sentence when rumors run wild and turn into hate. That's how it goes. That's how it is. We warned you, we would have tried, we would have lamented our difficult lot, and we would have tried very hard, we promised we would try hard, we just didn't know what, why and what for, we do what we can, we would not have hurt, not even touched any creature or man, that does not belong to us, but we may not belong to you, you beware of us. You tolerate everything, it is only us you don't. You do not avoid insult, we served our foes' lust and scorn, we would have liked to avoid that, believe us, it was not possible. Forgive us. Housing we would have liked available to us, whatever the city would have wanted to give us. Burdens and duties would we have gladly accepted. Whatever advice father state would have given us, we would have preserved it, faithfully, in good faith, for shyness and modesty mean more to us than our lives, which we can't lead anyway. Okay. And now we'll be happy to also praise something, yes, your god too, we've been in his house after all, it looked nice, all cleaned up, at least until we crashed there and got pneumonia and several hunger strikes. We praise the city, may it never be flooded, it won't happen, it does not have an ocean, there is a stream, the current is strong, it generates a lot of power, the city is prepared, it has its own power grid and a floodplain, maybe even more grids and power plants, but it has only one in power, unfortunately we do not know him. He did not come, he did not have to, he was already here. There is a plan for everything, just not for us. Okay, we can understand that, you couldn't have known that we would come, we made no reservations, though you have many, we arrived unannounced. We are the unannounced. The supplicants. The nailed ones. No, we wouldn't let you go that far. You have your god who is up to that, but not us. Not many look with pity on us. Others lord it over us from up high and don't see us, even though they are right above us, they should be able to, even from an airplane, even as an eagle. But no! They turn away, they look another way, but with keen eyes, as always. The lust for hunting is stronger, it gets ever stronger, but they don't see us, the scale tips, it sinks with us, we were taken out of the icebox, the hunt was over long ago, so there we lie, a few pieces of flesh and it is happening now, maybe it has already happened by the time you see this, what fate dealt us, that is, the end. The disappearance. The turning away from us, on both sides, turning to one side and then to the other. It keeps us in motion. Okay. Unmoved are those who are easily moved, moved by cat videos, moved by puppies, still veiled the future approaches us, yet even veiled we can see it, we already got to the bottom of rock bottom, wasn't so bad, we had no grounds for it, while even the ocean has one, somewhere, we just wanted to take a look, yes, we can already see the future, yes, that one, over there, in the still more secret past, tell us what we should still beg for and most of all, why? Whom? That justice will be done to us, we pray for that, may it be the fulfillment of my prayer for safe conduct, for a better lot. But it will not happen. It will not be. It is not. We are not here at all. We came, but we are not here at all.

Aeschylus: *The Supplicants*
Ministry of the Interior, State Secretariat for Integration
Ovid: *Metamorphoses*
And a pinch of Heidegger, a must, can't do without it.

SCENES OF TRANSLATION
Notes on *Coda* and *Appendix*

After I finished translating *Charges* the refugee crisis in Europe quickly escalated into one of the biggest forced migrations in European history since World War II with scores of refugees—mostly from the Middle East, Afghanistan, Pakistan, and Africa trying to escape civil wars, terror and persecution—arriving everyday. For example, in 2015 Germany alone took in more than a million refugees. In her characteristic open dramaturgy Jelinek responds to the burgeoning crisis with addenda to the main text, similar to what she did with her earlier play *The Merchant's Contracts* (2015). A keen, compassionate observer of local and world events, she wrote the two brief sequels to *Charges* between September and October 2015.

The *Appendix* was triggered by the Hungarian government's closing of the borders to Serbia, which resulted in a situation where massive floods of refugees were fenced in under shockingly inhumane conditions. Coincidentally, at the same time international media broke the scandal that the Volkswagen Group violated various anti-pollution acts, which mandate emission levels for diesel cars. Always quick to respond to disturbing topical events, Jelinek interweaves these events, which she experienced mainly via media coverage, with similar tragedies echoed in canonical literature.

Coda reflects the contemporary refugees' voyage in 'splinters', the term she uses in the concluding quasi-bibliographical list of references—passages from the *Odyssey*, Euripides's *Iphigenia in Aulis* and Ezra Pound's variations on Homer in *Cantos*. For the latter she cites the most recent translation by Eva Hesse published in 2012. The quotes from the *Odyssey* are clearly from the canonic translation by the eminent German translator, philologist and poet, Johann Heinrich Voss (1751–1826). True to her sources, the opening lines of *Coda* set the scene as a translation—the writer struggling to find the right German word for "tremble" (*zittern*). "Something's trembling, it is trembling, isn't it, the boat, no there's another word for it, no that won't nail it either, it wobbles, the boat, it shakes, probably because Hermes and Athena are not installed as shaft of compass as something trembling between them," obliquely refers to Pound's Canto 7: "Gods, / Hermes and Athene, / As shaft of compass, / Between them, trembled— . . . " References to attempts of finding "the right term" are woven throughout the text.

Homebound due to agoraphobia, Jelinek experiences reality as translated by the media, triggering a series of eclectic literary associations. She acknowledges 'a pinch of Freud' in the *Appendix*; the 'pinch' both deliberately and literally gets out of hand to become 'oversalted' like the (sea) water referred to in *Coda*. Freud's analysis of the child's anal stage translates into Jelinek's anal humor which is her translation of the everyday crisis faced by the refugees—the absence of sanitary facilities in their camps—an absurd situation that is also employed by several xenophobic governments to induce fear in their citizens. It is the lived experience of the trauma that ultimately makes it impossible for a writer, or anyone who is not a refugee, to translate the enormity of the global refugee crisis.

CODA

Something's trembling, the boat, it is trembling, isn't it?, no, there's another word for it, no, that won't nail it either, it wobbles, the boat, it shakes, probably because Hermes and Athena are not installed as shafts of the compass, something is trembling between them, the boat trembles from fear, no it rocks because those people can't sit still; no one is holding the sails, it doesn't have sails, well they would come in handy, it still has air, the boat, and it will need it too, some air is still in it, but not for long. There still is air above, but not for long. Then it'll go downward, and then we'll take a bath. The body becomes thought becomes body, and the thought relates to its host like the edge to the knife. Is this the way to the marble forest with the stone trees, if so, we would like to be here, no this is the way to Greece, to the gods, you might never get there, you and your buddies, I mean this boat is like—now I can't think of the word, like a densely covered pincushion in the women's world, I don't want to say full, yes but full it is nonetheless. No pine forest nearby, the boat avoided it, the water is denser than glass but unbreakable—parting, merging—what belongs together flows together, all one, all the same, water. Only people, those who fall in, go kaput. They don't break, the water takes them in, it opens its trap, no, can't say trap, just as one can't say tremble, could somebody please hand me new words, many thanks, words are on the march, some have been written down here too, the kitchen is open, only there's nothing to eat, no, nothing to drink either, isn't that enough water for you here, you really want more?, but that one is so salty, it's clearly oversalted, can I send it back?, yes, it goes back but then it won't come again, let alone improved, that's not how we meant it. Calm down, you can drink it okay, you can drink up a storm but you can't scream while you are drinking, obviously. Silver floods of light above the waves, you've got to see that. I haven't seen it in a long time. The lament emerges from the dark, hell casts shadows, for there is light from the fire, the flames strive seawards, the people converge in the ocean's claws. Copper glow, gleam of waves drift under hulls at night, under the ships' bellies? But this ship has no belly, we are its belly, without us it would be a rubber rag, and if it were a belly, a few hundred would immediately drown, they'd drown on the spot, no, thank you, I hope this belly has eaten already, thank you, it did, it keeps the food inside, look here, there's air in it, I'd say it consists of air, it's an airliner but not in the clouds. Air is lighter than water, it just can't swim on its own, it needs a case, air does, a husk, which can be thrown out as needed. Every boat must be destroyed after use, I find that excessive, that's like pounding screws with a hammer into the water where they won't stick. The air in the boat is sometimes surrounded by people who have been breathing it, or by rubber if it's a rubber raft, which consists of air with a thin layer, the so-called top layer, so that the air can't escape, so it won't come out, sure you can do it, who is keeping you? What happens afterwards is proof of a sense for fine differences—some know how to swim, others don't. Fate. But, know-how is also part of it. Out with you, it's only water, you can't be afraid of that, most of the earth's surface consists of it, and without water you would die, in it too; nevertheless, at least you'd still have a chance there! I ask you, you aren't really afraid of water, are you? That would be a contemptible gift handed to you, fear is a contemptuous gift, fear likes contempt, it looks down on you and laughs its head off so you can keep it.

It is night now, no just a moment, don't be hasty—not yet. The drift pulls away below the boat's belly. This boat plays into the hands of the storm, even if it doesn't stretch its hands, it falls right into it, storm's hands are the boat's home, it whirls itself into them and ventures even further, into ashen greyness, into thick blackness when it's night or when the dark is deep enough, no ice weighing down its hull, this is a southern ocean—please pay attention to the zone of this water, please also pay attention to its owners— and yet around the heads nothing but the dense blackness we can't use for anything else later, therefore the word dense and the word black. The night is wide open, yes and happily so, even for this boat, it makes no difference to the night, no, we travel by day, no night, no blackness, that's below the water during the day, and at night anyway, if you absolutely want to get in there you will see it, the blackness, the impenetrable, which looks sort of blue on the outside, is this even blue, or is it AdBlue?, you can google it, if you aren't driving a modern diesel including its nitric toxics, but you don't have to. Over there, on the other hand, people suffocate because they've got nothing to breathe in, I can't really see it clearly, I am sitting in a chair, looking at the photo of a poultry transporter and there's a lot more on YouTube; several groups, even this boat could carry those, not me, I can't swim.

The water doesn't knock me out, I am high and dry, that's where I belong, it doesn't matter there if something knocks me out, but in the ocean, the water always only knocks over a boat on which I am not, I can't swim, so why would I get on a boat!, and now the boat can't swim anymore either anyway, I would not find it even if it scattered seeds along its way. Yes, the sea is wide open below the boat, come on in if you've bought a ticket, you've paid for the whole package—yes we are open, but that's the wrong ticket, it's not valid here, there it says passage from country to country but not which one—but we are not in the country and not in the city either, not in a city of our choice, not in a city we were assigned to, but neither are we waved through, no one catches us, no light to serve as a lasso, so then I sink, by morning I am sinking, says the sea spitting out its gum which could not improve its breath, sometimes I too have to eat something, says the sea. I can do whatever I want. The black-eyed beast Sea can simply do whatever it wants. Darkness is not only in the eyes, we also make the dark, so we can make it inside it, so we can ride on it, on the raft, on the river, in every water. The flesh is aglow in the dark, it has devoured the glowing ball, and what do we see now, what are we supposed to see now? Could it be railroad tracks we are seeing here?

Dark shoulders that triggered the lightning, that man in the swim trunks shows off for starters, though he doesn't take much time for it, how the motor works, no he doesn't want to come along, what for?, he's got his money alright, the young man, good body, he must swim a lot, good for the waistline, the ideal line, which he does not have to sail himself, he is lucky, that God, who is in control of the motor and also shows it to others, he knows the motor as he knows what's locked up in his swim trunks, still he must leave it now, he won't see it again, the motor will take off, the people have been loaded in, they're led on and if they don't like it they'll just have to transfer the forest to here. If they want shade, the forest will have to come here. So you'll just have to pull or tear at something here, throttle there, then threaten, then stop again, I don't know whatever it is a motor does when it works. But the fuel has been put in, it's the stuff that gets us going, the motor has ingested the fire, it snarls and now it's running, though spluttering right from the start, it's spitting at us, something's not right here. Why shouldn't it work, why not, after all it was fed with this good diesel so that it keeps warm, no, not watered, only fuelled, why shouldn't it run further than us who've got no fuel at all, for what fuels us is inside us, at least we have it right on hand there. Something is wrong here. Something is wrong with this motor. This is no motor, this is no branch, those are not tracks, those are not clouds, this is something that roars and spits, no berries ripen near it that's for sure, why am I saying this? Because someone else said it before me though not in front of me but I am on the safe side with him unlike this boat. The dolphin man, the supposed savior-hero, butterflies back to the shore, soon he'll be high and dry, he lets the boat take off by itself, it knows what it has to do, the people finally got the idea too, they know now how the motor works, they had an introductory course at a bargain rate, which the ocean is spared, it doesn't need a rate when something is imported. The others have to stay the course. The boat swims in the water like birds on the tips of trees, but that isn't swimming, they can get off any time, those lucky ducks! You are now on your own, ladies and gentlemen, I would like that too, I don't even own myself, I am the ship but not the owner, who just jumped ship and left me a wreck. Hey you, Water, can you give me a way-leave? Else there's no way for me to find my way across, all on my own. Someone would have to put me there. All alone. Just like a mountain, enveloped by the breath of life, enveloped by what?, no idea, but there are no mountains here, there is only the sea, there is the Lite, people dance on it like birds on the tips of trees, no, they are not dancing, they are barely kicking, at least not yet the bucket, they keep still, and don't move,—just don't move! The birds would rather go on foot than into the water, they know what to do, sitting down where bough is bent over bough, look, that crow would also like a piece of bread, like the one I am about to throw there, but now it's fallen in the water, where the crow can't land. The water isn't the land, there, there is the way to Naxos, to Lesbos, to Kos or wherever, where I have never been—it's a straight line but not to there—come along, guys! Yes, the children too. Come along but not that way! Ay, that way, that way leads there if we come along. Take a look over the bow, what do you see? You can't steer the ship eastward to Kythera or wherever—you won't be able to if the noise puts you to sleep—because nothing is happening, this ship doesn't move, at least not the right way, it doesn't sound right and now it doesn't move at all, stock-stiff in the whirl of waves, no ivy upon its oars, when should any ivy have grown there?, we don't have oars. They are superfluous. We've got the motor but that's a no-go. Who walks on water? I spare myself the answer.

The children get nothing to drink, they might as well get used to getting nothing to eat either, let them inhale the wholesome diesel smoke, that'll do, yes it is diesel, not a new word but, as if out of thin air, in everyone's mouth, hot breath that was to blow on the ankles, but it doesn't come, the ship can't breathe, it is still struggling for it, but nothing's coming, even though it's got the diesel, a modern fuel, which nonetheless has been around for a long time, you can even heat with it: but, it smells funny somehow when it gets burnt, when too much gets burnt up, when it doesn't get burnt all the way, that was not the plan, burning up that much, getting burnt that way, abused for fraud by the *Volk's* car, that's not how it works, cars being so cheap and not doing much, which isn't their doing. It doesn't work. This car does not drive quite right, the diesel is no good, the diesel is tainted, it drives only two power wheels, all of mankind has been put to the test as everyone trembles whether it will pass, will it fulfil its own specifications, how could this work with only two wheels? I ask you, what do we do with just two wheels, what do we do with the other two in the meantime?, we need at least two more for this vehicle, ideally each driven separately. Or another option, conversion to manual operation: then we'll still need at least one person to work on it. Unfortunately, none of those will replace a motor, it might run if it has to. But then the pollutant emission might be too much, who knows? If we adjust it to reduced pollutants and feed it enough then it will run poorly, it will splutter alright. However, if we adjust this person—who already exhausted himself looking for work—to optimal performance, he'll have to siphon less fuel for himself but he'll be able to race along, on the roads, on the assembly line, everything will glide, everything going down smooth, like honey, no jam as in traffic. It will create quite a stink and more dirt than before, it will pollute our environment, so then what are we going to do with it? No idea. What is the desired conduct? Depends. It depends whom you want to protect, yourself or your world around here, the forest, the meadow, the river, the lake. I don't read anything about people here. I know how much I can eat sustainably, that's enough for me. There is a lot I can't tolerate which the environment still could for quite some time.

The sky is leaden but at least it isn't falling, that's all we'd need, we are on our way down ourselves. Wherever we are, it's going deeper and deeper. The board of directors steps up its damage control, luckily it's not stepping on us. So let's say, the supervisory board is in session but the cars don't want to go by the board, be supervised; they want the air we breathe to become foul and sinewy like cats so it can carry us, the air-filled boat. For that, however, we lack the super-vision for all these people here. They do what they don't want to that's all they can do. The boat is crammed up to the rim with them even when they are lying down there is noth-ing to get a grip on, polluting the air won't help the motor if it still won't start!, it could do that also when it's working, please motor, poison us but run, just start running!, away from us isn't possible, so just run for the hell of it like the city marathon runners, they are also running, come hell or high water, who else would do that voluntarily?, only the one who must. Nothing but water around here, the motor has a defect, that much is obvious. Those Volkswagens are not defective, they are just too cheap for what they must be able to do and they are too expensive for what they cannot do but should be able to. I want to buy such a diesel car please, I'd take out the engine, pour in the diesel and put the engine into this boat with the spluttering motor. So that it finally can move on, it's about to give up, the motor, you'll see, it'll give up completely in a moment and be done with. it. And what will we do then? Honesty does not cause us any dam-age, a busted motor does, especially when we must move on. On this oar ivy is slowly growing after all, but we don't even have this oar, we assured you several times that's no reason to insure us for what would we do with an oar. But we are in a hurry, we are in a hurry for nothing. We can't live forever without breathing. Hello, can someone lift the fog, can someone give us a lift, any plastic container would do, there are so many drifting about here, the fog bothers us. Though we see as little without it. But that's not fog, that's just breath, you are welcome to use it, if you don't need anything else. Oh, you also need your hair wax, which you always carry with you in your backpack, so that you always look pretty and fashionable when you have to present yourself any-where. I understand. The desire for beauty, I can understand that. The child inhales the diesel exhaust gases, it feels nau-seous, can we please put it some place else? No we can't or we'll upset the balance, besides we have to take care of the wrecked motor. But if it's wrecked anyway there's nothing to take care of! There is nothing we can do. We have the swim vests alright but we'll drown nonetheless, no idea how but we'll manage. And if we don't, we will be rescued, we'll arrive and throw out the vests at the beach as if they had not been little lifesavers, which kept us afloat for a while, we won't need them anymore, those airy wraps which could have saved us if it had come to that, if that fishing trawler had not come and taken us in tow. We cannot know that yet, some-one would have to first make a call and reach someone.

We throw everything out but ourselves. The throwing out is over now, now comes the taking, crouched at the fence, wrapped in the barbed NATO wire, just move a few moments, for a test only, between Hungary and Slovenia, you'll see how that hurts!, and you'll take it down again right away, that didn't work, the ingenious Ulysses wouldn't have messed with it to begin with, he'd have invented something else. Now life is approaching us again, we had given up already, now suddenly arms are embracing us, our hearts burst at the sight. Is this life at all?, we still can't see very well, at long last, welcome!, the sea is deep blue but now at least signs of aliveness are increasing—mud, junk, trash—as if we had anything to throw out, a cast net?, no our innermost product, that's what we are throwing out like weapons, their shells, crouched down, always crouched down in the deepest shadow of fences and gates. Compared to that the sea was still deep and blue, but we do welcome the shallowness and the beach beyond it, with still more junk, that's what people love to produce the most, not cars, no, junk, also comes partly from the cars, it's all very confusing.

We teeter like ants under the carcass bits of beasts they are lugging, but we aren't falling yet. That's good. The motor is dead. We aren't yet. There is a sun lying on the water, can someone rescue it please? It might be drowning too! No it won't. The motor is down too, it won't come back no matter what we do. It can't be revived. The morning sun overtakes the shadows, but that does nothing for us, there's nothing in it for us! We swim into the light like that dolphin-man, the motor didn't work properly then either, not as the man had told us, he promised that the motor will hold up for a while. It's not- functioning might actually be the way it functions, like your so-called functional clothing or something like it, something that functions, but only when tested in storms and water, so that your parka, your functional pants will prove themselves when put to the test, you'll see! But I doubt it, all we knew about this boat was where it was to be cast off. Now it is time to tell our names, only no one wants to hear them. What city will thrive all around us tomorrow? None whatsoever? Only water? Say, by what name were you called back home? Maybe it'll be the last word you'll say. Everybody is called something as soon as his mother gives birth to him. That's right. That's how it should be. And tell me the name of your land, your people, your city too, so that our ships—with all thoughts directed there—will not take you there again. Because they are supposed to get you to another place. The Phaeacians' ships don't need a pilot— well, maybe theirs—but ours do, not even because of the rudder, reportedly, they don't have that either; you know in advance where our people need to be steered to; one look at us is all you need. And now we must steer ourselves but without a motor we can't do it and and with a motor we wouldn't know how. There are ships, we don't know them, those ships, however, do know their mates' intentions without being told and all ports of call and all the rich green fields, with wings of the wind they cross the sea's huge gulfs shrouded in mist and cloud. Okay, fine. But unfortunately we can't do that. At least the sea is still silent. Still! No idea, what ideas it'll get once it notices that on this ship we were steered into danger so as to never arrive. An escort would really be nice now, we could talk to the guys, we could yell something to them, they could throw us a rope, not a bad idea in this darkly swelling sea, we surely could use one. Dragging an enormous, protective mountain range around the city wouldn't be bad either. Well yeah, but not here. Here we can only dream about mountains.

The swell now smooth and shiny because it's not a swell. The dolphin-man who explained the motor to us, though not while it was running because it never ran properly, that man is now swimming back to the shore, he is already properly dressed for it. We are yet to reach the shore, the other shore where we want to get to, I don't know if we can make it there, there are lawns and pretty creeks, which we don't have back home. But surely we shall see big hotels and well-lit restaurants. And good people who'll bring us something, a pizza maybe, a bottle of water, a piece of bread with something on it. And say something to us. It means nothing to me but there are some who understand them. There we can finally let lose the vehemence of our desire. If only the motor would run better! Do something about it! The man in the green swim trunks steps ashore and pulls out the money he made with and from us. And when we will have disappeared, there'll be no more evidence, once we drift pale below the algae, there are none here?, say we, the jellyfish. The swimmer's arms turned into branches, wish I could swim like him! He'll celebrate with his milk-brothers tonight, hey, he did it again!, once again he made a kill collecting from people the breath of life, it was their entrance fee into the sea. They all paid, otherwise they wouldn't have made it into the boat. The sea will collect on top of it. First the cash, but the sea must be paid as well, we'll have to think of something, we still owe it the rent, we've spent almost everything already, fifty dollars to sit on a chair, three-hundred-fifty dollars for sleeping three hours in a bed, it says so here on a slip of paper, it has been checked so it is true, I only just read it, supposedly it is correct but what good is such a check! Can't say that about the motor, can't say it overspent itself, and one certainly can't say it had been checked even though we paid for it in advance, that was also one of our expenses, we, however, are so many. How much is the ride per meter? Specification and reality diverge, but we won't notice, because it wasn't us who had to tank up. Now it's filled with diesel, the motor, it's about to puke, and that was also an expense, the fuel, a considerable one, and that doesn't yet include your food, does it?, and no, it does not overspend itself, it doesn't even give what it has. It gives nothing. The Volkswagen at least gave what it was given, it owes nothing to anyone. Not even a zappy way of driving will get you more, for then you'd have to constantly refill that little tank with that conveniently clear emission-cleaning fluid! A small wonder, this car can't even do a thousand kilometers with it the way you ruthlessly race this capable road raft as if Diana with her dogs were after you to turn you into a stag. She's got a lot of work to look forward to. What are you saying? Those who created it, this condrivance, were also capable of something? That's probably true, still, they were in no way incapacitated, there is no evidence whatsoever. Then the surprise at the gas station where we suddenly owed something they had promised us before! It was to be a saving. Some kind of clean world, and this particular vehicle would produce it with this clear liquid, it will contribute also to your life, unfolding bright and clear, oh yes, indeed you can be absolutely sure of it. All you have to do now is pay. But that's not too bad, you can fill her up yourself, no problem, check the manual where the tank is, one and a half liter will get you up to thirty thousand kilometers, that thing about one thousand really was too pessimistic, so why all that fuss? That's how far the purity will get you, which you can pour into your tank like a few last prayers into your soul, that's also how far the purity takes you with a catalytic converter, that's the other option for purification, in that case however you'll you have to get the converter clean again with the diesel-fuel injection, but that'll also work albeit not by itself. Everything works but nothing works by itself except yourself. Everything always works, just not for everyone. And the best thing about it: you can do it yourself, no need to get all worked up! You can personally pour it in, all you need is a funnel, a canister or a fuel nozzle and everything will be clean and pure again. Or there will be a cleanup. And while we are at it: who says we are to blame? And who are you to put the blame on us?

This boat won't give or say anything, it spits for a while, long enough to get off the shore and not having to look at sand or rocks anymore, and then it is silent. People were so happy it did anything at all, the motor, but it didn't do it right because now it's completely silent. It only started with difficulty and it must not stop at all or you'll never get it going again and then you'll have to keep going yourself, but whereto?, as long as it's running, it stays warm just like a human. As long as it can run it maintains the proper internal temperature to survive, it could not warm up but it had enough residual heat to run, hundred, two hundred kilometers, this one can manage, but the other one over there doesn't, nothing can be done about it, but the one I put my money on can do it. Just that it should also be able to swim, but that's too much to ask from any motor, they all run out of steam in water. And consider this: because of the rocking of the boat, which is not its own doing, dirt must have been washed up into the tank which cannot be removed, that's like those madmen back home who are granted status by the people, on borrowed time that is, and thus must be returned again. A loan is a loan. Wealth could do a better job but that's not been borrowed. You better remember that because I am not going to say it again. More often than not you can get old wrecks like me into gear only if you get them warmed up somehow, like that marine engine, so now I am just running hot until you put a stop to me. You can hold a lamp up to me, well maybe not an open light, but a shaded lamp, because I cannot hold on to me, I can't do that, yes this is how you have to hold the lamp!, so that I can warm up a bit and then get going. You don't want to? But I would like that.

One can no longer hear the motor, no wonder it's no longer doing anything. It had been running just long enough as a promise to get these people to the island of Kos or any of its neighbors, now it can keep this promise just like carmakers who give in to any pressure, first the air's which also would like to breathe, then to the customer who is able to breathe on his own, then to the sea, then to the emissions calculator. Oh no, that can't be right! And those people also gave in to the pressure and bought swim vests and small water bottles and energy bars, but you won't get energy from them, we already consumed the energy and then barred the gates behind us, that is to say all the energy when we still thought it was cheaper.

When I think of the drama they made of Hector's corpse! And that was just one man and nine days of outrage from the gods. But our motor not running doesn't concern them at all, it doesn't concern anyone but us. Because of one man who is now a corpse they have been arguing for nine days now, and because of thousands of men, women, children they don't create nearly such a riot, oh well, those will rot all on their own. I have to look up how that works in water where they will bloat, men, women and children who are also corpses as of now, and soon we'll join them, thirty or so more and another thirty or so and still thirty more, more or less right over there a few more and surely today many more boats will arrive! Those are the lucky ones, they won't become the deceased here, not yet anyway, that was the prophesy and the gods collided, screaming, but luckily those people didn't get between them, yes, exactly, lucky them, the gods didn't fight about those for a change. The gods are fighting over this Volkswagen's lie, and that one's too, a car from which one should be able to demand high standards cannot be that cheap. Our expectations of this boat were much more modest, it was the minimum require-ment, it should run, it shouldn't run out, but it does not run. So there it guzzled diesel until it almost puked, it rattled a few times and now it won't run for the life of it. Who'd want to quit running? But if it must be, if it is the water's wish, if it wants to fetch us in our youth's greening year to follow Ulysses's trail in the water. Something isn't working. I think fate decided perdition. In case it has decided something else

I'll find out in this magazine, which is our mirror, our *Spiegel* which always brings in the big guns, and I will sing how the cities were destroyed by the refugees until the real guns will be hauled out, there won't be any other way. And the wind, what does it say to that? The wind won't work—can one say it like that? Does it let its back get savagely beaten by its enemies, the various vehicles? That won't be necessary. The wind won't blow, no matter what, no matter what pitiful lot you threaten it with, if it will not blow. It doesn't move us along either. The wind doesn't start. The motor doesn't start. It is as if everything conspired against us. Perhaps, a small sacrifice? Sacrifice, anyone? We don't want to become victims but maybe that girl over there who is making such a pretty drawing right now? You want to sacrifice that girl? Come on now, that's ridiculous! That's not a sacrifice! We make that kind of sacrifice every hour, in case it is required. So how do we go about the sacrifice, we have to start somehow and somewhere. What star travels its steep course right there? Why does it climb up to the zenith, while we must go down? Not a sound all around, well now, are we getting on with the sacrifice or what? The wind, that idiot wind is silent, it wants screams, so it can pass them on and that's why it is silent now, so it can hear something when it starts. We are stuck here with twenty-seven people and a dead motor, do you understand? We must have a victim, any volunteers? That girl, well, that's not a lot, maybe the gentleman over there?, the lady with the headscarf?, no? So this girl must suffer, I mean, suffice as pledge for our crossing? Well, I don't know but in any event we won't let ourselves be crossed. So then Victim, over here, would you like a stone? What for, a stone? For you to lay down on? Whoever is not assured of divine help will plummet into the abyss. And the crowd? It's shimmering, never satisfied senses cause nothing but chaos. And you are a human whether you like it or not.

Well, if our children have to lie in their own shit and breathe sick diesel smoke from a sick motor, then we have no room for you girl, there, lie down!, we'll tell you where to lay and off we go, don't stall. I am running, I am running, where on earth do you want to run, you can't even stand here, can't even lie down for the sacrifice, and yet there must be a sacrifice. Don't let slumber beguile you, you sacrificial victim you, you wouldn't be one if you were to experience this unconsciously, that's not how it works. No wind, we wouldn't have any sails for it anyway, no motor, but you are here, our sacrifice, you were called and now you will be killed. No rolling by on speedy wheels, my child, to the ships of the Greeks, there one is coming already but we are not Greeks, but that's who we want to get to, and that's not a ship, that's a car that's also rolling along, only it has too much power, it burns up too much for that power and that doesn't even include that effective fluid; yes, exactly, the one for cleaning, the cleansing fluid which must be clean itself, no, you can't use water, even though it's as clear as it is invisible. It won't happen to us, that we, like the capitalists, will be allowed to love change and to settle here among you for a change. We are driven out everywhere, we drift away, it happens all by itself, it happens on this ship, it's the only one we have. Before we go, dinner in the orange grove, that's listed in the program, we insist on it!, dolphins dancing around the prow, I declare, the party is over now. Favorable winds to Naxos, Kythera or one of the neighbors, what are their names? Donkey boys, dust, deserts, Jerusalem, baksheesh and an endless fuss over passports. We haven't got that far and we won't get that far because we don't have passports. First we must journey to the far- away ocean, oh here we are already! On our boat trip think of us, you—our sacrifice, think of home, think what you want, maiden sacrifice. What are you saying? Mother is coming along, isn't she? So you are seeing your mother there? No. So she doesn't seem to be there. No father, no mother, you all alone, off to other people into a foreign house, but first the sacrifice, that will save you all your troubles while we will invest our savings in taxi rides, to Germany for instance, and if we can't pay, the taxi driver will cut half a pound of flesh out of us, but we only go to the border, we must also walk across alone, all alone, all of us alone, all of us.

Not so fast, we are not there yet, we still have quite a ways to go. And we don't yet even know which way. So far there's no way for us to even be on our way. We'll just have to ride the surf on those boards, then a quick selfie before it's too late, because the boat doesn't want to go on, it bucks, it needs to get rebooted, well, it had to come to that. We'd be happy to just get one meter further with the same diesel, that is the same amount your Volkswagen inhales per minute. Five million cars are affected, we aren't. No one cries for us. Just a moment, something pallid fell into the moon shaft, let's do a count if it was one of us! Only one? Do colors clash in your blood because you aren't affected? We however are destined for consumption by the ocean and we are against it. No matter what the ocean wants, we don't want it. Sure, shyness and love belong into the heart, who does glory belong to? I am told to the Peleid and his Pallas, the Germans' goddess, fine with me, but what's left for us? What's left for us humans to do? In his heart's madness the former held Hector beside the curved-beaked ships and did not redeem him; beaked?, weren't they curved and also resplendent?, whatever. All I know is: our boat is not beaked. It is packed with people, chock-full of mortals, simply too full, but resplendent it is not. What? With gifts we should please, no tease, no, appease the gods? Anything else? What's left for us to give? Ourselves probably, that's what the gods always want, well, okay, then we'll give ourselves to them if the girl we chose is not enough, we said that all along. Unfortunately, one of the gods has already left, he had to be home for dinner, that's what he promised his divine wife. The one who has power over us because the boat belongs to him, yes, also the motor, he already jumped ship, no not the motor, that—how shall I put it—that man who made promises it's not his fault, the boat isn't his, the money is, we could have bought many boats with it, one for each of us, who wants to do the math, please?, on the other hand: the boat is made for sinking, if sinking it must be, then rather there, where people are swimming naked in rivers, snuggling up to more beautiful ships, which don't need coastguards because they are in a marina. There, now he swims like a dolphin, the owner of this boat, but he also bought it used, from a third party, it'll be sunk anyway or sink all on its own, why spend money and for a motor that works we could find a better use, we better put it to use where we can get more out of it for a longer time. Now he jumps high up in the air, that man, straight from the water, I can clearly see his tight green swim trunks, I seem to be obsessed by such trunks, always have been, well, by what's in it, it warms my blood tank which does not have to be refilled, I am self-cleaning, I don't need to booze to run smooth. Now the man who got us the boat is swimming ashore, away from us, as quickly as possible, far away from us so he wouldn't get into the maelstrom created by us. But we also want to quickly get away from here, though in the opposite direction without approaching traffic, because everybody wants to go there, we drive on water as if it were land, we drive, wrath is duty, but no one around to receive it, no god to throw dice for us, not even for our robe, no society that would exchange us, we wouldn't know for what. We are worth nothing, we could be given away, sure, but no one would exchange us for anything. We are doing everything we are told to do, everyone except those cars on their wrong track, all doing exactly what they are told except it was the wrong thing. Those motors were promised long lives, they understood, their life was competition to which they were challenged mockingly because they were too cheap, they are ready now just like their buddies, okay, and now all the buggies, no, bugs and boats will be taken back, taken home. We however depend on their help to get away, obviously, without wrath nobody's body, possession and liberty are safe, so lets get this wrath here, it won't do us any good either but we'll take it along to be on the safe side, it's in this waterproof plastic bag, not the Peleid's one, together with the phone with the pictures of family, house, land, diploma, all gone, all gone, but the pictures want to stay a little longer, not for long, just for a short time, our wrath lies right next to it, that's where we put it, because inside us it's of no use right now, it will stretch and purr, it will jump up with a snarl, I am amazed it didn't do so sooner but there is too little room here for sure. Lynxes and leopards, sure, they jump. Not us, so—are we sheep, as it seems we have no rage? It must be somewhere, we took it off somewhere, we did, and at least the boat isn't yet sinking, it does everything it shouldn't, but it does not sink yet. So the motor is in place but useless, so what about our wrath, where did it go? We haven't yet told whom to direct it against! If you want wrath, you'll get it! I want to see the day when slaves—no I'll say it another way, I'll say something else—the day when wrath won't be necessary anymore. Here it is, I found it, it was next to the last jar of baby food, here's the wrath, but even that won't get the motor going. I don't understand. The energy is in these bars, locked in behind bars and this wrath is—not the Peleid's, not this time either, sorry—nothing again, our wrath is in these baggies. It must have everything in its proper order even if this car uses up more energy than it took in. That diesel rides in this car here, in the one over there a swig of diesel also goes down smoothly, only our diesel here in the boat stays put and does nothing. Maybe it would do something on concrete. Maybe we would do something else had we enough to eat.

The man in the swim trunks explained the motor to them, that must do, he is already stepping ashore, he swam across and now he steps ashore, he steps up to the beach, to his friends. If deeds are not bundled and stockpiled in the heart, exhaustion will follow. Should I be indebted to that man in a swimsuit? Well, not I, that's for sure. So I don't owe him. He must own up. But who cares. And the sea couldn't care less. The motor has had it and the people have to have it, something to eat, that's not possible, go some place else. The motor did eat, it ate the diesel, which didn't do our darling Volksbuggie any good because it lied about the amount, it wanted more and it got it too. But we should have been told! Yes, you, but not everyone. As punishment the motor will be torn out of it alive, ouch, with its two golden eyes it had covered the land and cut through the air and sawed through the woods and it lied all along. It can no longer do it, period; it cannot run as cheaply as it claims, it ran afoul of its own specifications. Wrong. Its brain, the soft ware must decide what it wants, it's always only one or the other. More foul air or more fuel in the tank, one or the other. Minimal fuel consumption for good performance, so why not go hog wild, beautiful nature right and left, she'll hold up a while longer, yes and the lungs too, no worries! And what's with that body there, under the water, it can no longer accomplish its task, we are really sorry. Alright then—it's either carefree racing along dry roads or, other alternative: less pollutant emission, it'll just have to guzzle more, that speedster, there's no other way. Well, he's got problems! Everything that costs is a problem. I would know what I would choose. I would definitely choose carefree. And that wouldn't only do for the test station, it would always work, for normal operation we simply switch the consumption of Spic and Span and Mr. Clean, of Pronto and Besto or AdBlue to almost zero, and whoop-de-doo off we go, makes our hair fly backwards, you won't know what hit you, it's a great feeling for the car too of course, it won't have to worry about anything anymore.

Unfortunately this boat can't do any of this, it can't choose, this boat can't pick its own motor, and if it does, it can't do much, and it doesn't have to do it for long; it's operator designated this motor for the boat and now it's supposed to make it work, not much, really, that's not necessary. And if it croaks we don't have to pay for a funeral, it gets a burial at sea. The manual for this motor and that one too— for everything that has a permit for the sea and won't stay calm if water seeps in—states, keep going all the way to the other shore. But when the motor has had it, the whole thing doesn't work. Between mountains that aren't here, between the water that's aplenty all around, and through clouded blackness, the poor boat works itself into the ground. It can't go on. The people, who must keep going, can't do it either, but at least they don't need any fuel, they are fuelled by something I don't know and that's what we will hang on to now. We'll hang together and will be saved while the brothers are still torn apart.

And we forget how to return, we forget how to get ahead, our eyes see what had been told to us back home but now we are looking at something completely different. There used to be a military power before us, behind us, everywhere, it stood in front of our soul. Now we fear every cat of the wood and the lynxes on our hats, no, no, the German armored *Luchse* looking out for us, leopards eating grapes, vines growing in our worship. Come on now! Stop it! Okay. Considering that something can be said any time, I might as well stop now. Oh evil bird hovering over my speech. Do you still want to say something now? I must die, so many standing around here and I have to die, what, you too? How so? And does anyone dare to bear down on you? Everyone! All of them! All!

Only a few splinters, no more, out of:

Ezra Pound, Cantos

Euripides, Iphigenia in Aulis

Homer, Odyssey

Thanks also to Philip Hagmann and the Deutsches Theater Göttingen and to Wikipedia *with its many cars*!

APPENDIX

The conquest of the world as image, that's history, for an image is made to stay. People however, are not made and they don't stay where they were made to stay. They fight for their position, that's not a position as you might imagine, that's just staying the way they are. They gave up on setting a new standard for *being*, for the set has not yet been set up, the one they will walk into. But they walk. They keep walking. No suntanned cheeks but sore hearts, tear-trained, they weep, they know how to, they better do, they have to, all of them except doctors and seers who are already drained of tears. What, you had three children and now there are only two, the third, who also happens to be three years old, is suddenly missing? That's nothing compared to others who are no more, calm down! They are moving along. Those few men who once were so important to me, so dear, like kin on their terrified flight, many already gone, some accused, they took someone along on the train, the train did not complain but here they were stuck with a claim, I don't know, I forgot how it turned out, they probably are still around or maybe not, those men who remained, some even here with us, I don't know. Whoever drew the line, judge, savior or smuggler, there had to be a line, something's always on the line, for them, pulling them, this way, that way. And they also get in line, lining up, moving on. They do have a goal that crashes against the Hungarians' Christian arrogance, but our tribe still takes care of them. Internally raging greed but we are still fighting against it. I was overwhelmed, compassion overwhelmed me and also other things, for example, this morning I was overwhelmed again but what of it, what of it, I am sitting here in my little house, I get overwhelmed just by a single gust of wind knocking on my window but not coming in as soon as it sees me, or the drunk, probably someone from the neighborhood whom I don't let in, I shut the window, I shut the door, period.

They wander around, those people, there are so many, no one can overlook them, they are talked about, no one can understand them. They are, like, you know, they don't know how people talk here. No wonder no one bothers to listen to them, not to their suffering, not to their songs which are of no use to anyone but them, those songs one hears, to the guitar, to an orchestra, you get to hear in a show, where people present themselves, those who really are presentable and real, and even more than that: who produce sounds of sorrow they've drilled into themselves in front of a mirror like shards of glass one has stepped on, something's hurting and it must be looked at whether one likes it or not. Isn't it piercing, the rehearsed pain of the woman singing in this show?, she would gladly let it get inside, if it came in person, that obscure pain of desire. Life is so hard, she sings breathlessly, but she still has enough air, luckily they all got airs, what torment in those songs soaring from the device, the torrent sears through it, such torture, those songs, and the woman sings so beautifully, yes the man too, but that's not what I wanted to say, this program was going on without me and will come back three more times this year, I don't mind. How loudly they wail, those are real cries of suffering, yes go ahead, hold on to them!, those folks camping here—let's hope just temporarily until they go away again—are measured by how real they get their wailing across, such loud cries of woe, glaringly shrill, dark, dull sounds, tear-dewed. Those tones of woe are sung now by that other woman too, I did not see her yesterday, tomorrow I'll see others, but today it's her turn, please, where is her third child, her three-year-old daughter, where, I ask you, who can hear it, tell me, really hear it, please! No idea. It's easier on TV, and even more on social media, there you can choose your own visiting hours. In reality those are only bytes, bitter bytes, not in foreign sounds of language unknown to us, no the woman, the singer sings in German and they all now want to learn German as fast as possible, those camping out here, wrapped in blankets, scarfs, foils, oh no, they are so stiff, they can hardly be twisted around. The singer's wailing sounds are so loud, you have to tear open the window so that the sounds can get out again, or they'd shatter the panes.

Alright, anyone else shattered here? This mother, who lost the third child along the way gets comforted, provided for, something gets written down to help find the child again. Or she'll just be gone and that's that. Then it will be a funeral song. That's okay too. More than they deserve, the way they sit there picking shoes from the pile nobody sorted. Are those the right songs, the right tears?, is this the right kind of suffering? I wouldn't be surprised. They hope that something, ideally everything, will still turn out to be their hell, I mean *Heil,* and Germany has not yet started to shoot, at least not in the sense of buds, well, okay, but of butts, it constantly kicks butts while the Bud keeps flowing and everyone stays put, Germany is there to stay and it is at the helm, it fights the salty waters, which isn't hard, their sea is way up north, but that's where they want to reach too, those besieging are beseeching us now. They want to get to Germany or Sweden. In Sweden they can complete their studies and after five years become citizens of that land. Who asks, who wants to know what happened before, in the ship's house, to others, to no one, to many, what happened that even without a storm a gentle breeze brought them here and still they capsized, whose fault was it, it was their own. They never complain about it, they have to put up with it and now they are here alright. They produce volcanoes of shit and dirt and waste, it looks as if a mountain of waste had exploded, go ahead take a look at the mess they make and something like this is to live among us now, and for good? They don't pass the German course, because they don't get in, so they make it to us without a pass, and did not pass the course that all of us would pass, because we can flee unscathed to wherever we want, so instead of learning their lesson they produce a lot of trash, for good advice comes at a price, waste is free, since WCs have not yet been invented in Hungary, maybe invented but didn't yet make it all the way there, I just heard that Serbia has exactly the same problem, only worse, so I should not talk about Hungary, but I will anyway. The fence is closed now. A train came and closed it with NATO wire, now I should say something about *NAHTOD*—near-death experience, that is—it would fit well, they often really are near death—if they haven't already died at sea—even though near enough, so that they would get to have experiences, and if they did they wouldn't say.

Calculations always contain violence. Ulysses, for example, one of the most famous travellers had calculated his journey to and back from Hisarlik Hill in Turkey but was delayed by so many events, yet he had a return ticket—I've no idea how long it was valid, and how often it had been punched. The world must find an indispen-sible form, otherwise nothing will move, but how many lack any form on the paths they follow, on the tracks they move on from sleeper to sleeper, not to here, not to there, not this time, they obediently follow the tracks that determine their route, but this is also why the trains can't run anymore because the people did not take their seats but occupied them instead. Those tracks have been occupied. Someone always gets the bum rap because he is the last one. Only yesterday Mercedes was in the factories of those Germaniacs and sorted their human stock into useful and useless kinds, that's quick and easy for them, or they wouldn't have been so successful, sure thing, their god is not a remote god, God knows, that one there isn't even a god, who on earth believes in that one? We wouldn't be so successful if we believed in him, says the Lord of Daimler and takes down the names of the men who know how to do things, who arrived as supplicants, each waving a branch, soon they'll hold screwdrivers or whatever, which that robust messenger, that union buster, the robot, man's priceless helper, that's pricier than any human and enjoys replacing him, does not want to put in their hands because then he would be replaced by humans!, and we, once again we are getting the waste left behind by Mercedes, the used Skoda or the refrigerated truck that changed owners a few times and now doesn't have one at all, at least he doesn't come forward, our star points somewhere else, and it's not a lucky star, speed unknown; no, nonsense, known, we all know how fast this car can drive when it wants to! But people can't catch up that fast, they don't catch on so quickly, they press on, but—no, not to get to the battle of worldviews, they might win that one. But not security. They cannot win that prize. Not against us, because we can't include them into our lives or conclude that they are us or relate to them as ours and our lives as theirs.

We already have relationships, we don't need anymore. We would like to relate to this breathless singer not the naturalized one, that one does not have to be naturalized, she already is, she has a right, she is just right when she sings and dances and laughs and wails. Unfortunately, a good view is no longer an option for me, there are too many viewpoints now. One has to first review what there is to view, this program: yes from the bottom of my heart, yes! The way she sings she must have settled here long ago, because evil peoples don't have such songs and they don't want them either. I am not watching her, that singer and her super show in which she comes flying through the air, what a lucky duck! I could—no, not fly—watch her, I have a device for that. If I'd ever want to hang myself, I wouldn't want to be strangled in that singer's slings but there's no danger of that. The danger comes from others, thank God, they got away, and where to? To us. So there. A better view can still be worked out, no, another view won't work, I already have one, I'll be happy to hand it in, in case you need one. I already have one view, I don't need a second view, I already viewed my fill, the second one would be too much even for me, even though I secretly have several for different looks, those I have up my sleeve, let's see what happens, in an emergency, I'll pull one out and hit someone over the head with a knock-out argument. The next one better not be my brother or it'll be a real hit, I'll smash his head in. It cannot be my brother and he can see that too. You can see, it's just awful what I have to look forward to, and every day a different look, I've got my back-up views well in advance, in case one, the older, outdated one, needs to be updated or cleaned. Now I am looking through my eyes of the day, I see my views of today and I present the following to you—yesterday all of them were still human. Today I cannot look at them since yesterday thousands, tens of thousands more arrived, and already the charge of injustice has arisen. We make spot check-like controls, which, however, are not very controlled. It is pure willfulness, but it's useless anyway. I have quite a different view of control, right, mommie dearest? How can thousands be controlled, how's that supposed to work, those spot checks do not hit the spot though we have the best removers, I can't bear the sight anymore, I can't stand it but at least I haven't been befallen—by grudges, by anything, I've sprung from a new mold, I offer you something new, don't you see, be happy, here you get only the newest, otherwise you'd have to get it from the papers or the TV or the hystery book, the only place where you won't find me, my nerves wouldn't be able to take it, but the radio will tell you too, I always say what others are saying, I wait until something new presents itself to me and then I throw everything into the same empty bottomless pit where you also throw anything you have no use for. And already I resort to my latest view, shouldn't I better take the other one, the one from yesterday? I don't know, there simply are too many, and too many people remain who were not here before, that's not possible. That many are not possible for us. Where could they go to, where did they come from? That's how they imagined it, but that's not the way it goes. Just getting here was troublesome enough, because they lie so much, they are not the ones who they are, but their getting *to* and getting *in* is a no go for now, for we go by the book, our hystery book, from now on there will be controls. The getting here will be stopped and thereby also the getting ahead. Maybe this baby, this child can get out, one got lost already, a three-year-old, I am curious whether she will be found, and many others didn't get away at all, not even by the skin of their teeth. We will have to change our knowledge about people, but the knowledge resists. Whatever it knows it wants to keep to itself. It will never be as it was before again, just the fact that it knows of these people, of these objects will make a difference; consciousness, I am afraid, will have to change its knowledge, there won't be another way, and that knowledge alone will also change the object itself, it will change us all, please listen to me, as long as I still speak, as long as I am the one I am, as long as I find these objects, these people as objects, my knowledge still pertinent, not pertinent— rather pertaining to my knowledge, which is very small and least of all I would find them appealing, I wouldn't even know in what language—so, as long as I find them, the people, not language, I have it with me, I always have it with me, here it is, hello, my language can handle it, it'll manage alright. Nonsense, I know where to find them, the people, the objects of my thinking, no, can't call that thinking, as long as I find them as presented to me, how do I find that?, much reduced and in this device and exactly at 9 am, 1 pm, 5 pm, and then three more times in the evening, and when I find them, these fleeing folks, none of them will stay on, because they are so fleeting, then nothing will hold on and I won't be able to hold on to myself, I can't even now, as you can see. But I won't find anything for me to hold on to either. Neither will I find my own standard for that. That's what happens when one embarks on a journey, so and so many of them don't make it all the way, the rest make it to here or they die because they wanted the rest of the family to get here, too and were it only away from here. Then why do they come here first, if all they want is to get out?

Transportation? Discontinued. But now what?, what's up now, now it will be resumed, but also controlled, tomorrow controls will be reinstalled and transportation stalled again. For now the train has been taken out of service, in an hour it might resume service again, I don't know. Who would want to be of service to those people? Good folks with food and clothes they can do without, want that, let me express my special thanks to you and I have many special expressions for that but I'll save myself the trouble, for which you'll soon thank me, maybe already tomorrow! Inscribe my words in your hearts if you don't have any paper at hand or any other device that records them and stores them, at least my words should have a place to stay. No not those, we want other words, from others. Who, I ask you, should record them? There aren't enough devices anywhere to record them, even though their stories are interesting, and even more so, if they are made up. Oh God, now that crowd gets moved towards me! What should I do? Turn off the device before it overheats? But it will get lukewarm at best, like me. There are so many, so many people, who have found their destination at their earlier stops, but, not anymore. Now, we are their destination. Those are humongous crowds, they require planning and guidance and being led—on and off—, if they cannot be kept here any longer, like in Hungary. They are a needy lot who are a lot of work, many won't do the work, and then they shit in front of our house and dump their waste right there. Where should they take it, seeing as how they haven't yet invented the john in Hungary, much less in Serbia; I mean the portable john, one of the most important inventions of mankind, who wants growth, construction, production, reproduction, where are construction workers to go, but those are a manageable lot, they also manage to see the john right away—always in eyeshot, so that too much valuable construction stock(s), meaning construction time, is not lost, right?, that little blue loo we all know hasn't yet made it to Hungary. I think it was intentional. Ulysses, come here, take a leak, I mean, look, no, I mean: listen! The song of those creatures can be somewhat distracting, if one wants to be distracted, we could use those singing females now, not the sirens, those are all yellow, dressed in sequins and they get pulled upwards through the air as they sing, they are singing in the skies, like that woman who sings very loudly and amplifies it too, so that absolutely everyone can hear it, well, basically we need such women, we'd need many more women, but none would be like that breathless woman, who can breathe much easier than us nonetheless; women who sing that way and divert the gaping crowd, that would be the way, maybe we should fill the packed station platforms, those are very dangerous, with her smoky sound, no, you can't smoke here, that's a no-no here, and it is in force. Let her go elsewhere—who?—well, that one there, though it does not have to be exactly that one, but she should know how to sing. Yes, it would help if singing women could manage to go some other place where they have johns since we do not make any available to you because as soon as we get overwhelmed with such giga-planning, we'll stop planning altogether, right, huh? And in Serbia nobody plans anything, who'd want to go there? Right. So then we'll just discontinue planning.

That gigantic mass of people, they make 'giant-like' a quality of its own, I think, this actually makes a mockery of the quality of those people for having none. This mass moves here, because it was told to, then there, because it was told something else, then it stops again, nothing doing here, nothing to be done here and there, where they had arrived, nothing either, and the children play with stones at the soldiers' feet. Those stones have been there for an eternity, like the name of the Lord, it stays forever and ever, it stays with us. Those fleeing have another Lord, they take him with them when they leave. The altar, even during times of war, provides protection to all fugitives in dolorous distress wherever gods are feared. Yes, so? The Hungarians have no such fear, and now they no longer let them pass through either, and soon they'll have a fence, a brand new one, which they are building right now. Those people must go elsewhere and there are many other countries people are assigned to, but not all of them accept those foreigners, those lost ones, at least those they found, holding their smartphones as unreliable shields, which often tell them something wrong, just as we do. Those are people just like us. Those are phones just like the ones we have. No, this country is not Australia. Germany is over there, across the green border, which you, however, will not find, for it is green no more. They don't care, I mean, those countries don't care what skills those people have. Who needs them? Okay, they might have qualities, which could possibly be brought to bear, but Mercedes has already grabbed those, and their quota already maxed out. We don't need more people now. We already have enough. We have enough of them already. I always say that at this point. If you are interested in me, you know this, this is the truth of my mind, which is very small.

The void gets stretched until it screams and then it finally gets filled. And still it isn't content. Let me help stretch this emptiness, so that more people can fit in, but it's not possible. This void is already full. Everything is full. Everything is brimful, so many, so many, they might be amazing in their way, well, okay, in their ways maybe, but now they are just emaciated, so first let's get them something to eat, yes, thank you, they can have that and also something to drink and a roll mat or a sleeping bag. They do get what they need, if not right away. Patience please! If that's all you need. Because we need to move on. No, we don't have beds at the moment, they have those in the Swedish camp, unreachable, but we still have bits of floor in stock. Floor is on sale today, patience now, there'll still be plenty left tomorrow. Not only is every humangous mass of people different in size from other humongous quantities, it also invents its own definition of size. This one here is simply too big for me, not only for me, don't you have a smaller one? Even Hungary might have portable toilets for a smaller one. If only it were smaller, that mass, if only they were fewer, these people, they could at least enjoy their excretions, those can compensate for a lot. They could compensate for father and mother, for there is much to learn from the sexual activities of children. The lips suck food, if there is any, as to other zones, pleasure must be compensated by muscular activities. And this creates the following problem: where to put it, if one isn't a child, but just plain small, an insignificant member in a humongous crowd, there isn't much that member can do with it either. Genital excitability could be the lifelong consequence if excretion can't find its place—wish I had your problems!—and in case of a child, it does not want that place, it wants to take advantage of this excitability of the anal zone. I am telling you, in case you have no children, I don't have any either, but I read about what's going on with them. Yes, the child likes doing that, maybe that three-year old, the one missing, does it too, let's hope it has been found already, even though it's a little girl, she counts for something and has genital urges. It wants to hold back those pressing masses, the child, you can read up on this, you won't know more than I do, holding it back, so it can enjoy the strong sensation on the mucus membranes, that's a nice activity for our little ones and smallest ones, but what do the grown-ups do, if they don't have a place and the function of discharge is prevented, after they had already been deprived, freed of everything they had, house, apartment, business, family, relatives, friends, what do our grown-ups do in Hungary? They have taken this route, they were right, right so far but not anymore, as of today. Tomorrow I might no longer able to tell who is right, then a new pass will be trampled down, a trail marked by the sign of the supplicants, which they will travel along harmlessly, but nonetheless in some state of agitation. A new trail, coming from the messenger in their device, according to the messenger's word, as to what's where, how should they know?, informed by the electronically winged messenger's word in their hands, they are now travelling along this path that gets them where, just a moment, I have to check, it must be Croatia or Slovenia or both, but not today.

It has only started today, their going elsewhere. But today is no longer yesterday and yesterday the following was true: what a way to start!, I mean, things started yesterday, hold it, not so fast, I can't keep up with myself, but those people must think on their feet, still, their device is faster, it must be, for who else should tell them what road to take, which path to stay off, lest they'd be beaten and now it's already a wide road with white swathed—the supplicants'— signs, Refugees Welcome!, but first another look at the display which tells them something, it tells another story because Hungary doesn't want them, Hungary itself is a gut that wants to purge itself of those unclaimed people. Who's supposed to stomach that? I ask you. Like it or not, it doesn't work. This country says: Get it all out. Even the Church is powerless against that. Get it all out. That's not what a child tells its gut because it wants to keep it all in as long as possible, its shit is its first gift, it has nothing else, the child, it is a gift whose refusal expresses the child's defiance of its environment. But who wants the defiance of all those adults? There is no destination for them, there is only the road they trampled down themselves, after they were trampled on by the Hungarian photographer, oh no, that was just one or two people plus their respective children, they have experienced worse. It doesn't even have to be broken, that anger, there is no more need for it, that's why it gets nipped in the butt. It doesn't have a destination, what destination could it be?, even though those defiant ones have lost everything, where should they direct what they can't keep inside forever? It has to come out at some point, it can't be helped; what would help: the porta-potty. Welcome, little blue friends, there you are, nicely lined up, people never line up so orderly as those guys do, what else can they do, they have to line up to get into those little cabins. For the least little bit they have to get in line, and that's nothing! They should be happy it's not worse. Here you won't find one portable Dixi potty, an entire Dixi band, a cohort of those blue Dixies would not be enough to take in those crowds without sword or cross to shield them, that is, who don't have the guts to fight the real shit—anyway—no Dixies here to take them all in for even just a moment, no, take them out in just one moment.

How then should he express himself, that angry man in need to press on, if all he's got is right inside him? No one is interested in what he's got in him, it's too much already that he is in here at all. He can't even let go of his shit after he held it inside for so long? And that woman with the red spot on her pants? She is ashamed! The child knows no shame, but that woman is ashamed. She sits on the side of the road and is bleeding. Only a grown woman could come up with such a thing! And what got into that one over there, a thunderstorm's brewing and it also erupts, and off we go, hurry up, the bus is waiting already, and of course the woman doesn't want to miss the bus, she has been waiting for it forever, attention, breaking news! That one's in labor, can you believe it, really!, only grown women could get into that. Okay. She's taken to the hospital, let's see what I can find out about her condition, at least in the hospital nothing will happen to her. And I've been sitting here for such a long time, I sit and sit, though I know how unhealthy this is for grown women, sitting, ask anyone. I'll die of it, sitting here, but not yet, that can take quite long, thank you, she is doing alright at the moment, the woman, yes I am too. Let's take a look what the crowd is doing, what these people here in the crowd are doing. They board the bus minus one woman who is in the hospital now, having become two persons, get two for one. Those folks must make do with what they get, or they just head out on their own, when the train doesn't come or is an hour late, they don't want to wait that long. They head out, there is nothing brazen in their voice they know they must control themselves or the Hungarians will lock them up too. They don't want to lose their place, in fact they haven't had one in a long time.

No way to get over that fence, but if that one's already too high for you, you haven't seen the fences in Bulgaria or Greece!, nevertheless!, please use the regular crossing and, most importantly, do not use the irregular toilet, which calls itself nature but in the meantime has turned into a far cry from nature. And now? What will we do now, if we are not children, get no children and have no place for what we have honestly acquired with the food, if we got any, which we now want to birth through the bowels, to bring into the world, it's not as bad as a birth, but it still must come out, and this end product, which is what becomes of donated meals no one is in charge of, there is nothing and no one, it is a loose end, what's man to do if he can't tie ends together, he would have to connect his mouth to his ass, in a sort of short circuit. Oh well, money, shit and the word. If we could spare ourselves these three it would be okay, but unfortunately we have nothing to spare and nothing to save. They do have mobile phones, the supplicants, but the body also wants to decide and defecate, oh no!, those two American students are already holding Kleenex to their nose against the stench. Let's be honest, that stench really is unbearable. Special masks are already available, policemen wear them in Hungary, I don't think those protect against infections, they use it against the stench. Here you see, there you smell an activity that doesn't know its destination, well, yes it does, but—where to? It would be better if those folks knew their goal even better, they really should, where will the stench go, where is everything supposed to go, including that which isn't even there?

We do know where to put the telephones, first to the charging unit, then to the ear and then back again. But where to put the bodies that come with telephones? Nobody can be imagined without a body, but by their phones you will recognize them. If the escape is to be free of bloodguilt, a smartphone is needed at the very least, which tells you when, whereto and how. Their shit, on the other hand, they would like to get rid off, the flight-ridden, because without such letting-go everything's a no-go, without letting-go everybody would burst. What am I saying? No one wants these people, that's the long and the short of it, there is no place, there is no place for anything or anybody. Excuse me, just now a hall has been opened here, military tents over there, and there we opened the waiting room for bicycles for them, let the bikes wait some place else, many, no, not many bikes which had taken their spot, their place, many have the runs already. Where to put it, a bit here, a bit there? How those people bop around with their poop is revolting. We can do that much better, but we don't do it. We bop and bounce elsewhere, we run to wherever a marathon takes place. There are so many camping here, they'd have so much to give but don't even have a little room where it could all flow into, where they could be at rest while it happens. I have my own notion of size but here it falls short, it doesn't cover this kind of mass. I also have my own notion of beauty, which you can read in my face, still!, it won't hold up much longer just as Hungary can't hold so many people or would want to, so much vanity showing on my forehead, right there, where the eyebrows are, I do smear quite a bit around there when I adorn my face with color, no peace in my eyes, my gaze restlessly flitting about, am I beautiful enough to go outside, even if it's just to the supermarket. I like being indolent, I am not hesitant. While I write I can do anything and I take advantage of it, who could do me any harm?

But you, I do not recommend this to you, who are on the run, for you are foreign and fleeing your country, the weaker ones better remove their big mouths before they let it rattle on, I'll remove my make-up only afterwards, after the people will have seen me. But I am all by myself so I can easily do something others are not permitted to. If you beg for pity from a stranger, you shouldn't be too loud, but not too soft either, lest you won't be heard or left unanswered. You should simply be, you should just *be*, that's all, take it or leave it. What else can one do? There'd be a lot left behind but it should not be ablated, it should rather be sublated. Or better still: leave it to Hegel.

The crowd is gigantic, it has grown humongous, but it must not be growing here, it must not take roots here; and all the planning, calculating, I mean all the facilities they need, starting with eating, sleeping, education, defecation, all those installations for security, they go way beyond my notion of *calcul,* I am not good at math, but this wrecks my brain, and what must be calculated becomes incalculable. And what needs to be said becomes unspeakable, well, I can't say it, I should be able to but I can't. This mass of people is surrounded by an invisible shadow, another mass hidden away, an uncouth, ungainly shadow that's cast wherever food is thrown at them, where their feed flies through the air, hey, there it flies, a drone?, no, what is it?, that's a roll, you want it or not? Someone else will love to have it if you don't want it. This decision is taken off your shoulders, someone else has caught it, he was faster, we are sorry. If you don't want the next one I'll take it, yes and the water bottle too, it's even more useful; if you don't watch out, it'll crash on your head! Your shit's running down on you, don't you notice?, where, I ask you, should it go?, where do you want to put it now? They are always in such a hurry, thus man becomes subject and the world an image, but the hurry is not the reason for it and what's to become of this subject I don't know either, it should join the line maybe it will get its turn for something, no idea. I don't know, I don't know, I can no longer oversee it, no not even overlook it, I can't, I just can't. But I don't have to either. Its not my call, I can recall it and then watch TV or browse along, I don't have to do anything, I have to sit here endlessly, in front of my device, forever, which as I said isn't good at all for me and my body. And it wouldn't be for you either. If you know nothing, shut up, shut your mouth already, I hear, I can't really see it, the direction it's coming from; we have it coming from so many sides. If you can't see through it, keep looking at the screen, yes the big one or the small one, whatever you've got, there the world gets shot from a fox hole, big or small whichever you've got on just now, so now you've seen it, there is no more and now you're on your own with the picture, serves you right if you can't grasp it, not even if it's small. What you can't grasp, we grab.

A fence, after all, is also a grab bag. And it will now be locked up before a few million Hungarians are up for grabs because they are under such massive threat.

This gigantic space, this gigantic mass has long gone way beyond my imagination, and even the unpredictable has disappeared, someone else has already computed it, there's no way out but those people are still on their way, even if every clock were to stop, they'd still be going, they are moving ahead, but that's got to stop!, are the borders open, are they closed, are the trains running, are they not, is the highway open, is it not, are there check points, are there none, are there checks now or in five minutes?, randomly or thoroughly?, all unpredictable, all more than I could know but no more than what I could find out on the radio, on TV, on the small social market in my hand, that's always open, that's more than I could find out but did not have to pass on because you saw and heard exactly the same without being able to figure it out. You now must go to the Department of Revenue, where you'll be told whether things will end up well or badly for you, whether the eyes of finance, not of high finance of course, can look at you full of grace or if you will have to pay more than some others who haven't paid anything yet. Come on in hurry up! Already by noon everything could be different, that's what makes it so hard for fiction, there's hardly time for a photo!, it's running out everywhere, the shit is running out everywhere, in Hungary where they don't yet have porta-potties, where you can't get them anywhere, yes, yes you can, I have seen them in some places, not in person, naturally, out there in nature it's all different again. The trains are running again but there are controls, because of them you got stranded in Salzburg and you got impatient, so you walked to the town of Freilassing, it's name suggests it sets you free and it surely will live up to it and not lock you up, last stop, end of the line, no, not last stop, still moving on. Nonetheless, it's a good idea to have something ready that proves who one is, it would be best the world would rise beyond its present space towards a new determinacy, which I definitely won't be told about, but I don't want to go on a trip, especially now, that the trains are so full, a determinacy, which won't be determined for me, let alone for thousands, don't read the old odes, my son, but the train schedules, they are more accurate, but more accurate than what? They are not told anything and I am only told what I could hear just now—most recently a quarter of an hour ago, the next one I won't wait for anymore, on the radio and on TV and won't see on my tablet which has nothing on it or everything when it's turned on, they don't say anything to them, they do tell me, but it does nothing for me, it is too much, it's too much for me. It would be best, if I can make a suggestion, they could rise beyond their predestined, designated space, those people, then they would finally have room, which they would have made for themselves, they do not wish to be seated close to God, for they'd be dead then. Then all this would finally be finished, their determinacy would become something unique, which, however, will not be visible. Could it be seen, everyone would immediately clear the way for them, but there are too many, no one stands alone and no one stands out as unique, there simply are too many moving along here, and there as well and over there more than ever.

Those who were in the church back then, who requested sanctuary, they are nothing now, they weren't even a beginning. Now all the world's the stage and it expands into a space not predetermined as theirs, so that everyone can come in, so that their shadows can also come in, so that their dead can also come in, who've also become shadows, rushing over the living, they can't be considerate, they have to take care of their own determinacy, which we determine for them but they have to find out nonetheless, and then we have to tell them their destination, which does not coincide with the one they had in mind! Mind you, there is nothing we can do about that. You have to find it on Google Maps which your relatives sent you, who are already in Sweden, they do know their location, the GPS does it for them and from that location one can let oneself be sent via various routes, you can enter anything, what would you like, what means of transportation do you want to take, and this is what you want to get computed for your destination, so you always enter the latest positions, the device always knows where you are except if it is an outdated device, so then you have to enter it, then you must tell it, your mother in Syria doesn't know, but the device knows exactly where you are, and then those in Sweden, who are already in the best location will choose the best route, the fastest route, no traffic jams, no weekend traffic, the best routes are searched by those who are already in the best place and in safety. So it goes back and forth because you are moving back and forth. Everything gets determined elsewhere. So it ends. And then it continues again. Maybe you'll have to wait. You and all the others who are walking with you.

Not even your shadows point to where you should go, the shadows are made for you by the sun, but where you are is told to you by hand-painted town signs, no, they use templates for that, and then they enter the names of the towns for Sweden, and then the route kicks in on your device all the way from Sweden, showing you the way to get away from those who want to kick you out, sorry, that was cheap, but true. Cheap but true. Even you can afford it. Those masses of people won't even find out what has been denied to them. What's been denied, I've said it already, are those potty-cabins. They really did it to me!, they don't do me any harm, they don't do anything to anybody, you might wonder why I am so obsessed with toilets, because I sit on one so frequently, that's why, and the Hungarians deny them to people who would like to have control over their excretions, but they always miss the mark. The toilets are never where the people are to begin with and that is also where it ends. The way in is up front, and in the rear the people are coming out again and it's coming out of them, now please, where should it go? Now look, this place here is as good as over there. This escape, do you think it it's true that it happened out of a mix of humbleness and arrogance? Is this the reason why everything is denied to you? Is it here right now, the moment in history that belongs to you and that god, the Sun god, who is also a refugee from heaven, he knows such bitter destinies, but does not want to share them, he wants to drive alone in his fast vehicle, it is a two-seater, but he drives by himself, he is driving across the heavens, he knows his destiny and the human lot, those lots of humans, yes, that's why a lot of others want to get rid of them, people, when they become too many and it becomes too much for us.

And the ground where they are staying, that's the only one they got? Did I, by spreading garbage all around, garbage everywhere, crap, shoes, parkas, caps of the dead whom I conjure though I shouldn't, could I have ruined the ground?, but wasn't it already ruined before? By spreading the rotten, the misbegotten and exposing the dead and forgotten, you can easily call attention to yourself, you are somebody, after all you shot and uploaded this picture and now it is working for you. Make up your mind if you want to publish it, if not, it won't matter either, it has no consequences unlike this text which might be followed by a sequel. No. No worries! Zero consequences. Just this one I think, nothing will come to my mind. Too many people are coming here, I can't wrap my mind around them, I gladly welcome them to our land but what else can I do? I never even share my house, not even with friends. I don't share, I just let you have it. Haven't I said that somewhere already? With absolute certainty. But that only comes with death, he'll soon be coming to me, I am certain. Just you wait, you won't hear much more from me and then you'll have to respond yourself, not my way but yours. Take a look and say something about it, say what you are going to do, what are you doing tonight? Avoid hostile blood relatives? That's no problem. You simply say you don't have time today, period. But those people won't listen. Not your relatives. I mean those foreigners. Those people flooded the lands, they are here, they are there, they are foreign and they are in-between— no the in-between is the screen, that's where I watch them, on-screen and I scream—in print, watching out for oneself is better than meeting friends. The screen comes in-between, we need better screening, but screening won't help. There is no time. The child is dead. The other one has just been born. There is no time for lingering on the cold shore. The picture has been taken, it will be shown to the world, period. Only one, a little boy. Big deal.

No answer. Just now something is brought in again, no idea what. The current inflow will have to be stemmed, no, the Danube won't stop flowing, well okay, you can channel her, on the left and the right, it must be done or she would be the ocean, but you can't stop her course, she just keeps flowing along, no doubt about that. The soul, oh yes, it can swing wherever it wants to, we swing ourselves over this fence even though it was meant to be insurmountable, we use every hole, we can also crawl, we throw a blanket over

it so it won't tear into us, the fence, no the fence won't tear,
it'll rather slash us, who knows how long they'll still be there,
those natural loopholes. And today they are already gone,
and fourteen people have already been arrested and will be
locked up, soon there'll be more. What does Europe say?
Europe says nothing. What's there to say, we founded it but
sadly we have no longer control over this construct, someone has to execute judgement unto these crimes, but no one
does. The God of the Dead? Is there one? And if so, which
one? Anubis, the jackal that eats dead matter? Well everyone
knows that one. Take one that isn't that well known: Thoth?
Controls the weight of hearts and writes down the results?
What are you saying? He is the judge of crimes, I can't think
of his name, oh right, Thoth, I just said it, and who is he?,
but who judges the living? Supposedly, he does that too. And
anyway, how am I to talk to you, says this or that helpless
god, it doesn't matter. That hole in the fence might pop up
some other place, no that's another one, who knows
how long that one will last. We have to get through them.
The operation. The processing. The jurisdiction, but not for
the conditions, we mean the location, which more often
than not does not even fall under Germany's jurisdiction.
The national specifications, the national explications, the
national abominations. There are so many, they'll just have
to accept that they don't have the choice as to where they
want to seek shelter, because our helpfulness must not be
overextended, no, no that's true because it is written right
here otherwise I wouldn't know it. Something should be
imported again, which we've already exported, border controls, so that not everything we don't need can be imported,
which Mercedes doesn't need either, that star who classifies
people into usable and unusable. Points of departure, of
origin, need to be established, but those don't even know

themselves, where they are coming from. The border control will find out, everything must be accounted for. No mortal eye has ever seen so many fake Syrians in one place. It doesn't matter anyway, that woman here is lying for sure, yes, and that man over there is too, they all lie. They speak the wrong language. There are too many, we can't control them anymore. The place of refuge must be moved, it is no longer here, look for one yourself. That's what you thought, wasn't it, didn't you, when you set out on a ship, maybe because it wasn't a ship, not even a boat, just a dinghy made of inflatable rubber, one prick and it is gone. The smuggler jumps out in his swim trunks, no not out of them, he swims away and gone he is. It's not that bloodguilt drove you into banishment, oh yes, it was bloodguilt, whatever, what are you saying, oh, it wasn't yours?, doesn't matter either!, and we also carry a lot more bloody guilt, a heavy debt that cannot be paid off. By the city folk's decisive resolution something must be done, I won't bother writing down what that is, for in an hour those city folk's masters will have resolved something else again. Which woman rejects which man, who lost his child, who's losing his right now, who is having one right now, during a severe thunderstorm no less, the word severe goes with storm as the word heavy does with punishment. It's all one. Sometimes there are more. To me they have seemed more than all for quite a while. Like spectral appearances, they can't be compared either to anything else that appears. The people flee, they have been fleeced, that means they have no funds at all, doesn't matter, they'll get more gifts of fleece en route, no not the golden one, that came ashore in Greece, not to the shore where the dead are lying now, that is if they ever made it to there. I don't know. Yesterday it was Germany and Sweden, I don't know what it is today.

This city here, that country there, the graves they've been dwelling in so long, the crap they throw out, that corner where they shit, that foot on the ground. What ground? Was that yours? I'm sorry, then I will look for another ground for my fast rowing vehicle, let me through, I am its auxiliary motor, something must help them!, no, the ground is for myself, I no longer have a vehicle, though it certainly brought me here, but now I have to manage on my own. I was sent by the sea, and that was lucky. The tornado, thunder and lightning, the rain-heavy hurricane, the howling wrath with which we faced the salty waves only to be able to finally face you here, you whom we never wanted to face, all over, twenty- three, no, I just hear twenty-seven of us are dead, they dropped, they drowned, thus deceased, they ceased to count, we however, we seize every bed we can get, for the ocean certainly won't leave his for our sake. There are no dry diapers for the ocean. And we are now boarding this train despite your refusal, but you will get us out again, we can see it coming, right after we cross the border, if ever we will get that far. Our God shall be our Savior, but you don't like that one either, you don't like anything, we can see that already. So we call out the name of our God, we've brought the mobile phone, we call him, on your flowery ground where nothing will grow again, after we will have risen again, we are thinking of our forefathers, we are thinking about our foremothers. We step before the inhabitants of this land but we want to get to Germany or Sweden. That's probably not believable, or rather that is what we really want, but we don't believe we'll ever get there, we just hope. Whatever is believable, if anything at all, will be revealed tomorrow, when we'll know the new regulations and time will have torn up what's been said, then we will find out too. Then the sounds of our mobile phones will roar into our ears and we'll be able to understand the call, we interpret the flight of maps on the displays, always a new one, it depends, thus they fly past as the falcon chases the nightingale. Driven from our country's groves, our river's banks, we grovel for a new home, no wonder you can't hear it anymore. Today you still can but tomorrow it will be getting too much even for you. And we, we are beat as well. So you don't have to do it anymore, the beating. That's at least something we can relieve you of. Anything that goes beyond our immediate being here, we can relieve you of, because soon you will no longer be able to do it. The progression of our destinies is unstoppable, oh if only we could be there already, where our destinations are! By then, our destinations will have progressed further than us, you'll see, so will we, unfortunately. The destination will be where we won't have to go beyond our limits, where it will find itself and the notion of Germany corresponds to the destination Germany and the notion of Sweden to the destination Sweden. Our progression thereto is unstoppable, you can control as much as you like, it will always be limited to our natural life, you cannot control more than that. If we get torn away to death, you no longer have a say. You are too dense for that, yes and there's already another one of your dense fences. We'll climb over it or crawl through from below, and on we go beyond the barrier, it's behind us already, and the void ends or a new one begins. We shall see.

The usual as before. With a pinch of Freud. Well, that's all we needed!

EPILOGUE
My Coffees with Elfriede

Elfriede Jelinek leads an increasingly secluded life ever since she received the 2004 Nobel Prize in Literature, and no longer gives interviews in person. As her authorized translator I have had the opportunity of many visits and inspiring conversations at her homes in Vienna and Munich. In this context she agreed to the extensive conversation reproduced here for the first time. The informal tone reflects the nature of our relationship as collaborators and friends.

We met on three consecutive afternoons in the modest two-story house in Vienna-Hütteldorf on the outskirts of the Austrian capital. It is her family home where she continues to live after the death of her mother. It is important to note that Jelinek does not see any productions of her work due to an acute anxiety disorder and thus depends solely on reports from her friends. Spring and summer 2014 turned out to be an especially active period. Six weeks after *Charges* opened the quadrennial Theatre of the World Festival in Mannheim, Jelinek's *Faust/In and Out*, opened in Munich as part of the Residenz Theatre's Spring season. The repertoire was devoted to contem-porary explorations of and responses to Goethe's *Faust* (on which he worked throughout his professional life). The program included lavishly provocative productions of *Faust, Part I* and *Part II*, as well as variations on their themes by new playwrights. Jelinek's text is one of her so-called secondary plays. It is an addendum to Goethe's *Urfaust*, his early version of *Faust, Part I*. In her characteristic dramaturgy, topical concerns and canonical texts, motifs of Goethe's youthful tragedy of underage Margaret, seduced by the middle-aged scholar (based on the legends surrounding the medieval story of Dr. Faustus) and driven to infanticide and madness, provide the basis for her take on the monstrous case of Josef Fritzl that shocked the world when it came to light in 2008. Fritzl had lured his eighteen-year-old daughter into the basement of the family home, where he kept her locked up for twenty-four years and fathered seven children with her, one of which he allegedly burned when it died a few days after birth.

At the time of my visit Jelinek was greatly relieved that she had just finished her most recent and longest performance text: the 230 typescript pages of *The Silent Maiden* (*Das schweigende Mädchen*). Johan Simon, the artistic director of Munich's Kammerspiele, had already begun rehearsals for the play's premiere scheduled for the following fall 2015. The play is based on the long-running trial of Beate Zschäpe, in Munich. Zschäpe was one of the young leaders of a Neo Nazi cell called the National Socialist Underground (NSU), that had begun to organize in the eastern states of Germany after the fall of the Berlin wall and continues to attract skinheads and other disillusioned youth across the country. Suspected NSU members were routinely recruited as spies by the German equivalent of the FBI and local government agencies. During the trial it was revealed that government agents were aware of murders and assaults planned by rabidly racist skinheads groups in both eastern and western parts of Germany, but did not intervene. Pertinent files in these matters were quickly destroyed. The title of Jelinek's play refers to the defendant Beate Zschäpe, who so far has not said a word during the entire trial. For twelve years she and two friends, who had also been her lovers, Uwe Mundlos and Uwe Boehnhardt were on a murderous rampage against people with a migration background, killing at least ten, possibly more. After the police was closing in, the two young men were found shot dead in their charred camper. Police investigators reported that the gun in Mundlos's hand indicated a murder–suicide.

At the time of our conversations the trial was still proceeding without an end in sight. As a consequence the text of *The Silent Maiden* was very much on Jelinek's mind, while I was still deeply affected by the Munich opening of *Faust/In and Out*, which I had attended the evening before our first meeting. Consequently, references to both works kept slipping into our conversation which was, however, primarily focused on the text of *Charges*.

Gitta Honegger
May 2016

GREIFVOGEL: I AM A BIRD OF PREY

In Conversation with Elfriede Jelinek

GITTA HONEGGER. In your performance texts, you inter-
weave topical events with canonical texts, from the
Greek to the Bible to Nietzsche, Freud and Heidegger,
to name just a few. How do you find and construct your
themes and their cultural framework?

ELFRIEDE JELINEK. It was clear in the case of *Charges*. It had
to be *then* and it will annoy me for the rest of my life
that it couldn't happen right away. Because it was
planned to be performed right then and there. I wrote
it for a special occasion, for Nicolas's (Stemann's) project *Commune of Truth. Reality Machine* (*Kommune der
Wahrheit. Wirklichkeitsmaschine*) for the Vienna Festival
in May 2013. I did not ask what he wanted to do with
my text and it simply didn't fit in. The project was supposed to be an immediate response to current events
and Nicolas only worked with original soundtracks and
direct quotes, news and such things, and mine was a literary text and that didn't work. Looking back, I think
it still should have been done then with two or three
actors, just setting up somewhere, Nicolas would have
certainly participated in the reading, and I would have

probably read as well and that's how it should have happened. And then it was done in a church in Hamburg, which was already a half-religious act in a way, it was very beautiful, apparently and it had a ceremonial quality, but now it no longer has that subversion and topicality. Now it's just a play.

GH. But when I am reading it now—and translating it, I read it very intensively. It is absolutely urgent and topical.

EJ. Yes, now it just happened again, those unaccompanied children, five-year-old children, who travel alone by freight train to the US, since there is no specific law concerning children traveling alone, they can't be deported and there are graves all along the way. There are special DNA teams now, they take the DNA of the children—that would already be another play, the DNA plants—and create DNA data banks, so that when parents search for their missing children, they can be located. And just today, in the Mediterranean they pulled thirty dead people out of the water. They were all in one boat; all of them were dead. And that happens every day. Thousands, thousands, so the play is almost too polished, too beautiful—one can't really grasp such things, as I can't really grasp this NSU [National Socialist Union] terror and only now, after I finished writing the text am I reading a standard book about it, which presents a chronological breakdown of it all since the re-unification and I would not have been able to finish the play *The Silent Maiden* had I known it all before. Because realities are so extreme, complicated and complex I could not have captured them with my approach, which is always standardizing [*typisierend*], lumping together and does not explore an individual but, rather, shows a general political perspective. I could never have written it otherwise, I'd be totally meshugge.

GH. How do you respond when directors or producers approach you with an idea?

EJ. For *Charges*, Nicolas did not come to me with an idea, he just said, do you want to write something for the *Commune of Truth* and since I already was pretty certain that I wanted to write something about the refugees in Votiv Church and their move to the monastery, I thought, that works out well, what I want to write about is happening right now, that'll fit and I didn't ask him. What he really wanted was of course not anything literary, not a play, he probably thought I would put some newspaper clippings together. I don't really know what he had in mind.

GH. As you were contemplating to write about the refugees' predicament, before Nicolas contacted you, did you already think of the myth of Io, that her story can be merged with the refugees'?

EJ. But that happened independently of what he did with his *Commune of Truth*. I took his project simply as an inducement to write what I had in mind. Because I thought, that it was absolutely topical, so it would fit into Nicolas's project. But it did not.

GH. If Nicolas had not talked you into—

EJ. I would have waited longer. I would have taken more time. And then I did write it at an insane speed, two or three weeks. Some things require that kind of speed and the haste of the language. The text itself has a breathlessness [that suggests both the writing process and the situation of the "real" refugees]. Then there are ideas for texts, which were triggered by others. Usually I don't accept assignments. Usually I write what I want to write. Sometimes somebody says don't you want to write a play for us again, there is and that, could you imagine writing about it and then I say no. Now *Winterreise* [Winter Journey], I don't know where that came from. Ideas were often triggered by the Munich Kammerspiele, where *Winterreise* also premiered. But now I can't really imagine it could have come from there. Because I have been dealing with Schubert's *Winterreise* almost my entire life, accompanying the most different singers on the piano, sometimes I sang it myself, I practically know it by heart. *Rechnitz* was interesting, because the Kammerspiele and Jossi Wieler, the director, wanted something on Luis Bunuel's film *The Exterminating Angel*. I hadn't seen the film in ages, so I watched it again and it was clear to me what to do. David Litchfield's book about the Thyssen dynasty, *Art Macabre*, had been published, and before that I saw the documentary about the massacre at Rechnitz castle, *Totschweigen* [Wall of Silence].

GH. And there also are appropriations of Nietzsche's *Thus Spoke Zarathustra* and Euripides's *The Bacchae*. Were those then free associations?

EJ. Yes, they were. Sometimes, as in the case of *The Silent Maiden,* I consider quite specifically what additional material I could read, Agamben or different interpretations of the Bible. Those are now pure linguistic investigations of Aramaic, which I don't know (*laughs*). But it's so interesting, that Bible research has shifted completely to linguistic questions. There are all those disputed issues in the Old Testament; those are purely linguistic investigations. It's hardly a question of content anymore but, rather, miniscule shifts, whether the Angel was here or there and said this or that, or if angels really existed. I wouldn't have thought that in the end everything is a matter of language.

GH. It also is your primary focus. And the Bible, I noticed, is an increasingly prominent source in your performance texts.

EJ. Yes, it surprises me too. I mean, I am not religious at all, I absolutely don't believe in a God, but as bodies of speech those texts simply are—you can't kill them and I certainly don't want to kill them, because first of all, they are incredibly revolutionary, Jesus was a revolutionary, one can't just ignore that. Some of the disciples were too reactionary and too narrow-minded to understand that right away, or too cowardly, it was truly enormous, what Jesus spoke of, I do want to keep that for its revolutionary potential.

GH. And you don't really put religion down.

EJ. Well, let's say I preserve the greatness, for example of the "Sermon on the Mount," those are incredibly literary texts, nonetheless, greatness has to be cut, down, but without making it little. It remains, unlike Brecht: "The Big will not stay big / the little won't stay little . . . "[1] I preserve the big and I take it down as the big. So it is a certain reverence, not the one of God or religion, but of the greatness of the texts.

---

1 Eric Bentley, 'The Song of the Moldau', *Eric Bentley: Songs of Hanns Eisler* (New York: Folkway Records, 1964). Available at: https://-goo.gl/zH9ENO (last accessed on November 28, 2015). Original German lyrics was wriiten by Bertolt Brecht with music by Hanns Eisler for Brecht's play *Schweik in the Second World War* (1943).

GH. Did your mother raise you religiously or was Catholicism just an important aspect of Austrian culture?

EJ. I attended Catholic elementary school. Actually, I did grow up quite Catholic since earliest childhood. During vacations in Styria, there were our long walks from our house to the cathedral, the famous, huge Cistercian Minster, that's four kilometers one way and then back, even as a small child, I probably owe the last little bit of physical conditioning to [those walks]. Yes, Catholic traditions did have quite a formative impact on me. And of course, it is so much more mystical, as it is also in convent school, those quiet hallways with the nuns disappearing in their locked wing of the building. After all, I was only four years old when I entered convent school.

And my mother's mother, my grandmother tended toward religious mania. And my mother actually had visions—I sneaked that, partly hidden, into my plays—well, I think she really was crazy, angels really appeared to her and talked to her, so let's say, to some extent I grew up in a very mystical environment, which was counteracted by my scientific, Jewish father who was completely atheistic. He and his family did not believe in anything religious, they tore Catholicism apart, in addition, he was a Socialist, such a staunch socialist, like many Jews, that for the workers parade on May 1, I had to have red ribbons in my braids and then, on Corpus Christi Day my braids had to be tied with white ribbons for the procession. In the US they probably don't know all those traditions, Corpus Christi processions and such, in Boston they probably do, and in Chicago with their Irish and Polish population and the Italians—

GH. —and Mexicans, especially in the Southwest, where I live.

EJ. Yes, of course! Mexicans have a completely different Catholicism. They perceive death as marvelously colorful, while for us it is quite dark. Death. Even if you believe in eternal life, in seeing your loved ones again and on Judgment Day, when even our bodies will rise, I don't know what'll happen to those who let themselves be cremated (*laughs*)—they'll rise as clouds of ashes; repressed matter, the repressed ash clouds of Auschwitz, they'll be coming on Judgment Day.

GH. The image of the ovens haunts your texts, I am thinking of the production of *Faust/In and Out,* which I just saw, about Josef Fritzl, who burned one of the babies he fathered with his daughter. It was almost unbearable to watch Johan Simons's minimalist staging of the parallel monologues—the daughter's haunting mediations on what happened and the father, the self-assured *pater familias* as her un-God. It was a theatrical experience that literally took everyone's breath away.

EJ. Really!

GH. It was that powerful. *Charges* is equally overwhelming, differently, because the text has such tragic immediacy.

EJ. Yes, that one happened in one throw. There are such things, they are written in one throw. They are just tossed there, very quickly, since it was written for this specific occasion, within two weeks or so, it is like a chorus, an oratory.

GH. Your text of *Faust/In and Out* features two speakers. The feminized Ghost and the feminized Faust, based on motifs of Goethe's *Urfaust. Charges* has no designated speakers. It raises the question, as in many of your more or less choral texts, who are the "we."

EJ. That depends. It has to be discovered who the speakers are at any given moment. That's probably what makes analyzing my text interesting, determining who those "we" are. Sometimes it is I who speaks in the *pluralis majestatis*, sometimes it's an ironical "we", it's something the masses appropriate, when everyone actually says "I," sometimes it is an abstract "I," so there are many "we's." There is "Bravo, we did it again!" (*Na, wir sind wieder einmal toll gewesen*) That's the collective, mocking I, that thinks it can do anything. And then there is the "I" that accuses, the I that indicts. Of course that's quite tricky in *Charges*, because everybody asks who is that "we," since I presume to speak as if in their voices in a way they'd never speak. But this "we" is probably the interesting thing in all my writing. Sometimes it is a role I am presumptuous enough to take on by turning myself into one of those refugees, something I am not at all entitled to, I live comfortably in prosperity and peace, I practically throw myself at them.

GH. Nicolas struggled with that during his preparatory work.

EJ. He was very concerned about me, a white woman speaking for people of color. I suggested he should read Frantz Fanon, the North African intellectual, communist and psychiatrist. But a black person can speak differently about blacks than a white one. And I suggested, that the whites should put on white make up and the blacks black, that is, they should make themselves up as themselves, so to speak, not the blacks as white and the whites as black, they should reinforce themselves.

Moreover, strictly speaking, I am not talking about Africans. I refer to a specific incident, which involved mostly Afghani and Pakistani.[2]

GH. Interestingly, while I was working on *Rechnitz* and *The Merchant's Contracts*, it actually was postcolonial literary discourse that helped me understand your position as an activist, poststructuralist literary figure. The way you deconstruct and reconfigure the male canon, it's grammar, idioms and imagery, the dynamics of your relationship to the dominant language brings to mind Homi Bhabha's notion of certain writers as "comedians of culture."[3] The dominant culture sees itself reflected in the other, but still different, "distorted"—

---

2 The Hamburg Thalia Theatre prepared for the first production of *Charges* in the fall 2013, two years after Jelinek had written *Charges* in response to the specific situation in Vienna in 2011. In the meantime, the refugee crisis had escalated. By 2013, thousands of African migrants had tried to reach the Italian island of Lampedusa, many of them refugees from the civil war in Lybia. Hundreds of them drowned in shipwrecks in the treacherous waters surrounding the island. News about Lampedusa shook Europe almost on a daily basis. Hamburg had accepted about 300 of migrants from Lampedusa. The public's reactions were comparable to the situation in Vienna. In fall 2013, eighty of those migrants lived in the Lutheran Church in the district of St. Pauli. The urgent situation inspired the *"Urlesung"* [*ur*-reading] of *Charges* at the church prior to the production. Resident migrants performed with actors from the Hamburg Thalia Theatre under the direction of the theatre's artistic director Joachim Lux. Stemann, who then directed the subsequent world premiere continued to include local refugees during the production's international tours. In one scene, the actors put on make on stage, each in a different shade of random color.

3 See Homi Bhabha, "Articulating the Archaic: Cultural Difference and Colonial Nonsense," *The Location of Culture* (Oxon: Routledge, 2004), pp. 175–98; here p. 195.

EJ. Yes, and as a woman; in any case, as a woman one is colonized. One is doubly marginalized. On the one hand it is a burden one always has to carry: that a woman is not able to pull off a cultural creation, at least not one that counts, on the other hand it gives you—the woman—an anarchic freedom, of course, because it doesn't oblige you to anything, that's the point. And you are right with regard to the colonizing, especially in English, because everyone first learns English as a foreign language and there are so many pidgins and that is exactly what liberates the English language; well and American English is freer to begin with, British English is somewhat more fixed, but it too has this tradition of playing with language.

GH. And postcolonial writers confront the challenge, how do we speak this language now, the dominant language, can this be done without showing the rupture—

EJ. Yes, *discourse de maitrise*, the master's discourse, as the poststructuralists call it, language itself gets subverted by breaking it open or remaking languages for oneself.

GH. And this is what makes you especially provocative as a woman.

EJ. Yes, because it's not simply a matter of gendering, as is happening right now in this ridiculous debate about the Austrian national anthem [whether the line about being "the land of sons" should be changed to "the land of daughters and sons"], that's really dumb. The point is to subversively transform language, not just the use of "his/her" and things like that.

GH. It's also important to remember what you mentioned in one of our recent conversations, that you want to put your figures, or rather language itself on cothurns.

EJ. I enlarge my figures.

GH. Isn't this also due to your musical background? Those are not psychologically developed characters, but a composition of voices.

EJ. They are linguistic agitators [*Sprachkörper*] like agitators, *Rührkörper*[4] [literal translation, "language-bodies"; also "mechanical agitators"] which turn people into language [*die Versprachlichung von Personen*]. Basically, my characters are linguistic templates [*Sprachschablonen*]; that's of course exactly what I get criticized for—everything I say gets used against me. Everything I say about myself is used against me. It's like the Miranda warning.

GH. What makes it difficult for the uninitiated reader to follow your dramaturgy—at least while reading it—is to see the change in perspective, the "we" of the refugees and that of the local people.

EJ. Call and response as in Catholic antiphony.

GH. That brings us back to the astonishing religious resonances in your texts. There is a moment in *Charges* Nicolas brought out chillingly in his production. It is the line "Let the little children come to me." In your text

---

4 One of the wordplays that are not readily translatable. A crassly literal translation, "linguistic bodies like stirring bodies." Jelinek's email response to Honegger, with reference to an editor's query on the German term *Rührkörper* (March 20, 2016): "There are many different sorts . . . they are small things, little balls, which help in the process of liquefying something, eye drops for example [that's what rattles when you shake the bottle]. There are many forms, also in tech- nology." [Such as agitators in treatment plants, which Jelinek did not have in mind, though she might enjoy the connotation, albeit in a different context.]

the speakers represent the local community. I quote: "Let the children come to me, we swiftly revoke their being if they call for their mommy, we drown them and on top of each coffin we put a little teddy bear. Yes, we top it off with more! Five coffins, five teddies! That'll do. They probably did not have those before. They had no coffins to play with and no teddy bears . . . " Nicolas turned the whole passage into a song, with the eerie refrain "And on top of each coffin we put a little teddy bear." During the very sweet mellow song that was sung by the performers along with projections of rows of small coffins, with a teddy bear placed on each one.

EJ. Yes, the teddy bear has become a common thread through several texts, maybe because they sit in that chair with a gleeful grin (*points to the transparent swing chair in her living room. [See image on the facing page.]*) They also found a teddy in the charred camper of one of those NSU guys, it was half burned, the teddy, they blew up the camper, the two NSU killers. An artist painted the whole scene, she also painted the teddy with those burned legs. Yes, the Teddy seems to pursue me.

GH. The "Teddy" turned out to be a minor translation problem. Your first reference to it is the Austrian diminutive term for *Bär* / bear: "*Bärli*" specifically for stuffed toy bears.

EJ. Yes, that would interest me—how did you translate "*Bärli*," the French say only "*un ours*".

GH. What came to my mind as an equivalent to the feel of "*Bärli*" was the sound of Pooh Bear. But Nicolas clearly had teddies on the coffins, which I did not know when I worked on the surtitles for the German premiere. And the image was so chilling in performance that I did not pay attention to the titles. Afterwards I was torn, since I really love that "Pooh" sound.

EJ. It has to be a bit childlike—as I wrote in the play, in their real lives those children never had a toy and when they are lying in the coffins, they get a toy bear put on them. It is eerie.

And then here are these two NSU murderers who killed ten people, maybe even more, which haven't been linked to them and there is this teddy bear one of them probably had as a child and he took it with him, that's even eerier. There you have the teddies on the coffins completely depersonalized—they were not the children's, after all, they were just put on the coffins to indicate that children were inside them, which was obvious anyway from the smaller size of the coffins, but that two Nazi killers also took a *Bärli* with them, that's really eerie—and the role of bears in my dramatic work . . . (*laughs*)

GH. And in your life, you have them right here!

EJ. And those aren't the only stuffed animals I have. Downstairs I have 200 monkeys, they belong to a friend of mine, but they occupy everything here—every window, everything, filled with monkeys, the hammock, the chairs, everything.

GH. Well, for the publication of *Charges* I kept the teddy, since that is the common image of the toy.

God takes on several meanings in *Charges*. Frank Stronach, the real person behind the unnamed figure of the Austrian Canadian millionaire, entrepreneur of automobile spare parts, and recently maverick candidate for the Austrian parliament—represents a sort of God figure. That was a bit confusing for my editor.

EJ. Well, that's the "we" talking—that's this one God, the "we" also speak of their God and that there also is a Jesus in Islam, there he is just a prophet that's why I realized I can't say "Christ," I must say Jesus, the Christ has been cut in Islam, and that's become Jesus, the prophet, he is not a savior, he is not God, only a prophet. God is Allah. Mohammed is also a prophet. And there are also angels in Islam, that's what I was told, I don't know much about Islam, only that what [Christianity and Islam] have in common.

GH. We have been talking about Catholicism in your work. That gets us to Heidegger, who keeps returning in your texts, who still is quite important in Catholic discourse.

EJ. Well, he studied religion, he was in a Catholic seminary. But he didn't last there very long. I think it was boarding school rather than religion he couldn't take.

GH. He is one of the main inspirations for your language based cultural critiques. Since your play *Totenauberg* [*Death/Valley/Mountain*],[5] which features Heidegger and Hannah Arendt, he haunts all your texts. I got to know him primarily through you.

EJ. Of course, I can't say either that I really know him. But I use him selectively, so to speak. In *Totenauberg* [Heidegger] is the "leading text", so to speak as is Goethe in *Faust/In and Out* and Aeschylus in *Charges*. Actually I started around the time of *Totenauberg*,

---

5 *Totenauberg* is a play based on Todtnauberg, a village in the Black Forest, where Heidegger lived. See also "Death/Valley/Mountain," *Drama Contemporary Germany* (Gitta Honegger trans. and Carl Weber ed.) (Baltimore, MD: Johns Hopkins University Press, 1996), pp. 217–63.

because the German reunification has, of course Germanness [*das Deutsche*] as its subject, which I dealt with in my earlier play *wolken.heim* (cloud.[cuckoo]-home).[6] There, I started with just using quotes, in *Totenauberg* it was Heidegger, the philosopher, the philosopher of *being* and Hannah Arendt, who basically had already lost out, but who already said one shouldn't take existential philosophy too seriously, one should also be able to laugh about it, this gives you a special sovereignty over it. With Arendt it is the story of emigration and the outsiderness of Jews, who must always wander—

GH. From then on Heidegger haunts all your texts.

EJ. But most of the time I make an ass of him.

GH. And Paul Celan, he also wanders through your work.

EJ. Not recently. But when he did, his presence suggested itself: all those stateless people, who persist against this self-assured notion of homeland (*Heimat*). That is, the thinker of *being*, in *Totenauberg,* who walks with his backpack through the Black Forest and Paul Celan, the Jew, who desperately tries to get a word of regret out of Heidegger, an admission of his entanglement with the Nazis, but he never got it, no one ever got it. Heidegger, who was a proponent of pure thought, who, after all, was very precise, in his inaugural address for example, would not let himself be pinned down to such a thing. Now in his *Black Notebooks*, which I didn't see, there apparently are more concrete passages, which I probably

---

6 *Wolken.heim*, literally, "cloud.home." In German the saying "you live in the clouds" means "you are crazy."

wouldn't have used anyway. But there you have a philosopher who thinks he can lead the *Führer*, the leader, and that an Adolf Hitler and his gang were just waiting for a thinker, that's so grotesque, gushing about his beautiful hands and blue eyes—but *Ungeist* cannot be led by *Geist*.[7] Nevertheless, I still see that Heidegger is a great thinker, I mean, I am not one, who kicks him down, down from the Black Forest. (*Laughs.*) It's making an ass of him with a certain awe.

GH. Did you learn from his method, did it influence you?

EJ. Well, if it did, I made fun of it. But of course, that's easy. Countless school classes made an ass of Heidegger. That's not too difficult once you get going.

GH. What is it that fascinates you about him?

EJ. The thinking. Pure thinking though that's, of course, mathematics—the purest thinking, and because it is not accessible to me.

GH. But through your musical training you do have a strong connection to mathematics.

EJ. Well, not really. Music is a mathematical system, but the mathematical part of composing was always very difficult for me. You have to count and calculate all the time, how long is this now, is this now a quarter note, even if you work without measure lines or with different measures, you always have to calculate, how does it add up, if it's twice as long, what does it have to be then, a sixteenth or a thirty-second. A professional composer has

---

7 An untranslatable term in this context because the meaning of the German "Geist" is "mind and soul," and the prefix "un-" denotes its antonym.

that down. Olga got it down.[8] She no longer needs to count, but she has a mathematical mind. She once told me she has a counting compulsion, she always has to count everything and she can only have a telephone number that consists of uneven numbers. So, I am obsessed with language and with the mutations one can derive from it. Olga with numbers.

I am too impatient for that, as I am also too impatient to cook. Composing, you never can write down your ideas directly. There is always a complicated process of transposition until you can put it all together. Painting is the most direct process. You can put everything that comes to your mind directly on the canvas— one to one, simultaneously, writing is almost as fast and I think I am writing out of impatience. I can type very quickly because of my playing the piano and the organ, I actually type at the speed of my thinking, that is, I think somewhat slowly and I type very fast, (*laughs*) so it works out, I can put down what I think in real time, so to speak. But then it is many times. I mean, I don't leave it at that, but I don't tinker with it, I do it all over, again and again, and always very fast. That is, like someone who draws a sketch and then, by shading the things from the outside peels them out, so to speak.

GH. Whereas Peter Handke, your fellow Austrian—I think the two of you are such perfect opposites—

---

8 Olga Neuwirth, award-winning Austrian composer, collaborated with Jelinek for several projects, such as the libretti for *Bählamm's Fest* (*Baa-lamb's Holiday*, premiered in 1999) based on the play by the Surrealist artist and writer Leonora Carrington, and *Lost Highway* (2003) based on the film by David Lynch and Barry Gifford's novel of the same name.

EJ. Handke writes everything by hand, in beautiful hand-writing and he actually draws little sketches, while I write nothing by hand—

GH. He says somewhere that sometimes if he succeeds writing one sentence that's just the right one, it is a good day.

EJ. Hmm—but the pieces he writes, the way he writes them by hand, actually look as if they'd flow, you don't notice any hesitation or any starting anew, it all flows so smoothly. Perhaps they are already copies, I don't know. But he writes everything by hand, which I really admire, because I couldn't do that.

GH. You two—

EJ. Yes, we are antipodes.

GH. I find the comparison between the two of you, because of your completely opposite but equally indefatigable forging of a language, the German language, more specifically the Austrian German language after the Holocaust much more interesting than the comparison between you and Thomas Bernhard.

EJ. Seeing Austria critically connects Bernhard and me, but others do that too.

GH. The three of you are Austria's unholy trinity.

EJ. Yes, but I don't really belong there. I am the outsider, most definitely, among the three of us; [Handke and Bernhard] are perfectly sure of themselves and it's this self-assurance with which Bernhard writes, always in a spoken language, which I only use in my plays. With Bernhard you have the feeling it's written at a crazy speed as if he first dictated it and then wrote it down. It's always spoken.

GH. He loved to talk—

EJ. Oh yes, he could talk ten to twelve hours non-stop, people would beg him to finally stop—I know that, I know some of his friends—and Bernhard would say, "Well, then I'll top it off with the thirteenth hour." (*Laughs.*) The others were all already lying on the floor. I am not like that at all. I am the silent woman.

GH. But the three of you have written the Austria of the twentieth century.

EJ. Still, this dominant discourse of men is something a woman cannot do. She has to somehow sidle through subversively or find other ways . . . They will add my name now, probably because I got the Nobel Prize. Otherwise, they wouldn't mention me in the same breath with Handke and Bernhard. I am absolutely sure. If I am sure of anything, this is it. A woman does not represent when she is talking, while a man does represent. It is speaking-to-all, while a woman, even if she speaks to others, probably always speaks to herself, into herself. And probably this "we" [that I tend to use], this "we" is always a camouflage for what one cannot say, because a woman doesn't have that "I," she has to construct herself.

GH. And a man?

EJ. They all stand behind him, the [male] academics; he stands in front and the others are behind him—a wall.

GH. Many people who know your work assume that you have a special connection to Derrida.

EJ. No, no, I read very little by him. But it is not my job to interpret, others can do that.

GH. I see your connection to Derrida via Heidegger.

EJ. Derrida is also a stranger, a foreigner. Jewish, oriental, French, African—

GH. —who then lives in Paris.

EJ. I have to say, I don't understand [his work]. It is all very difficult, very dark.

GH. Hmm, I still think you come together through Heidegger.

EJ. A lot comes together through Heidegger, Sartre, who even learned German to be able to read *Being and Time*, Simone de Beauvoir too, and Arendt. It's interesting that the women arrived at a rather political way of philosophizing—Beauvoir, through her femi- nism, *The Other Sex*; and Arendt with her political thinking about totalitarianism. While abstraction, pure thinking, remained with the men. Roland Barthes in his *Mythologies* describes this with very specific examples, such as the famous American photo exhibition "The Family of Man."[9] It's been quite some time since I read the *Mythologies*. But I did use Barthes's *Michelet* in my most recent text [*The Silent Maiden*], where he delineates how the historian Michelet feminizes history, how he biologizes it, how he compares history with old aunts, with sexless old aunts or with menstruating women; it's pretty unusual, after all, that a historian takes the

---

9 "The Family of Man" was curated by Edward Steichen in 1955 at the New York Museum of Modern Art. The photographs included in the exhibition focussed on the people and cultures around the world as an expression of humanism in the decade following World War II. In *Mythologies* (1956), Barthes criticized the exhibition as being an example of his concept of myth—the dramatization of an ideological message.

human body as a paradigm for historical processes. So, while writing the play, *The Silent Maiden*, I couldn't resist taking something from there (*laughs*).

GH. How do you use your sources?

EJ. It works like that: I have the book in front of me and I thumb through it, and then it is a sort of lunging for something that will be useful for the text, that'll move the text forward, one bears down like a bird of prey, one claws oneself in like a sea eagle, who catches his fish, in flight so to speak, its claws barely touching the water and then flies right up, or like the buzzard catches the mouse. So then I am—and that's a metaphor, which really fits me—a bird of prey that hacks out the stuff.

GH. The German term "Greifvogel"—a bird that uses its claws to catch and kill—illustrates the action much more accurately.

EJ. It really works like that, I hack my fish out of the water, as it were, and this could be a different fish in a different spot.

GH. That reminds me of Peter Brook who once said in one of his workshop demonstrations, he doesn't "invent" things, rather, he is a vulture who picks them up from everywhere.

EJ. Interesting that he also compares his work to that of a bird of prey. Though, the vulture isn't really a bird of prey. A vulture hacks his stuff out of a carcass, while I, in flight, so to speak, grab the living thing, the living, bleeding prey out of the water or the mouse, like the buzzard, out of the ground.

GH. Makes sense, as a director he works differently.

EJ. As a director he works on a text, so actually on dead matter, as a vulture, while I have to still create something.

But what's really important to me is that I am not an authority of secondary texts. I can't say I know Nietzsche so well that I know exactly what to look up, my knowledge is not concrete, it's rather a kind of *sample*, like the cloud, which is a storage space, from where you take things out later. Maybe my brain is such a cloud, where I search around out of a vague inkling and then I might find something completely different and I immediately know—that's it. At any rate, what I am after is language per se. Of course [my texts] are not collages; it's always only just one quote, which I frequently alter as well. So it's not exactly as in Heidegger, or only rarely, but rather like a marker on the way one is taking, and then one ties Ariadne's thread around it and continues with the thread, knowing one can return if necessary, in case one loses the way.

GH. Those are beautiful images.

EJ. Images—it's all I have, because I cannot think.

GH. Well, I am not going to write that . . . (*both laugh*)

EJ. There you go, I am telling you a profound truth and then you don't want to use it.

GH. How do you arrive at the sources you use? In *Charges* you weave Aeschylus's play about the fifty Danaid virgins fleeing from forced marriages and the myth of Io— who was turned into a shiny white cow by her lover Zeus to protect her from his jealous wife Hera, who in turn has her guarded by hundred-eyed Argos who in turn is killed on Hera's command, who then has Io chased by a gadfly from Europe to Asia.

EJ. I really can't say. Of course, I am thinking about what I could use to provide the rhythm for the text, so to speak.

GH. And that's already in your head or are you then reading a lot?

EJ. Well, I've got to have it in my head, I couldn't start reading all Greek plays.

GH. Does that go back to your high school education?

EJ. No, we did not have ancient Greek and we hardly dealt with Greek tragedies, Greek drama in school.

GH. So, then, how do you get to these sources. You just have them in your head?

EJ. No, otherwise I would not be a writer, I would be a theorist. I don't really have an academic education, I am an autodidact, I did study, but I did not finish— *Theaterwissenschaft* [Theater History/Theater Studies] —and you know what you learn there (*both laugh*). At least here, I am sure it's different where you are—

GH. No comment. —But you do read a lot, I assume.

EJ. I read a lot of mysteries.

GH. I know. But where—

EJ. Well, of course, once I decided to write *Totenauberg*, I read Arendt and Heidegger, but I read them from a different perspective than a philosopher who is trained to make completely different connections. I read them as literature and Heidegger himself was literary minded, he has written a lot about poetic language and he also penned awful poems, like Hegel (*laughs*). When philosophers produced poetry, it was terrible poetry. Yes, it's interesting to see who becomes a thinker and who processes all this in a poetic language.

GH. As translator, I have to do my homework. Because of you, I read a lot more of Heidegger, also in English.

EJ. But you really don't have to use the existing Heidegger translations. Or you can change the translations, after all, I change Heidegger too.

GH. Yes, but you come up with such terrific terms—

EJ. (*laughs*). But you do too. You've got them.

GH. So then, how do you finally decide on your "secondary" material?

EJ. I really can't answer that. Because it happens in a kind of in-between-zone of thinking, trying to grasp it with logical thinking would not work. When I send one of my texts to Bärbel Lücke for example, most recently it was The *Silent Maiden*, she has a thousand ideas and insights and associations; that's different, yes, because she has a more profound education than I and then, in the case of the NSU, she uses René Girard for her interpretation.[10] I have also used him before, for *Rechnitz*, but he would have been wrong for *The Silent Maiden*, because I made it an allegory and that would have been a doubling, I would say once again what's said in the play, so then, it has to be something that works against the text, which I can sink my teeth in. But those things occur in an in-between zone.

GH. Sometimes that happens with translating.

EJ. Sure, you also work with associations.

GH. Yes, those are fun and you encourage me to go way over the top with them and I do, in the first draft. But

---

10 Barbel Lücke is a German author and literary critic. She has written extensively about Jelinek's linguistic deconstructions.

in the next drafts of texts such as *Rechnitz* and *Charges* and your great novel *The Children of the Dead,* which are culturally so specific and linguistically so precise—you don't ever cheat, no matter how far out you drive your associations—I am eventually taken back to the text by your rhythm and logic and syntax, almost automatically, albeit via some detours.

EJ. Yes, you can trigger such linguistic associations as you work with them in English, you can trigger them and once that happens, they keep coming, also in English.

GH. But the other language also can take you in a completely different direction.

EJ. Sure, but English has a tradition of punning, of silly word games, while in the German theater culture I get constantly beaten over the head by the critics for mine. But I think using language as such to tell the truth, even against its will, is a literary tradition. If it's granted to Arno Schmidt, to James Joyce—they can grant it to me too. It is an acknowledged [literary tool] even in German-language cultures as in the case of Arno Schmidt and his punning was much more outrageous than mine.

GH. In *Charges* there is a term, which of course plays a big part: *Einbürgerung*, which translates idiomatically into naturalization—

EJ. Yeah and that's absurd, because naturalization—it's also used in German, "he is a naturalized German"—but that's the opposite of *Ein-bürgerung*, which is an over-acculturation, to squeeze someone into a nation, while the other is a natural condition.

GH. Yes, but when you take American culture at large, there is nothing "natural," everything has to be artificially "improved," your skin, your hair, your breasts, your eyelids so that it looks "natural." In Arizona, where I live, you can get a facelift at any shopping mall.

EJ. NOOH!

GH. Food is processed to make it taste better than natural.

EJ. You are ahead of us there.

GH. Now you push the term *Einbürgerung* further and further. You also would have pushed "naturalization" way over the top, had you used that term. But you are not using it, so *Einbürgerung* pops up in different contexts with different meanings, based on the prefix *ein-*, which connotes both the number one and the action of infusing something into something else and even "preserving" as in preserving fruit (*einmachen*). So crassly literal, "*Ein–bürgerung*" translates into "infusing citizenship." Now citizenship needs a verb to suggest the act of obtaining it, which would break your rhythm. It's not a very flexible term, at best "ship" could be connected to the "boat" of the refugees. But they are nowhere near their respective places in your text where I could spin a chain of wordplays which will take me back to the point you are ultimately making. And those points are astutely targeted.

EJ. Well, you are also such a processed citizen (*laughs*). Now you are finally naturalized, away from Vienna, stuffed into your nature—the true one!

GH. Hmm, I have to think about that. We were on the subject of untranslatable terms. We talked about Celan before. Now, the correspondence between Heidegger and Celan has just been published and was discussed in the media this week. There is the word *Andenken*, which you love too. It usually connotes memory, it also means souvenir, but that doesn't play into what I am getting at. In the case of Celan and Heidegger the issue of course is the different meaning of memory for the Jewish poet and for the philosopher as an early, [at least publicly] unrepenting admirer of Hitler. Now Heidegger teases out the verb in the noun *An-denken*, which suggests the mental process of approaching a subject, a "thinking toward." You also introduce the term in that sense as a starting point for further transformations of meanings.

EJ. Yes, thinking-toward, sure, some things will work in translation, some just won't, then you just have to make up for it in some other place, where the English term may trigger a wordplay, but not its German equivalent.

GH. Well, yes, it seems quite logical talking about it, but in actuality, once you start playing, the word stays in the game, so to speak, and for a long period of time. And each time with a different, context-depending connotation. So what do I do then, in case I ignored it before? The sentences won't make any sense, because the meaning emerges strictly out of the chain of mutating words.

EJ. Hmm. When you take language by its word and then "twist it around in the mouth," as we say here, that is when it starts getting interesting.

GH. That is how the picture emerges.

EJ. First the word, that's already different than the figurative meaning and then turning it all around.

GH. And even if I manage to find only one equivalent pun in translation, it just sits there, for no obvious reason, let alone necessity, but it continues—

EJ. No, it's not simply about one wordplay. It always serves some message, whatever it may be.

GH. And your playing with certain terms, idioms, quotations weaves through the entire text, sometimes getting entangled in utter nonsense, which turns out to actually be the point of your take on a given situation and the "true picture" emerges only once the tapestry is completed. And your linguistic strategies are so precise, so tightly intertwined—the translator has to pay the closest attention not to drop a stitch.

EJ. That's because of my training in music; my treatment of language is compositional. As we discussed earlier, I have studied composition. I can sense when something isn't right, rhythmically. Sometimes I can't say why, but I know there's a snag, it just isn't working, I notice right away, that's something that's been drilled into me since earliest childhood, I have learned that from scratch. Basically, it is a compositional process, I often said that, but I haven't talked about it in ages.

GH. That's how it works for me in translation as well. A sentence may be grammatically correct, but something's still wrong about it. The Dutch director Johan Simons, who is now rehearsing *The Silent Maiden* at the Munich Kammerspiele, who has staged several of your plays, said that he approaches your texts through music, through the body.

EJ. That's because he doesn't know German very well, there must be another level where he understands me, maybe as I understand Derrida or Heidegger on another level of cognition.

GH. It's somewhat ironical that Derrida died the year you received the Nobel Prize.

EJ. Yes, it's crazy. They say he had hoped to get it.

GH. Oh yes.

EJ. I hope it wasn't disappointment (*laughs*) he died from because I got it. That would be terrible. But it really is a little spooky.

GH. Considering his way of writing, I think he'd have wanted nothing more than transforming his thinking into a *Dichtung*, a poetic work, a work of literature.

EJ. I often hear about the profoundest thinkers—whom I can't follow at all, not even their simplest sentences—that they actually just wanted to be artists. Their great ideal—but for that you really don't have to know anything.

GH. Well—

EJ. Writing functions on a different cognitive level. You have to leave yourself behind yourself, even if you are talking about yourself and throw yourself into something else, which is the music of language. And since I am able to concentrate extremely well and have this compulsion to associate, this obsessive twisting and turning of language to tap it for another meaning, that goes so far that I sometimes read a completely different word from what's written, and then I see it is different, it just sounds similar.

GH. You have a moment like that in *Charges*, when the refugees try to read the brochure and instead of "unprejudiced," they first read "unperjured."

EJ. Yes, yes, that brochure was a real treasure trove, of course.

GH. It really exists?

EJ. It sure does. You couldn't even make that up! I got it
from the web.[11] That's what people receive who apply
for citizenship, meaning refugees who have no status.
They have to read this, apparently it's been written by a
lawyer, a law professor, it's totally insane. Now that
opens all connections to free-associating.

GH. That brings me to a choice of wordplay I want to double check with you. The speakers are the refugees, imitating the mindset and the voices of the local people,
who think that asylum seekers need to be reined in
[*eingezäumt*]—in German, the term relates to horses,
which takes you to fenced in [*eingezäunt*] by just changing one letter from *m* to *n*. So you play with "*einzäu-
men*" that suggests reins and "*einzäunen*" [to fence in]
which leads you to refugees must be tamed "*gezähmt*"
like savages.

I start with "to be barred from" which gets me to
bars as a misunderstanding, but I lose the taming "like
savages." So, since you weave in allusions to Catholicism
and Islam [the latter more or less veiled—pun not
intended here] I can sneak in a [silly] allusion to the
religious prohibition of drinking. You say: *Menschen
wie wir gehören eingezäumt, nein, eingezäunt, Entschul-
digung, gezähmt gehören wir Wilden, damit wir Sie nicht
überschwemmen . . .* [Folks like us must be barred, put
in bars, no, behind them (we don't drink), fenced in like
savages, so that we won't flood you, no, no, that must
not be . . .]

---

11 *Zusammenleben in Österreich* [Coexistence in Austria], the
brochure published by the Integration Centre, Interior Ministry of
Austria in 2013–14. Available at: http://goo.gl/gGP7al (last accessed
on April 26, 2016).

It seems a small matter, but still, I am moving far away from your images here, so I thought, I should put my additions in parentheses—in this case "we don't drink"—so it is clear that they are not in your text.

EJ. You don't have to use parentheses. Those are your creative contribution, your linguistically creative contributions. And sometimes it takes you to a completely different place simply because it is already embedded in the text. Translating really is a fascinating process. *Über-setzen*—crossing by boat.

GH. The refugees . . . Wow . . . There are other kinds of insertions into *Charges* I want to run by you. You refer to well-known people without mentioning their names. For example the Russian soprano—I love the resonance of Tony here,[12] but of course, you are talking of Anna Netrebko. You also talk about "the thinker," who is Heidegger. I felt I needed to give the reader–audience some cue. I thought that people often don't recall names instantly, which lends itself to the oldest shtick routines of trying to remember, so Netrebko took me to neb— nebbish.

EJ. Exactly, that's wonderful. But she certainly is also known in the US.

GH. Yes, but you never mention her name, or Heidegger's.

EJ. Of course I am quite aware that I am a provincial author. Since I do not travel, I claw myself into what happens here. Yes, Heidegger "Why do I stay in the provinces?" that's also by Heidegger—why didn't he accept the call to Berlin, why did he stay in Freiburg, so there is a

---

12 Refers to Tony Soprano, the protagonist of the internationally popular TV series *The Sopranos* (1999–2007).

certain kinship here. Well, and then there was Hannah Arendt, when she came back. He would have wanted to seamlessly resume their relationship. So now she was the American Jewish woman, so to speak, and what is the Jews' special expertise? Money. And immediately he gave her the task of auctioning his *Being and Time*, so that he can get money. That was, that is, I mean that is an anti-Semitism that was so deeply rooted in the Germans that they weren't even conscious of it. But since I come from a Jewish family, I was very much made aware of it since earliest childhood.

GH. Provincial, especially for our generation in the wake of the Nazi's "blood and soil" glorification, has a very negative association—"country bumpkin" versus "the urbane".

EJ. Yes, that's exactly what happened to me. When I got the award, everyone said, of course, "she calls herself provincial." What I never meant as a negative, but used in order to explain my horizon, was used against me to brand me as a "provincial cow," though I have always lived in Vienna, and Vienna is a cosmopolitan city, a small one, relatively, but one of the cultural capitals. So they can't say I come from the provinces. Maybe they think I am from Styria, because I was born there, but that was just the family's country place and my parents happened to be there when I was born.

GH. I am very interested in the perception of "provincial" in postcolonialist discourse. The Indian historian Dipesh Chakrabarty's influential book *Provincializing Europe* was very important to my understanding of the notion of "where we come from."

EJ. I would be very interested in that.

GH. It s not about "provincialism" in the sense we are talking about here, but rather about the postcolonial world's continued generalizing perception of Europe as one cultural–hegemonic power. Instead it should also be seen as broken down into regions, provinces. Chakrabarty then discusses India's history from a Heideggerian and Marxian perspective as a precarious balance between place, origin, tradition on the one hand and contemporary social challenges on the other. It seems to me that this dialectic also defines the "provincialism" of your literary themes.

EJ. I think, one either penetrates a very small space very deeply or remains on the surface and enters big spaces.

GH. But isn't it precisely that depth that makes it universal?

EJ. Yes, but the universal is not the place. Because in my novels, for example—my plays, at least in that sense are abstract—the province is really present, Styria, where I actually spent all vacations, the Styrian woods, all that was the uncanny to me. *The Children of the Dead* take place in Styria. [Austria's] history culminates in the provinces. And that goes back to some extent to early childhood experiences. Because I have come to Styria since I was a baby. To condense it, literary speaking [*um es zu verdichten*] it has to be brought home. That's what's so un*heim*lich [uncanny] about *Heim*at. The word *Heim*—"home," features in both.

GH. Now we have entered Freudian territory. I usually try to avoid Freud when I am talking about your work, especially to you, so you won't think, 'now she uses the most obvious cliché,' I mean, with regard to your staging of familial relationships.

EJ. Well, I did read Freud. He was of course a magnificent writer. And I quoted him in several plays, again and again, where he fits in—or doesn't fit in, sometimes I consciously denied myself the opportunity—because it was too obvious, as I [denied][13] myself René Girard in the NSU play.

—Aha, there we have it—*vergreifen-verkneifen* and *vergreifen*. A typical slip of tongue, which could happen to anyone, but it's absolutely typical for me.

GH. I really had to laugh about the term "*verkniffen*." It sounds so funny hearing it with an "Americanized ear" so to speak, and I haven't heard this word since my childhood.

EJ. Yes, those are childhood words, the Austrian language we speak, you at any rate, you conserved it like in a time capsule, while I continued to speak it. But young people don't understand it, because language gets depleted. That beautiful old Viennese my father spoke, and those idioms! "Strain yourself through the sewer cover," (*sich im Kanaldeckel passieren*) things like that. He was half Jewish and therefore able to survive the holocaust in Vienna as a forced laborer of sorts, a chemist at Siemens, during the Nazi time, when all the new bosses were German, so everyone had to sing "We are sailing against England—ahoy!" and instead of "ahoy" my father always used to sing "*amoy*," Viennese dialect for *einmal*, some time, whenever, meaning never, as in

---

13 Here Jelinek intended to say, "denied," a repetition of the previously used, somewhat quirky German term for "denying oneself something" [*sich etwas verkneifen*]. Instead she says "*vergreifen*" which usually connotes a sexual assault.

"[Elfriede], you are going to America!"—"Yeah, when-ever." *Ahoy–Amoy*. Exactly the opposite. Don't you know it?

GH. I had to hear you say it a few times until I heard the subtext.

EJ. Exactly. And that's what he sang out loud. In his precarious position, it was a pretty subversive act. I would surely not have dared to do that. And that language— that's truly absurd—that language can say "some time", when it means "never."

GH. You do that all the time.

EJ. Yes, exactly. Maybe I've really got it since early childhood, from my father and my aunts, his two sisters, who always praised me for my little language jokes, maybe that's what triggered it in me. "Ahoy-amoy" that's genius, really!

GH. Yes, and you keep repeating it and I am desperate! "*Macht nichts*," for example. means, depending on the tone of voice, "it doesn't matter" or "don't do anything." And there are a few other such seemingly innocuous idioms. So, it all goes back to your family's dinner conversations!

EJ. Yes, yes. And the praise. When children can show off and everybody laughs about the funny things they say, they'll get more and more into it, because every child will try to go even further, if she gets rewarded or admired for it, that's normal. "Ego gratification" an old school friend of mine told me; she is a psycho-analyst in the Californian prison system.

GH. So, there are the Freudian slips, the father's survivor's humor and Heidegger's digging up of word roots—

EJ. Oh yes—"*Das Nichts nichtet*," that's a play on words.

GH. Sure! "The Nothing noths," as I read in one of the Heidegger translations. If I used that in any of your texts, it would just be a bad translation.

EJ. Yeah, but in context it will become clear that it is not, because if it were, everything would be badly translated, but in context you can see how it develops and where it comes from and how in the end it all makes sense.

GH. And then there is the reference to the nameless "thinker" in *Charges* who probably is easier to recognize in the original German, than in translation. So I tried to sneak in a couple of cues, which I ran by you via email: Heidegg-whatever, Heidegghead, Heideggman.

EJ. Yes, those are the huge questions of our times! (*Laughs.*)

GH. Well, that's the problem—when do I get too cute, too silly, too "funny"?

EJ. Okay, you can't ever be funny enough!

GH. Okay—

EJ. Don't be shy!

GH. That's a really important point.

EJ. No, don't ever hold back, that is the first commandment. I tell all my directors—by now most of them don't have to be told anymore—it must be comical, that's what's most important. So, if you have two solutions, you always must take the comical one.

Even if it's perhaps not as good as the other one, but it must be used—it's a stylistic tool, it's not satire, it's a tool of mockery: Language that grins about itself, so, actually, it is a bitter, mocking laugh.

GH. But at other times you can be quite endearingly funny. For example, when you insert yourself in the text, such as in connection with a quote: "I'll have to look that up myself."

EJ. Yes, that was true. I still had to look something up about the virgin, but the book hadn't yet been delivered, it came the afternoon after I had written this.

GH. And this time I even dared to insert myself as the translator—

EJ. Of course, after all, you are me in that sense.

GH. So, when you write: "I have to write," I add "And I have to translate!"

EJ. Yes, exactly, you are I.

GH. And then your "*Zug*" [train] kept me busy. In German you can do a lot with this term. There's "train of refugees"—I first used "column," because the picture of all the refugees on foot seemed clearer—but then the meaning mutates into *Zug* for "draught," Zug, the town in Switzerland, etc. In the end, since *Zug* sounds funny when pronounced in English, I played with the German word as well.

Perhaps the most problematic term to translate is the German, "*man*" as in "one does that." Commonly used in German, it instantly comes across as "un-English." It's a big problem in *Charges*, since it indicates the speaker's de-individualized perception of refugees and how the refugees eventually see themselves.

EJ. Yes, one is "we," the other is "you" in English.

GH. Or "they." So the editor asks, "who are the 'they'," which relates to my earlier question "who are the 'we'." It gets more tricky because of Heidegger haunting your language; and Heidegger's definition of "*man*" as the "*uneigentliche Mensch*," or the "inauthentic man," in Heideggerian terminology. Therefore, losing the "one" in English or not being as consistent with it as you can be in German, "one" loses an essential psychological aspect in the play. And the question is: where to preserve the foreignness of the text. Generally, it is expected that one shouldn't notice that it is a translated text.

EJ. What doesn't fit in must be made to fit in.

GH. It gets naturalized! I wonder whether it reveals an attitude towards anything foreign. At the risk of generalization, "one" versus "they" might reflect the notion of American individualism versus a German emphasis on "one's" responsibilities towards society as a whole.

In any event, I thought that the "one" problem can only be solved dramaturgically, in performance. It depends on the director and the ensemble's understanding of social responsibility. They have to find the right balance in rehearsal. Those are really challenging questions for a theater company.

EJ. You already had the experience with the New York production of *Jackie*. Although it still is relatively simple there, because it is a real monologue and it's clear who is talking. One would have to see how that works in a more abstract text, such as *Rechnitz*.

GH. But the really good directors have filled what you call "linguistic templates" very excitingly, even psychologically in a non-naturalistic way as Jossi Wieler's work, or, like Nicolas, who found his own associative stage language, which is the theatrical equivalent of your linguistic strategies.

EJ. Nicolas adds more voices, because he is also a musician. That's what's important. And then he adds his improvisations, they are incredibly comical, but he knows what he can add.

GH. And you have Johan Simons, the artistic director of the Munich Kammerspiele until the end of the 2014–15 season, who staged the premiere productions of your *Winterreise*, and *The City. The Street. The Attack* about Maximilian Strasse—Munich's exclusive shopping street—the murder of the famous fashion designer Rudolph Moshammer, and the brutal search of your home by the Bavarian police. As we speak, Simons is rehearsing *The Silent Maiden*. And of course there is Jossi Wieler, the defining director, most recently, of *Rechnitz*.

EJ. Unfortunately, Jossi has no longer the time to direct plays since he took over the Stuttgart Opera. He is very precise and he distills characters from my lin-guistic templates. Not psychologically, but on another level. Terrific. I work with a hammer, Jossi with tweezers and awl, to pull out the fishbones, so to speak—

GH. —which become absolutely real human beings.

EJ. It's amazing that he can do that. It is something the others can't.

GH. It just shows that the way you talk about linguistic templates is somewhat misleading. Your texts are multilayered, they can be processed in many ways.

EJ. Yes. Directors can take what parts they want to work on. I offer them the whole thing. One takes this, the other that. It's possible to make many plays out of a single one.

GH. How do you react to directors who cut as much as two-thirds of your plays?

EJ. I am always very thankful. I always worry that the audience will begin to get bored, and that would be terrible. But I also want my plays to exist as [complete] texts and that they get read, but that hasn't happened. Because for a reading audience those are still plays, and plays are hardly read by the general reading audience. But my plays are texts, basically like the novels, just that the ones are texts for speaking, the others for reading. And that's the only difference. The methods are the same.

GH. You said earlier that you revise a lot, that is, while writing. But not anymore when the texts go into production.

EJ. Yes, I rewrite several times. That leads to more associations. In the second version one can be much freer with them. What was just an allusion in the first one, can become too rich in the second version, it happens, it can get overloaded, I tend to do that, I try to rein myself in (*laughs*) but then it gets more and more and each time more targeted because there's already something to work with.

GH. It's similar with translating. One gets more daring the second time around.

EJ. Yes, yes, then one can see where it goes, where it works and where it can sustain some more and where it gets too much again. I always tend toward the too much, all editors know that, I mean Nils [Tabert, the editor of Rowohlt Theater division] cut 30 pages of *The Silent Maiden*, that's cutting thirty of 240 manuscript pages.

GH. *Charges* by comparison is a very compact play, 58 pages in your manuscript.

EJ. It was a rush job.

GH. How long do you work on a performance text?

EJ. That varies quite a bit. As I said, on *Charges* no longer than two to three weeks. *The Silent Maiden* took the longest ever, six months with interruptions.

GH. It is interesting that since you received the Nobel Prize you have written primarily texts for the theater and brief prose texts—

EJ. Yes, and funny enough, I received the Nobel specifically for a play, which has rarely been performed and it was the final push so to speak.[14] Christoph Marthaler directed it. I heard in an interview, that the Nobel committee made a special trip to Zürich to see the production, since Kjell Espmark, the chair of the committee always thought that my plays are undramatic, they are not plays. So they all flew to Zürich, they didn't go to Munich where it premiered, they wanted to be incognito, it's all very secret. And afterwards Espmark said, it was one of the most powerful theatrical experiences in his life. He would have never imagined that such texts could function on stage. So, actually, I got the award as a dramatist. Well, it was the final impetus.

GH. Why are you writing so many texts for the theater now?

EJ. As a substitute for living probably, because I always let others speak for me in other places, since I can't go

---

14 *In den Alpen* [In the Alps] premiered at the Munich Kammerspiele in association with the Zürich Schauspielhaus in 2002.

there myself. I haven't seen productions of my plays in the theater in many years—only on DVDs. So it is an ersatz life so to speak.

GH. But you've always been politically active. Intervention was always important to you and you do intervene—

EJ. Yeah, it would be nice if I could believe that one can really intervene, I am trying, but I don't have the feeling that it effects anything, especially in Austria where people are extremely negative towards me. Maybe not so much so after the Nobel, critics have become more cautious, but you just have to read the posts against me—

GH. Well, you disturb and that's an important task of the theater. I often wonder how you can deal with the issues you confront, such as the case of Josef Fritzl, who kept his daughter locked up for years in his basement and fathered her children or the NSU murders—

EJ. Fritzl and the murder of the baby, his daughter gave birth to twins and he flung one of them into the fire, infanticide, that this man could kill his own child—well, it was already dead, but I certainly wouldn't put this beyond him. The Nazis used to do that, they threw babies against the wall or—they did everything one couldn't even imagine.

GH. How can you live in this world?

EJ. I can't, I can't anyway. I am ill, after all.

GH. But it takes incredible courage.

EJ. Well, I don't know. But one processes these things as a text, a play. Sure, it takes you in—but maybe I would be better off if I weren't writing such things. I have no idea. I don't want to blame [my interests for my condition]. But I have been asked a few times, by my publishers:

how can you expose yourself to all that, no wonder you are not well (*laughs*). I don't want to make this connection [between my work and my condition], but it is strange, I always have to instantly rip out things that are buried, in the cellar or in the ground as in *Rechnitz*.

GH. I think your body of work is the strongest testimony of the times we live in.

EJ. Yes, but I don't offer anything positive, one should see that too, but it doesn't interest me, I am only interested in things I need to work through, but not in anything positive, unlike Yasmina Reza, who actually does see the abyss in the idyll, but her plays are still comedies. That's a completely different kind of theater, masterly, of course, but different. Or Allen Ayckbourne's comedies, they are terrific, and Woody Allen's films, they are certainly great and evil is already in them too, but—still, my work always turns comical too, if that weren't possible, I probably wouldn't do it. Especially, the NSU piece.

GH. Sometimes it takes very careful reading to discover the comedy in your intricate wordplays.

EJ. And it takes directors who know how to direct that. Nicolas pushes it further into the comical, grotesque. Jossi [Wieler] takes it more seriously and stays closer inside the text, that's different again.

GH. When people ask me about the absence of hope in your writing, I tell them that the hope is in the fact that you keep writing about matters that need to be confronted and worked through. That literature and theater can still do that.

EJ. Well, and then I have Oscar Wilde to recuperate [from my plays]. That happens when I translate Eugène Labiche, Georges Feydeau, and Wilde.

GH. Last, but not least, you are also a translator.

EJ. I translate only comedies.

GH. Do you pick the plays or are those assignments?

EJ. Those are assignments, first by my former publisher, [Bansemer & Nyssen] also by directors.

GH. And how was your knack for that kind of comedy discovered? Did you express your interest?

EJ. No, no, it was the publishers. The copyright had just expired, so they asked me if I'd be interested in translating Labiche. And I was, those plays are brilliant.

GH. You also translated Thomas Pynchon's *Gravity's Rainbow* [*Das Enden der Parabel*] in 1981, your first major translation project.

EJ. That was pure hubris, because of course I was not able to do that, but I just did it. One has to be totally solid in the target language, but one also has to have a real sense for the source language, such as you for mine—and since I know you, I know with absolute certainty, that only a native speaker of German, that is of Austrian German can really translate me. No one else. I learned this through you. It was clear to me earlier, but in you I found the embodiment, you grew up exactly as I did, you are almost the same age, you experienced the same things and then, at age 20 or so, you threw yourself into a totally different language, which you probably know better than your mother tongue, because your vocabulary expanded and still you preserved your sense for the mother tongue. Well, in my case that's the only way it works. It's different with other authors, I am sure that it's not a problem with them. But with me it doesn't work in any other way. That's just the way it is.

GH. I think I had the advantage that both my daughters were born and grew up in the States. I was pregnant with my first daughter when I moved there. So we practically arrived at the same time. I had 10 years of English in school and I always loved the language. So I thought that with the birth of my daughter I could also absorb English as the language of childhood. I think it is very important for a translator to experience the language of childhood in both languages.

EJ. Do your daughters speak German?

GH. No.

EJ. Funny, I never asked you this. It just occurs to me now.

GH. It was an act of rebellion in a way against the language of guilt, as I perceived it then. It was embarrassing to speak German in the 1960s.

EJ. Yes, I am convinced it was a question of guilt.

GH. I remember a column in *The New York Times* by Peter Schneider, the German writer who lived in New York for a while during the 80s. He wrote that if your child ran into the street you'd be embarrassed to shout "*Halt!*" That's so true.

EJ. Oh! Is it still that way?

GH. No, it has changed.

EJ. Since Germany's soccer World Cup victory this summer Germany finally is innocent.

GH. Have you been watching the games?

EJ. Only the final matches.

GH. This time I watched every single game for "cultural studies," so to speak.

EJ. It's not easy. But I think baseball is a lot more difficult. I made a terrible fool of myself in my Pynchon translation. There was a baseball expression, which I had not recognized as such and it was pointed out to me rather unkindly that it was stupid.

GH. It seems to me you put yourself down a bit much with regard to Pynchon. After all, you introduced him to German readers.

EJ. Well, let's say I have my merits, but when I worked on it, I didn't know what I was doing. In the end I realized that I did not see the difficulties. I had wonderful helpers, there was an American friend, he had the same cultural background as Pynchon and like him he was interested in the soldiers' songs of World War II, so he could explain them to me. Then, there was a member of the OSS [Office of Strategic Services], he was Jewish and served once in the US Intelligence Service. I didn't know the names of the individual parts of a gun. He was my expert in weapon technology. He explained to me how a revolver works.

GH. How do you always find these people?

EJ. I found the OSS agent in the Austrian Communist Party. (*Laughs.*) The Americans had even sentenced him to death for espionage for the Soviet Union. He was eventually released. He was a valuable resource for my translation. He is dead now.

GH. What were your mistakes?

EJ. Countless, simply because I don't know American culture well enough. As we have said before, translating isn't only language—you have to live in that culture. Luckily, *Gravity's Rainbow* does not take place in America. It's about American GIs, but it is set in the Zone, in occupied post–World War II Germany, and in the Nazi period, and there is a lot of German stuff—otherwise I would have been lost. I could have never translated his later works, say *Mason & Dixon*.

GH. But your translation of *Gravity's Rainbow* is still the most current translation.

EJ. Well, my friend helped me with the translation and I had asked Thomas Piltz to revise it. Otherwise I'd have been up the creek. But it really was a killer. I literally worked a couple of years four hours every morning, four hours in the afternoon—every single day.

GH. Yeah, tell me about it! You also translated Marlowe's *The Jew of Malta* for Peter Zadek's 2001 production at the Vienna Burgtheater.

EJ. Yes. I had just finished my first so-called secondary play to [Gotthold Ephraim] Lessing's *Nathan the Wise*, which is always performed as this peace vision (between Jews, Arabs and the Knights of the Temple, set in Jerusalem) and I responded by showing the insanity in the Middle East between Palestinians and Israel. And Peter Zadek wanted to show this as well in his production of *The Jew of Malta*. So he asked me to translate the play.

GH. Can you explain your concept of "secondary play."

EJ. This idea came to me like a flash. I don't know, it was a real inspiration. I thought why shouldn't it be possible to write continuations of plays. They could be either short continuations or dialectical juxtapositions. I had done this with *Nathan the Wise*. The fact that Zadek then asked me to translate *The Jew of Malta* rather than his wife, Elizabeth Plessen, who is an excellent translator, seemed like an indication that he had something specific in mind. I don't know. Maybe it was because he had staged it in Vienna. It was a magnificent production, which, unfortunately, never got the attention it deserved.

GH. Marvin Carlson, a distinguished American scholar and critic questioned the production together with Zadek's brilliant staging of *The Merchant of Venice* [in Plessen's translation, 1988] in the contemporary Venetian banking world because of suspected traces of anti-semitism. [Zadek is Jewish.] Carlson's misreading of the director's dialectical dramaturgy is a perfect example of the problems of cultural translation. Perhaps in an effort to soften the shock for American audiences about a headline published in Theater Heute, in July 1990: "*Ich möchte lieber Verbrecher als Opfer sein*" (I'd rather be a perpetrator than a victim)—quoting Zadek from the magazine's interview with Zadek about his interpretation of Shylock—Carlson mistranslates the director's statement as quoted in the headline, replacing the term "perpetrator" with "rebel" so that it reads "I'd rather be a rebel than a victim."[15]

EJ. It leaves a trail of facts behind, doesn't it? The Israeli are the people who were the victim and never want to be victim again, they rather makes others the victims than

---

15 See Gitta Honegger, "Lost in Translation," *The Routledge Companion to Dramaturgy* (Magda Romanska ed.) (Oxon, New York: Routledge, 2015), pp. 282–7.

becoming victims again. Psychoanalytically, this is completely understandable. It is horrible, but it is understandable.

GH. Yes, and that was completely misunderstood. And Zadek of course is as uncompromising as you and incredibly smart.

EJ. Yes, yes, we understood each other completely. We were in full agreement. I really prepared thoroughly. I used to think only in blank verse those days and I think, I even was speaking it. My play *Ulrike Maria* is also written in blank verse.[16] But only a few people noticed it. Which is a sign that it's right.

GH. Actually, the play you just finished, *The Silent Maiden*, about Beate Zschäppe the surviving leader of the National Socialist Underground, brings post–World War II terrorism in Germany to full circle: from *Ulrike Maria Stuart* about the Baader-Meinhof group's Red Army Fraction of the 1970s that started out as a rebellion against the legacy of Germany's Nazi past to the contemporary neo-Nazis' deadly attacks on members of minority groups, with *Charges*, a powerful lament over the plight of refugees, to Aeschylus and Greek mythologies. What's next?

EJ. Vacation! I'll spend it in my backyard reading crime fiction.

---

16 Refers to Ulrike Meinhof, Gudrun Ensslin and Andreas Baader, based on Friedrich Schiller's verse play *Maria Stuart* (1800).

ACKNOWLEDGEMENTS

First off, my thanks go to Elfriede Jelinek for her collaborative generosity and many stimulating conversations over the years about issues of cultural translation in performance.

During a one-year fellowship at the International Research Center "Interweaving Performance Cultures," at the Free University Berlin, I had the unique opportunity to further explore the dramaturgy and politics of translation in performance with distinguished scholars and artists from around the world as I was translating *The Merchant's Contracts*. Erika Fischer-Lichte and Christel Weiler, the directors of the center and my cohort of fellows provided challenging feedback and arguments from a wide range of cultural perspectives and performance practices.

The translation of *Rechnitz* was fine-tuned in collaboration with the London-based aya theater company during rehearsals for their first workshop presentation of scenes from *Rechnitz* at the company's space in London in July 2012. Under the direction of aya founder Ryan Kiggell, the company's daringly imaginative visual approach in combination with a deep understanding of the powerful performativity of Jelinek's language opened up new windows to the text.

I am indebted to Megan Carter (the dramaturg of Jelinek's *Jackie*, the first fully professional North American premiere of any play by Jelinek at the New York Women's

Project Theater in March 2013), whose dramaturgical skills and affinity to the drama inside Jelinek's language made her an ideal editor of the translation of *The Merchant's Contracts*.

During my stay in Berlin and briefer research travels through Germany, Austria and to Tel Aviv, I saw not only several performances of Jossi Wieler's and Nicolas Stemann's premiere productions of *Rechnitz* and *The Merchant's Contracts*, respectively, at their home theater and on tour, but also productions of both plays by other directors in several cities. Conversations over the years with Stemann and Wieler kept me in touch with their ongoing explorations of Jelinek's works. Dramaturg Julia Lochte and the cast members of *Rechnitz*, Katja Bürkle, André Jung, Hans Kremer, Steven Scharf and Hildegard Schmahl offered invaluable insights on- and off-stage during the tour to Tel Aviv. Karoline Exner, the dramaturg of the St. Gallen Theater's production of *The Merchant's Contracts* provided very useful information about her research of the connections between the Meinl dynasty and the University of St. Gallen's business school, and about the more or less site-specific staging of the text.

I am most thankful to Carol Martin, the editor of Seagull Books' In Performance series, for both her strong commitment to plays in translation and her sensitive, expert editing of the introduction. Seagull publisher Naveen Kishore's openness to expanding the scope of the book has been most helpful and energizing, as has been Nils Tabert's love of Elfriede Jelinek's work and support of this project as the editor of Rowohlt Theater Verlag.

Finally, these translations owe to Manfred Laubichler, my husband, for his challenging feedback from a scientific perspective on Jelinek's linguistic strategies and our shared native culture.